STATS™ BASEBALL SCOREBOARD 2001

Don Zminda, Tony Nistler, Editors

Tim Coletta, Marc Elman, Thom Henninger,
Jim Henzler, Chuck Miller, Assistant Editors

STATS™ INC.
PUBLISHING

Published by STATS Publishing
A division of Sports Team Analysis & Tracking Systems, Inc.

I want to dedicate this book to the following:
The three ladies in my life:
my wonderful wife Allison, who if there was such a thing
as a Jewish saint would be canonized
for putting up with all of my mishigas;
and my two daughters, Devin, whose caring and love makes my heart
smile every day, and Maya, whose spit and fire reminds me what the
joys of life are all about.
I love you all.
To the memories of Chester Lanin and Lester Teich, two men who
loved sports, not just for the competition
but the good times it allowed them to spend with their families.
I miss you both.
To the 1980 New York Islanders,
thank you for allowing my boyhood sports dreams to come true.

—Howard Lanin

Cover by Ryan Balock, Marc Elman and Chuck Miller

Cover photo by Allsport/Otto Gruehl
The photographs which appear in the *STATS Baseball Scoreboard* were furnished individually by the following Major League Baseball teams: Baltimore Orioles, Boston Red Sox, Chicago Cubs, Cincinnati Reds, Colorado Rockies, Houston Astros, Montreal Expos, New York Mets, Pittsburgh Pirates, St. Louis Cardinals, San Diego Padres, San Francisco Giants, Seattle Mariners and Toronto Blue Jays. Also supplying photos for the book were Lovero Photography (Anaheim Angels) and Ron Vesely Photography (Chicago White Sox).

© Copyright 2001 by STATS, Inc.

All rights reserved. Printed in the United States of America. No part of this book may be used or reproduced in any manner whatsoever without written permission except in the case of brief quotations embodied in critical articles and reviews. For information, address STATS, Inc., 8130 Lehigh Ave., Morton Grove, IL 60053

STATS is a registered trademark of Sports Team Analysis and Tracking Systems, Inc.

First Edition: March, 2001

ISBN 1-884064-91-4

Acknowledgments

The process of putting together the 12th edition of the *STATS Baseball Scoreboard* takes a full major league season and some postseason work. We'd like to thank those people who contribute to this effort.

The STATS team is successfully anchored by President Alan Leib. Senior Vice President Steve Byrd steers our consumer divisions while Vice President Robert Schur directs our interactive and commercial divisions.

Marc Elman is the Director of the Publications Department that produced this book and all of our other sports titles. Tony Nistler oversaw editorial responsibilities and received help with the written word from STATS employees Don Zminda, Don Hartack, Thom Henninger, Jim Henzler, Sam Lubeck, Craig Rolling, Barry Rubinowitz and John Sasman as well as Bill James, Jim Callis and Steven Schulman. Getting the numbers programmed appropriately fell into the hands of Tim Coletta. Chuck Miller painstakingly manipulated the many columns, tables and graphics that are key to the book's design. Taylor Bechtold, Marc Carl and Norm DeNosaquo were invaluable in their attention to detail in the stat checking process. Getting the word out about and fulfulling orders for *STATS Baseball Scoreboard* and other STATS publications requires the hard work of Ryan Balock, Mike Janosi, Antoinette Kelly and Mike Sarkis. Ryan also designed this book's cover.

We couldn't publish this book without our Data Collection Department run by Director of Operations Allan Spear. Special thanks to Jeff Chernow, who oversees the accuracy of our MLB data. Thanks also to the vast network of reporters who cover each and every major league game.

Keeping STATS at the forefront of sports information on a daily basis are Senior Vice President of sales Jim Capuano; Assistant Vice President of Information Technology Jeff Smith; Vice President Bob Meyerhoff; Director of Finance/Administration Howard Lanin; and Director of Fantasy Sports Mike Perlow.

Our Research Department for Fox Sports in Los Angeles is headed by Don Zminda. His team of sports researchers and technical staff provide many of the stats that are broadcast daily from the Fox Sports studios, as well as from remote game telecasts on Fox and Fox Sports Net.

Thanks to everyone else at STATS who insures the machine runs smoothly each day: Jeremy Alpert, Herson Arriaga, Athan Arvanitis, Arthur Ashley, Megan Bennett, Scott Berg, Mike Berger, Matt Brown, Bill Burke, Sean Bush, Jon Caplin, Li Chen, Karen Christensen, Walt Cohen, Ethan D. Cooperson, Jim Corelis, Michael Dreckmann, Chuck Durvis, Khalid El-Bayoumy, Kevin Feng, Jay Fleck, Dan Ford, Eddie Garcia, Mary Ellen Gomez, Tracey Graham, Ryan Gunn, Mike Hammer, Brian Hogan, Matt Jenkins, Derek Kenar, Fred King, Greg Kirkorsky, Gregg Kosieniak, Scott Kraatz, Stefan Kretschmann, Tony Largo, Tracy Lickton, Joe Lindholm, Walter Lis, Roger Liss, Jennifer Manicki, Patrick Markey, Will McCleskey, Angie Melecio, Marc Moeller, Betty Moy, Jim Osborne, Oscar Palacios, Jon Passman, Dean Peterson, Jim Pollard, Pat Quinn, Corey Roberts, Eric Robin, Carol Savier, Jeff Schinski, Joe Sclafani, Matt Senter, Meghan Sheehan, Mindy Singer, Stephanie Sluke, Paul Sobaje, Brian Spisak, Nick Stamm, Jake Stein, Bill Stephens, Joe Stillwell, John Strougal, David Thiel, Brian Tolleson, Michael Trakan, Aneel Trivedi, Andy Tumpowsky, Randy Williams, Zachary Williams, Chris Witt and Susan Zamechek.

—Chuck Miller

Table of Contents

Introduction 1

I. TEAM QUESTIONS 3

Anaheim Angels: How Impressive Was Erstad's Improvement?............4
Baltimore Orioles: Did the O's Need to Sign Segui? 6
Boston Red Sox: How Unusual Are Martinez' Control "Lapses"? 9
Chicago White Sox: What's the Future For the Sox
And Their Young Sluggers? 11
Cleveland Indians: Will Gonzalez Drive 'Em In Like Ramirez? 14
Detroit Tigers: Is Comerica Park the New Astrodome?........................16
Kansas City Royals: How Common Is the Sophomore Slump? 19
Minnesota Twins: How Long Can Kelly Last? 21
New York Yankees: What Can We Expect From Their Fab
Foursome? 24
Oakland Athletics: Are Chavez And Tejada the Best Young
SS/3B Combo Ever? 28
Seattle Mariners: Is Martinez an Overshadowed Legend? 31
Tampa Bay Devil Rays: How Critical Is Up-The-Middle Offense?.....34
Texas Rangers: Can A-Rod Create Enough Runs
to Justify the Funds?...36
Toronto Blue Jays: Is Batista the Littlest Big Bopper? 38
Arizona Diamondbacks: Is Finley's Post-30 Power Surge
Unprecedented? 40
Atlanta Braves: How Extraordinary Was Furcal's First Season? 42
Chicago Cubs: Can Sosa Keep Swinging Away And Still Hit .300? 44
Cincinnati Reds: Do Decent Teams With Unexceptional
Pitchers Fade? 47
Colorado Rockies: Can Hampton And Neagle Survive
in the Thin Air? 49
Florida Marlins: Is Castillo the New Enzo Hernandez?.......................52

Houston Astros: Can Lima Come Back? 55
Los Angeles Dodgers: Does Experience Matter
For a New Manager? 59
Milwaukee Brewers: Is Hammonds An Upgrade Over Grissom? 61
Montreal Expos: Is Guerrero's Combination of Power
And Discipline Unmatched? 63
New York Mets: Is It Time For Piazza to Come Out From
Behind the Plate? 65
Philadelphia Phillies: How Damaging Are Poor Starts? 68
Pittsburgh Pirates: Is Kendall Better Suited to Bat Leadoff
Than Any Catcher Ever? 70
St. Louis Cardinals: Can Ankiel Overcome His Control
Difficulties? 72
San Diego Padres: Is There Hope For Rivera? 75
San Francisco Giants: How Good Was Kent's Season For a
Second Baseman? 77

II. QUESTIONS ON OFFENSE   79

Does Coors Hurt Rockies' Hitters When They Hit the Road? 80
Who Hits the Most Late-Inning Clutch Home Runs? 83
Are Veteran Hitters Better Than "Youngsters" in the Clutch? 86
Are Aaron's Records Safer? 88
Who Bagged the Most Runs Created? 91
Who's Second to None? 93
Who Puts 'Em Ahead? 96
Who Are the Real RBI Kings? 98
Can a Change of Scenery Be Good For the Heart? 101
Who Gets the Slidin' Billy Trophy? 103
Who's the Best Bunter? 105
Who Is the New Millennium's First Man on the Moon? 108
Who Are the Human Air Conditioners? 110
Can a Team Strike Out a Lot And Still Win? 112
Are Hitters Taking More Pitches These Days? 114

Are Hitters More Patient in the Postseason? 117
Who Plays It Smart on the Bases? 119

III. QUESTIONS ON PITCHING   121

Who Are the Top 300-Win Candidates? by Bill James 122
What Might We Expect From Wells in 2001—And Beyond? 124
Has Any Pitcher Started Hotter Than Hudson? 127
Who Are the Game's Best "Stoppers"? 129
Are Tall Pitchers Really Better? 133
Which Pitchers Love Home Cookin'? 136
Who Are Baseball's Best-Hitting Pitchers? 139
Who's Toughest to Pull? 141
Which Pitchers Scored the Highest? 143
What If a Staff Has Quality, But Not Quantity? 145
Who Gets the Red Barrett Trophy? 147
Whose Heater Is Hottest? 149
Has Anyone Ever Dominated Hitters Like Martinez Did in 2000? 151
Why Are Managers Using So Many Situational Relievers? 153
Who Gets the Easy Saves—And Who Toughs It Out? 156
If You Hold the Fort, Will You Soon Be Closing the Gate? 159
Who Knows How to Handle His Inheritance? 161
Which Relievers Prevent the Most Runs? 163

IV. QUESTIONS ON DEFENSE   167

Which Catchers Catch Thieves? 168
Who's Best in the Infield Zone? 170
Who Can Turn the Pivot? 174
Which Outfielders Know How to Hold 'Em? 176
Who's Best in the Outfield Zone? 179
Which Fielders Have the Best Defensive Batting Averages? 182

V. GENERAL QUESTIONS — 187

What's Been the Role of Parks In Increasing Offense
In the Years 1990-2000? by Bill James 188
Is It Easier to Win in a Pitchers' Park? 192
Was Getting Swept a Bad Omen For the White Sox? 195
Which Teams Were 2000's Biggest Overachievers And
Underachievers? 197
Have Hall of Fame Standards For Pitchers Gotten Too Strict? 199

VI. AWARDS — 203

Which Players Cleaned Up at the Awards Banquet? 204

Appendix — 211

Glossary — 293

Index — 301

About STATS, Inc. — 306

Introduction

This is *Baseball Scoreboard* No. 12, and we think you'll find the book as topical as ever. But there's been a been a few changes made.

The first thing you'll notice is that a couple of familiar names are missing from the cover. One is Jim Callis, a *Scoreboard* co-author for the last couple of years and a major contributor to STATS publications since the late 1990s. Jim has returned to his first love, *Baseball America*, as Executive Editor. Fortunately for us, Jim still is doing a little "moonlighting" for STATS, and he's contributed a number of essays to this year's book.

The other change is even more significant: John Dewan, co-editor of the *Scoreboard* since the first edition and the man who built STATS into the sports giant it is today, left our company to pursue other opportunities. To say he'll be missed is like saying the Seattle Mariners will have a little bit of a void at shortstop this year. John was involved in every aspect of the company during its period of phenomenal growth, and none of us at STATS would be where we are without him.

My own roots with John go back to the 1980s, when he became executive director of Project Scoresheet, an outfit started by Bill James to collect major league play-by-play data. I was one of the original volunteers, scoring White Sox games off television and radio. Eventually John decided to use some of the Project Scoresheet data in a pair of Cubs/White Sox sister publications called *The Chicago Baseball Report*. I became the chief commentator and analyst. Our first year, the White Sox edition had exactly 12 subscribers. But they liked what they were getting, and you have to start somewhere.

A short time later John moved over to STATS, which at the time was a small company collecting data for a handful of major league teams. John expanded the operation to cover every major league team on a live basis, and the game was on. Success took a little while, and it was hardly assured at first. When STATS began a Publications Department in 1989, the business was so small that I was able to handle the job of director while working part-time. Our first books rolled off the presses that fall: the *Major League Handbook*, the *Scouting Report* (later to become *The Scouting Notebook*) and the very first edition of the *Baseball Scoreboard*.

From the beginning, the *Scoreboard* was a favorite publication among the people who worked at STATS, and it quickly became a hit with readers as well. The 1990 edition featured questions on the best leadoff hitters in baseball, pitchers with the most quality starts and second basemen who were best at turning the double play—issues which continue to be discussed in the *Scoreboard* today. There

Baseball Scoreboard

were also gems like the one called "What Good is a Foul Ball?", an article which showed that the more foul balls a batter hit after two strikes, the better his chances were of getting a hit. That was the type of article that made the *Scoreboard* a must-have among people interested in unlocking the mysteries of baseball. People took notice, and the word began to spread: these STATS guys know what they're doing.

In the early days I wrote every essay in the book (all 101 of them), and John did pretty much everything else: supervising the programming, laying out the pages of the book, working with illustrator John Grimwade, and most importantly, adding his expertise to the analysis. As the company grew and the *Scoreboard* continued to find an audience, other voices joined the choir. We're proud to say that over the years, such distinguished baseball analysts as Rob Neyer, Mat Olkin and Steve Moyer contributed essays to the book—not to mention Bill James, who always has considered the *Scoreboard* one of his favorite books. But the most important voice was always John's. He had the vision to see that the *Scoreboard's* real importance to the company was that it was a showcase for the kind of unique data that STATS collected, and for the kind of insightful analysis that we could provide. Because of that vision, the company grew in ways few of us ever could have imagined.

A year ago that growth culminated in the sale of STATS to a division of News Corporation. With the success of the company assured for the long run, John eventually decided to move onto another phase of his life, but he left the company in capable hands. He left the *Scoreboard* in capable hands as well. My own role in the book is diminishing, as my new position as the company's Director of Research for FOX Sports in Los Angeles is taking up most of my time. Tony Nistler and company have taken over, but not to worry: it's still the same *Scoreboard*, filled with fascinating questions and analysis. Along with the familiar articles on subjects like the pitchers with the most tough saves and the batters with the most go-ahead RBI, we look into whether Juan Gonzalez will be an adequate replacement for Manny Ramirez, whether Mike Hampton and Denny Neagle can survive in Colorado's thin air and which teams play it smart on the bases. As always, there's a whole lot more.

Twelve years after the *Scoreboard* started, we're still going strong. More than anyone else, one person made that possible. To John Dewan, we'd like to say thanks for being what you were: visionary, innovator, and on a personal level, friend. Thank you, John, from the bottom of our hearts.

—Don Zminda

I. TEAM QUESTIONS

Anaheim Angels: How Impressive Was Erstad's Improvement?

Darin Erstad always has had a knack for getting hits. While starring at the University of Nebraska, he batted .356 and set school records for hits in a game, season (since broken) and career. After the Angels made him the No. 1 overall pick in the 1995 draft, Erstad kept producing. He batted .328 in the minors and reached Anaheim barely more than a year after he turned pro.

Erstad continued to succeed in his first two and a half big league seasons. He batted .295, stroking 379 hits in 329 games. When he earned an All-Star berth in 1998, it appeared to be just the first of many.

He didn't come anywhere close to the All-Star Game in 1999, however, bottoming out like few would have expected. Erstad hit just .253, as pitchers learned to take advantage of the aggressiveness that permeates his game at the plate, on the bases and in the field.

Consider his lesson learned. Erstad exhibited more calm in the batter's box last season, refusing to chase pitches he couldn't turn into line drives. A year after not even matching the prowess of former journeyman Dick Sisler, Erstad chased history made by Dick's father George, a Hall of Famer.

Erstad had 240 hits in 2000, tying Wade Boggs (1985) for the most in a single season since 1930. Erstad chased Sisler's record of 257, which has stood since 1920, before cooling off in the final two months. As a consolation prize, he did set the mark for the biggest increase in hits from one year to the next by a major league regular (defined as having 500 at-bats).

Biggest Single-Season Hit Improvements—1876-2000

Player	Years	Yr1 Avg	Yr1 H	Yr2 Avg	Yr2 H	Diff
Darin Erstad	**1999-2000**	**.253**	**148**	**.355**	**240**	**92**
Paul Molitor	1995-96	.270	142	.341	225	83
George Sisler	1919-20	.352	180	.407	257	77
Omar Moreno	1978-79	.235	121	.282	196	75
Keith Hernandez	1978-79	.255	138	.344	210	72
Billy Shindle	1888-89	.208	107	.314	178	71
Lenny Dykstra	1989-90	.237	121	.325	192	71
Al Simmons	1924-25	.307	183	.387	253	70
Earl Averill	1935-36	.288	162	.378	232	70
Pete Rose	1964-65	.269	139	.312	209	70
Dave May	1972-73	.238	119	.303	189	70

(minimum 500 AB in Yr1)

That's an eclectic list, to say the least. Like Erstad, Paul Molitor, Omar Moreno, Keith Hernandez, Lenny Dykstra, Earl Averill and Dave May all followed the worst full year of their careers with their best. Hall of Famers Sisler and Al Simmons went from merely solid to spectacular seasons. Billy Shindle and Pete Rose rebounded from their worst years by improving significantly, then hit even better the following campaign.

Darin Erstad

Shindle and Rose were the exceptions on this list, as all but one of the other eight players (not including Erstad, who has yet to provide an encore) came back in the third season with a batting average somewhere between their previous two. May plummeted to .226 in 1974, then was traded to the Braves in the deal that brought Hank Aaron back to Milwaukee.

While Erstad may never hit .355 again, the company he keeps on this list bodes well for his career. Moreno, Shindle and May were the only players who were flukes. Everyone else had a standout career, with Averill joining Sisler and Simmons in Cooperstown. Molitor almost certainly will join them in 2004, and Rose obviously would be enshrined as well if not for his lifetime ban.

—Jim Callis

A more complete listing for this category can be found on page 212.

Baltimore Orioles: Did the O's Need to Sign Segui?

The Orioles took a lot of heat for the players they acquired when they packaged veterans Mike Bordick, B.J. Surhoff, Harold Baines, Mike Timlin, Charles Johnson and Will Clark for a host of youngsters during the 2000 season. It's hard to argue with the O's critics, as those five vets didn't translate into a single top-flight prospect.

Chris Richard

Instead, the Orioles loaded their system with catcher Brook Fordyce, utility player Melvin Mora and mostly roster-filler minor leaguers, many in their mid-to late 20s. The best of the lot were a pair of hard-throwing, 22-year-old righthanders, Luis Rivera and Leslie Brea. They have legitimate promise, but Rivera has been plagued by injuries and Brea suffers with command issues. If some progress is made on those fronts, both could pitch in Baltimore in 2001.

Some of the sting of that criticism may have been diminished when 26-year-old Chris Richard, acquired from St. Louis in the Timlin deal, stepped in for the departed Will Clark and hit 13 homers and slugged .563 in 199 at-bats with Baltimore. He passed a younger Calvin Pickering on the Orioles' depth chart at first base, but is he their long-term solution at first?

How likely is it that a lightly regarded 26-year-old rookie will develop into a productive major leaguer who has a solid career? In the history of the major leagues, only 21 rookies who were seasonal age 26 (as of June 30) or older have hit as many homers as Richard's 14 (St. Louis and Baltimore combined) and have slugged .500 or better in their rookie campaign. They range from Buck Freeman, who led the National League in homers and hit .318-25-122 as a rookie with the Washington Senators in 1899, to current players Benny Agbayani and Brian Daubach.

Among those 21 players, half reached or surpassed their rookie home-run total in a subsequent season, though only nine ever slugged .500 or better again over a full campaign. Six played baseball in at least 10 big league seasons. Just seven hit as many as 100 homers in the majors while only two—Indian Bob Johnson (288) and the senior Earl Averill (238)—surpassed the 200-dinger mark during their career.

Averill is the only Hall of Famer of this group of 21, although Bill James made a case a few years ago that Johnson's career, in the context of its time, was probably better than Hall of Famer Hack Wilson's. Johnson did manage to hit at least 25 homers in six of his 13 seasons, and he slugged .500 or better nine times.

The truth is, though, other than the success of Averill, Johnson, Al Rosen (seven seasons, 192 career homers) and a Baltimore first baseman of 40 years ago, Jim Gentile (nine seasons, 179 homers), there's little in the numbers to suggest that Richard is going to develop into a big-time power threat.

That also remains true when you look at the players who enjoyed rookie seasons similar to Richard's in modern times. Since the major league rules were changed to counter the success of pitchers at the end of the 1960s, seven rookies other than Richard have debuted with double-digit homers and a .500 slugging percentage at seasonal age 26 or above.

Let's first take a look at what those seven players did in their first and second full seasons, which may shed some light on whether Richard will be productive his second time around the American League:

Rookie And Sophomore Seasons—1970-2000

Player	Age	Year	AB	H	2B	HR	RBI	Avg	Slg	AB/HR
Hal Breeden	29	1973	258	71	10	15	43	.275	.535	17.2
	30	1974	190	47	13	2	20	.247	.347	95.0
Jim Morrison	26	1979	240	66	14	14	35	.275	.508	17.1
	27	1980	604	171	40	15	57	.283	.424	40.3
Bob Hamelin	26	1994	312	88	25	24	65	.282	.599	13.0
	27	1995	208	35	7	7	25	.168	.313	29.7
Ron Coomer	29	1996	233	69	12	12	41	.296	.511	19.4
	30	1997	523	156	30	13	85	.298	.438	40.2
Curtis Pride	27	1996	267	80	17	10	31	.300	.513	26.7
	28	1997	164	35	4	3	20	.213	.341	54.7
Benny Agbayani	27	1999	276	79	18	14	42	.286	.525	19.7
	28	2000	350	101	20	15	60	.289	.480	23.3
Brian Daubach	27	1999	381	112	33	21	73	.294	.562	18.1
	28	2000	495	123	32	21	76	.248	.448	23.6

(minimum seasonal age 26, 200 AB, 10 HR, .500 Slg in rookie season)

There's a Rookie of the Year here in Bob Hamelin, but an inability to make contact and weight issues quickly sidetracked a promising career. His second year was a disaster—some of it spent at Triple-A Omaha—and he finished with a .246 career average and 67 homers in six seasons.

Hamelin's sophomore struggles actually were quite typical of this group, as slugging percentages and home-run rates dipped significantly in each player's sophomore campaign. It didn't seem to matter whether these guys became regulars or were exposed even less to big league pitching the second time around. Scouting reports allowed pitchers to make adjustments and counter their rookie success.

While he didn't maintain his home-run pace as a second-year player, Jim Morrison is the success story in this group. His career lasted longer than the musician's with whom he shared a name. The ballplayer's career spanned 12 seasons. He hit double-digit homers seven times—including a career-high 23 for the Pirates in 1986—and finished with 112 longballs.

The other side of the coin is Hal Breeden, who emerged to hit 15 homers with Montreal in 1973 in his third cup of coffee in the majors. He struggled in '74 and his career was over after a 5-for-37 stint in '75. Curtis Pride didn't fare much better after an unlikely power surge in his first lengthy exposure to major league pitching, but he does continue to surface for a brief spell most seasons.

While there's an outside chance that Richard will erupt and have a string of good years like Johnson or Rosen, it's more likely he'll follow the career path of current peers such as Coomer, Daubach or Agbayani. None of them are certain to be big league regulars throughout their career, but they can be valuable components of a major league team.

Does that mean the Orioles were smart in signing first baseman David Segui to a four-year deal in December? It's hard to see the sensibility of the signing, considering the O's aren't likely to be competitive any time soon. Why not take the time to find out if Richard is a late bloomer? After all, he could be the next Bob Johnson. Then again, he might be the next flash-in-the-pan incarnation of Bob Hamelin.

—Thom Henninger

A more complete listing for this category can be found on page 213.

Boston Red Sox: How Unusual Are Martinez' Control "Lapses"?

Pedro Martinez almost threw the first official no-hitter of his major league career last August 29, not yielding a hit until Devil Rays catcher John Flaherty singled to lead off the ninth inning. But the game actually may have been more memorable for all the acrimony between the two teams. With his fourth pitch of the game, Martinez hit Tampa Bay center fielder Gerald Williams, who charged the mound. By game's end, there had been two bench-clearing fracases, four hit batsmen, two Red Sox sent to the hospital and eight Devil Rays ejected.

"It seems that there are some guys who can do whatever they want to do and it's all right," Tampa Bay DH Greg Vaughn said afterward. "[Martinez] throws 95-96 MPH and he decides he wants to hit you, and you have to stand there and take it? It's not right."

Vaughn wasn't the only Devil Ray who suggested that there's a double standard involving Martinez, who was tagged as a headhunter when he was breaking into the majors with the Dodgers and Expos. Reggie Sanders once charged the mound after being hit by Martinez, though getting hit had broken up a perfect game in the late innings.

Several opponents have said Martinez continues to throw at batters. They wonder how he can show exquisite control most of the time yet annually rank among the major league leaders in hit batsmen. In 2000, he ranked second in the American League in fewest walks per nine innings—as well as in hit batsmen. He plunked 14 hitters and walked just 32 in 217 innings. How unusual was his .438 ratio of hit batsmen to walks last year? It was the fifth-highest single-season mark since 1900.

Highest HB/BB Ratios, Season—1900-2000

Pitcher, Team	Year	IP	HB	BB	Ratio
Bill Wolfe, NYA-Was	1904	160.1	13	26	.500
Kevin Brown, Fla	1996	233.0	16	33	.485
Jesse Tannehill, Bos	1904	281.2	15	33	.455
Danny Darwin, Pit-Hou	1996	164.2	12	27	.444
Pedro Martinez, Bos	**2000**	**217.0**	**14**	**32**	**.438**
Jesse Tannehill, Pit	1902	231.0	10	25	.400
Jesse Tannehill, Pit	1900	234.0	17	43	.395
Chief Bender, Phi	1903	270.0	25	65	.385
Nick Maddox, Pit	1909	203.1	15	39	.385
Don Drysdale, LA	1966	273.2	17	45	.378

(minimum 150 IP)

Hall of Famer Don Drysdale was known for his fondness for throwing at hitters, and even he never approached Martinez' .438 ratio. The king of this category obviously is Jesse Tannehill, who has three of the top seven single-season HB/BB ratios and ranks second among pitchers with at least 1,000 innings with a career .282 ratio.

Neither the single-season nor career leaders ever had a winning campaign in the majors. In 1904, Bill Wolfe became the only pitcher in the 20th century to hit half as many batters as he walked in a season. He spent just four years in the big leagues, going 21-37. Jack Warhop, a 69-93 pitcher over eight seasons, holds the career mark at .285.

It's interesting that while Martinez has a reputation for being malicious, ornery Kevin Brown does not. Brown has the second-highest single-season ratio (.485 in 1996), and his career .160 mark is slightly higher than Martinez' .156. Yet it's Martinez who seems to get under hitters' skin like few other pitchers can.

—Jim Callis

A more complete listing for this category can be found on page 214.

Chicago White Sox: What's the Future For the Sox And Their Young Sluggers?

In another essay (see p. 195), we examine the question of whether the White Sox will be able to recover from getting swept in the first round of the 2000 playoffs. Based on historical precedent, our conclusion was they ought to be just fine. But there's another reason to be optimistic about the club's future: it's brimming with young talent. Consider the slugging threesome of Magglio Ordonez, Paul Konerko and Carlos Lee. All three players were 26 years old or under last year, and all three batted better than .290 with at least 20 homers and 90 RBI. Since most players don't peak on offense until around age 27, the trio figures to be even more productive over the next few campaigns.

The exploits of Ordonez, Konerko and Lee made us wonder how many other teams in baseball history had a trio of sluggers, all seasonal age 26 or younger (based on their age as of June 30) and all producing at least 20 homers and 80 RBI. More to the point, how did the players and their teams perform over the next few seasons? There were only a handful of such teams, including one with overlapping personnel, as a new young slugger joined the group. Here's a rundown on most of them:

1938 New York Yankees (Joe DiMaggio, Joe Gordon, Tommy Henrich)
1940-41 New York Yankees (Joe DiMaggio, Joe Gordon, Charlie Keller)

The Yankees dominated baseball in the late 1930s and early 1940s, and a big reason was that the club had a bevy of young sluggers. Take the 1938 team, which included 23-year-old center fielder Joe DiMaggio (.324-32-140), 23-year-old second baseman Joe Gordon (.255-25-97) and 25-year-old right fielder Tommy Henrich (.270-22-91). By 1940, DiMaggio and Gordon were only 25, and they were joined by 23-year-old outfielder Charlie Keller (.286-21-93) to form a second trio. Though DiMaggio was the only Hall of Famer in the group (at least to date), all four players remained productive through most of the 1940s. By then Gordon was gone, but the player the Yanks received in return, Allie Reynolds, proved equally valuable. They all helped the Yankees win five pennants from 1938 to 1943, and two more in 1947 and 1949.

1940 Boston Red Sox (Bobby Doerr, Jim Tabor, Ted Williams)

When Ted Williams joined the Red Sox as a 20-year-old rookie in 1939, Boston fans had hopes that the Sox soon would rival the Yankees for American League supremacy. The '39 Red Sox also had a promising 21-year-old second baseman in Bobby Doerr, and another young slugger in 22-year-old third sacker Jim Tabor. A year later all three topped the 20-

homer/80-RBI mark, and the optimism was even more rampant. Tabor proved to be a flash in the pan, but Doerr and Williams went on to have Hall of Fame careers. The Sox won only one pennant with Doerr and Williams in the lineup (in 1946), but they had near-misses in 1948 and 1949, and might have won another flag or two had Williams not missed three full seasons during World War II.

1962 Los Angeles Dodgers (Tommy Davis, Willie Davis, Frank Howard)
The Dodgers of the 1960s were led by the power pitching of Sandy Koufax and Don Drysdale, but they had some talented hitters as well. In 1962 the Dodgers' outfield threesome of Tommy Davis (.346-27-153), Willie Davis (.285-21-85) and Frank Howard (.296-31-119) terrorized National League pitching despite the handicap of playing in Dodger Stadium. None were older than 25. The Dodgers lost the NL pennant in a playoff in 1962, won it all in '63, and took two more flags and one World Series in 1965-66. Willie Davis was a key performer for all those teams, and Tommy Davis remained one of the team's top hitters, though he was slowed by an ankle injury that caused him to miss almost the entire 1965 season. Howard was gone by 1965, but he contributed indirectly to the club's success; he was traded to the Senators in a deal that brought the Dodgers star lefthander Claude Osteen, among others.

1969 Boston Red Sox (Tony Conigliaro, Rico Petrocelli, Reggie Smith)
What is it with these Red Sox? They always seem to have a flock of young sluggers who appear destined to lead them to a dynasty. . . but one pennant is usually all they're good for, if that. The Sox of the late 1960s to mid-1970s were slightly more fortunate. Tony Conigliaro, Rico Petrocelli and Reggie Smith all were regulars on the "Impossible Dream" Red Sox club that came out of nowhere to win the 1967 AL pennant, though none reached the 20-homer, 80-RBI mark. By the time they reached the 20-80 mark as a trio in 1969, Conigliaro was recovering from a fearful eye injury that would soon recur and derail his career. Smith was dealt to the Cardinals after the 1973 season, but the players the Sox received in return, Rick Wise and Bernie Carbo, helped Boston win another flag in 1975. The third baseman on that '75 pennant winner? Rico Petrocelli.

1969 Cincinnati Reds (Johnny Bench, Lee May, Bobby Tolan)
The Reds of the 1970s were one of the most powerful teams of all time. The seeds of that dynasty began to sprout in the late 1960s, when Johnny Bench, Lee May and Bobby Tolan began to develop into stars. Bench and May were products of the club's farm system; Tolan had come from the Cardinals in a trade. Bench, May and Tolan all helped the Reds win the NL flag in 1970. A year later, May was traded to the Astros, but the key

player the Reds received in return, Joe Morgan, helped lead Cincinnati to flags in 1972, '75 and '76, as well as a division title in 1973.

1979 Montreal Expos (Andre Dawson, Larry Parrish, Ellis Valentine)
1986 Toronto Blue Jays (Jesse Barfield, George Bell, Lloyd Moseby)

Call these teams "The Canadian Teasers." The Expos of the late 1970s and early 1980s and the Blue Jays of a few years later were perennial contenders who never could seem to get over the hump. The Expos contended for several seasons but made only one trip to the playoffs, in 1981. The Jays seemed similarly cursed for many years, and it wasn't until 1992 that the Blue Jays became the first Canadian team to win a World Series. By that time, the slugging outfield of George Bell, Lloyd Moseby and Jesse Barfield was long gone. Still, the trio helped the Jays win a division title in 1985, and Bell and Moseby were regulars on the 1989 AL East champs.

1999 Kansas City Royals (Carlos Beltran, Jermaine Dye, Mike Sweeney)
2000 Chicago White Sox (Paul Konerko, Carlos Lee, Magglio Ordonez)
2000 Oakland Athletics (Eric Chavez, Ben Grieve, Miguel Tejada)

The last few seasons have been a period of big hitting, so it's not surprising to find several teams with a trio of young sluggers. The Royals seem some distance away from serious contention, despite the breakthrough of Carlos Beltran, Jermaine Dye and Mike Sweeney in 1999. (It didn't help that Beltran had a miserable year in 2000.) The future looks bright for the A's and White Sox, however. In keeping with the times, the A's already have dealt away one of their young sluggers, Ben Grieve, in a three-team deal that brought them another young star (though already 27 and not yet a 20-80 guy) in Johnny Damon. Building a lasting dynasty will be a tall task for the White Sox and A's, since they might have difficulty affording the salaries of their stars once they fully mature.

Two other teams had a trio of young 20-homer/80-RBI sluggers. One, the 1970 San Diego Padres (Ollie Brown, Nate Colbert, Cito Gaston) never came close to contending. . . in part because none of their young sluggers proved to be a lasting star. The other, the 1991 Texas Rangers with Juan Gonzalez, Rafael Palmeiro and Ruben Sierra, eventually made it to the postseason a couple of times, starting in 1996, but they never got past the first round. A cautionary note for the A's and White Sox?

—Don Zminda

Cleveland Indians: Will Gonzalez Drive 'Em In Like Ramirez?

When the Cleveland Indians announced the signing of Juan Gonzalez in early January, general manager John Hart suggested a big season might be in store for the man he chose to replace the departed Manny Ramirez. After all, Hart said of his new cleanup hitter, "Juan has never had the fortune to hit behind the best 1-2-3 hitters in the league."

Replacing a run producer who has averaged 144 RBI a year over the last three seasons is a daunting task, but is it likely that Gonzalez gains a significant edge by hitting behind Kenny Lofton, Omar Vizquel and Roberto Alomar in 2001? It certainly seems so when you consider the career on-base percentages of Lofton (.383), Vizquel (.342) and Alomar (.375). Vizquel may seem like the weak link here, but his on-base rates the last two seasons have been .397 and .377.

To further explore this notion, let's take a look at the on-base percentages for all No. 1, 2 and 3 hitters for Gonzalez' two previous teams and his new club over the last five seasons:

On-Base Percentages For Nos. 1, 2 And 3 Hitters—1996-2000

Team	No. 1	No. 2	No. 3
Texas	.346	.356	.390
Detroit	.336	.346	.345
Cleveland	**.357**	**.364**	**.385**

On-base percentage hasn't been a team strength for the young Tigers of recent seasons. Still, the club's on-base percentage near the top of the order has been climbing steadily since 1998. Last summer, in Gonzalez' only season with Detroit, the top three in the order generated more respectable on-base percentages of .342, .351 and .375. That wasn't much of a benefit for Gonzalez, however, whose 2000 season was compromised more by foot, ankle and back injuries than happenings on the field.

Obviously Cleveland's first three hitters have been the most productive of these three teams at setting the table for their cleanup hitter. But has the threesome of Lofton, Vizquel and Alomar been that much better than, say, the 1998 Texas trio of Tom Goodwin (.378 OBP in a career year), Mark McLemore (.362 OBP since '98) and Rusty Greer (career .392 mark)? The Texas group obviously was critical to Gonzalez' MVP performance in '98.

To cut through all the percentages, here is the number of baserunners on the sacks when the cleanup hitter has come to bat for these three teams over the last five years. This includes *all* baserunners, not just those generated by the three men at the top of the order.

Runners on Base When No. 4 Hitter Comes to the Plate—1996-2000

Team	1996	1997	1998	1999	2000	Total
Texas	**568**	**534**	**554**	543	508	2,707
Detroit	463	440	467	471	**545**	2,386
Cleveland	524	527	499	588	564	2,702

(Gonzalez' teams in bold)

The truth is, the Rangers set up their cleanup hitter better than the Tribe over the first three years of this five-year span, including Gonzalez' two MVP seasons with Texas in 1996 and '98. That helps to explain how he drove in 144 runs in '96 and led the league with 157 RBI in '98.

While Texas has the highest five-year total of the three teams, Cleveland provided more RBI opportunities for the No. 4 man than Texas during 1999 and 2000. The last two seasons in Cleveland mark the arrival of Alomar and the surge in Vizquel's on-base percentage. Those 588 baserunners on the sacks in '99 helped Ramirez drive home 165 runs—the highest total since Jimmie Foxx generated 175 RBI for the Red Sox in 1938.

With the tablesetters more productive in Cleveland in recent years, Gonzalez has a chance to see as many RBI opportunities as he saw in Texas during his two MVP seasons. But it's doubtful that he will see significantly more. It's also likely that Gonzalez won't be as productive with his opportunities in Cleveland as Ramirez was. The departing Ramirez delivered on a higher percentage of his RBI available in each of the last three campaigns, with RBI available defined essentially as the number of runs a player would drive in if he homered every time he came to bat (see essay on page 98 for a more thorough definition). That includes 2000, when Gonzalez actually had 20 *more* RBI available (799) than Ramirez (779) but delivered 55 fewer total RBI (67-122).

Clearly, Gonzalez wasn't the same player last year, largely due to his back ailment that was diagnosed late in the season as a bulging disc. He eventually may need surgery, which serves as a reminder that Gonzalez' success in 2001 probably has more to do with his health and his ability to adjust to a new environment than who is hitting in front of him in the lineup.

—Thom Henninger

Detroit Tigers: Is Comerica Park the New Astrodome?

Baseball lost one of its most eccentric parks last season when the Houston Astros moved from the Astrodome into Enron Field. When they did, the Astros relocated from one of the game's best pitching venues to one of its best hitting parks. Wait. That probably doesn't do the Astrodome justice. After all, for most of its existence, the "eighth wonder of the world" ranked as the Death Valley of major league stadiums. The Astrodome was the place where flyballs went to die. Home runs were harder to find there than Republicans at a "People for the American Way" convention.

The Astrodome opened in 1965, though it was called Harris County Domed Stadium then. Whatever you called it, the enclosed ballpark simply refused to allow cheap home runs. The Astros and their opponents managed only 57 longballs in Houston that season, as opposed to 163 in Astros road games. For his Astros career, Jose Cruz hit twice as many homers on the road (92) as at home (46). In 1984, all 12 of his dingers were slugged away from Houston. As recently as 1999, Jeff Bagwell connected for 30 homers on the road and only 12 at home. Think about that. Had the Astrodome been a normal park, Bagwell may have clubbed 60 that season.

That all changed in 2000, however, when the Astros christened Enron. The Astros and their opponents hit 49 more homers at Enron than in Houston road games last year. This followed 35 years in which there was an average of 44 *fewer* homers at the Astrodome than on the road each season. Bagwell got into the act, as well, blasting 28 at Enron as opposed to 19 on the road.

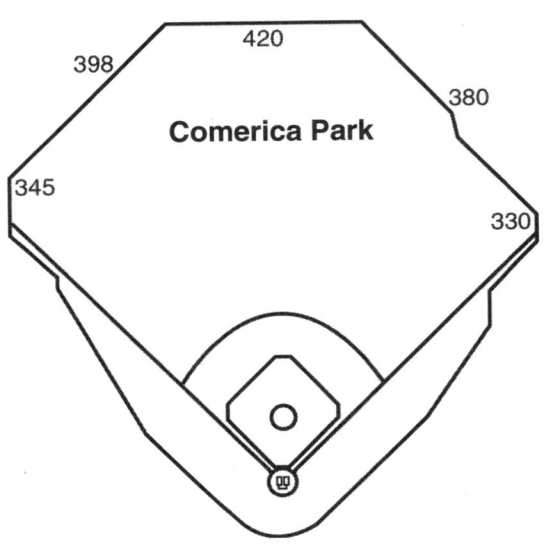

Although fans of offense likely welcomed Enron into the pantheon of new stadiums, some baseball purists may have mourned the Astrodome's passing. They probably didn't miss the old park's phony surface or the playing of the game indoors. Still, its demise marked the retirement of one of the few remaining parks that depressed scoring. New stadiums such as

Jacobs Field, The Ballpark in Arlington, Coors Field and Enron have only abetted the offensive explosion of recent seasons. But while hitting surged in Houston last season, it diminished in Detroit, where the Tigers opened Comerica Park.

The Tigers had played at Tiger Stadium for most of the 20th century. The park at the corner of Michigan and Trumbull generally was considered a fairly decent park for offense, especially for home runs. But in its inaugural season, Comerica could hardly be considered a hitters' haven. Fifty-eight fewer runs were scored in all Tiger's games at Comerica compared to on the road. Even more telling, a whopping 80 fewer homers were smacked in Detroit.

STATS has been printing park indexes in its *Major League Handbook* for years. Those indexes, which are based on non-interleague games only, are computed on a per at-bat basis. We have breakdowns of home and road at-bats going back to 1987. Last year, Comerica's home-run index was slightly under 61, the smallest in all of baseball. And that rate ranks as one of the lowest of the past 14 seasons.

Lowest Home-Run Indexes—1987-2000

Year	Team	Index
1991	Indians	49.2
1991	Astros	51.4
1989	Royals	53.5
1992	Royals	56.0
1987	Astros	58.0
1990	Astros	58.1
2000	**Tigers**	**60.8**
1992	Dodgers	62.3
1991	Cardinals	62.6
1991	Royals	62.6

Although Comerica's home-run index was low, it was not historically low. The Astros produced three of the six lowest rates since '87, as well as six of the lowest 14. Cleveland's 1991 mark was the product of a one-year endeavor to concentrate on speed and defense. The Indians moved the fences back at old Municipal Stadium that season, resulting in far fewer home runs. The Tribe also lost 105 games, the most in its history.

Because Detroit predominantly was a righthanded-hitting team last year, the Tigers may have been most disappointed in the effect that Comerica had on righthanded hitters' power. Seven Tigers reached double-digits in home runs last season. Five of them are righties, while a sixth, Tony Clark, is a switch-hitter. Detroit pinned much of its hopes on Juan Gonzalez, whom they had traded for and hoped to sign to a long-term contract. But Gonzalez criticized the dimensions of Detroit's new park, wound up hitting a meager total of eight home runs there, and later signed with Cleveland for 2001. Judging from the numbers, Gonzalez' concerns appear justified. Comerica's home-run index for righthanded hitters was an unsightly 51.9 last season.

Lowest Righthanded Home-Run Indexes—1987-2000

Year	Team	Index
1991	Astros	48.9
1992	Dodgers	51.0
2000	**Tigers**	**51.9**
1991	Indians	53.7
1993	Brewers	56.1
1990	Astros	57.6
1987	Astros	58.0
1989	Royals	59.8
1988	Cardinals	61.4
1994	Rangers	62.4

If the second chart is any indication of Comerica's true characteristics, the Tigers may want to think twice before investing in righthanded power. Righties almost certainly will find the distant left-field fence an intimidating target. In fact, Comerica's dimensions are 345 feet down the left-field line and 398 feet to left-center. That's quite a change from Tiger Stadium, where it was a cozy 365 feet to the left-field alley. Among current ballparks, only Yankee Stadium is deeper, albeit by only one foot.

Teams often talk about building with speed, pitching and defense. Considering Comerica's behavior in 2000, the Tigers may be advised to heed that old maxim. We don't want to go overboard after only one year, but it does appear as though Comerica may be the logical successor to the Astrodome. It may not be exciting for fans who are used to slugfests, but Detroit might enjoy greater success by concentrating on areas other than offense.

—Jim Henzler

A more complete listing for this category can be found on page 216.

Kansas City Royals: How Common Is the Sophomore Slump?

Carlos Beltran appeared to have everything going for him as he entered the 2000 campaign. He was young, talented and successful. He didn't turn 23 until last April. He possessed an impressive mixture of power, speed and center-field defense. He was the reigning American League Rookie of the Year. Not a bad combination to have.

The Royals were counting on Beltran to remain a vital part of their offense. He opened last year as Kansas City's No. 3 hitter, but he got off to a sluggish start, hitting just .213 with six extra-base hits through the team's first 20 games. He slid to the No. 5 spot in the lineup and continued to struggle. On May 13, in the midst of an 0-for-24 skid, he was dropped to No. 7. In June, Beltran was disciplined for one game due to a lack of hustle. In July, he went on the DL with a bone bruise in his knee. In August, the Royals suspended him for refusing a rehab assignment. In September, he returned to the team and slugged a meager .303 in his final 22 games.

A successful sophomore season it was not. After generating 111 runs created in 1999, Beltran slumped to 39 RC last year. Only one other Rookie of the Year had ever fallen farther in his second campaign.

Largest Decreases in Runs Created For Rookies of the Year—1947-99

Player, Team	Year	Lg	RC	RC-2	Diff
Walt Dropo, Bos	1950	AL	120	40	-80
Carlos Beltran, KC	**1999**	**AL**	**111**	**39**	**-72**
Joe Charboneau, Cle	1980	AL	71	11	-60
Sandy Alomar Jr., Cle	1990	AL	62	4	-58
Willie Mays, NYG	1951	NL	75	18	-57
Todd Hollandsworth, LA	1996	NL	82	30	-52
Bob Hamelin, KC	1994	AL	67	15	-52
Albie Pearson, Was	1958	AL	69	18	-51
Al Bumbry, Bal	1973	AL	68	24	-44
Roy Sievers, StL	1949	AL	85	44	-41
Benito Santiago, SD	1987	NL	73	32	-41

To refresh your memory, runs created are based upon formulae developed by Bill James that attempt to gauge how much a player has contributed to an offense. For our purposes, we're considering position players only. Beltran's sophomore slump was deeper than usual for most Rookies of the Year. Injuries had something to do with that, as did immaturity, perhaps. Still, it's hard to put a smiley face on a season in which his average dipped

46 points and his slugging percentage plunged by 88. The only ROY to tumble further was Walt Dropo. "Moose" slumped from a .322 average and 144 RBI in 1950 to .239-57 in '51. By June of '52, he was traded.

Dropo's and Beltran's experiences were exceptional, but it's clear that poorer second seasons are not uncommon. In fact, of the 80 Rookies of the Year between 1947-99, 51 (64 percent) created fewer runs in their follow-up year. Now, the players on the above list created *far* fewer runs their second season. For the most part, it's a collection of players who never came close to fulfilling their early promise. That isn't a good sign for Beltran.

There is one exception: Willie Mays missed most of the 1952 season while serving in the military. He had a non-baseball excuse for his decline. When he returned in 1954, he blasted 41 homers and led the majors with a .345 average. From there, nothing could keep Mays from the Hall of Fame. While we shouldn't expect Beltran to duplicate Mays' experience, we probably can expect Carlos to have a better season in 2001. A look at the combined totals for Rookies of the Year indicate they tend to regain some of the production in Year 3 that they had lost in Year 2:

Rookies of the Year—1947-1999

Category	Year 1	Year 2	Diff	Year 3
Runs Created	82.2	70.1	-12.2	69.7
Batting Average	.286	.275	-.011	.278
On-Base Percentage	.349	.340	-.009	.346
Slugging Percentage	.449	.423	-.025	.441

In general, Rookies of the Year do endure a sophomore slump. Their runs created drop by about 12, while their percentage stats decrease, as well. The players do rebound a bit in Year 3, though not to the levels of their rookie performance. The fact that their runs created average in Year 3 is slightly lower than their mark in Year 2 probably is due to decreased playing time resulting from their poorer sophomore showings.

If Beltran is like the typical Rookie of the Year, he'll enjoy a bit of a renaissance in 2001. With Johnny Damon out of the picture in Kansas City, the Royals hope Beltran picks up some of the slack, possibly as their leadoff hitter. His showing in the Puerto Rican Winter League was not overwhelming, though, as he hit just .227 in 66 at-bats. While it's far too early to give up on him, he needs to prove he wasn't just a one-year wonder.

—Jim Henzler

A more complete listing for this category can be found on page 217.

Minnesota Twins: How Long Can Kelly Last?

For manager Tom Kelly and the Minnesota Twins, it's been a long, hard road since they won World Series titles in 1987 and 1991. Those championship Twins teams were built around a core of talent that was produced by the farm system, but the era of Kirby Puckett, Frank Viola, Chuck Knoblauch and Kent Hrbek is long gone.

Despite having one of the richest owners in the game, the Twins play small-market baseball. The talent leaving almost always is greater than the talent arriving, and the steady departure of quality ballplayers during the 1990s shows in the team's winning percentage over the last eight seasons.

Worst Winning Percentages—1993-2000

Team	W	L	Pct
Tampa Bay	201	284	.414
Minnesota	**528**	**699**	**.430**
Detroit	543	687	.441
Florida	551	678	.448
Pittsburgh	554	675	.451

Only the newborn Devil Rays have had a worse winning percentage than the Twins since 1993. Yet, Kelly has the longest tenure of any manager with his current club.

A Minnesota native, Kelly came on the scene in 1986, taking over for Ray Miller with 23 games remaining in September. The Twins were 71-91 that year, and in his first full season in '87, Kelly directed the team to an 85-77 finish that was good enough to eke out the West Division crown. With just one regular in the starting lineup over the age of 30, the 37-year-old rookie skipper led his young club to a stunning five-game upset of the Detroit Tigers in the ALCS before managing the Twins to their first championship in a seven-game World Series against the Cardinals.

That remarkable season and Kelly's second run to the title in '91 have solidified his place in Minnesota sports lore and his reputation as a big league manager. In light of free-agent flight and the ownership's unwillingness to pay enough to keep its own developing players or sign free agents, it's hard to blame the team's deepening slide over the last decade on the manager.

On the other hand, through the eight losing seasons since the Twins last posted a winning record in 1992, Kelly has developed a reputation for being impatient with young players and quick to criticize them in public. While Kelly has stood by LaTroy Hawkins and Matt Lawton through thick and thin, others including Todd Walker and Dave McCarty struggled under Kelly's handling. His effectiveness as a teacher has been questioned by some of his players and by members of the front office.

That's a serious issue for a club loaded with kids. After all, sixteen rookies surfaced on the Twins' roster during the 2000 season. Rumors were abound all summer that the end might be near for Kelly, but he will return in 2001 after signing a one-year deal in October.

The relationship between Kelly and owner Carl Pohlad has endured, and that has given the manager security over the years. It's obvious he's had more job security than most of his big league peers, especially when you look at the list of skippers who have suffered through eight or more straight losing seasons in major league history:

Managers With Most Consecutive Losing Seasons—1876-2000

Manager	Team(s)	Years	Losing Seasons
Connie Mack	Phi (AL)	1934-46	13
Jimmie Wilson	Phi-ChC	1934-38, 1941-44	9
Bob Ferguson	4 Tms	1879-84, 1886-87	8
Rene Lachemann	Sea-Mil-Fla	1981-84, 1993-97	8
Phil Garner	Mil-Det	1993-2000	8
Tom Kelly	**Min**	**1993-2000**	**8**

No one ever has had more job security than Connie Mack, who was an owner of the team he piloted for 50 years. His tenure as a manager is one record that may never be broken. Mack won six American League pennants in the first 14 years of the league, but on two occasions he dismantled strong clubs by selling off his stars. His fire sale at the end of the 1932 campaign led to those 13 straight losing seasons, a mark that Phil Garner and Kelly still are a long way from equaling.

With the notable exception of Kelly, none of the other managers on the above list achieved their dubious losing streaks by sticking with one club. Jimmie Wilson's nine losing seasons (he was gone after a 1-9 start in 1944) were split between the National League clubs in Philadelphia and Chicago. Bob Ferguson had four major league jobs in his eight years, and his managing career was over after his New York Metropolitans of the American Association started 6-24 in 1887. Rene Lachemann was fired three times during his eight consecutive losing seasons, managing Seattle and Milwaukee in the 1980s before serving as Florida's first skipper in the early '90s. The expansion Marlins tolerated just four losing campaigns before replacing Lachemann with Jim Leyland.

Only Mack surpasses Kelly for losing seasons with one club, and he didn't have to worry whether management remembered his successful years. Garner nearly equaled Kelly's eight straight losing seasons with one club, but the Brewers cut loose Garner after seven campaigns in Milwaukee. Gene Mauch, known as a patient man and a teacher, skippered the expansion Expos through their first seven seasons in the National League.

With a managing career that began much like Kelly's, nice guy Bucky Harris managed the Washington Senators to six straight losing seasons from 1937 through 1942. He probably was cut some slack in this second tenure with the Senators, considering he had led the franchise to its first AL pennant and World Series title as a rookie manager in 1924. Harris was 27 years old and also played second base while directing Washington to its only world championship. He served five seasons as a player-manager before he was traded to Detroit, and his second run with Washington ended after his sixth losing season in '42.

There are five big league managers who managed five straight losing seasons with the same club: Wilson with the Phillies (1934-38), Rogers Hornsby (Browns, 1933-37), Casey Stengel (Braves, 1939-43), Gil Hodges (expansion Senators, 1963-67) and Joe Torre (Mets, 1977-81). But only Hodges and Torre finished their fifth season. That makes a total of 10 managers in the history of the major leagues who survived more than four losing seasons with one club. Three or four losing campaigns are the norm after which managers' heads roll.

Minnesota's status as a small-market, talent-challenged franchise obviously takes the pressure off Kelly to some degree, but he still has his detractors inside the organization who believe his demanding nature no longer is getting the best out of his players—especially the young guys who need a patient teacher.

As it is for all managers, winning cures everything. Most veterans enjoy playing for Kelly, which suggests that his approach is hardly any different than when he took over the club 15 years ago. When the manager's approach doesn't work, however, we know who takes the fall. Eventually that time will come, even for the only manager in club history to lead the Twins to the Promised Land.

—Thom Henninger

New York Yankees: What Can We Expect From Their Fab Foursome?

When the New York Yankees signed Mike Mussina to a six-year, $88.5 million contract at the end of November, they suddenly had four starters who each had a career winning percentage better than .600. The impressive foursome of Mussina, Roger Clemens, Andy Pettitte and Orlando Hernandez enters the 2001 season not only with a collective winning percentage of .643, but also with a combined total of 548 victories.

Yankees' Top Four Starters—2001

Pitcher	W	L	Pct
Roger Clemens	260	142	.647
Mike Mussina	147	81	.645
Andy Pettitte	100	55	.645
Orlando Hernandez	41	26	.612
Total	548	304	.643

Few major league rotations ever have looked so dominating heading into a new season. Several rotations in big league history have had four starters with 50 career decisions and winning percentages of .600 or better, but none have approached the win total of the current Yankees foursome.

Let's take a look at the winningest rotations that have started a season with each member owning at least 50 decisions and a .600 winning percentage. To gauge what we might expect in 2001 from the Yankees' rotation, the criteria for the rotations below also require each pitcher to secure 15 decisions in that season. The rotations are ranked by their career win totals prior to the season in question.

1907 New York Giants

Pitcher	Career Prior to 1907			1907 Season	
	W	L	Pct	W	L
Joe McGinnity	217	116	.652	18	18
Christy Mathewson	150	83	.644	24	12
Hooks Wiltse	44	20	.688	13	12
Red Ames	40	24	.625	10	12
Total	451	243	.650	65	54

In both 1904 and '05, the first two seasons this foursome was together, the Giants won more than 100 games and claimed National League pennants. In '04, Joe McGinnity went 35-8 and Christy Mathewson was 33-12 as the club's star hurlers. They combined for 52 wins in 1905, and Red Ames

(22-8) and Hook Wiltse (15-6) added key contributions. In 1906, the Giants "fell" to 96-56, 40 games over .500, and finished second behind the 116-36 Cubs. Again, McGinnity (27-12) and Mathewson (22-12) led the way. The slide continued in 1907, the only year in which a 36-year-old McGinnity and Ames failed to produce winning records over a full season with New York. McGinnity was more hittable than in past seasons, yet the New York staff allowed the same number of runs as it did in '06. The offense scored 51 fewer runs in '07 en route to an 82-71 mark and a fourth-place finish.

1950 St. Louis Cardinals

Pitcher	Career Prior to 1950			1950 Season	
	W	L	Pct	W	L
Harry Brecheen	105	59	.640	8	11
Howie Pollet	83	49	.629	14	13
George Munger	63	34	.649	7	8
Max Lanier	79	51	.608	11	9
Al Brazle	57	34	.626	11	9
Total	387	227	.630	51	50

Essentially the same Cardinals' rotation during 1948 and '49 qualified as well. This group includes four southpaws—only George Munger was righthanded—and another righty, Ted Wilks, began the 1950 season with a career record of 49-20 (.710), but was lost for nearly the entire year after elbow surgery. After Howie Pollet went 21-10 and Harry Brecheen won three World Series games to spark the Cards to a world title in 1946, the rest of the 1940s were a frustrating dogfight with the Brooklyn Dodgers and Boston Braves. The Cards finished second in the National League in '47, '48 and '49. Pollet (20-9), Munger (15-8) and Al Brazle (14-8) were solid in 1949, but the loss of Wilks and the team's second-half fade in '50 resulted in the Cards' first second-division finish since 1938.

1956 Brooklyn Dodgers

Pitcher	Career Prior to 1956			1956 Season	
	W	L	Pct	W	L
Don Newcombe	85	41	.675	27	7
Sal Maglie	95	44	.683	13	5
Carl Erskine	100	57	.637	13	11
Clem Labine	44	22	.667	10	6
Total	324	164	.664	63	29

Out of six World Series battles between the Dodgers and Yankees shortly after World War II, the Dodgers won only one world title in 1955. They went 98-55 that year, outscoring all National League opponents and posting the best team ERA. The staff was led by ace Don Newcombe (20-5), Carl Erskine (11-8), Billy Loes (10-4) and reliever Clem Labine (13-5). While the Dodgers were in first place for all but two days in 1955, they barely survived a tight three-team race in '56 in which they held the top spot in the NL for just 18 days. En route to a 93-61 finish, the Dodgers dealt Loes to Baltimore and Erskine's chronic arm troubles were especially acute. They also lost an up-and-coming Johnny Podres to military service. Brooklyn probably wouldn't have repeated without trading for former nemesis Sal Maglie in May. Newcombe capped his career year by clinching the NL flag with his 27th win on the final day of the season.

	1990 New York Mets				
	Career Prior to 1990			**1990 Season**	
Pitcher	W	L	Pct	W	L
Dwight Gooden	100	39	.719	19	7
Ron Darling	87	55	.613	7	9
Sid Fernandez	69	45	.605	9	14
David Cone	39	17	.696	14	10
Total	295	156	.654	49	40

The Mets improved from 87-75 in 1989 to 91-71 in 1990, but both seasons produced second-place finishes in the National League East. With the acquisition of Frank Viola from Minnesota late in the 1989 season, better results were expected in '90, and a 20-22 start cost manager Davey Johnson his job in late May. The team rebounded under new skipper Bud Harrelson, but the club fell short of the eventual NL East champs, the Pirates, by playing .500 ball in September. Viola went 20-12 in his first full season in New York, and Dwight Gooden won 19 games. While Sid Fernandez went 14-5 in '89 and dropped to 9-14 in '90, his .200 opponent batting average allowed ranked first in the National League. The Mets' rotation wasn't the problem for this underachieving club. The pitching staff was plagued by poor work from relievers trying to maintain leads for closer John Franco.

	1908 Chicago Cubs				
	Career Prior to 1908			**1908 Season**	
Pitcher	W	L	Pct	W	L
Three Finger Brown	88	47	.652	29	9
Carl Lundgren	85	45	.654	6	9

Pitcher	Career Prior to 1908			1908 Season	
	W	L	Pct	W	L
Ed Reulbach	54	22	.711	24	7
Jack Pfiester	35	21	.625	12	10
Total	262	135	.660	71	35

The Cubs of 1907 won 107 games and easily secured their second straight National League pennant with this foursome and Orval Overall combining for 92 wins. Overall was the big winner with 23 victories, and his career mark was 57-39 (.594) heading into the '08 season. Still, the Cubs faced a tough race in '08. Engaged in a seesaw battle with the Pirates and Giants, the Cubs pulled into a first-place tie with Pittsburgh on September 22 by defeating the Giants twice. The next day's match-up featured the legendary Merkle's boner in which New York's Fred Merkle failed to advance to second base on a game-winning hit and was forced out by Cubs second baseman Johnny Evers after fans had rushed onto the field with darkness descending. The game was ruled a tie, but in a replay of the game on October 8 to determine the outcome of the race, the Cubs beat New York's Christy Mathewson to earn their third straight trip to the World Series.

If the 2001 Yankees get career seasons from two of their four aces, as the 1908 Cubs did, the Bronx Bombers may be on their way to their fourth straight World Series title. On the other hand, the New York lineup is an aging group, and the production of Tino Martinez, Scott Brosius and Paul O'Neill has been in decline. A drop-off in production by the 1907 Giants hastened the team's fall to fourth place despite a 24-12 performance from Mathewson. And the story of an aging McGinnity in '07 could repeat itself for a 38-year-old Roger Clemens.

The Yankees' bullpen also has some questions this spring after stud setup man Jeff Nelson departed for Seattle. The bullpen was a weak link for the 1990 Mets, and it didn't matter that Viola won 20 and Gooden won 19.

The 1956 Dodgers, however, were an aging group that won the pennant despite getting a career year from only the staff ace. All of these scenarios simply demonstrate the unpredictable nature of pennant races and the many facets of team play that must mesh for a championship club. Signing Mussina doesn't guarantee another division title for the Yankees, nor does it assure success in three rounds of postseason play. Still, there's hardly a team in baseball that doesn't covet the New York rotation.

—Thom Henninger

Oakland Athletics: Are Chavez And Tejada the Best Young SS/3B Combo Ever?

The youngsters anchoring the left side of Oakland's infield, shortstop Miguel Tejada and third baseman Eric Chavez, always were highly regarded prospects who seemed destined to have big league careers. Yet it's remarkable how both have progressed year to year in the majors and have emerged as budding stars at such a young age.

Miguel Tejada—1998-2000

Year	AB	R	H	2B	HR	RBI	Avg	OBP	Slg
1998	365	53	85	20	11	45	.233	.298	.384
1999	593	93	149	33	21	84	.251	.325	.427
2000	607	105	167	32	30	115	.275	.349	.479

Eric Chavez—1998-2000

Year	AB	R	H	2B	HR	RBI	Avg	OBP	Slg
1998	45	6	14	4	0	6	.311	.354	.444
1999	356	47	88	21	13	50	.247	.333	.427
2000	501	89	139	23	26	86	.277	.355	.495

That's impressive progress considering Chavez just turned 23 in December and Tejada is 24 until late May. Both already have surpassed 25 homers in a season and Tejada had his first 100-RBI campaign in 2000.

If you were to isolate shortstop-third base combos in which both players were seasonal age 25 or younger (as of June 30), and each already had had either a 25-homer season or reached the 100-RBI plateau, history reveals there have been just three such pairs, including Tejada and Chavez.

One of those pairs was shortstop Glenn Wright and third baseman Pie Traynor of the Pittsburgh Pirates in the early 1920s. At age 23, Traynor batted .338 and drove in 101 runs in his second full season in the majors in 1923. Wright was 23 the following year, when he recorded 111 RBI as a rookie. Both broke the 100-RBI mark in 1925, collecting 24 homers and 227 ribbies between them.

The other pair was Cleveland's Lou Boudreau and Ken Keltner at the end of the 1930s. Third sacker Keltner was 21 in his .276-26-113 rookie year in '38. He's probably best known, however, for two impressive defensive plays to stop Joe DiMaggio's 56-game hitting streak in '41. Boudreau, who turned 23 during his first full major league campaign in 1940, drove in 101 runs that year. By the end of that season, Keltner was a month shy of turning 24 and already had collected 54 homers and 288 RBI.

The impressive 1925 season by Traynor and Wright suggests a search of the best seasons by young left sides may be revealing. How do the Traynor-Wright and Chavez-Tejada combos compare to other young left sides? Here's a look at the best seasons among young shortstops and third basemen, when on-base and slugging abilities are considered:

Highest Combined OPS, Primary SS & 3B (Age 25 or Younger)—1876-2000

Player, Team	Pos	Age	Year	OBP	Slg	OPS	Comb OPS
John McGraw, Bal	3B	21	1894	.451	.436	.887	
Hughie Jennings, Bal	SS	25	1894	.411	.479	.890	1.777
Jumbo Davis, Bal	3B	25	1887	.353	.485	.838	
Oyster Burns, Bal	SS	22	1887	.414	.519	.933	1.770
Fernando Tatis, StL	3B	24	1999	.404	.553	.957	
Edgar Renteria, StL	SS	23	1999	.334	.400	.734	1.691
Eric Chavez, Oak	**3B**	**22**	**2000**	**.355**	**.495**	**.850**	
Miguel Tejada, Oak	**SS**	**24**	**2000**	**.349**	**.479**	**.828**	**1.678**
Freddy Lindstrom, NYG	3B	23	1929	.354	.464	.819	
Travis Jackson, NYG	SS	25	1929	.367	.490	.857	1.676
Freddy Lindstrom, NYG	3B	22	1928	.383	.511	.894	
Travis Jackson, NYG	SS	24	1928	.339	.436	.775	1.669
Bill Brubaker, Pit	3B	25	1936	.352	.384	.736	
Arky Vaughan, Pit	SS	24	1936	.453	.474	.927	1.663
Pie Traynor, Pit	3B	25	1925	.377	.464	.840	
Glenn Wright, Pit	SS	24	1925	.341	.480	.822	1.662

(minimum 400 PA and 80 G at position; age as of June 30)

While the pair of Traynor and Wright was the only one to have both players surpass the 100-RBI mark, the twosome ranked eighth in on-base-plus-slugging among young left sides. Ranking first on the list is a scrappy pair of colorful Hall of Famers, John McGraw and Hughie Jennings. They were the leaders of the National League's rough-and-tumble Baltimore Orioles club, players known to play hard and dirty. They baited umps, spiked opponents and stepped in front of baserunners or grabbed their belts when the game's sole umpire wasn't looking. They also were gifted players, and together they contributed 46 doubles, 30 triples, 201 RBI and a combined 1.777 OPS to the NL champs of 1894.

McGraw, of course, made his Hall of Fame mark as a manager. He was the skipper of the Giants when youngsters Travis Jackson and Freddy Lindstrom took over the left side of the New York infield in the early 1920s. Like McGraw and Jennings, both Jackson and Lindstrom are Hall of Famers, and they produced two of the top eight OPS totals among these young left sides. Their performance in 1927 ranked 10th in this study.

The McGraw-Jennings and Jackson-Lindstrom tandems received nearly equal production from both positions, which wasn't as true with the combinations of Fernando Tatis and Edgar Renteria in St. Louis and Pittsburgh's Arky Vaughan and Bill Brubaker. Despite weaker percentages from Brubaker, who replaced an aging Traynor at third for the Pirates in 1936, he delivered 102 RBI compared to Vaughan's 78.

As for the modern-day combos of Tatis-Renteria and Chavez-Tejada, no single player tops Tatis' .553 slugging percentage or .957 OPS. And no duo matches the 56 home runs by Chavez and Tejada. However, when you look at how productive these left sides were in terms of OPS, compared to league average, the modern-day left sides don't rank significantly above league average. By dividing a tandem's combined OPS in half, then dividing it by the league average in OPS, Tatis-Renteria as a group average nearly 10 percent above the league average while Chavez-Tejada are six percent above the league average—the smallest difference among the eight left sides in the chart.

The group most productive compared to league average is the Baltimore left side of Jumbo Davis and Oyster Burns from the American Association club of 1887. Not only did they collectively generate 56 doubles and 38 triples—a league-best 19 a piece—Davis and Burns produced an impressive 1.77 OPS that, when averaged by dividing in half, was nearly 26 percent above the league average that season.

Although he had a decent career, Burns wasn't a Hall of Famer, and Davis was a flash in the pan whose major league days were over four years later. Considering the growth in their numbers through the 2000 season, Chavez and Tejada seem certain to have much longer, more productive careers. For now, they rank among some of the best young players at their positions in history, some of whom went on to generate Hall of Fame credentials. If Chavez and Tejada continue to make progress as they have in their first three seasons, the comparisons someday will be addressing their own Hall of Fame chances.

—Thom Henninger

A more complete listing for this category can be found on page 218.

Seattle Mariners: Is Martinez an Overshadowed Legend?

The shadows have departed from Seattle. And no, the situation is not related to the retractable roof at Safeco Field.

Nor is it a reflection of the rainy climate in the Emerald City.

But over the past two years, Ken Griffey Jr. and Alex Rodriguez have moved on—along with their ever-present shadows—to much greener pastures. Both seem destined to rank among baseball's immortals. Griffey ultimately may threaten Hank Aaron's all-time home-run record, while Rodriguez may wind up being the greatest offensive shortstop in history. No doubt about it, they cast huge shadows while playing for Seattle.

However, as painful as Griffey's and Rodriguez' exits have been for Seattle's faithful, they finally may allow the spotlight to shine brightly on another terrific hitter. It's hard to remain anonymous when you've been as productive as Edgar Martinez. But try as he might, Edgar probably hasn't received as much recognition as he has deserved.

Over the past six seasons, Martinez has been one of the most consistent players in baseball. Year in and year out, he could be counted on to come close to or reach triple digits in runs, RBI and walks. Even more glamorously, he has delivered 20 or more homers and a .320-plus batting average like clockwork.

Edgar Martinez

The combination of power and average that Martinez has provided on a routine basis is more rare than you might expect. Oh sure, in this era of 500-foot home runs and record-breaking offensive seasons, clouting 20 homers seemingly has become an effortless milestone. Barry Bonds, for instance, has blasted 20 or more homers for 11 consecutive seasons. Rafael Palmeiro and Albert Belle have done so for 10 straight campaigns. Guys like Dean Palmer and Henry Rodriguez have managed the feat in each of the last five years. But how many of them are .300 hitters, much less .320 batsmen? Very few actually.

In fact, 26 players batted at least .320 last year (minimum 502 plate appearances), the most in any season since 1937. In addition, Jeff Cirillo and Derek Jeter have reached the mark each of the past three seasons. But they have only one career 20-homer campaign between them. In general, players with exceptionally high batting averages, like Tony Gwynn and Wade Boggs, aren't noted for their power.

So that's why Martinez' streak of homers and batting average is so remarkable. As you can see from the following chart, few players in history have been able to match Edgar's achievement, and check out the names of those who have:

Longest Streaks With 20-Plus Home Runs And .320-Plus Batting Average—1876-2000

Player	Years	Span
Lou Gehrig	1930-37	8
Ted Williams	1939-42, 1946-49	8
Babe Ruth	1926-32	7
Stan Musial	1948-54	7
Joe DiMaggio	1936-41	6
Edgar Martinez	**1995-00**	**6**
Chuck Klein	1929-33	5
Jimmie Foxx	1932-36	5
Ted Williams	1954-58	5

Well, there's no doubt that Martinez is dwelling in the land of the legends. You know you're living in the high-rent district when the other residents have names like Lou Gehrig, Ted Williams, Babe Ruth, Stan Musial and Joe DiMaggio. Yet those are the only players who generated streaks of 20-plus homers and .320-plus batting averages as long as Martinez' six. All of them are in the Hall of Fame, as are Chuck Klein and Jimmie Foxx, who produced five-year streaks.

Special mention must be made of Williams. The Splendid Splinter arrived as a rookie in 1939 and promptly hit .327 with 31 home runs. He eclipsed 20 homers and a .320 batting average each of the next three seasons, before leaving for military service between 1943-45. After returning from the war, he picked up right where he left off, with four more 20 HR-.320 BA seasons in succession.

Then in 1950, missing much of the campaign with a broken elbow, Williams hit .317. He hit .318 the following year, before missing most of the next two seasons while fighting another war. In 1954, he began another five-year run of 20-.320, which reached its peak with 38 homers and a .388 batting average in 1957. He was *40 years old* by the end of that streak. So, if he hadn't missed most of five seasons defending our country, and if he had managed only a couple more hits in 1950 and 1951, it's conceivable that Williams would have compiled a 19-year streak of 20-.320. Amazing.

Since Williams retired, 20-.320 streaks have become quite rare. Don Mattingly produced a four-year run between 1984-87, as did Mike Piazza between 1995-98. In the last 40 years, only Kirby Puckett, Larry Walker, Bernie Williams, Ivan Rodriguez and Nomar Garciaparra have produced streaks of exactly three years. Rodriguez' and Garciaparra's runs both are active. The only other players with active streaks of exactly two years are Todd Helton, Manny Ramirez and Mike Sweeney.

Though Martinez turned 38 years of age this January, he shows few signs of slowing down. He hit 37 homers last year, a career high, and led the American League with 145 RBI. He still walks a lot and collects his share of doubles, helping produce an OPS around 1.000.

Considering how devastating an offensive force he is, it's amazing that Edgar didn't firmly establish himself in the big leagues until he was 27 years old. He had been an All-Star third baseman in Triple-A for two seasons prior to establishing his footing in the majors. Had he gotten to the majors a couple years earlier, he almost certainly would be past 2,000 career hits, and well above 1,000 runs scored and RBI. He probably would be a stronger Hall of Fame candidate, as well.

For now, Edgar may be remembered as the third-best player on the Mariners during this era. That might be unfortunate, considering the rarified air of his particular accomplishment. But now that Griffey and Rodriguez are gone, Martinez at last might begin casting a longer shadow of his own.

—Jim Henzler

A more complete listing for this category can be found on page 220.

Tampa Bay Devil Rays: How Critical Is Up-The-Middle Offense?

The mess that was Tampa Bay's offense last season was offensive in the worst sense of the word. It ranked last in the American League in hits, total bases and on-base percentage. It was the only offense in the majors to generate a slugging percentage *under* .400. Most importantly, it produced the fewest runs in the AL. The Devil Rays' lineup was an albatross around the team's collective neck, helping doom the club to just 69 wins. Clearly, there was much dysfunction to go around. But one particular facet was hard to overlook. Tampa Bay's lineup featured a few black holes sprinkled throughout its order. Consider the overall statistics of the players who saw the most playing time for the Devil Rays at the following positions:

Tampa Bay Devil Rays—2000

Pos	Player	OBP	Slg	OPS
C	John Flaherty	.296	.376	.671
2B	Miguel Cairo	.314	.328	.642
SS	Felix Martinez	.305	.298	.603
CF	Gerald Williams	.312	.427	.739
MLB Average		**.345**	**.437**	**.782**

Tampa's regular catcher couldn't produce a .300 on-base percentage, its shortstop couldn't slug .300, and none of these players could generate an OPS that came close to the major league average. You often hear the phrase "strong up the middle" used when describing the desired qualities of a major league team. The term usually applies to defense when assessing the club's up-the-middle talent. Clearly, fielding ability is important at these positions. But defensive wizardry may not be able to overcome questionable offense if it's too far below average. Tampa Bay's offensive output from its corps of up-the-middle performers definitely was substandard.

Worst Up-the-Middle OPS—2000

Team	W-L	Pct	Place/Tms	OBP	Slg	OPS
Phillies	65-97	.401	5/5	.317	.360	.677
Devil Rays	**69-92**	**.429**	**5/5**	**.309**	**.368**	**.677**
Twins	69-93	.426	5/5	.308	.385	.694
Padres	76-86	.469	5/5	.323	.374	.698
Brewers	73-89	.451	3/6	.324	.383	.706
Blue Jays	83-79	.512	3/5	.315	.396	.711
Royals	77-85	.475	4/5	.338	.377	.715
Cubs	65-97	.401	6/6	.340	.375	.716

Each team's place is based upon its division finish. The number of clubs competing in each division also is listed. It's certainly hard to find a truly good team on the list. None of them finished higher than third in their division, and none finished more than four games over .500. In fact, the three teams ranking worst in up-the-middle OPS last year—the Phillies, Devil Rays and Twins—posted the fewest wins in their respective leagues.

The Phillies' and Devil Rays' experience follows the general rule. Among the most recent 10 teams to finish last in their leagues in up-the-middle OPS since 1996, not one has finished better than 10 games *below* .500.

Teams Finishing Last in Up-the-Middle OPS—1996-2000

Year	Team	Lg	W-L	Pct	Place/Tms	OBP	Slg	OPS
1996	Blue Jays	AL	74-88	.457	4/5	.318	.350	.667
1996	Giants	NL	68-94	.420	4/4	.320	.348	.668
1997	Blue Jays	AL	76-86	.469	5/5	.300	.338	.638
1997	Cubs	NL	68-94	.420	5/5	.313	.382	.696
1998	Devil Rays	AL	63-99	.389	5/5	.304	.359	.663
1998	Phillies	NL	75-87	.463	3/5	.308	.358	.667
1999	Angels	AL	70-92	.432	4/4	.309	.358	.666
1999	Cardinals	NL	75-86	.466	4/6	.325	.389	.714
2000	**Devil Rays**	**AL**	**69-92**	**.429**	**5/5**	**.309**	**.368**	**.677**
2000	Phillies	NL	65-97	.401	5/5	.317	.360	.677

This clearly shows how difficult it is for a team to overcome abnormally poor offense at the "defensive" positions. That makes sense, since nearly half of the lineup is producing at a subpar level. STATS has offensive data broken down by position since 1987. Since then, the 28 teams ranking last in their league in this category have combined for a .453 winning percentage, or roughly a 73-89 record.

Now, before we get carried away with this information, any team will tend to do poorly overall if its combined OPS at *any* four positions ranks last in the league. In fact, teams ranking last in their leagues at the "corner" positions—1B/3B/LF/RF—have combined for a .448 winning percentage since 1987. That's even worse than the record for poor up-the-middle teams. Nevertheless, the study indicates that teams shouldn't overlook the offense when trying to build the best possible defense.

—Jim Henzler

A more complete listing for this category can be found on page 221.

Texas Rangers: Can A-Rod Create Enough Runs to Justify the Funds?

They like to do things big in Texas.

Big state.

Big oil.

And now, the biggest contract in baseball.

The Rangers landed perhaps the best player money could buy when they signed Alex Rodriguez to a 10-year, $252 million deal this past offseason. By doing so, they also strengthened one of their weakest positions. Last year, Texas shortstops combined for 15 homers, 62 RBI and a .238 batting average. By comparison, Rodriguez hit .316 and dwarfed those home-run and RBI totals with 41 and 132, respectively.

Multimillion-dollar contracts are nothing new, of course. In recent years, players like Albert Belle, Mike Piazza and Kevin Brown each have taken turns raising the compensation bar with salaries that average eight figures per year. The difference with Rodriguez, however, is that he signed his huge deal possibly two or three years before he even reaches his peak.

Rodriguez now has scored at least 100 runs in five seasons. He's driven in 100-plus runs four times. He's slugged 40-plus homers in each of the past three campaigns. And yet, remarkably, he didn't turn 25 years of age until last July. A player as talented, accomplished and young as Rodriguez is truly a rare combination. A-Rod's seasonal age (as of June 30) was 24 in 2000. He already has generated 627 runs created in his career. Few players have achieved that level of production through the same seasonal age:

Most Runs Created Through Seasonal Age 24

Player	RC	\multicolumn{10}{c}{Next 10 Seasons}	Total
		1	2	3	4	5	6	7	8	9	10	
Ty Cobb	763	148	99	80	154	123	144	90	100	81	120	1139
Mel Ott	756	143	130	140	120	134	107	105	110	124	71	1184
Jimmie Foxx	713	166	144	139	152	119	172	142	115	97	33	1279
Mickey Mantle	700	155	138	110	118	157	114	46	116	65	69	1088
George Davis	689	105	133	85	82	80	87	98	1	80	87	838
Joe Kelley	650	127	98	122	102	88	75	77	77	46	49	861
Alex Rodriguez	627	—	—	—	—	—	—	—	—	—	—	—
Ted Williams	622	—	—	166	161	160	174	98	144	4	34	941
Ken Griffey Jr.	603	45	132	148	135	140	108	—	—	—	—	708
Jimmy Sheckard	592	58	78	85	74	55	79	79	115	86	30	739

(age as of June 30)

Even on a list containing some of baseball's legends, Rodriguez is unique. He's the only one of the 10 who primarily was a middle infielder through seasonal age 24. George Davis soon would become one, but he had played mostly the outfield and third base prior to turning 25.

As good as Rodriguez has been, it's entirely possible that he'll get even better in the future. It's common knowledge that players, as a group, don't reach their peak until seasonal age 27. While that may be the case for Rodriguez, it's interesting to note that of the nine other players besides A-Rod to make the list on the previous page, only Ted Williams and Ken Griffey Jr. managed to produce a season after age 25 that surpassed their single-season high through age 24.

Still, these are the kind of players teams want to keep. In general, if a player is young and possesses great ability, clubs are reluctant to discard him. True, three of the players listed, Davis, Joe Kelley and Jimmy Sheckard, switched teams at some point through seasonal age 25. But they're also the only ones among our 10 who played in the 19th century.

In fact, there now have been 16 players who generated at least 400 runs created through age 24 and also switched teams at some point through age 25 (like Rodriguez). Twelve of those 16 players began their careers before 1900. Two others—Joe Jackson and Doc Hoblitzell—started their careers in 1908. The only other one, besides Rodriguez, to begin his career after 1908 is Roberto Alomar. Special mention should be made of Babe Ruth, of course, who was sent from the Red Sox to the Yankees before turning 25 in 1920. But Ruth had pitched in 158 games before then and had created just 259 runs through seasonal age 24.

The players who created at least 400 runs through age 24 averaged roughly 88 runs created per season between ages 25-34. For the nine players besides A-Rod on our top 10 list, the average was about 104 per year. Since Rodriguez has created at least 130 runs twice over the past three years, 88-104 runs created may be a bit disappointing. Then again, $252 million only goes so far.

—Jim Henzler

A more complete listing for this category can be found on page 223.

Toronto Blue Jays: Is Batista the Littlest Big Bopper?

Tony Batista

Bigger, stronger, bulked-up players are one of the many explanations given for the offensive explosion in recent years. Of course baseballs will be flying out of the park, the thinking goes, when every lineup has hitters like Mark McGwire, Frank Thomas or Mo Vaughn. These are guys that look like they would be more at home on the football field than the baseball diamond.

The Blue Jays' Tony Batista flies in the face of that theory. Following an impressive 1999 season in which he clubbed 31 homers and drove in 100 runs, Batista affirmed himself as one of the game's premier power hitters in 2000. Sure, he hit only .263 and still pretty much refuses to take a walk, but Batista launched 41 homers last season, tied for fourth most in the American League.

All this from a guy who perhaps is more likely to be mistaken for the bat boy than a major league power hitter. After all, not only does Batista have the oddest-looking batting stance in the majors (as "open" a stance as is possible), but he's also only 6-feet and 185 pounds. At least, that's his listed weight in the Toronto media guide.

Even if Batista really does tip the scales at 185 pounds, it places him as one of the leanest home-run hitters in recent years. In 2000, 16 players hit 40 or more home runs. Of those 16, only three weighed in at less than 200 pounds—Richard Hidalgo, Jeff Bagwell and Batista—and none weighed less than the Toronto third baseman. Excluding Batista, the average height of the 40-homer hitter in 2000 was better than 6-foot-2 and the average weight was almost 215 pounds. Batista is giving away several inches and nearly 30 pounds to these players!

While Batista is one of the slightest power hitters in today's game, how does he stack up to the players of the past? If we limit our study to just the past 25 years, Batista's accomplishment is pretty impressive. Check out the list of the lightest 40-homer hitters since 1975:

Lightest 40-Homer Hitters—1975-2000

Player	Ht	Wt	Season(s) (HR)
Ben Oglivie	6-2	160	1980 (41)
George Foster	6-1	180	1977 (52), 1978 (40)
Tony Batista	**6-0**	**185**	**2000 (41)**
George Bell	6-1	190	1987 (47)
Ryne Sandberg	6-2	190	1990 (40)
Rafael Palmeiro	6-0	190	1998 (43), 1999 (47)
Richard Hidalgo	6-3	190	2000 (44)
Reggie Jackson	6-0	195	1969 (47), 1980 (41)
Mike Schmidt	6-2	195	1979 (45), 1980 (48), 1983 (40)
Jeff Bagwell	6-0	195	1997 (43), 1999 (42), 2000 (47)

Yeah, Ben Oglivie was the Spiderman, wasn't he? Batista joins him and George Foster (was he really that skinny?) in the select company of the most impressive little power hitters of the last quarter-century.

Of course, if we compare Batista to the hitters of more than a generation or two ago, he doesn't seem too out of the ordinary. In fact, looking at the weights of players from the '50s and '60s, there's no doubting that today's players are much bigger and stronger. While Batista is small by contemporary standards, he's nothing special when compared to the home-run hitters of a generation or two ago. Ernie Banks, for one, tipped the scales at 180, Hank Aaron also weighed only 180, while Willie Mays was listed at 170 pounds.

Of course, all measurements need to be taken with a grain of salt. Did Mays really weigh 170 throughout his career? Maybe. Did Hank Aaron really weigh less than your average starting shortstop does today? Maybe. Is Tony Batista your best pound-for-pound power hitter in today's game? Sounds like a good bet.

—John Sasman

A more complete listing for this category can be found on page 224.

Arizona Diamondbacks: Is Finley's Post-30 Power Surge Unprecedented?

By the end of the 1995 season, Steve Finley pretty much had cemented his reputation. After seven major league seasons, he had established himself as a stellar center fielder and a legitimate stolen-base threat. Usually a leadoff hitter, his on-base percentages didn't stand out because he didn't walk enough for the role.

As for power, Finley wasn't counted on to provide much. He always ranked among the leaders in triples because of his speed, though he had hit just 47 homers in 919 games. Sure, the Astrodome had muted some of Finley's longball ability, but he also hit just 10 homers in 1995, his first season in San Diego.

Having turned 31 just before the 1996 campaign, Finley didn't figure to suddenly blossom into a power hitter. But that's exactly what he did. He used weightlifting to get stronger and started to turn on inside pitches more aggressively. He broke out with 30 homers in '96 and has averaged 28 in each of the last five years. In other words, he has hit 141 (75 percent) of his 188 total homers (through seasonal age 35) from ages 31-35.

Over the course of baseball history, the typical hitter hit 25 percent of his career homers (through seasonal age 35) after turning 31. Finley's surge is the third-greatest ever among players with 150 homers through age 35.

Highest Percentages of Career Home Runs (Through Seasonal Age 35) Hit Between Ages 31-35—1876-2000

Player	Before Age 31			Age 31-35			31-35
	AB	HR	HR Pct	AB	HR	HR Pct	HR Pct
Hank Sauer	169	7	4.1	2,671	165	6.2	.96
Ken Williams	995	16	1.6	2,496	135	5.4	.89
Steve Finley	**3,364**	**47**	**1.4**	**2,963**	**141**	**4.8**	**.75**
Edgar Martinez	1,940	49	2.5	2,434	125	5.1	.72
Ken Caminiti	3,035	57	1.9	2,416	139	5.8	.71
Brady Anderson	2,717	56	2.1	2,766	126	4.6	.69
Sid Gordon	1,932	57	3.0	2,306	126	5.5	.69
Mike Stanley	1,583	50	3.2	1,930	104	5.4	.68
Brian Downing	2,603	56	2.2	2,598	110	4.2	.66
B.J. Surhoff	3,884	57	.64	2,850	103	3.6	.64

(minimum 150 HR though seasonal age 35; age as of June 30)

Five of Finley's contemporaries also make the top 10 list: Edgar Martinez, Ken Caminiti, Brady Anderson, Mike Stanley and B.J. Surhoff. Homers are being hit with more frequency than ever, but that's only a minor cause for these players' improved performance.

Steve Finley

There are five main reasons that the players on the chart suddenly upped their longball production: military service, the lively ball, opportunity, better health and increased strength.

Hank Sauer hit an unmatched 96 percent of his homers from ages 31-35. He lost most of 1944-45 to World War II, and a bigger problem was that he was trapped in the minors until he was 31. Finally given a chance, he hit at least 30 homers in his first five full big league seasons and was named National League MVP in 1952 at age 35. Military service also cut into the pre-age-31 production of Ken Williams (World War I, 1918) and Sid Gordon (World War II, 1944-45). Williams also battled injuries and benefited from the end of the dead-ball era when he turned 30.

Like Sauer, Martinez and Stanley had to wait longer than they should have for the chance to play regularly in the majors. Martinez was 27 when he got his first shot, while Stanley was 30.

Not coincidentally, Martinez' power blossomed when he became a full-time DH at age 32, putting an end to a string of injuries that had plagued him as a third baseman. Similarly, Surhoff has been a healthier and more effective hitter as his defensive responsibilities have lessened. He moved from catcher to third base at age 28, then to the outfield at age 30 (though he did return for a final season at the hot corner a year later).

Surhoff missed most of the 1994 season with an abdominal strain, and he used his rehabilitation time to get stronger. Weightlifting also was the primary factor in the power surges of Caminiti, Anderson and Downing, helping to alter their approaches at the plate, as well as their reputations.

—Jim Callis

A more complete listing for this category can be found on page 225.

Atlanta Braves: How Extraordinary Was Furcal's First Season?

In his major league debut last season, Rafael Furcal gave the Braves the leadoff hitter they lacked, ran wild on the bases and provided quality defense at both shortstop and second base. Observers obviously were impressed, as Furcal was named National League Rookie of the Year.

But the magnitude of Furcal's accomplishments, for the most part, escaped notice. Not only did he bat .295 with a .394 on-base percentage and 40 stolen bases, he did so while making the jump from Class-A at age 19. Furcal wasn't just the top rookie in the NL last season. He also turned in one of the best performances by a teenager in baseball history.

Highest Batting Averages, Teenagers—1876-2000

Player, Team	Year	Age	Avg
Mel Ott, NYG	1928	19	.322
Ty Cobb, Det	1906	19	.316
Cesar Cedeno, Hou	1970	19	.310
Rafael Furcal, Atl	**2000**	**19**	**.295**
Buddy Lewis, Was	1936	19	.291

(minimum 300 PA)

That's pretty nice company. Ty Cobb and Mel Ott are in Cooperstown. Cesar Cedeno seemed destined for the Hall of Fame before his skills rapidly deteriorated once he reached 30. Buddy Lewis, the former Senators third baseman, had 1,112 hits through age 24, then lost 1942-44 to World War II and played parts of just four seasons afterward.

Highest On-Base Percentages, Teenagers—1876-2000

Player, Team	Year	Age	OBP
Mel Ott, NYG	1928	19	.397
Rafael Furcal, Atl	**2000**	**19**	**.394**
Ty Cobb, Det	1906	19	.355
John McGraw, Bal	1892	19	.355
Tony Conigliaro, Bos	1964	19	.354

This list may have even more impressive names than the first. Ott and Cobb are joined by a third Hall of Famer, John McGraw. While McGraw made it to Cooperstown primarily for his managerial skills, he also was a lifetime .334 hitter who might have been enshrined as a player had leg injuries not truncated his career. Conigliaro was one of the best young sluggers the game had ever seen before a beaning at age 22 ruined his career.

Most Stolen Bases, Teenagers—1876-2000

Player, Team	Year	Age	SB
Rafael Furcal, Atl	**2000**	**19**	**40**
Ty Cobb, Det	1906	19	23
George Davis, Cle	1890	19	22
Taylor Shaffer, Phi	1890	19	19
Ben Conroy, Phi	1890	19	17
Cesar Cedeno, Hou	1970	19	17

No teenager ever stole as many bases in one year as Furcal did in 2000. Only Hall of Famers Cobb and George Davis even swiped half as many.

Most Runs Created, Teenagers—1876-2000

Player, Team	Year	Age	RC
George Davis, Cle	1890	19	90
Buddy Lewis, Was	1936	19	87
Mel Ott, NYG	1928	19	85
Phil Cavarretta, ChC	1935	18	81
Rafael Furcal, Atl	**2000**	**19**	**73**

Runs created is a Bill James statistic that takes a player's total offensive performance and determines how many runs he contributed to his team. Besides Furcal, this chart features two Hall of Famers, as well as Lewis and Phil Cavarretta, the only 18-year-old on any of the four lists.

Furcal made all four of these top fives, while several notable teenagers couldn't crack one. Ken Griffey Jr. and Hall of Famers Travis Jackson, Al Kaline, Freddy Lindstrom, Mickey Mantle and Robin Yount are absent despite playing regularly as teenagers. In fact, the only under-20 hitters at any position to have a clearly better year were Ott (.322, 18 homers and 69 runs in 1928) and Conigliaro (.290-24-69 in 1964).

We would be remiss if we didn't point out that HBO reported last summer that Furcal actually was three years older than believed. He and the Braves insist that isn't the case. If they're telling the truth, Furcal's future looks extremely bright indeed.

—Jim Callis

A more complete listing for this category can be found on page 226.

Chicago Cubs: Can Sosa Keep Swinging Away And Still Hit .300?

Don't blame it on El Niño, or La Niña. Lake Michigan wasn't at fault, either. There were no unusual Canadian air masses hovering overhead. No, not even the best Chicagoland weatherman could have forecasted the ill wind that swirled around Wrigley Field last summer.

The Cubs got off to a disappointing 20-33 start under new skipper Don Baylor, done in by everything from weak hitting to an injury-riddled starting staff to a horrendous bullpen. General manager Ed Lynch resigned shortly after the All-Star break, and the team unloaded Glenallen Hill, Ismael Valdes and Henry Rodriguez before the trade deadline. A 16-42 finish did little to calm the storm. At the center of the season-long tempest, however, was none other than Sammy Sosa. His contentious contract talks, controversial trade demands and public "disagreements" with both Baylor and current GM Andy MacPhail did wonders for columnists around the city, but did little for the organization's chemistry.

Still, despite the distractions off the field and the losing streaks on it, Sosa continued to do the two things that have cemented his reputation at the plate: hit lots of home runs and swing away with impunity. He did both so well that he led the majors in home runs (50) *and* number of swings and misses (422). What was surprising was that he also finished the 2000 season with a career-high .320 batting average despite striking out 168 times. That .320 mark was the highest figure ever for someone who struck out more than 155 times in a season, and the 168 whiffs represented the third-highest strikeout total in history for a .300 hitter.

Most Strikeouts While Batting .300 or Better, Season—1876-2000

Player, Team	Year	AB	H	SO	Avg	Next Yr Avg
Bobby Bonds, SF	1970	663	200	189	.302	.288
Sammy Sosa, ChC	1998	643	198	171	.308	.288
Sammy Sosa, ChC	**2000**	**604**	**193**	**168**	**.320**	—
Andres Galarraga, Col	1996	626	190	157	.304	.318
Mo Vaughn, Bos	1996	635	207	154	.326	.315
Mo Vaughn, Bos	1997	527	166	154	.315	.337
Andres Galarraga, Mon	1988	609	184	153	.302	.257
Greg Luzinski, Phi	1975	596	179	151	.300	.304
Dick Allen, Phi	1965	619	187	150	.302	.317
Mo Vaughn, Bos	1995	550	165	150	.300	.326

The only .300 hitters to ring up more whiffs in a season than Sosa did in 2000 were Bobby Bonds and Swingin' Sammy himself—he fanned 171 times while posting a .308 batting average during the Great Home-Run Race of 1998. Sosa also struck out 171 times in 1999, but he couldn't keep his batting average from falling 20 points. Bonds is an interesting case, as he reached this 189-.302 level in 1970, his third season in the bigs. For the next 11 campaigns, he never struck out more than 148 times in a year, but neither did he hit better than his '71 mark of .288.

The next-year drops in batting average for both Bonds and Sosa were not indicative of our top 10 as a whole, however, as five of the next-year batting averages actually were higher than they were in the big strikeout year. The batting-average improvements in the the next year didn't really come at the expense of the strikeouts, either. For example, Andres Galarraga hit .318 in 1997 but still struck out 141 times, Mo Vaughn hit .337 in 1998 but piled up 144 whiffs, and Dick Allen jumped to .317 in '66 while striking out 136 times.

While it may appear as though Sosa is becoming the King of Swing among this group, he actually has a long way to go to catch the trio of Galarraga, Vaughn and Allen. Sosa has broken the 125-strikeout, .300 plateau just twice, but Galarraga has reached those levels six times in his career, including the pair of instances in our top 10 where he fanned more than 150 times. Vaughn and Allen each have produced four 125-.300 campaigns.

Sammy Sosa

The point is, it's just not that common to rack up big strikeout totals while maintaining a high average. It's even less common to do it year in and year out. Take a look at the breakdown on the following page:

125-Strikeout, .300-Average Seasons by Individual Players

Decade	No.
1960s	5
1970s	7
1980s	8
1990-2000	19

Just 25 players in major league history have reached 125-plus strikeouts and a .300 batting average in a single season a total of 39 times. Besides Galarraga, Vaughn, Allen and Sosa, only Greg Luzinski and Phil Bradley have done it as much as twice. With the exception of Bradley, those names carry some impressive credentials, but the short list illustrates just how few players are able to balance high strikeout totals with a high average on an annual basis.

Not surprisingly, this also is a more recent phenomenon, as higher strikeout totals and lower batting averages are increasingly overlooked as long as baseballs keep flying out of the park and big contracts continue to go to home-run hitters. More 125-.300 seasons have happened in the last 11 years than in the entire history of baseball prior to 1990.

So the question is whether Sosa will be able to maintain his average, or is .300 an unrealistic expectation? Certainly, guys like Galarraga, Vaughn and more recently Manny Ramirez (131 strikeouts, .333 average in 1999) have shown that big strikeout totals and a .300 average don't have to be mutually exclusive, especially in this era of big swings and even bigger offense.

What is certain is that Sosa will continue to rack up the strikeouts, as he has fanned an average of 159 times during the past six seasons. His strikeout totals may even *increase* now that Major League Baseball has told umpires to call the strike zone as it's defined in the rule book, which in essence means that umpires may actually enforce the high strike beginning this year. Perhaps a better question is whether Cubs fans really care if Sosa maintains a .300 average. Our guess is probably not, just as long as the wind that blows out at Wrigley this summer is generated by his bat rather than a jet plane taking him to "greener" pastures.

—Tony Nistler

A more complete listing for this category can be found on page 227.

Cincinnati Reds: Do Decent Teams With Unexceptional Pitchers Fade?

There was rejoicing on the banks of the Ohio last February when the Reds traded for Ken Griffey Jr. After finishing a game behind Houston and losing a one-game playoff to the Mets in '99, Cincinnati thought it may have acquired the missing piece to its championship puzzle. Griffey was the native son returning home, and possibly the best player in baseball to boot.

As we know, the story didn't have a happy ending last year, at least not if you're a Reds fan. Griffey got off to a slow start and was batting just .212 through May. The Reds went 10-17 in June and fell 8.5 games behind the Cardinals. At the All-Star break, Cincinnati traded its best starter, Denny Neagle. Nevertheless, without Neagle the Reds fared better in the second half (42-33) than they had in the first (43-44). Overall, they finished eight games over .500 despite not having a pitcher who won more than 12 games. By doing so, Cincinnati bucked the odds. The other 10 teams without so much as a 13-game winner in 2000 finished an average of 16 games *under* .500.

So even though the Reds didn't have a clear ace last season, they enjoyed relatively greater success than most teams in similar situations. What does that mean for 2001? To get an idea, we'll consider only those clubs since 1900 that finished at least six games over .500 without any single pitcher winning more than 12 contests. Because of the tricks that strike-shortened seasons can play with the results, we'll exclude 1981, 1994 and 1995. The 2000 Reds became the 11th team to qualify, based on our parameters.

Teams Six-Plus Games Over .500 Without a 13-Game Winner—1900-2000

Team	Year	W-L	Pct	Place	NextYr	Pct	Place
Red Sox	1940	82-72	.532	4	84-70	.545	2
Angels	1967	84-77	.522	5	67-95	.414	8
Red Sox	1980	83-77	.519	4	59-49	.546	*5
Red Sox	1984	86-76	.531	4	81-81	.500	5
Phillies	1986	86-75	.534	2	80-82	.494	4
Cardinals	1987	95-67	.586	1	76-86	.469	5
Reds	1987	84-78	.519	2	87-74	.540	2
Expos	1990	85-77	.525	3	71-90	.441	6
Cardinals	1991	84-78	.519	2	83-79	.512	3
Angels	1998	85-77	.525	2	70-92	.432	4
Reds	**2000**	**85-77**	**.525**	**2**	—	—	—
Totals		939-831	.531		758-798	.487	

(*based on combined 1st/2nd half records; excludes '81, '94, '95 strike years)

Not surprisingly, most of these seasons have occurred since the advent of the five-man rotation. With five-man rotations, starts are spread between more pitchers, at least relative to four-man rotations. So the chances are higher that their wins will be more spread out, too.

Of the 10 teams on the list before 2000, only three managed to produce better winning percentages in Year 2. None improved by more than 3.5 games (though the Red Sox were on pace to improve by four games in '81 if not for the strike). Interestingly, the club that improved the most was the other Cincinnati contingent on the chart. The 1987 Reds captured 84 games despite not having a single pitcher win more than 10 games. Bill Gullickson, Ted Power and Tom Browning won 10 games apiece, yet each finished below .500. The next year, Danny Jackson joined the Reds and finished second in the National League Cy Young race after posting 23 wins. Jose Rijo also climbed aboard via a trade and won 13 times, while Browning improved to 18 victories. Cincinnati wound up going 87-74 in 1988.

Taken as a group, the teams on the list dropped from a .531 winning percentage in Year 1 to .487 in Year 2. That translates to a slide of seven wins—from 86 to 79—in a 162-game schedule. Perhaps even more ominous from the Reds' perspective is the fact that no club on the list managed to capture any kind of league or division race in Year 2.

In fact, only one club even rose in the standings. You have to go all the way back to the 1940-41 Red Sox to find that feat. If that time frame isn't depressing enough for Reds fans, they may want to know that the 1941 Red Sox didn't come close to sniffing first place, finishing 17 lengths behind the Yankees that season.

The 2001 Reds must hope one or two of their pitchers can emerge as Jackson, Rijo or Browning did in 1988. The best candidates may be Rob Bell and Seth Etherton, though they have a combined total of 12 major league victories between them. Otherwise, Cincinnati's top returning starters appear to be Elmer Dessens and Pete Harnisch.

If the historical experience of similar teams is any guide, it's likely the Reds will have less success this season compared to last. But hey, maybe they can find another player like Griffey who wants to return home. Perhaps this time, it'll be a starting pitcher.

—Jim Henzler

Colorado Rockies: Can Hampton And Neagle Survive in the Thin Air?

We've been hearing it ever since the National League expanded into Denver in 1993: the Rockies have lousy pitching. How bad has it been? Well, they've had a staff ERA of 5.42 over the last three years. That's pretty bad. When they get away from the horrors of Coors, however, their ERA is a respectable 4.49 over that span. In fact, that's better than the 4.57 mark put up by all other pitchers in baseball when not throwing in Colorado.

Mike Hampton

Still, the club was bound and determined to upgrade its starting staff this winter. Colorado spent big-time dollars to acquire the services of Mike Hampton and Denny Neagle. After all, these are two quality veterans. How much could the thin air really bother them?

Possible short answer: a lot. Just ask Darryl Kile.

Over his career, Hampton has a 4-1 record at Coors, but his ERA in those five starts is 6.48. What is potentially telling, however, is that he averaged 6.7 innings per Coors start, which is slightly better than the 6.5 he averaged in all of his other lifetime starts. This might indicate that the intense hitting environment does not bother Hampton that much. As for Neagle, he is 3-3 with a 7.30 ERA in seven Coors starts and has averaged just 5.8 innings per start (6.3 elsewhere).

What is particularly interesting about the two southpaws is that their pitching styles are so different. Since 1998, Hampton has a groundball-flyball ratio of 2.59, one of the highest in baseball. Meanwhile, over the same three-year span, Neagle has one of the lowest ratios in baseball (0.75).

So how has Coors treated pitchers with these respective styles over the last three years? Because Hampton and Neagle are on opposite ends of the spectrum, we divided pitchers into five categories. Normally, we call anyone with a groundball-flyball ratio under 1.0 a flyball pitcher, guys who are over 1.5 groundball pitchers, and all those in the middle neutral. For this study, we've further defined the margins by calling those at .75 or less extreme flyball pitchers and anyone over 2.0 an extreme groundball hurler.

Flyball And Groundball Pitchers, Coors Field vs. All Other Parks—1998-2000

Pitcher Type	Coors ERA	Non-Coors ERA	Diff
Extreme Flyball	7.14	4.65	2.49
Flyball	7.14	4.64	2.50
Neutral	6.65	4.64	2.01
Groundball	6.35	4.46	1.89
Extreme Groundball	4.62	4.12	0.50
All Pitchers	**6.52**	**4.57**	**1.95**

While this is a rather small sample, it clearly shows that the flyball pitchers suffer more damage in the thin air. Makes sense.

Another aspect about pitching in Denver is the physical toll caused by the stress of pitching with men on base. Some have suggested that every start in Coors is like a 120-pitch start somewhere else. How do pitchers fare in the start *after* they make a start in Coors? Overall, not too badly. Visiting pitchers allowed a 4.65 ERA in their next start after pitching in Coors over the last three years, while their overall non-Coors ERA was 4.67.

However, when we look at this on a case-by-case basis, there might be something to it. For instance, Hampton has allowed a 6.63 ERA in Coors since 1998, with a 3.02 ERA everywhere else. In his starts immediately after pitching in Denver, his ERA was 4.82. Neagle's splits have been more dramatic; his Coors and non-Coors ERAs are 8.44 and 3.98, while in his next starts after pitching in Denver, it's 6.17. Greg Maddux is the only National League guy with a higher groundball-flyball ratio than Hampton over the last three seasons and he struggles more in his next start after Coors than he does in Colorado itself (4.67/5.40/2.83). Other groundball specialists include Kevin Brown, who seems mostly unaffected by the thin air and is even stronger the next time out (3.53/1.96/2.60), and fellow Dodger Darren Dreifort, who also handles Coors but may be worn out a bit by the effort (3.44/5.50/4.48).

One last factor in pitching in Coors is the weather. Hampton got off to a horrible start last season in New York and some surmised that the cool weather may have had something to do with it. A poor start on a chilly night in the Bronx last October did nothing to dispel that idea. Hampton really struggles with his control and command when temperatures drop.

Mike Hampton by Game-Time Temperature—Career

Temp	W-L	ERA	SO/BB
30s	0-1	13.50	0.5
40s	3-3	6.17	0.9
50s	4-1	3.49	1.7
60s	10-7	2.87	1.6
70s	59-33	3.44	1.9
80s	8-6	3.23	1.7
90s	1-2	3.54	1.6

When the game-time temperature is 49 degrees or less, Hampton is 3-4 with a 6.69 ERA and a 0.8 strikeout-walk ratio. At 50 and above, he is 82-49 with a 3.34 ERA and a ratio of 1.8. On the other hand, Neagle has had success at lower temps. He's 15-1 when the temperature is 59 degrees or below.

Denny Neagle by Game-Time Temperature—Career

Temp	W-L	ERA	SO/BB
30s	0-0	1.50	4.0
40s	5-1	3.45	2.6
50s	10-0	3.96	2.4
60s	15-17	4.35	2.3
70s	45-27	3.87	2.7
80s	27-18	3.78	2.3
90s	2-6	3.95	2.5
100+	1-0	4.76	2.5

So how many cold days and nights will they face in Colorado? Actually, not as many as one might think. In 615 games at Coors Field, only 38 (6.2 percent) have started when the temperature is 49 degrees or below. Of course, that says nothing about how chilly it is when the slugfests reach the later innings. Then again, not many starting pitchers last that long. A surprising side note is that the temperature at game time in Denver has been 90 degrees or above (39) more than it has been under 50 degrees.

So how will the newest Rockies starters perform? Hampton's reliance on groundball outs, not to mention his bulldog personality, would seem to give him a better shot at success than Neagle. It's just good to keep in mind that Pedro Astacio, who arguably has been the most successful Colorado starter since the franchise was formed, has a 7.05 home ERA over the last three seasons.

—Don Hartack

Florida Marlins: Is Castillo the New Enzo Hernandez?

It was a season-long quest, pitting a .330-hitter against one of the most remarkable records in baseball history. The race wasn't decided until the final month of the campaign, when Luis Castillo staged a furious rally. Though he ultimately fell short, his season should be remembered for quite some time.

No, it won't go down in history in the same breath as Ted Williams' .406 batting average or Mark McGwire's 70 home runs. But Castillo's 2000 season was an extraordinary exhibition of contradictory forces. A quick glance at Castillo's final statistics will leave you scratching your head. The Florida second baseman topped .300 for the second straight year, ranking fifth in the National League with a .334 average. He also posted a .418 on-base percentage and led the Marlins with 101 runs scored.

Looks good, doesn't it? But then you notice the number in his RBI column—17. Huh? How can somebody who collected 180 hits and scored more than a hundred runs drive in such an embarrassingly low total?

Castillo averaged less than one RBI per week, and about one for every 32 at-bats. But as poor as that rate was, it was not the worst in history.

Highest AB/RBI Rates, Season—1876-2000

Player, Team	Year	AB	RBI	AB/RBI	Avg
Enzo Hernandez, SD	1971	549	12	45.8	.222
Billy Sunday, Pit	1888	505	15	33.7	.236
Clyde Milan, Was	1910	531	16	33.2	.279
Luis Castillo, Fla	**2000**	**539**	**17**	**31.7**	**.334**
Morrie Rath, CWS	1912	591	19	31.1	.272
Ivy Olson, Bro	1918	506	17	29.8	.239
Richie Ashburn, Phi	1959	564	20	28.2	.266
Doc Casey, Bro	1907	527	19	27.7	.231
Greasy Neale, Cin	1916	530	20	26.5	.262
Larry Bowa, Phi	1971	650	25	26.0	.249

(minimum 500 AB)

Enzo Hernandez' 1971 season was a piece of work. In 549 at-bats, the San Diego shortstop mustered only 12 extra-base hits and 12 RBI. Considering his weak stick, you might think he was a fielding wizard. He may have been, though the fact is that Hernandez committed 33 errors, which tied for the most in baseball. It's hard to have a more pitiful season than that.

Castillo's season, on the other hand, was far from pitiful. He hit .333 in April and only got hotter in May and June. By the All-Star break, he was cruising along at .369. Still, he had gathered a mere four RBI in the season's first half. At that point, he looked like a shoe-in to shatter Hernandez' mark. But Castillo picked up the pace with three RBI in July and three more in August. Any chance to break the record evaporated when he delivered RBI in three straight games at the beginning of September.

Though he settled for 17 RBI overall, Castillo appears a little out of place on the first chart. He's the only player to have batted at least .280, let alone .334. Many of the others who made the list were weak-hitting stiffs. In fact, if the chart had rated the highest hit-RBI ratios of all time, Castillo would have topped it with a mark of 10.6.

Considering all those hits, how did Castillo convert so few into RBI? Well, the simple fact that he served as Florida's leadoff hitter had a lot to do with it. He averaged 0.41 runners on base and 0.20 runners in scoring position per plate appearance. Only Montreal's Peter Bergeron had fewer men on base.

But from the Marlins' perspective, maybe that's a good thing. Castillo certainly didn't come through in the limited chances he had with ducks on the pond. Consider his splits. While his batting average was a robust .380 with nobody on base, it plunged to .217 when at least one of the bases was occupied. No other player with 500 or more at-bats last year suffered a dip larger than 67 points. Actually, Castillo's difficulties with men on base last year were the most pronounced since STATS began tracking such information in 1987.

Largest Batting Average Drop-Offs, None on vs. Runners on—1987-2000

Player, Team	Year	Total AB	None on	Runners on	Diff
Luis Castillo, Fla	2000	539	.380	.217	.163
Kevin McReynolds, NYM	1987	590	.325	.222	.103
Kevin Mitchell, SF	1990	524	.341	.241	.100
Joey Cora, Sea-Cle	1998	602	.308	.215	.093
Fernando Tatis, Tex-StL	1998	532	.317	.224	.093
Mark McGwire, Oak-StL	1997	540	.318	.226	.092
Derek Jeter, NYY	1996	582	.355	.263	.092
Lou Whitaker, Det	1987	604	.297	.207	.090
Phil Bradley, Sea	1987	603	.333	.244	.089
Omar Vizquel, Cle	1997	565	.318	.230	.088

(minimum 500 total AB)

As if that wasn't telling enough, Castillo also hit just .211 with runners in scoring position, while batting .359 in other circumstances. That drop-off in higher-profile situations also was the largest since '87 (minimum 500 AB). Castillo may be a nice tablesetter, but please don't ask him to clear it.

One shudders to think what Hernandez must have hit with men on base or in scoring position in 1971. It must not have been pretty, in order for him to collect so few RBI. While Enzo still owns the worst single-season AB/RBI mark of all time, Castillo may yet own a record even more grand, if not more dubious. Luis has driven in 71 runs in 1,606 career at-bats, a rate of roughly 23 at-bats per RBI. Not even the legendary Hernandez (20.6), nor anyone else with at least 1,500 at-bats, can top that.

—Jim Henzler

A more complete listing for this category can be found on page 229.

Houston Astros: Can Lima Come Back?

For two seasons—1998 and 1999—Jose Lima was one of the most consistent and reliable pitchers in the majors. During that span, Lima made 68 starts, pitched more than 475 innings, walked only 76 batters, won 37 games and carried a very respectable 3.64 ERA. In '99, he finished tied for fourth in the National League Cy Young voting after going 21-10.

Jose Lima

However, the 2000 season was not kind. His record dropped to 7-16, and he reached career worsts in ERA (6.65), walks (68), base runners per nine innings (14.7), earned runs allowed (145, a ML high) and home runs allowed (48, also a ML high). Granted, Lima suffered partially due to a new home stadium, Enron Field, which proved to be a tremendous hitters' park. But his 2000 road ERA was an unsightly 6.32, while his home ERA was just out of sight at 6.92.

So one of the key questions facing the Astros as they prepare for the 2001 campaign is whether Lima can bounce back? One way of investigating his chances for recovery is to look at other pitchers who experienced similarly drastic ERA rises on the heels of a 20-win season.

Lima is one of 17 pitchers since 1920 who followed up a 20-win effort by raising his ERA by more than two runs over the previous season while working at least 100 innings in the follow-up campaign.

On the following page you'll find the list of those 17 hurlers, starting with the year they won 20 or more games:

20-Game Winners With 2.00-Plus ERA Rises the Following Season—1920-2000

Pitcher	20-Win Yr	ERA	Yr 2	Yr 3	Yr 4	Yr 5
Sloppy Thurston	1924	3.80	5.95	5.02	4.47	—
Jesse Haines	1928	3.18	5.71	4.30	3.02	4.75
Bill Sherdel	1928	2.86	5.93	4.71	4.25	3.68
Lefty Grove	1933	3.20	6.50	2.70	2.81	3.02
Howie Pollet	1946	2.10	4.34	4.54	2.77	3.29
Ewell Blackwell	1947	2.47	4.54	4.23	2.97	3.44
Gene Bearden	1948	2.43	5.10	4.99	4.64	4.30
Johnny Sain	1948	2.60	4.81	3.94	4.20	3.46
Warren Spahn	1963	2.60	5.29	4.01	—	—
Luis Tiant	1968	1.60	3.71	3.40	4.85	1.91
Juan Marichal	1969	2.10	4.12	2.94	3.71	3.82
Ron Bryant	1973	3.53	5.61	16.62	—	—
Ross Grimsley	1978	3.05	5.35	6.59	5.25	—
Danny Jackson	1988	2.73	5.60	3.61	6.75	3.84
Dave Stewart	1990	2.56	5.18	3.66	4.44	5.87
Jack Morris	1992	4.04	6.19	5.60	—	—
Jose Lima	**1999**	**3.58**	**6.65**	—	—	—

(minimum 100 IP in Year 2)

Just seven of these hurlers were able to rebound from their big drop-off to again reach a reasonable level of dominance. Let's take a closer look at those seven:

Jesse Haines pitched more years (18) in a Cardinals uniform than anyone in history. After picking up his third 20-win season in 1928, Haines faltered a bit his next season, giving up a career-high 114 earned runs and 21 home runs. His 5.71 ERA in 1929 at the age of 35 would convince most pitchers to retire. Haines declined on that option and two years later went 12-3 with a 3.02 ERA, mostly due to his improved knuckleball.

Lefty Grove could have taught Mike Hampton about smashing a water cooler with his temper, but between 1925 and 1933, Lefty led the American League in wins four times, in ERA five times, in strikeouts seven times, and saves once. So, after seven consecutive 20-plus win seasons for the Philadelphia Athletics, Grove was sold to the Red Sox. He struggled with arm troubles in his first season with Boston, posting an 8-8 record with a 6.50 ERA. He bounced back to his Grove-esque numbers in 1935, going 20-12 with a 2.70 ERA. He then went on to win a total of 105 games in eight seasons as a member of the Red Sox.

Howie Pollet's baseball career felt the repercussions of World War II in 1943, as he left a pennant-winning St. Louis team with an 8-4 record at mid-season. When he returned in 1946, he showed his true skills, going 21-10 with a 2.10 ERA, while the Cardinals won the World Series. Those lofty totals faltered a bit in 1947, when Pollet went 9-11 with a 4.34 ERA. In 1949, however, Pollet returned to the top of the NL leader boards in most pitching categories, with a 20-9 record and a 2.77 ERA. A couple of years later, he was bounced around a few different teams, which definitely seemed to tarnish his focus.

After picking up an NL-high six shutouts in his 1946 rookie season, **Ewell Blackwell** truly came into his own in 1947, going 22-8 with a 2.47 ERA and 193 strikeouts. He set an NL record with an incredible 16 consecutive victories. Unfortunately, his delivery led to arm troubles that hampered him his entire career, including 1948 and 1949, when his ERAs rose to 4.54 and 4.23, respectively. The 1950 All-Star game was proof that Blackwell still had signs of life, as he picked up the victory.

Johnny Sain actually was the better half of the Braves' "Spahn and Sain and pray for rain" pennant drive in 1948. Sain won 24 games that year for Boston, but he slumped badly in '49 and went 10-17 with a 4.81 ERA. He quickly righted his ship, however, and gave the Braves 20 wins in 1950 before being shipped to the Yankees in 1951. He went a combined 25-13 for pennant-winning New York clubs in '52 and '53, and he posted an AL best 22 saves in 1954.

Luis Tiant fashioned a 21-9 record with a 1.60 ERA for the 1968 Indians. After their star pitcher impressed the baseball world in 1968, the Indians wanted to protect Tiant's arm and ordered him to skip his yearly routine of winter ball. Tiant struggled the following year, leading the AL with 20 losses, while still carrying a respectable 3.71 ERA. After 1969, Tiant found himself pitching for the Twins, and then the Red Sox. He recaptured his brilliance in 1972, going 15-6, 1.91 and winning the Comeback Player of the Year Award.

Juan Marichal picked up six 20-plus victory seasons, while taking NL titles in wins, innings pitched, shutouts, ERA and complete games. The 1969 season was a typically dandy one for Marichal, who went 21-11 with a 2.10 ERA and 205 strikeouts. Unfortunately for him, in the spring of 1970 he suffered a severe reaction to penicillin that later led to a bout with chronic arthritis and a back injury. While he managed to still win 12 games that season, his ERA rose to 4.12. Marichal overcame his troubles, completing one last magical year in 1971, going 18-11 with a 2.94 ERA.

While we have looked at several pitchers who bounced back to regain their form, there are several who failed to do so, including some well-known hurlers. Warren Spahn, Jack Morris and Dave Stewart were among our 20-game winners who experienced the dreaded 2.00-plus rise in ERA never to respond. Granted, each of these hurlers was forced to deal with their respective "jumps" at the tail-end of their careers—Spahn was 43, Morris 38 and Stewart 34.

A more comparable case to Lima's could be that of Darryl Kile. After a 19-7, 2.57 season in 1997, Kile left the cushy Astrodome mound for hitter-friendly Coors Field. Two sub-.500 records and two 5.00-plus ERA seasons later, Kile bolted the mile-high city for much thicker Busch Stadium air. He rebounded in 2000, as he went 20-9 with a 3.91 ERA for the NL Central Division champion Cardinals.

Time will be the test in showing us if Lima can rebound from a horrible 2000 campaign. The ability is certainly there. A major injury didn't account for his drop-off, so there are no health issues that should prevent him from bouncing back. He simply must prove to himself he can still pitch in all parks, including Enron Field.

—Sam Lubeck

Los Angeles Dodgers: Does Experience Matter For a New Manager?

When the Dodgers hired Jim Tracy as manager on November 1, Los Angeles showed as much enthusiasm as it usually gives the NBA's Clippers. Here's a sampling from local newspaper columnists:

> Kevin Modesti, *Los Angeles Daily News*: After "Jim who?" is answered, I'm afraid we'll still be left with "Jim why?"

> Bill Plaschke, *Los Angeles Times*: This elicits the same reaction given those who show up at Halloween parties in plain orange sweaters. Nice, but that's the best you can do? Upon attending the introduction of their new manager Wednesday, your first impulse was to order Dodger executives to march back into their room and try again.

> Lyle Spencer, *Riverside Press-Enterprise*: It is my cynical suspicion that they also liked how Tracy would work for much less than the high-profile names such as Baker, Valentine and Lou Piniella.

The crux of the disappointment surrounding general manager Kevin Malone's decision to hire Tracy centered on two points. First, that the club didn't hire a former Dodger with a successful managerial resume, such as Dusty Baker or Bobby Valentine. And second, that if Los Angeles was going to tab a first-time skipper, it should have opted for a bigger name. Among the candidates who didn't get the job were Chris Chambliss, Orel Hershiser, Eddie Murray and Willie Randolph. Tracy, who played 87 games for the 1980-81 Cubs and served as the Dodgers' bench coach in 1999-2000, was far more anonymous.

Fame aside, how much does prior managerial experience matter? Larry Dierker led the Astros to the National League Central title in his 1997 debut, but Modesti pointed out that the last skipper to win a World Series in his first job was Cito Gaston with the 1992-93 Blue Jays. The last rookie manager to start the year and reach a League Championship Series was Houston's Hal Lanier in 1986.

We decided to take a look at the broader picture, and we do mean "broader." We went all the way back to 1920 and examined the performance of every new manager, defined as anyone who began a season as a club's skipper after not running that team the year before. We separated the field generals into those with prior managerial experience and those with none, and the results can be found on the following page:

Inexperienced vs. Experienced Managers in First Three Years With New Team—1920-2000

Year	Inexperienced			Experienced		
	W	L	Pct	W	L	Pct
Before Hiring	10,948	12,312	.471	11,645	13,087	.471
Year 1	11,071	12,006	.480	12,002	12,793	.484
Year 2	7,647	8,007	.489	9,048	9,218	.495
Year 3	5,442	5,520	.496	6,308	6,442	.495
Total Years 1-3	24,160	2,553	.486	27,358	28,453	.490

As the chart shows, experience has made almost no difference in the performance of new managers. The two groups inherited similar situations, as the combined winning percentages for the teams in the year before they hired a new manager was .471 for both.

The rookies lag slightly behind their more seasoned counterparts in years one and two, then have a small advantage in year three. Over the entire period, the experienced managers had a .490 winning percentage, while the first-timers had a .486 mark. Over the course of a 162-game season, that .004 difference translates into about two-thirds of a win.

While he may not have a lot of name value, Los Angeles fans and media need to cut Jim Tracy a little slack. His inexperience shouldn't be a handicap as he takes over a Dodgers team that hasn't won a postseason game since 1988.

—Jim Callis

Milwaukee Brewers: Is Hammonds An Upgrade Over Grissom?

Well, you can't blame the Brewers for wanting to make a change in center field this season. Marquis Grissom rarely has been an acceptable offensive performer, especially in recent years. Sure he has speed, but he hasn't stolen more than 30 bases since 1994. At age 34, he won't be getting any faster, either. Given his paucity of walks, he doesn't contribute much to the lineup, particularly at the top of the order.

Grissom split his time primarily between the first two slots in Milwaukee's lineup last year. Not coincidentally, the Brewers' No. 1 and 2 hitters scored a grand total of 190 runs. Only the Phillies (189) mustered fewer among National League clubs. Now, Grissom can't be blamed for all of Milwaukee's run-scoring problems. But he certainly bears his share of responsibility. His OPS (on-base plus slugging percentage) was a pathetic .640 last season, the second-worst in baseball.

Worst OPS—2000

Player, Team	OBP	Slg	OPS
Rey Sanchez, KC	.314	.322	.637
Marquis Grissom, Mil	**.288**	**.351**	**.640**
Desi Relaford, Phi-SD	.351	.300	.651
Mike Lansing, Col-Bos	.292	.365	.657
Mark McLemore, Sea	.353	.316	.669
Peter Bergeron, Mon	.320	.349	.669
Rickey Henderson, NYM-Sea	.368	.305	.673
Scott Brosius, NYY	.299	.374	.673
Doug Glanville, Phi	.307	.374	.681
Chris Singleton, CWS	.301	.382	.683
MLB Average	**.345**	**.437**	**.782**

(minimum 502 PA)

Grissom was an offensive drain last year. He failed to hit for average (.244), didn't walk (39 bases on balls in 640 plate appearances) and didn't hit for much power (34 extra-base hits). That's why Grissom is the only non-middle infielder who ranked in the bottom five of OPS in 2000.

The Brewers can find a better hitter to patrol center field, can't they? They hope they landed that player when they signed Jeffrey Hammonds to a three-year, $21.75 million deal in December. Hammonds is coming off the finest season of his career, having batted .335 with 20 homers and 106

RBI. His on-base percentage of .395 and slugging of .529 added up to a respectable OPS of .924. But before we go overboard, we should remember that Hammonds produced those numbers in his first and only season with Colorado. And the Rockies didn't even offer him arbitration after the campaign. One look at his home-road breakdown may tell you why:

Jeffrey Hammonds—2000

	Avg	AB	R	H	2B	3B	HR	RBI	BB	SO	OBP	Slg
Home	.399	218	61	87	11	1	14	71	29	27	.465	.651
Road	.275	236	33	65	13	1	6	35	15	56	.325	.415

Clearly, this is a case of a hitter taking advantage of Coors. Hammonds' OPS at home (1.116) was a whopping 375 points higher than his road mark (.741). Among players with 502 plate appearances last season, only Manny Ramirez (1.194) and Barry Bonds (1.189) had higher home OPS. In fact, if we simply double Hammonds' production in "neutral" parks—his road games—we'll find that he and Grissom were fairly even.

Grissom vs. Hammonds—2000

	Avg	AB	R	H	2B	3B	HR	RBI	BB	SO	OBP	Slg
Grissom Total	.244	595	67	145	18	2	14	62	39	99	.288	.351
Hammonds Road (doubled)	.275	472	66	130	26	2	12	70	30	112	.325	.415

If the Brewers really think Hammonds will match last year's overall production, they could be in for a major disappointment. When the gas of his Coors numbers is eliminated from his overall record, we're left with an offensive player who could hardly be described as electric.

Sometimes it can be argued that analysts take the easy way out when predicting the adverse effect that leaving Colorado will have on hitters. Many predicted doom for Andres Galarraga, Dante Bichette and Vinny Castilla when they departed the Rockies. Yet only Castilla can be described as truly stumbling in his new environment. The sample size (three players) is relatively small, so perhaps we shouldn't draw too large a conclusion from their experience. Hammonds obviously benefited from playing in Denver, and it's likely that his numbers will tumble a bit in 2001. Still, considering the production Milwaukee received from Grissom last year, anything Hammonds provides probably will be considered an improvement.

—Jim Henzler

A more complete listing for this category can be found on page 230.

Montreal Expos: Is Guerrero's Combination of Power And Discipline Unmatched?

In the *STATS Baseball Scoreboard 2000*, we pondered whether Vladimir Guerrero was on the way to immortality. We noted that he had just become the fourth player ever to have a 30-game hitting streak and 30 homers in the same year, and the ninth player to have a .300-40-120 season at age 23 or younger. We also revealed that the most similar player to Guerrero through age 23 was Willie Mays, one of the very best players ever. Our conclusion was that, indeed, Guerrero was destined for greatness.

Taking our cue, he did nothing last season to change our minds. Guerrero set new career highs in batting average (.345), home runs (44), on-base percentage (.410) and slugging (.664) while driving in 123 runs. He also showed extreme discipline for a power hitter, striking out just 74 times.

In the first 40 years after the lively ball was introduced in 1920, baseball was rife with sluggers who made consistent contact. Joe DiMaggio, Lou Gehrig, Ted Kluszewski, Johnny Mize and Mel Ott all had at least one season in which they went deep at least 40 times and had more homers than strikeouts.

Vladimir Guerrero

Since the expansion era began in 1961, both longballs and whiffs have risen steadily. Only Hank Aaron in 1969 (44 home runs, 47 strikeouts) has come even close to having more homers than strikeouts, and it's not uncommon to see sluggers fan three times as often as they leave the park.

Guerrero is far from common, however. He hit more than 40 homers in both 1999 and 2000, and struck out just 136 times in 1,315 plate appearances during that time. His .103 strikeout-plate appearance ratio is the best of any player with consecutive

40-plus homer seasons since 1961.

Lowest SO/PA Ratios, Players With 40-Plus Home Runs in Consecutive Years—1961-2000

Player	Years	HR	SO	PA	SO/PA
Vladimir Guerrero	**1999-2000**	**86**	**136**	**1,315**	**.103**
Willie Mays	1964-65	99	143	1,303	.110
Frank Thomas	1995-96	80	144	1,296	.111
Carl Yastrzemski	1969-70	80	157	1,405	.112
Rafael Palmeiro	1998-99	90	160	1,383	.116
Willie Mays	1961-62	89	162	1,365	.119
Barry Bonds	1996-97	82	163	1,365	.119
Hank Aaron	1962-63	89	167	1,381	.121
Harmon Killebrew	1969-70	90	168	1,374	.122
Albert Belle	1995-96	98	167	1,346	.124
Average, 1961-2000 (44)		**94**	**231**	**1,331**	**.174**
Average, before 1961 (31)		**92**	**146**	**1,326**	**.110**

(Mickey Mantle 1960-61 counted in 1961-2000 group)

Once again, we see a striking similarity between Guerrero and Mays. The other players on this list include several of the elite all-around hitters of the expansion era, including Frank Thomas, Hank Aaron and Barry Bonds.

As the chart shows, the 1961-2000 sluggers have fanned 58 percent more often than their predecessors. But while disciplined power hitters haven't remained in vogue, one thing has remained constant: Guerrero's ability to amaze us.

—Jim Callis

A more complete listing for this category can be found on page 232.

New York Mets: Is It Time For Piazza to Come Out From Behind the Plate?

The talk started a few years ago, when Mike Piazza was still catching for the Los Angeles Dodgers. The word was that Piazza, who was developing into one of the best-hitting catchers of all time, would be better served by coming out from behind the plate before his backstop duties compromised his batting skills.

Mike Piazza

The New York Mets catcher turned 32 last September, so he now is at an age when most major league hitters start showing signs of decline. But not Mr. Piazza.

Yet there were warning signs that maybe he *should* start thinking about manning another position. When May came to a close last season, Piazza looked like the leading man for National League MVP honors. He was batting .372 with 14 homers and 36 RBI, and he had generated a whopping .731 slugging percentage. While he still enjoyed one of his best seasons in 2000, Piazza's success at the plate may have been stunted a bit by a rash of minor injuries he suffered. He was struck in the head by the follow-through of a Gary Sheffield swing, and he was beaned by Roger Clemens in July. Then he played with a bruised hip and shin for much of August. While he batted .342 and slugged .534 that month, his offense took a dive in September. He hit just .231 in the final month, and his .462 slugging percentage was more than 150 points lower than his .614 mark for the season.

One month doesn't mark a permanent decline, but should it be a wake-up call about Piazza's long-term future? After all, the Mets' star caught his 1,000th game during the 2000 campaign, becoming only the 91st backstop in major league history to do so. Only five active catchers have done it, but among the five, just he and Ivan Rodriguez remain starters.

So let's take a look at this group of 91 warriors who held up through 1,000 games of foul tips and home-plate collisions. The chart below shows the hitting percentages of these catchers leading up to their 1,000th game, and for the seasons that follow:

**Hitting Percentages For All Catchers
With 1,000 Games Behind the Plate—1876-2000**

	Avg	OBP	Slg
Career through season of 1,000th game caught	.267	.332	.392
1st season after catching 1,000th game	.268	.341	.394
2nd season after catching 1,000th game	.260	.336	.383
3rd season after catching 1,000th game	.254	.327	.366

This sturdy group of backstops held up well through the first season after it surpassed 1,000 games behind the plate. The decline starts to show in the second season following the 1,000th game. The change in percentages doesn't appear to be dramatic, but the sample size is fairly large and it took some serious drop-off in performance to alter the percentages this much. The decline continues in the third year, particularly in terms of power.

Among the 91 catchers who make up the above chart, Piazza and eight others were seasonal age 31 (as of June 30) during the summer in which they caught their 1,000th game. The drop-off after catching 1,000 games is more rapid for this group.

**Hitting Percentages For Catchers Who Caught
Their 1,000th Game at Seasonal Age 31—1876-2000**

	Avg	OBP	Slg
Career through season of 1,000th game caught	.275	.335	.396
1st season after catching 1,000th game	.253	.312	.335
2nd season after catching 1,000th game	.254	.323	.340
3rd season after catching 1,000th game	.246	.307	.315

(age as of June 30)

Piazza arguably is the best-hitting catcher of all time, so it's not surprising that no one in this group was anywhere near as productive as he was at age 31. While Piazza launched 38 homers as a 31-year-old catcher, the best of the rest were Terry Kennedy (18) and Tony Pena (10). Neither Kennedy nor Pena ever hit double-digit homers or saw 500 at-bats in a season again.

All of the other eight backstops clearly were in decline by age 31, although four players—Jerry Grote, Muddy Ruel, Frank Snyder and Ivy Wingo—had what could be labeled as one of their best two or three seasons at seasonal age 31 or 32. Grote, Snyder and Wingo turned in solid performances as part-time players, and a 31-year-old Ruel still managed just 22 extra-base hits in 428 at-bats and slugged a mere .376 for the 1927 Washington Senators. Their four decent seasons combined totaled 81 extra-base hits; Piazza collected 64 during the 2000 campaign alone. Only Kennedy, Grote, Ruel and Pena caught at least 100 games in a season after the age of 31. And only Kennedy and Pena did it beyond age 32.

As for the issue of Piazza stepping aside to preserve his bat speed and physical skills, it's worth noting that he is so productive as a hitter that he would be a valuable asset behind the plate even if his numbers were to drop off by as much as 25 percent. That's not likely to happen overnight.

That's good news for the Mets, considering the organization has no prospect in line to replace Piazza if he were moved to first base. The pipeline to Flushing has no one who will be ready anytime soon.

Sure, it may save Piazza some wear and tear to play first base 15-20 times a season. Plus, the Mets should continue to monitor the frequency of those minor injuries that seem to accumulate as catchers age. Long-time Minnesota backstop Earl Battey, who was among the other eight but was battered and forced to retire at age 32, can attest to the high price of the constant, nagging ailments that are inherent to catching. So far, Piazza hasn't let them slow him down, and it would be hard to justify removing such a productive player from a position that he still can handle and has no desire to abandon.

—Thom Henninger

Philadelphia Phillies: How Damaging Are Poor Starts?

If baseball imitated fables, the Phillies may have had a chance last year. As we recall from the story "The Tortoise and the Hare," a sluggish beginning didn't doom the tortoise in his grudge match against the fast-starting hare. Behind early, the tortoise gradually gained ground and emerged victorious.

Unfortunately, the 2000 edition of the Phillies Phable bore little resemblence to anything Aesop might offer. The Phillies started slowly, fell behind early, rarely overcame initial deficits, and were doomed to the worst record in baseball. It wasn't a happy ending.

The Phillies simply had a hard time scoring runs in the first inning in 2000. They pushed across a grand total of 69 tallies in the opening frame, a very low sum. Not surprisingly, Philadelphia was outscored in the first inning by 51 runs. No other team was outscored by more than 42 last season.

Worst Run Differentials After First Inning—2000

Team	Own	Opp	Diff	Trailing After 1 Record	Pct	Overall Record	Pct
Phillies	69	120	-51	12-37	.245	65-97	.401
Rangers	112	154	-42	15-36	.294	71-91	.438
Dodgers	103	135	-32	23-33	.411	86-76	.531
Brewers	88	110	-22	11-31	.262	73-89	.451
Angels	99	119	-20	14-32	.304	82-80	.506
Cubs	91	111	-20	13-30	.302	65-97	.401
Astros	114	132	-18	19-32	.373	72-90	.444
Red Sox	87	103	-16	19-22	.463	85-77	.525
Twins	87	102	-15	8-34	.190	69-93	.426
Expos	100	115	-15	10-30	.250	67-95	.414
MLB Totals				418-833	.334		

The Phillies' first-inning deficiency ranks as the fourth largest since 1987. Only the 1998 Tigers (-72), 1991 Orioles (-67) and 1993 Athletics (-56) produced worse first-inning profit-loss statements than Philadelphia's ledger last year. Considering that none of those teams lost fewer than 94 games, we can see how devastating slow starts turn out to be.

In fact, the Phillies trailed after the first inning 49 times in 2000. They won only 12 of those games, a rate of less than 25 percent. In addition, the Phillies *led* only 31 times after one inning, the fewest in the majors. As you might suspect, such poor totals are leading indicators of a team's travails.

As a group, teams trailing after one inning went 418-833 last season, for a paltry winning percentage of .334. So any team that consistently puts itself in an early hole will have a hard time digging out. That's what the Phillies did in 2000, going into the second inning facing a deficit in nearly one-third of their games. It's hard to be successful that way.

In fact, there now have been 11 teams that were outscored by at least 41 runs in the first inning since 1987. Those 11 teams have combined for an overall winning percentage of .423. Predictably, successful first-inning squads tend to win more overall.

Winning Percentages by First-Inning Run Differential—1987-2000

		Win Pct by Situation After First Inning			
Run Diff	Teams	Trail	Lead	Tied	Season
-41 or less	11	.271	.614	.443	.423
-40 to -31	16	.301	.667	.456	.455
-30 to -21	46	.286	.658	.462	.455
-20 to -11	57	.301	.657	.485	.475
-10 to -1	60	.313	.673	.503	.496
0 to 9	74	.329	.690	.500	.506
10 to 19	44	.334	.699	.520	.524
20 to 29	41	.341	.694	.524	.531
30 to 39	19	.363	.719	.556	.565
40 to 49	12	.361	.748	.541	.568
50 or more	6	.364	.721	.559	.575

The overall winning percentages improve with each increase of the run-differential grouping. It probably isn't a mystery why that occurs. The better teams simply tend to jump out to early leads. And if they're good enough to "win" the first inning, it makes sense that they're also good enough to win the rest of the game. The winning percentages generally follow positive trends under any scenario, whether considering how teams do when trailing, leading or tied after one frame.

What it boils down to is that the 2000 Phillies were a bad team. They were outscored in every inning besides the third and fifth. In all, they scored 122 fewer runs than they allowed. No matter how tenacious the tortoise may have been, it would have been hard to gain ground when going in reverse.

—Jim Henzler

A more complete listing for this category can be found on page 233.

Pittsburgh Pirates: Is Kendall Better Suited to Bat Leadoff Than Any Catcher Ever?

The Pirates have been searching in vain for a leadoff hitter for a decade. They haven't bettered the National League average in on-base percentage out of the No. 1 spot since 1991. Since then, Pittsburgh has entrusted the top of its lineup to such ill-suited players as Carlos Garcia, Jacob Brumfield, Jermaine Allensworth, Tony Womack and Chad Hermansen.

The Pirates also have used Jason Kendall in the leadoff spot, though only on a sporadic basis. But other than the fact that he's a catcher and catchers don't typically fit the profile teams are looking for in a No. 1 hitter, there's no good reason why Pittsburgh should avoid turning to Kendall to fill that role.

A leadoff man's most important attributes are his ability to get on base and score runs. It's also nice if he has the speed to steal a base or two to get himself into scoring position when needed. Unlike most backstops, Kendall can do all of those things. He has a career .402 on-base percentage and has averaged 97 runs and 23 steals per 162 major league games.

How does Kendall rate among catchers in leadoff skills all time? Let's take a look:

Best Leadoff Skills, Catchers—1876-2000

Highest OBP		Most R/162G		Most SB/162G	
Player	OBP	Player	R/162G	Player	SB/162G
Mickey Cochrane	.419	Fred Carroll	117	Fred Carroll	29
Johnny Bassler	.416	Mickey Cochrane	114	Connie Mack	29
Jason Kendall	**.402**	Mike Piazza	102	Jack O'Connor	24
Wally Schang	.393	Jack Boyle	100	Con Daily	24
Mike Piazza	.392	**Jason Kendall**	**97**	Roger Bresnahan	24
Dick Dietz	.390	Jocko Milligan	92	Wilbert Robinson	23
Gene Tenace	.388	Ivan Rodriguez	92	**Jason Kendall**	**23**
Roger Bresnahan	.386	Yogi Berra	90	Mike Grady	20
Bill Dickey	.382	Connie Mack	88	John Wathan	20
Rick Ferrell	.378	Charlie Ganzel	87	Chief Zimmer	19

(minimum 500 G and 50 percent of G at catcher)

The names on the on-base percentage list are the most familiar, as they include four Hall of Famers (Mickey Cochrane, Roger Bresnahan, Bill Dickey and Rick Ferrell) and arguably the best-hitting catcher ever in

Jason Kendall

Mike Piazza. The runs and stolen-bases lists consist of several 19th-century players (Fred Carroll, Jack Boyle, Jocko Milligan, Connie Mack, Charlie Ganzel, Jack O'Connor, Con Daily, Wilbert Robinson, Mike Grady and Chief Zimmer). That's no surprise, because that era's environment (such as the rules, strategies and quality of defensive play) produced more scoring and steals than any other period in baseball history.

Kendall is the only player to make the top 10 among catchers in all three categories of leadoff skills. Only two other men were close to doing so. Carroll topped all backstops in scoring runs and stealing bases while ranking 16th with a .370 on-base percentage. Bresnahan was fifth in steals, eighth in on-base percentage and 27th in runs (76 per 162 games).

Adrian Brown performed decently when he took over Pittsburgh's No. 1 spot after Hermansen and Warren Morris fizzled last year. But new Pirates manager Lloyd McClendon still should consider writing Kendall's name at the top of his lineup card on a regular basis, even if it defies baseball convention.

—Jim Callis

A more complete listing for this category can be found on page 234.

St. Louis Cardinals: Can Ankiel Overcome His Control Difficulties?

If the Cardinals hadn't qualified for the playoffs last year, Rick Ankiel's offseason probably would have been a whole lot more peaceful. Without a postseason, he likely would have been brimming with confidence about his bright future. After all, he had enjoyed a strong rookie campaign that seemingly legitimized his status as one of the best pitching prospects in the game today.

But as we know, St. Louis didn't go quietly into the offseason. Neither did Ankiel. Instead, the Redbirds won the Central Division title and swept the Braves in the Division Series, before losing to the Mets in the National League Championship Series. Along the way, Ankiel's October performance drew national attention. And now many Cardinals fans, if not Ankiel himself, must have some degree of doubt about what lies ahead.

Rick Ankiel

The young lefthander seemed to self-destruct in the playoffs. After a regular season in which he had compiled an 11-7 record and a team-high 194 strikeouts, Ankiel drew the starting assignment for Game 1 against Atlanta. Things began well, as the Cardinals jumped out to a 6-0 lead. But the wheels came off for Ankiel in the third inning. He opened the frame by walking the opposing pitcher. After getting Rafael Furcal to foul out, Ankiel then uncorked two wild pitches before issuing another walk and unleashing another wild pitch. With two outs, the carnage continued: walk, wild pitch, single, wild pitch, walk, single. Finally, Ankiel mercifully was pulled.

He came back to start Game 2 of the NLCS, but with similar disastrous results. Three walks, two wild pitches and a double chased Ankiel after two-thirds of an inning. He returned in a mopup role in Game 5, though his finale was hardly encouraging. Two more walks, two more wild pitches, and he exited once again after recording only two outs. With that, his season was over. Ankiel entered the long winter knowing his nine wild pitches over four October innings were more than any other pitcher had thrown in a postseason *career*. Good luck, kid. See 'ya next spring.

History includes other pitchers who seemingly lost their control overnight. Perhaps the most famous was Steve Blass. Unlike Ankiel, Blass had tasted postseason success, helping lead the 1971 Pirates to the world championship. In 1972, he was 19-8 with a 2.49 ERA, and again he pitched well in the postseason that year. Then, all of a sudden, he lost it. In 1973, he went 3-9 with a 9.85 ERA while issuing 84 walks in 88.2 innings. By 1974, his career was over after he walked seven men in five innings. He simply couldn't throw the ball over the plate with regularity.

Mark Wohlers has repeated Blass' horror story. After saving 97 games between 1995-97, Wohlers lost utter command in 1998. A torn oblique muscle may have contributed to his misery, but he walked 33 men in 20.1 innings, tried to correct mechanical problems in his delivery in Triple-A, and landed on the DL when those corrections didn't work. He was traded to Cincinnati in April of 1999 after walking six men in two-thirds of an inning for the Braves. The change of scenery didn't help, however, and the control-monster remained that season until he went on the disabled list with an anxiety disorder. He pitched better in 2000, though it's still unclear if he'll ever come close to his previously dominating form.

Wohlers is the 10th pitcher who began his career since 1970 who also went from acceptable control one season to horrible control in a subsequent campaign. As you can see, the prospects for future success are fairly bleak, based on this chart:

Pitchers Who Averaged 4.00 BB/9 in One Season And 8.00 BB/9 in a Subsequent Season—1970-2000

Pitcher	Career	BB/9 Prior	Year	BB/9	BB/9 Thereafter
Pedro Borbon	1992-00	4.22	2000	8.21	—
Rob Dibble	1988-95	3.30	1993	9.07	15.72
Jason Grimsley	1989-00	5.40	1995	8.47	4.65
Dave Hamilton	1972-80	3.86	1980	8.40	—
Michael Mimbs	1995-97	4.42	1997	8.48	—
Bill Parsons	1971-74	3.16	1973	10.11	13.50

Pitcher	Career	BB/9 Prior	Year	BB/9	BB/9 Thereafter
Ken Reynolds	1970-76	4.38	1976	8.07	—
Dave Righetti	1979-95	3.74	1994	8.41	3.28
Bill Scherrer	1982-88	3.54	1986	9.43	4.33
Mark Wohlers	1991-00	4.06	1998	14.61	7.22

(minimum 20 IP in both seasons)

Borbon's major league career may not be over. But the careers were over for Hamilton, Mimbs and Reynolds, who never again pitched in the majors after averaging more than eight walks per nine innings. Similarly, Dibble, Parsons and Righetti worked only one more year. Only Grimsley, Scherrer and Wohlers pitched in more than one subsequent season, and none enjoyed any real success.

It's a little hard to know where Ankiel now stands in relation to this list. His sudden control outage occurred unexpectedly in the postseason. Immediately before, he had struck out 27 men while walking only four in his final three September starts. It's possible his playoff woes stemmed partly from the pressure of postseason action. But how will he react the first time he fires a fastball back to the screen this spring? Or the next time he issues a couple walks in succession? There certainly will be questions, if not pressure, when he experiences that kind of adversity.

Interestingly, Ankiel overcame similar bouts of wildness early last season. On April 20, for instance, he issued seven walks in five innings. Three starts later, he walked four and uncorked four wild pitches. But three outings after that, he struck out 11 while allowing nary a free pass. Though he struggled with command at times throughout the season, he generally overcame his initial tussle with wildness.

It's amazing how quickly outlooks can change in baseball. Two years ago, the Cardinals caught some heat when they kept Ankiel in the minors after he had proven to be perhaps the No. 1 prospect in baseball. His rookie season, though hardly breathtaking, still was superior for a 20-year-old. But now there are questions about his future. The Cardinals certainly hope Ankiel answers those questions positively this spring.

—Jim Henzler

A more complete listing for this category can be found on page 236.

San Diego Padres: Is There Hope For Rivera?

Ruben Rivera

When Michael Jordan was playing in the Arizona Fall League in 1994, he couldn't monopolize all of the attention. When people weren't gawking at Jordan, they were gasping at the prodigious talents of Peoria Javelinas center fielder Ruben Rivera.

Rivera, then 20, was fresh off a virtuoso Class-A performance that included 33 homers and 48 steals. One scout who saw him in the AFL said he was baseball's best prospect since Ken Griffey Jr. Said Peoria manager John Stearns: "The Yankees haven't had a talent like this guy since Mickey Mantle."

Rivera looked like a can't-miss prospect, but that's exactly what he has done. Miss and miss again. His inability to make consistent contact has limited him as a major leaguer. Rivera struck out in his first big league at-bat in 1995 against Dennis Eckersley, and he now has 368 whiffs in 445 games in the majors. Rivera also has a paltry .210 average to show for 1,115 at-bats through seasonal age 26 (as of June 30). No outfielder in baseball history has hit that poorly with at least 1,000 at-bats through that age.

Lowest Batting Averages, Outfielders Through Age 26—1876-2000

Player	AB	H	Avg
Ruben Rivera	1,115	234	.210
Dave Nicholson	1,394	296	.212
Joe Lahoud	1,142	244	.214
Ken Williams	1,055	227	.215

Player	AB	H	Avg
Bob Coluccio	1,095	241	.220
Pat Seerey	1,815	406	.224
Heity Cruz	1,404	316	.225
Ed Kirkpatrick	1,960	442	.226
Eric Anthony	1,606	363	.226
Rob Deer	1,126	255	.226

(minimum 1,000 AB and 50 percent of G as outfielder; age as of June 30)

There are some good stories behind the names on the above list. Dave Nicholson set a bonus record when he signed with the Orioles for $120,000 in 1958, and a major league strikeout record with 175 in 1963. Both of those marks have been broken, but Rob Deer still holds the American League standard for whiffs with 186 in 1987. Ken Williams was named general manager of the White Sox this offseason.

Pat Seerey is one of just 12 big leaguers ever to hit four homers in one game (though he needed 11 innings to do it). Heity Cruz' brothers Jose and Tommy and nephew Jose Jr. all played in the majors. And Ed Kirkpatrick is one of just three players in the expansion era who made their big league debuts at age 17.

Interesting as they might have been, none of the other nine players on the chart ever went on to earn so much as All-Star recognition, and only Kirkpatrick and Deer had much of a major league career beyond age 26.

If Rivera wants solace, he can find some in the examples of Brady Anderson, Bill Robinson and Gorman Thomas. None of the outfielders reached 1,000 at-bats until after age 26, but when they did they had similarly horrific batting averages: Anderson, .219 at age 27; Robinson, .213 at age 29; and Thomas, .214 at age 27. All three recovered to become productive hitters. Robinson, like Rivera, had been touted as another Mickey Mantle early in his career.

Rivera won't ever approach living up to that billing, and his prospects for turning his fortunes around at the plate don't look bright, either. His biggest claim to fame at this point is that he was the key player for the Padres in the trade that sent Hideki Irabu to the Yankees in 1997, a deal that didn't work out for either club.

—Jim Callis

A more complete listing for this category can be found on page 237.

San Francisco Giants: How Good Was Kent's Season For a Second Baseman?

After the 2000 season ended, the National League MVP race appeared to come down to two teammates on the Giants, whose 97 victories topped all major league clubs.

Barry Bonds batted .306-49-106 with 117 walks, a .440 on-base percentage and a .688 slugging percentage. Hitting cleanup behind Bonds, Jeff Kent finished at .334-33-125 with 90 walks, a .424 on-base percentage and a .596 slugging percentage.

When the voting was announced in November, Kent garnered 22 of the 32 first-place votes and beat out Bonds 392-279. Though Bonds' overall numbers were superior to Kent's, score one for the writers. Bonds had a great season for a left fielder, but Kent had one of the best ever for a second baseman.

Kent became just the fourth second baseman to post an on-base plus slugging percentage (OPS) of 1.000 or greater. His 1.021 OPS (he gains a point when his averages are added together and rounded) ranks 10th on the all-time list in baseball's modern era.

Highest Season OPS, Second Basemen—1901-2000

Player, Team	Year	OBP	Slg	OPS
Rogers Hornsby, StLN	1925	.489	.756	1.245
Rogers Hornsby, StLN	1924	.507	.696	1.203
Rogers Hornsby, StLN	1922	.459	.722	1.181
Rogers Hornsby, ChC	1929	.459	.679	1.139
Rogers Hornsby, BosN	1928	.498	.632	1.130
Nap Lajoie, Cle	1901	.463	.643	1.106
Rogers Hornsby, StLN	1921	.458	.639	1.097
Rogers Hornsby, StLN	1923	.459	.627	1.086
Rogers Hornsby, NYG	1927	.448	.586	1.035
Jeff Kent, SF	**2000**	**.424**	**.596**	**1.021**

(minimum 3.1 PA per team G and 50 percent of G at second base)

Rogers Hornsby monopolizes the list, claiming the top five spots and eight of the 10. He's arguably the best righthanded hitter in baseball history and unquestionably the most potent second baseman ever. Fellow Hall of Famer Nap Lajoie checks in in sixth place, with a 1901 performance that saw him become the only other second baseman to win a Triple Crown

Jeff Kent

(Hornsby won in both 1922 and 1925). Not shown on the list is another Cooperstown immortal, Joe Morgan, who had a 1.020 OPS in his 1976 NL MVP season.

This isn't the first time Kent has drawn comparisons to Hornsby. Two years ago, in the *Baseball Scoreboard 1999*, we showed that Kent's 249 RBI in 1997-98 were the second-most for a second baseman in a two-year period, trailing only Hornsby's 278 in 1921-22. Hornsby shows up five times on that top 10 list, while Kent's 229 RBI in 1998-99 are good for a tie for ninth.

Not bad for a player who hit .193 and .221 in his final two years at the University of California and was the 519th player taken in the 1989 draft. Most San Francisco fans were outraged when the club traded Matt Williams for Kent and three other players in 1996, but they're certainly not complaining any more.

—Jim Callis

A more complete listing for this category can be found on page 238.

II. QUESTIONS ON OFFENSE

Does Coors Hurt Rockies' Hitters When They Hit the Road?

It seemed like the safest prediction in the book. In an essay entitled "Can Cirillo Replace Castilla?" in last year's *Scoreboard*, we confidently predicted that in terms of overall offensive value, newly-acquired third baseman Jeff Cirillo would do as much or more for the Rockies as the man they dealt away, Vinny Castilla.

The argument went like this:

1. From 1997-99, Cirillo's on-base plus slugging (OPS) in Brewers' road games, .838, had been higher than Castilla's in road games (.817).

2. Virtually all hitters get a big boost playing in Coors' high altitude, and Cirillo's 1997-99 numbers, adjusted for the Coors park indexes for the same period, projected to an 1.003 OPS if he'd played his home games at Coors. Castilla's actual OPS at Coors during the same period was only .959.

3. While Cirillo wasn't likely to match Castilla's home-run output, he figured to hit in the .340-.350 range overall with an on-base percentage over .400 and a slugging percentage that topped .500. We thought he'd drive in 100 runs and score well over 100, with 17-20 home runs. Throw in his obvious superiority over Castilla in speed and defense, and you wind up with a clearly more valuable player.

In a lot of ways, Cirillo's 2000 season came close to matching our predictions. He scored 111 runs and drove home 115. While he hit only 11 home runs, his 53 doubles were second in the league to teammate Todd Helton. However, he fell a little short of our predictions in batting average (.326), on-base percentage (.392) and slugging percentage (.477). Given his all-around skills, not many people in Colorado were complaining about Cirillo's performance, but nonetheless, his .869 OPS fell a little short of what the Rockies had received from Castilla from 1997-99 (.889).

A deeper look at Cirillo's numbers reveals a season that was baffling in many ways. His performance at Coors surpassed even our glowing predictions, with 75 RBI, a .607 slugging percentage, a .472 on-base percentage and a major league-leading .403 batting average.

But it was a different story when he went on the road. A splendid road performer during his years with the Brewers, Cirillo hit .239 with only two home runs away from Coors. He did manage to drive in 40 runs on the

Jeff Cirillo

road, but his on-base (.299) and slugging percentages (.329) away from Coors were those of a 90-pound weakling, not an established star. If we'd had no previous knowledge of his major league career, we likely would have labeled him as yet another overrated Rockies hitter who looks better than he really is, simply because of playing his home games at Coors.

Cirillo's road struggles were so out of context with the rest of his career that it caused us to wonder if Rockies hitters have adjustment problems when they leave Colorado's high altitude. If that were the case, one would expect them to have a particularly tough time in their first game on the road after leaving Coors, or perhaps in their first road series. As the road trip continued, you would expect improved performance as the players became more accustomed to hitting in lower altitudes. Let's test the theory.

This chart shows the Rockies' OPS from 1995-2000 in their home games compared to their OPS in the first game on the road after leaving Coors, and then with all other road games:

Rockies Home OPS vs. First Game on Road—1995-2000

Home	1st Rd Gm	Other Rd Gms
.935	.711	.700

This is the opposite of what we expected. Rather than doing better after getting a road game under their belts, Rockies hitters performed a little worse. As you'll see on the following page, we get the same results when we compare how they perform in their first road series compared with subsequent road games:

Rockies Home OPS vs. First Road Series—1995-2000

Home	1st Rd Series	Other Rd Series
.935	.707	.699

A look at the hitters who logged at least 1,000 plate appearances for the Rockies from 1995-2000 shows no set pattern—some improved with more time on the road, some didn't:

Rockies Hitters OPS, Home vs. Road—1995-2000

Player	Home	1st Rd Gm	Other Rd Gms	1st Rd Series	Other Rd Series
Dante Bichette	1.041	.666	.748	.727	.743
Ellis Burks	1.035	.768	.870	.776	.910
Vinny Castilla	1.010	.708	.781	.780	.763
Andres Galarraga	1.040	.681	.838	.772	.846
Todd Helton	1.132	.840	.888	.899	.870
Mike Lansing	.883	.821	.584	.642	.601
Neifi Perez	.798	.717	.615	.616	.639
Jeff Reed	.893	.618	.791	.659	.843

(minimum 1,000 PA with Rockies)

Cirillo himself showed no pattern worth drawing any conclusions from last year. In his first game on the road after a Coors homestand, his OPS was .594. It improved to .633 in his subsequent road games. But comparing his first road *series* with subsequent series on the road, we see the opposite pattern: .705 OPS in the first series, .572 thereafter.

So Cirillo's road peformance last year remains baffling, given that it was so unlike the rest of his career. It may well have been just a fluke. While Cirillo may not hit .400 at Coors this year, he figures to continue to get a big boost from playing in Colorado. Meanwhile his road numbers can be expected to improve. If Cirillo has an overall average in the .350 range *this* year, we won't be a bit surprised.

—Don Zminda

Who Hits the Most Late-Inning Clutch Home Runs?

There are any number of measuring sticks one can use to try to measure clutch hitting, but here's a pretty basic one that we've never looked at before: Who hits the most late-inning clutch home runs?

Let's define a late-inning clutch homer as one that meets the following conditions: it comes in the seventh inning or later, with either the tying or lead run on base *or* the hitter himself representing the tying or lead run. By definition, a good number of these home runs undoubtedly comes in situations where a clutch single, double, etc., would have served the purpose of tying the game or giving the hitter's team the lead. Thus there's a built-in bias toward power hitters—you're unlikely to find Tony Gwynn at the top of this list, no matter how good a clutch hitter he might be. At the same time, few things in baseball are as dramatic as a late-inning homer that ties the game or puts the hitter's team in the lead with one swing of the bat. Just ask Bobby Thomson or Bill Mazeroski. So while this hardly is the only measure we would use to define coming through under pressure, it's *one* measure. . . and besides, it's fun. Here are the hitters who have belted the most late-inning clutch homers over the last three seasons:

Most Late-Inning Clutch Home Runs—1998-2000

Player	AB	HR	AB/HR	Overall HR	Overall AB/HR
Mark McGwire	123	15	8.20	167	7.58
Greg Vaughn	168	15	11.20	123	12.88
Sammy Sosa	187	15	12.47	179	10.46
Mike Piazza	146	13	11.23	110	14.34
Scott Rolen	151	13	11.62	83	18.13
Jeromy Burnitz	161	13	12.38	102	16.08
Jeff Bagwell	172	13	13.23	123	13.76
Eric Karros	174	12	14.50	88	18.97
Bernie Williams	119	11	10.82	81	20.09
Carlos Delgado	135	11	12.27	123	13.59
Rafael Palmeiro	138	11	12.55	129	13.56
Matt Stairs	139	11	12.64	85	18.00
Cliff Floyd	149	11	13.55	55	22.89
Todd Helton	158	11	14.36	102	16.55
MLB Average			**34.70**		**30.80**

(7th inning or later, tying or lead run at bat or on base)

Sammy Sosa (179 home runs) and Mark McGwire (167) have hit more homers than anyone else over the last three years, so it's not a big shock to find them tied for the lead in late-inning clutch homers over the same period. Or is it? Having spent most of our recent years in the Chicago area, we've heard plenty of talk-show grumbling about how "Sammy never hits them in the clutch." It's a bum rap. Along with hitting 15 late-inning clutch homers over the last three years, Sosa has homered at close to the same rate under late-inning pressure (one homer for every 12.5 at-bats) as he has overall (10.5 AB/HR). Similarly, McGwire's home-run rate under late-inning pressure was one for each 8.2 at-bats; overall, his four-bagger rate was only slightly better at 7.6 AB/HR.

Greg Vaughn, who tied Sosa and McGwire for the top spot, is a bit of a surprise. Vaughn has hit 123 homers over the last three seasons, far fewer than Sosa or McGwire, yet he has managed to hit the same number of clutch home runs. Vaughn's homer rate was better under late-inning pressure (11.2 AB/HR) than his overall rate (12.9). Along with Vaughn, the most interesting names on the leaders list are Cliff Floyd, Scott Rolen, Bernie Williams and Matt Stairs. None are big home-run hitters by current standards—especially Floyd, who has hit only 55 homers over the last three seasons, 11 of them in late-inning pressure situations. Floyd, Williams, Rolen and Stairs all had home-run rates which were dramatically higher in late-inning clutch situations than their overall four-bagger rate.

A few big-name sluggers just missed the leaders list, such as Alex Rodriguez and Mo Vaughn (10 late-inning clutch home runs each), as well as Barry Bonds, Ken Griffey Jr. and Chipper Jones (nine apiece). Some other names worth noting:

Darin Erstad. Erstad has only 57 homers over the last three years, yet 10 of them have come in late-inning clutch situations. His homer rate in the clutch (15.7 AB/HR) was nearly twice his overall rate (31.5).

Mike Lowell. The Marlins' oft-injured third baseman has outdone even Floyd and Erstad, as eight of his 34 homers over the last three years have come in the clutch.

Dave Hansen. Hansen set a major league mark last year with seven pinch homers. He obviously can handle the pressure: over the last three years, he's homered once every 7.5 AB in late-inning clutch situations.

Gary Sheffield. Sheffield is no Dave Hansen when it comes to dramatic late-inning homers. Over the last three years, Sheffield has hit only five of his 99 homers in the clutch.

Jim Leyritz. The postseason heroics of "The King" are no fluke. Over the last three years, Leyritz has hit only 22 homers, but five of them have come in late-inning clutch situations.

Brian Giles. Giles hit 90 homers from 1998-2000, but only four of them have come in late-inning clutch situations. That's not good.

Jason Giambi. Giambi's heroics under pennant-race pressure won him the American League Most Valuable Player Award last year. He clearly can come through in tough situations, yet only three of his 103 longballs in 1998-2000 came in late-inning clutch situations.

Richard Hidalgo. Hidalgo has 66 homers over the last three years, including 44 last season. Yet only one of those 66 dingers came in the clutch. You figure it out.

Frank Thomas. This one is painful for your author, a lifelong White Sox fan and almost as big of a Frank Thomas fan. Over the last three years, The Big Hurt has hit only one of his 87 homers in a late-inning clutch situation. And then he followed with a hitless performance against the Mariners in the Division Series last year. Remember that mocking nickname they gave him when he visited Wrigley Field—The Big Skirt? If the dress fits. . .

—Don Zminda

A more complete listing for this category can be found on page 239.

Are Veteran Hitters Better Than "Youngsters" in the Clutch?

It's the ninth inning, the tying run is in scoring position and you need a hit. You look down your bench and see a kid, still wet behind the ears, and a veteran, who's seen this situation a hundred times. Whom do you pick? Are veterans really better in clutch situations? Is there an advantage to "having been there before"?

One measure of clutch performance is how a hitter performs in "close-and-late" situations, defined as the seventh inning or later and the hitting team is ahead by one run, tied, or has the potential tying run on base, at the plate, or on deck.

A glance down our imaginary bench produced some interesting results in 2000. Veteran Mark Grace hit .280 overall last year, while rookie Pat Burrell hit .260—surely the steady Grace is the obvious choice under pressure. Well, Grace hit .213 and slugged a weak .348 in the clutch, while Burrell hit .242 while slugging a healthy .500. How about Frank Thomas vs. David Ortiz? Don't laugh. Thomas hit .268 in close-and-late situations and slugged .380, while Ortiz hit .292 and slugged .400. How about National League MVP Jeff Kent or second-year bust Warren Morris? Kent hit .268 and slugged .402, while Morris hit .284 and slugged .400.

These are selective choices, but they illustrate the point that for every over-matched youngster in the clutch last season like Eric Chavez (.154), there was a helpless veteran like Brady Anderson (.143). On an individual basis, the number of close-and-late at-bats over the course of a single season is not enough to be trustworthy. Even top hitters can have 60 or 70 bad at-bats. If you don't believe that, here is a lineup of veteran players who were less than reliable with the game on the line in 2000.

Selected Batting Averages, Close-And-Late—2000

Player, Team	Avg
Brady Anderson, Bal	.143
Craig Biggio, Hou	.160
Jeromy Burnitz, Mil	.161
Robin Ventura, NYM	.182
Alex Rodriguez, Sea	.203
Mark Grace, ChC	.213
Garret Anderson, Ana	.214
Mike Lieberthal, Phi	.243
Frank Thomas, CWS	.268

Eric Karros (.220) and Jeff Bagwell (.267) also could be added to the list. So a better way to answer our original question is to look at a larger group of experienced and inexperienced players over a period of time. Since 1988, here are the numbers for players who entered a season with less than 500 plate appearances (inexperienced), compared to the veterans who had at least 500 PA:

Overall vs. Close-And-Late—1988-2000

	Avg	C&L Avg	Slg	C&L Slg
Inexperienced	.256	.244	.386	.358
Experienced	.270	.258	.421	.388

Both types of players hit twelve points worse in the clutch than they did overall, and with less power. Since the veterans hit better in general, we could say they're better to have up at any time, but the fact is, if we had a veteran and a rookie with the same batting averages overall, there's no evidence to suggest that the veteran would hit better with the game on the line. The inexperienced hitters actually had *less* of a drop-off in slugging.

Here's another way to look at the numbers: take all major leaguers from last season whose careers started in 1988 or later and who have had at least 100 close-and-late at-bats. If veterans are better in the clutch, shouldn't most of them improve as they mature as big league hitters?

Batting Averages, Close-And-Late—1988-2000

	Avg
First 50 AB	.247
After 50 AB	.264

The difference starts to spread a little when we compare players to their own performance. We found that 45.2 percent of players hit more than 20 points higher after their first 50 close-and-late at-bats, compared to 32.1 percent who hit more than 20 points lower. Put another way, 58.5 percent of those with a difference of more than 20 points one way or another improved in the positive direction after the first 50 clutch at-bats.

Taking all of these numbers together, there appears to be some value to having experienced hitters at the plate in the clutch. On the other hand, if your choice is between a veteran with a .240 career average and rookie who is a potential .280 hitter, you might want to take a chance on the kid.

—Barry Rubinowitz

A more complete listing for this category can be found on page 241.

Are Aaron's Records Safer?

2000 wasn't a bad year for Hank Aaron. No, he didn't come out of retirement. So no, he didn't smack any more homers. Nevertheless, his record total of 755 home runs may have gotten just a bit more secure.

As you know, the last few years have been absolutely homer-happy. Throughout baseball history, only eight seasons have featured games that have averaged at least two homers. All but one of those seasons (1987) has occurred since 1994. As a result, we have shortstops hitting 40 homers a year, teams blasting 240, and seemingly annual assaults on the single-season record. All those longballs means that we now have 18 players who were active last season with at least 300 career home runs. For those players who are active, their lifetime totals are only going to increase.

In fact, there were more homers hit last year (5,693), and more of them hit per game (2.34), than in any previous campaign. Yet Hammerin' Hank just might be sleeping easier about the long-term security of his record total. How can that be? Because a few of the players who had entered last year as Aaron's biggest threats endured poor seasons. Well, "poor" is a relative term, at least when a couple of those players are swatting 40 and 32 homers, as Ken Griffey Jr. and Mark McGwire did last year. But when you're chasing a career record like Aaron's and you routinely had been blasting 52, as Griffey had, or 65, as McGwire had, then your 2000 campaigns qualify as disappointing.

As a result, Griffey's chances of catching Aaron dropped from 44 percent entering 2000 to 36 percent entering 2001. McGwire's chances have been cut by more than half, from 48 to 23 percent. This according to the Career Assessments system (see the Glossary) designed by Bill James.

Players With a 1% Chance For 756 Home Runs

Player	Age	Current	Chance
Ken Griffey Jr.	30	438	36%
Sammy Sosa	31	386	35%
Mark McGwire	36	554	23%
Alex Rodriguez	24	189	16%
Vladimir Guerrero	24	136	11%
Barry Bonds	35	494	6%
Manny Ramirez	28	236	5%
Carlos Delgado	28	190	1%

(age as of June 30, 2000)

The system is designed to estimate the chances players have of reaching career milestones. Sammy Sosa now ranks second on the list, although his chance has held at 35 percent for the second straight year. You'll notice that Sosa and Griffey are virtually tied, even though Griffey is a year younger and has 52 more career homers. That's because Sosa has established a rate of 57 homers per year, while Junior is at 45.3. So although Griffey currently has the career edge, Sosa has been gaining on him.

Ken Griffey Jr.

Meanwhile, at McGwire's advanced age, he cannot afford many more seasons in which he plays only 89 games. Still, given that Big Mac's home run per at-bat rate was the second best of his career, he hasn't lost his stroke. At exactly 201 homers behind Aaron, McGwire could be challenging the all-time record within four years. Since he had averaged over 60 homers per season between 1996-99, McGwire shouldn't be written off.

The system has written off Juan Gonzalez, at least for the time being. He had rated a 15-percent chance of catching Aaron entering last season. But a 22-homer campaign with Detroit dropped him off the radar screen. Now he must settle for a six-percent chance of hitting "only" 700 homers. Perhaps leaving Motown will recharge Gonzalez' batteries, though he also needs to remain healthy.

Last year at this time, we would have computed the probability that at least one player would break Aaron's record at roughly 87 percent. But, due primarily to the lower rates for Griffey, McGwire and Gonzalez, we now would reduce that overall estimate to 79 percent. That's still very high, considering it's nearly a 4-in-5 chance. The odds are good that *somebody* eventually will surpass 756. Still, the chances are significantly lower than almost 7-in-8.

Aaron's 2,297 RBI, another career record, also is a bit more secure this year:

Players With a 1% Chance For 2,298 RBI

Player	Age	Current	Chance
Ken Griffey Jr.	30	1,270	25%
Manny Ramirez	28	804	16%
Alex Rodriguez	24	595	15%
Sammy Sosa	31	1,079	14%
Vladimir Guerrero	24	404	9%
Carlos Delgado	28	604	5%
Juan Gonzalez	30	1,142	3%
Todd Helton	26	368	3%
Jeff Bagwell	32	1,093	2%
Frank Thomas	32	1,183	2%

(age as of June 30, 2000)

After driving in 118 runs last year, Griffey's chance has dropped from 30 to 25 percent. Manny Ramirez has dipped from 18 to 16 percent. And Gonzalez has plunged from 23 to 3 percent. Overall, Aaron's chances of losing his RBI record to some current player has fallen from 67 percent to 64. Still pretty high, but better from Hank's perspective.

The players to watch are Alex Rodriguez and Vladimir Guerrero. Both of them enjoyed terrific 2000 campaigns, both will be 25 this season, and both have improved their chances of catching Aaron in home runs and RBI. They're still a long way off, but they should be considered serious threats.

The concern that Rodriguez, Guerrero and others must share, however, is a work stoppage. A strike or lockout could cause lasting damage to someone chasing a longevity record. In the case of McGwire, who has said he'd seriously consider retiring in the event of a work stoppage, it could kill any chance he would otherwise have. That's just another factor that may work in Hank's favor. Of course, if the home runs keep flying over the walls, it may not make much difference.

—Jim Henzler

A more complete listing for this category can be found on page 244.

Who Bagged the Most Runs Created?

Though he finished just eight homers shy of winning the first National League Triple Crown since Joe Medwick in 1937, Colorado's Todd Helton still managed to capture the "percentages" Triple Crown in the NL in 2000. Helton paced the Senior Circuit in batting average (.372), on-base percentage (.463) and slugging percentage (.698), outdistancing his nearest opponent by a wide margin in the first two categories. His excellence in all three areas propelled him to the top of the list of the best run creators in baseball last season.

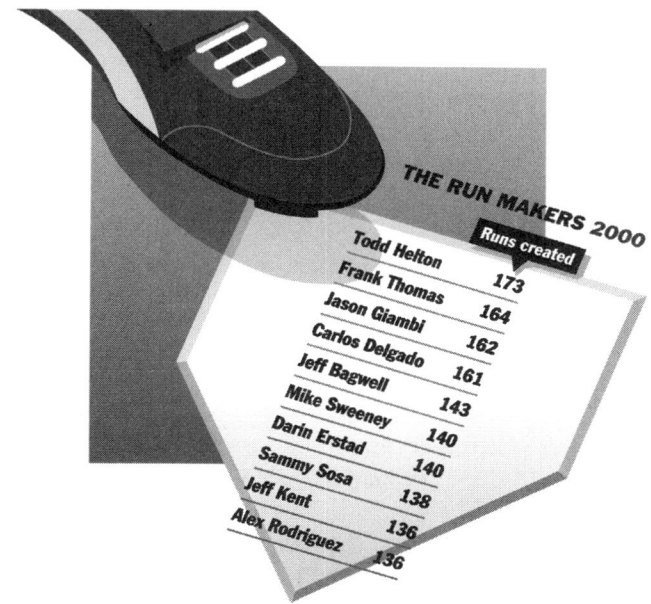

THE RUN MAKERS 2000

	Runs created
Todd Helton	173
Frank Thomas	164
Jason Giambi	162
Carlos Delgado	161
Jeff Bagwell	143
Mike Sweeney	140
Darin Erstad	140
Sammy Sosa	138
Jeff Kent	136
Alex Rodriguez	136

Runs created is the popular statistic devised by Bill James that has been as evolutionary as it has been revolutionary. James has made a number of refinements to the system over the years, but the essence of the statistic remains the same: measure how many runs a player actually contributed to his team. The runs created system accounts for a multitude of factors, but very high on the list are the ability to get on base and produce for power. Nobody in the majors did those two things better than Helton did in 2000. Also of import are the ability to curb strikeouts, come through with runners in scoring position and stay in the lineup every day. Helton struck out just 61 times, led the majors with a .392 batting average with teammates in scoring position and logged 160 games. It all added up to the best single-season RC total since Mickey Mantle's 174 in 1956.

A trio of AL sluggers also posted noteworthy totals in 2000. Frank Thomas set a new career high with 164 runs created. Jason Giambi and Carlos Delgado also cracked the 160 plateau, marking the first time since the 1937 campaign and only the third time in history that four players created 160 or more runs in the same year.

An offshoot of runs created is offensive winning percentage, which uses RC to estimate the winning percentage that a team of nine of one hitter would produce versus a club of nine average hitters, given that pitching and defense are equal. This category also is dominated by the big four.

Highest Offensive Winning Percentages—2000

Player, Team	OWP
Todd Helton, Col	.851
Jason Giambi, Oak	.840
Manny Ramirez, Cle	.826
Carlos Delgado, Tor	.813
Frank Thomas, CWS	.800
Barry Bonds, SF	.798
Gary Sheffield, LA	.792
Edgardo Alfonzo, NYM	.761
Vladimir Guerrero, Mon	.759
Nomar Garciaparra, Bos	.758
MLB Average	**.500**

(minimum 502 PA)

According to this measurement, a team of nine Heltons would have finished the 2000 campaign with roughly a 138-24 record, besting a team of Giambis by two games. It's interesting to note that besides Helton, Giambi, Thomas and Delgado, the other six players with the best offensive winning percentages did *not* make the top 10 in runs created. As mentioned earlier, an important component of RC is the ability to stay in the lineup, something that Manny Ramirez, Barry Bonds, Gary Sheffield and Nomar Garciaparra struggled to do in 2000. Ramirez and Garciaparra spent time on the DL, and Sheffield missed time due to a suspension. For his part, Bonds played in just 143 games, or 16 fewer than MVP teammate Jeff Kent. Those 16 games were the difference in Kent's superior RC total, and they just may have been the difference in the MVP voting, as well.

—Tony Nistler

A more complete listing for this category can be found on page 246.

Who's Second to None?

There's little that Barry Bonds can't do on the diamond, which is why he's headed to Cooperstown five years after he retires. A statistic known as secondary average neatly captures a player's all-around contributions, and Bonds led the majors in that category in 2000.

Barry Bonds

Bill James created the concept of secondary average when he was trying to express the contribution of a player beyond his batting average, which ranks with the save as perhaps baseball's most overrated statistic. Here's the formula:

(TB - H + BB + SB - CS) / AB

Bonds hits for average (.306 last year) and does so much more. He hits for power (slugging .688, or .362 above his batting average), draws walks (a National League-high 117) and steals bases at a good percentage (11 in 14 attempts). Do the math, and Bonds' 2000 secondary average was .642, the 16th-highest figure in baseball history.

Highest Secondary Averages—2000	
Player, Team	**Sec**
Barry Bonds, SF	.642
Jason Giambi, Oak	.586
Manny Ramirez, Cle	.542
Carlos Delgado, Tor	.534
Troy Glaus, Ana	.524
Gary Sheffield, LA	.515
Todd Helton, Col	.507
Jim Edmonds, StL	.497
Brian Giles, Pit	.494
Jeff Bagwell, Hou	.492
MLB Average	**.285**

(minimum 502 PA)

Baseball Scoreboard

The major league secondary average of .285 was the highest ever for a season in which all the pertinent data was available. The previous record was .281, set way back in 1999. With home-run and walk rates soaring, secondary average does the same.

Bonds' outstanding performance in 2000 was no fluke. It was the fifth time he had topped the majors in secondary average, also having accomplished the feat in 1991-93 and 1997. He improved his career mark to .530, the fourth-highest in baseball history.

Highest Secondary Averages—Career	
Player	**Sec**
Babe Ruth*	.594
Ted Williams	.552
Mark McGwire	.541
Barry Bonds	**.530**
Mickey Mantle	.487
Lou Gehrig	.481
Frank Thomas	.477
Jim Thome	.472
Bill Joyce*	.471
Ralph Kiner	.467

(minimum 3,000 PA;
* indicates incomplete CS data)

The career list is a mix of Bonds' contemporaries (Mark McGwire, Frank Thomas, Jim Thome) and some of the game's most devastating hitters ever (Babe Ruth, Ted Williams, Mickey Mantle, Lou Gehrig and Ralph Kiner). The only unfamiliar name is Bill Joyce, a 19th-century slugger who benefits from the fact that caught-stealing statistics weren't kept during his career.

Royals shortstop Rey Sanchez stands at the other end of the spectrum from Bonds. Sanchez has qualified for the batting title three times in his career: in 1995, when his .119 secondary average was the worst in the game; in 1999, when his .134 mark was the second-worst; and in 2000, when he again took top dishonors at .112.

Lowest Secondary Averages—2000	
Player, Team	Sec
Rey Sanchez, KC	.112
Mike Lamb, Tex	.160
Deivi Cruz, Det	.165
Fernando Vina, StL	.177
Neifi Perez, Col	.181
Doug Glanville, Phi	.184
Marquis Grissom, Mil	.190
Ben Molina, Ana	.190
Eric Owens, SD	.190
Joe Randa, KC	.198
(minimum 502 PA)	

Sanchez' .273 batting average was respectable, especially for a shortstop. But it also represented most of his offensive contributions because he doesn't hit for power, draw walks or steal bases efficiently. The same is true of his cohorts on this list.

Sanchez' partner on the left side of Kansas City's infield, third baseman Joe Randa, had one of the more misleading seasons in baseball. Randa batted .304 and drove in 106 runs. But he also had just 48 extra-base hits, 36 walks and six steals (in nine attempts) in 158 games. His on-base (.343) and slugging (.438) percentages were right at the American League averages (.335 and .436, respectively) for the hot corner.

—Jim Callis

A more complete listing for this category can be found on page 248.

Who Puts 'Em Ahead?

Though it may not seem like a big deal at a time in the game when many fans still are making their way to their seats, teams that took the lead in the first inning last year won nearly 63 percent of those contests. Of course, the winning percentages go up from there after taking the lead in subsequent frames. In fact, when a club took the lead in the seventh inning or later in 2000, it came away victorious nearly 87 percent of the time. Overall last year, teams that took the lead at any stage in a game posted a .678 winning percentage.

The point of all this is to highlight the importance of the idea that a team can't win if it never has the lead. To this end, we focus on the guys who produced the most go-ahead RBI (GARBI) last season:

Most Go-Ahead RBI—2000

Player, Team	GARBI
Mike Sweeney, KC	37
Barry Bonds, SF	35
Preston Wilson, Fla	35
Brian Giles, Pit	34
Vladimir Guerrero, Mon	33
Jeff Bagwell, Hou	32
Jim Edmonds, StL	31
Cliff Floyd, Fla	30
Andres Galarraga, Atl	30
Richard Hidalgo, Hou	30
Gary Sheffield, LA	30

The go-ahead RBI, an offshoot of the defunct game-winning RBI, is a measure of the number of times a player drove in a run that gave his team the lead at any point during the game. Nobody put his team ahead with greater frequency in 2000 than the Royals' Mike Sweeney, who finished third in the majors with 144 total RBI. Sweeney paced the American League with a .385 batting average with runners in scoring position. Unfortunately for Kansas City, however, only six of his GARBI came in the seventh inning or later.

Occupying second place on the list is Barry Bonds. Bonds (106) could not keep pace with MVP teammate Jeff Kent in total RBI (125), but 35 of Bonds' ribbies put the Giants ahead last season, while Kent's did so just 29 times. Still, the two were the second-most prolific teammates in terms of GARBI, just behind the Florida duo of Preston Wilson and Cliff Floyd.

We also consider the players who make the most of their go-ahead RBI opportunities. We compute go-ahead RBI percentages by dividing a player's total number of go-ahead RBI by the number of GARBI opportunities, or GARBI *plus* the number of times he stranded a go-ahead run in scoring position while using up an out (excluding sacrifice hits and sacrifice flies). Here are the best in 2000 among players with at least 25 opportunities:

Best Go-Ahead RBI Percentages—2000

Player, Team	GARBI	Opp	Pct
Jose Valentin, CWS	19	29	65.5
Ivan Rodriguez, Tex	22	35	62.9
Mike Sweeney, KC	37	59	62.7
Alex Rodriguez, Sea	29	47	61.7
Gary Sheffield, LA	30	49	61.2
Barry Bonds, SF	35	58	60.3
Carlos Lee, CWS	15	25	60.0
Mark McGwire, StL	23	39	59.0
Trot Nixon, Bos	18	31	58.1
Darin Erstad, Ana	20	35	57.1
MLB Average			**39.7**

(minimum 25 Opp)

Sweeney produced quantity *and* quality in 2000, coming through with a GARBI in nearly 63 percent of his opportunities. Bonds also made the most of his chances, as did Alex Rodriguez, whom the Rangers hope will team with Ivan Rodriguez to give Texas plenty of leads next year. Last year's surprise leader in best go-ahead RBI percentage, the White Sox' Jose Valentin, drove in 92 total runs, his best figure since 1996.

As for the worst GARBI percentages in 2000, those belong to B.J. Surhoff (20.7), Cristian Guzman (24.1), Doug Glanville (24.1), Royce Clayton (25.0) and Scott Rolen (25.8). The Braves—who had a major league-best .766 winning percentage when they took the lead at any point during a game last year—hope that Surhoff can turn his fortunes around in 2001, while the Sox hope that Clayton will learn a thing or two about GARBI from Valentin, the man Clayton is replacing at shortstop in Chicago.

—Tony Nistler

A more complete listing for this category can be found on page 249.

Who Are the Real RBI Kings?

The Run Batted In was adopted as an official statistic in 1920, a sign of baseball's original lively-ball era launched by Babe Ruth. From its beginning, the RBI has been a statistic of opportunity. Lou Gehrig's RBI totals from the '20s and '30s are substantial because Gehrig, in addition to being a great hitter, hit behind the incomparable Ruth.

Over the last several seasons, the sport has enjoyed another lively-ball era. Hitters are getting more and more RBI opportunities, and they are taking advantage of them. While nobody in this era has seriously threatened Hack Wilson's 1930 record of 191 ribbies, clearing the century mark has become noticeably more common in recent years. Last season, a baseball record was set when 18 players knocked in 120 runs or more.

Which of this new breed of RBI kings are making the most of their opportunities? Each year, the *Scoreboard* ranks the most opportunistic RBI men in baseball by comparing each player's RBI total to the number of runs available for the player to drive in. Our definition of RBI available, as suggested by reader Bill Penn, is the number of RBI a player would accumulate if he homered every time he came to bat. An at-bat with the bases loaded, then, counts as four RBI available, while an AB with the bases empty counts as one. A player is not charged with any RBI opportunities if he reaches base via a walk, hit by pitch or catcher's interference, unless a run scores as a result of the play.

Mark McGwire has owned this section of the book in recent years. In 1999, McGwire won his fourth RBI efficiency title in five seasons by knocking in 17.2 percent of his RBI available. In 2000, Big Mac was an even more efficient run producer, finishing with 73 RBI in 410 opportunities for a 17.8 RBI percentage.

However, McGwire failed to meet our traditional minimum of 80 total runs batted in necessary to qualify for the efficiency crown. Though he had 69 RBI at the All-Star break, tendinitis in his right knee limited McGwire to just 15 at-bats and four RBI afterward.

So McGwire is denied a fifth title in six years. As you'll see on the following page, our award for the most productive RBI man in 2000 goes to American League MVP Jason Giambi, McGwire's replacement at first base in Oakland:

Most RBI Per Opportunity—2000

Player, Team	RBI	Avail	Pct
Jason Giambi, Oak	137	869	15.8
Manny Ramirez, Cle	122	779	15.7
Frank Thomas, CWS	143	968	14.8
Todd Helton, Col	147	1,000	14.7
Edgar Martinez, Sea	145	1,005	14.4
Carlos Delgado, Tor	137	969	14.1
Alex Rodriguez, Sea	132	936	14.1
John Vander Wal, Pit	94	670	14.0
Moises Alou, Hou	114	816	14.0
Barry Bonds, SF	106	761	13.9
MLB Average			8.5

(minimum 80 RBI)

The other names on the list are all well-known RBI men, with the exception of Pittsburgh veteran John Vander Wal. Associated primarily with pinch-hitting prowess, Vander Wal had amassed only 197 career RBI going into the 2000 campaign, never finishing with more than 41 in a season. But the Pirates allowed Vander Wal to play every day against righthanded pitching, and Vander Wal rewarded them by knocking in runs at a higher rate than Barry Bonds, Sammy Sosa or Jeff Bagwell.

Vander Wal hit .335 when penciled in as the No. 3 or 4 hitter for the Pirates last season. However, it looks as if the 2001 Bucs will be entrusting one of those lineup spots—and some of Vander Wal's playing time—to free-agent acquisition Derek Bell.

Last season while with the Mets, Bell drove in 69 runs in 843 opportunities. Given 173 more chances than Vander Wal, Bell drove in 25 fewer runs. It seems that hitting Bell behind or between on-base machines Jason Kendall and Brian Giles could be a mistake.

Here are some other players who left their share of baserunners stranded during the 2000 season. All of the players listed on the following page spent most of the year hitting in the third through sixth spots in their respective batting orders:

RBI Underachievers—2000

Player, Team	RBI	Avail	Pct
Jeff Conine, Bal	46	674	6.8
Travis Lee, Ari-Phi	54	708	7.6
B.J. Surhoff, Bal-Atl	68	887	7.7
Troy O'Leary, Bos	70	888	7.9
Corey Koskie, Min	65	798	8.1
Juan Gonzalez, Det	67	799	8.4
Roberto Alomar, Cle	89	1,047	8.5
Todd Zeile, NYM	79	909	8.7
David Ortiz, Min	63	716	8.8
Ron Coomer, Min	82	930	8.8

(minimum 650 RBI Available)

The name that jumps out on this list is Juan Gonzalez, whose performance as a big-time RBI man earned him a pair of MVP awards in the '90s. In fact, Gonzalez had averaged 140 RBI over the previous four seasons before slumping to 67 last year. During the offseason, Cleveland signed Gonzalez to replace the departed Manny Ramirez in the cleanup spot. Hitting fourth for the Indians is sure to allow Gonzalez a ton of RBI opportunities. His ability to return to his run-producing ways will go a long way toward deciding whether the Tribe returns to the playoffs in 2001.

Finally, it should come as no surprise that baseball's least efficient run producer in 2000 was Florida leadoff man Luis Castillo, whom we look at in greater detail in the Marlins' team essay on page 52. Despite hitting .334 for the Marlins, Castillo drove in just 17 runs in 775 opportunities (2.2 percent). To put that in perspective, consider that Ramirez drove in over 100 more runs than Castillo despite a nearly identical number of RBI available. Although the RBI is indeed a statistic of opportunity, some hitters clearly are in a position to be more opportunistic run producers than others.

—Craig Rolling

A more complete listing for this category can be found on page 250.

Can a Change of Scenery Be Good For the Heart?

If home is where the heart is, then it didn't take long for the Astros and Giants to call their new ballparks *home* last season. The heart of the order of both clubs—the No. 3, 4 and 5 hitters—wasted no time christening Enron Field and Pac Bell Park, respectively, in 2000.

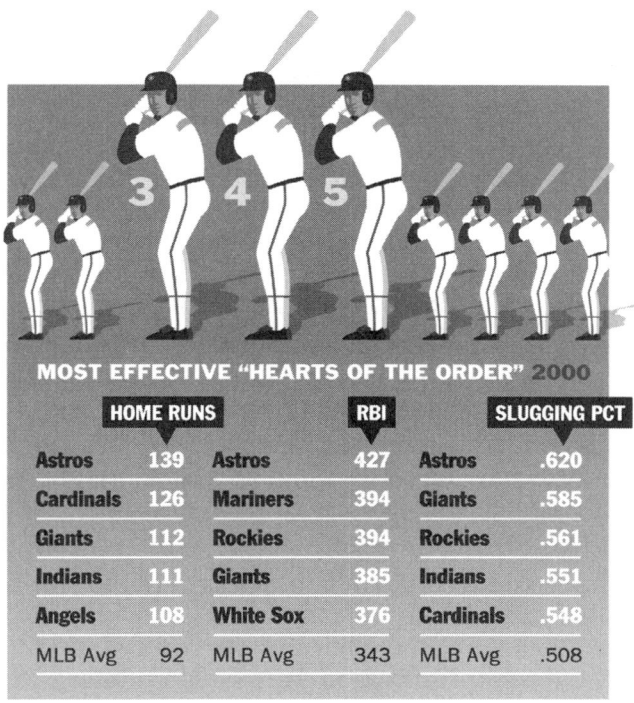

MOST EFFECTIVE "HEARTS OF THE ORDER" 2000

HOME RUNS		RBI		SLUGGING PCT	
Astros	139	Astros	427	Astros	.620
Cardinals	126	Mariners	394	Giants	.585
Giants	112	Rockies	394	Rockies	.561
Indians	111	Giants	385	Indians	.551
Angels	108	White Sox	376	Cardinals	.548
MLB Avg	92	MLB Avg	343	MLB Avg	.508

In fact, the Astros and Giants boasted the two most productive hearts of the order in the majors in 2000, propelled in part by their performances at their new pads (or launching pad, in the case of Enron). In fact, Houston's 3, 4 and 5 hitters were so enamored with their new surroundings that they became just the second group since 1990 to sweep all three of our heart-of-the-order categories, joining the 1997 Rockies. Here's our annual rundown of the top tickers in baseball:

1. Astros. Buoyed by the move from the spacious environs of the Astrodome to the more specious, for hitters at least, confines of Enron, the heart of the Houston batting order pounded out a gaudy .620 slugging percentage. The primary 3-4-5 trio of Jeff Bagwell, Ken Caminiti and Moises

Alou hit 92 home runs, with 54 (58.7 percent) of those longballs coming at home. Both Richard Hidalgo and Lance Berkman spent time in the cleanup spot last season along with Caminiti, and both should help Houston's heartbeat remain strong in 2001 despite Caminiti's departure.

2. Giants. The heart of the San Francisco order also took very kindly to its new surroundings, though Barry Bonds, Jeff Kent and J.T. Snow also were terrors on the road. You know your heart is in good shape when your No. 3 and 4 hitters finish 1-2 in the voting for National League MVP. The Giants were the only other team besides the Astros to rank in the top five in all three heart measurements.

3. Indians. Powered by the steady bats of Roberto Alomar, Manny Ramirez and Jim Thome, Cleveland's heart worked its way into our top three for the second straight year. The final numbers proved to be disappointing, however. In 1999, the heart of the order for the Indians drove in 439 runs, but the group produced "just" 374 ribbies in 2000. Still, that's an impressive total, and one that will set the bar high for new transplantee Juan Gonzalez.

4. Cardinals. The Cardinals' heart could have stopped last year after Mark McGwire succumbed to a bum knee in early July. But, in stepped Will Clark, who pumped new life into the heart of the St. Louis lineup just in time to lead the Cards into the postseason. Of course, it didn't hurt that Big Mac averaged one homer in every 7.4 at-bats while hitting third or fourth, or that Jim Edmonds smacked 42 dingers during the 2000 campaign.

5. Blue Jays. The Jays edged the White Sox in a photo finish for the fifth spot, as Toronto's heart placed sixth in the majors with 107 homers and a .544 slugging percentage. Carlos Delgado provided plenty of punch from his cleanup spot, but a surprise season from Brad Fullmer in the No. 5 hole tipped the scales for the Blue Jays.

A check-up on the weakest hearts in the league once again reveals the Twins, whose 3-4-5 batsmen produced just 39 homers for the second consecutive year. More surprising, however, was the failing heart of the Orioles. Regulars Delino DeShields, Albert Belle and Jeff Conine finished with just 38 heart-of-the-order home runs between them. With all three expected to remain in Baltimore in 2001, the Orioles must be hoping that a change of scenery is good for the heart—and bat—of free-agent acquisition David Segui.

—Tony Nistler

A more complete listing for this category can be found on page 253.

Who Gets the Slidin' Billy Trophy?

The Yankee dynasty continues, even in the face of age and injuries. But whether the Craig Biggio dynasty can continue is another matter. Prior to the 2000 campaign, Biggio had won our Slidin' Billy Trophy as the game's best leadoff man for three consecutive years, but a torn knee ligament may well have put an end to that.

Biggio wasn't the only contender to end up in the hospital rather than in the lineup in 2000. Quilvio Veras was having a big year for the Braves when he tore *his* ACL. Fernando Vina's hamstring put him on the disabled list and kept him from running after that. Things got so bad at the No. 1 spot that while 1999's top 10 in leadoff on-base percentage had seven players with at least 400 at-bats in the leadoff role, last year's list contains just two players who reached the 400 plateau.

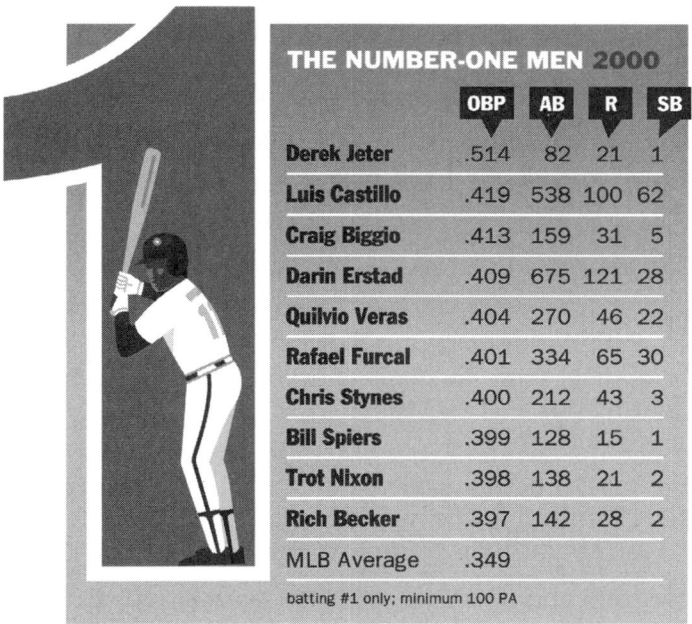

THE NUMBER-ONE MEN 2000

	OBP	AB	R	SB
Derek Jeter	.514	82	21	1
Luis Castillo	.419	538	100	62
Craig Biggio	.413	159	31	5
Darin Erstad	.409	675	121	28
Quilvio Veras	.404	270	46	22
Rafael Furcal	.401	334	65	30
Chris Stynes	.400	212	43	3
Bill Spiers	.399	128	15	1
Trot Nixon	.398	138	21	2
Rich Becker	.397	142	28	2
MLB Average	.349			

batting #1 only; minimum 100 PA

Impressive as Derek Jeter's .514 on-base percentage in the leadoff slot was, he only had 100 plate appearances while batting No. 1, so let's concentrate on the full-time table-setters. After all, the Slidin' Billy voters need to find someone worthy of the great legacy of Billy Hamilton, who scored 100 runs 10 consecutive years in the 19th century. The quintessential leadoff man, he had a career on-base percentage of .455 and scored a mind-boggling 192 runs in 1894. Here are the top candidates in 2000:

Luis Castillo. If this were the Slidin' Billy Play-Alike Trophy, Castillo would own it. Hamilton averaged 35 extra-base hits per 150 games in his career, never hitting more than 25 doubles or seven homers. Castillo has averaged 24 extra-base hits per 150 games, with a season high of 23 doubles and two homers. Castillo topped all regular leadoff men in 2000 with a .419 on-base percentage and led the league with 62 stolen bases.

Darin Erstad. Hamilton would be proud to have Erstad receive this award, as few players did more sliding in 2000 than Erstad. Whether into second on one of his 39 doubles, into third on one of his six triples, or into both on one of his 28 steals, Erstad was the ultimate example of the modern leadoff hitter, as he flashed both power along with speed.

Johnny Damon. Damon scored 136 runs and drove in 88 teammates. A .327 batting average, 42 doubles, 10 triples and 16 homers didn't hurt his cause, either. He stole 46 bases in 55 tries and now stands to make a large sum of money after his 2001 campaign with the Athletics. That should enable him to build a pretty nice trophy case, should he ever need one.

Ray Durham. The catalyst for the White Sox on their way to the AL Central crown, Durham scored 121 times. He could be described as the Poor Man's Johnny Damon, with 35 doubles, nine triples, 17 homers and 25 steals. Add 75 RBI to the mix and you have a mighty nice No. 1 hitter, despite his slightly low .361 on-base percentage.

Eric Young. Young finished with a .370 on-base percentage and only scored 96 runs while hitting leadoff. But combine his 40 doubles, two triples and six homers with 54 steals and you have a leadoff hitter who put himself in scoring position 102 times.

Before we open the envelope, a word about Rich Becker. Only three players made our top 10 in this category in each of the last two years—Craig Biggio, Luis Castillo and the well-traveled Mr. Becker. If Becker could only run. . . Good luck finding employment, Rich.

When all was said and done, we were left with a tight choice between Erstad and Damon. In a cloud of dirt, the winner of the 2000 Slidin' Billy Award is Erstad. We can't ignore the big margin in on-base plus slugging (.950 to .877), and the 100 ribbies from the leadoff slot is a nice bonus.

—Barry Rubinowitz

A more complete listing for this category can be found on page 254.

Who's the Best Bunter?

It may not be the stuff of boyhood dreams, multimillion-dollar contracts or highlight reels, but like peanuts, popcorn and Cracker Jacks, bunting remains an integral part of the game. Just ask the Mariners. In the third and final game of last year's Division Series sweep of the White Sox, pinch-hitter Carlos Guillen poked a drag bunt to the right side of the infield in the bottom of the ninth of a 1-1 contest that scored Rickey Henderson from third. Game over. Series over. Good night. No home run necessary.

Of course, most bunts don't carry that kind of drama. Still, in close contests, the ability to execute a sac bunt or lay one down for a base hit can be the difference. For that reason, we recognize the men who aren't afraid to *not* swing away by awarding the STATS FlatBat to the game's top bunter. We begin our annual salute with a look at the top sacrifice bunters in 2000:

Highest Sacrifice Bunt Percentages—2000

Player, Team	SH	Att	Pct
Dan Wilson, Sea	11	11	1.000
Kirk Rueter, SF	10	10	1.000
Rick Reed, NYM	14	15	.933
Garrett Stephenson, StL	13	14	.929
Javier Vazquez, Mon	13	14	.929
Doug Glanville, Phi	12	13	.923
Felix Martinez, TB	12	13	.923
Chris Singleton, CWS	12	13	.923
Shawn Estes, SF	11	12	.917
Shane Halter, Det	10	11	.909
Jon Lieber, ChC	10	11	.909
MLB Average			**.769**

(minimum 10 Att)

Speaking of the Mariners, catcher Dan Wilson, of all players, turned in the top performance in this category in 2000. What's this, Lou Piniella turning into a little-ball fanatic? Actually, the M's did an outstanding job of adjusting to their first full season at pitcher-friendly Safeco Field, finishing second in the league in both sacrifice bunt attempts (73) and sacrifice bunt percentage (87.7). New Seattle hitting coach Gerald Perry required everyone to practice bunting on a daily basis, and the extra work obviously paid dividends. Besides Wilson, the Mariners' David Bell was 6-for-6 in sac bunt attempts during the regular season, while the aforementioned Guillen was 7-for-8.

The rest of the percentages list is dominated by pitchers and center fielders, including a pair of San Francisco hurlers. Kirk Rueter and Shawn Estes did an outstanding job of moving runners along, helping the Giants to a major league-best 90.7 sac bunt percentage. Neither Doug Glanville nor Chris Singleton had outstanding seasons offensively, but they did rise to the occasion when called upon to give themselves up.

Perhaps the biggest surprise was not who made the list, but rather who did *not* crack the top 10. The Indians' Omar Vizquel was not at the top of our percentage leaders for the first time since 1996. Not only did Vizquel fail on a sac attempt for the first time since that '96 campaign, but he also failed to reach the 10-attempt minimum. He *did*, however, crack the leader board for most bunts for a base hit last season.

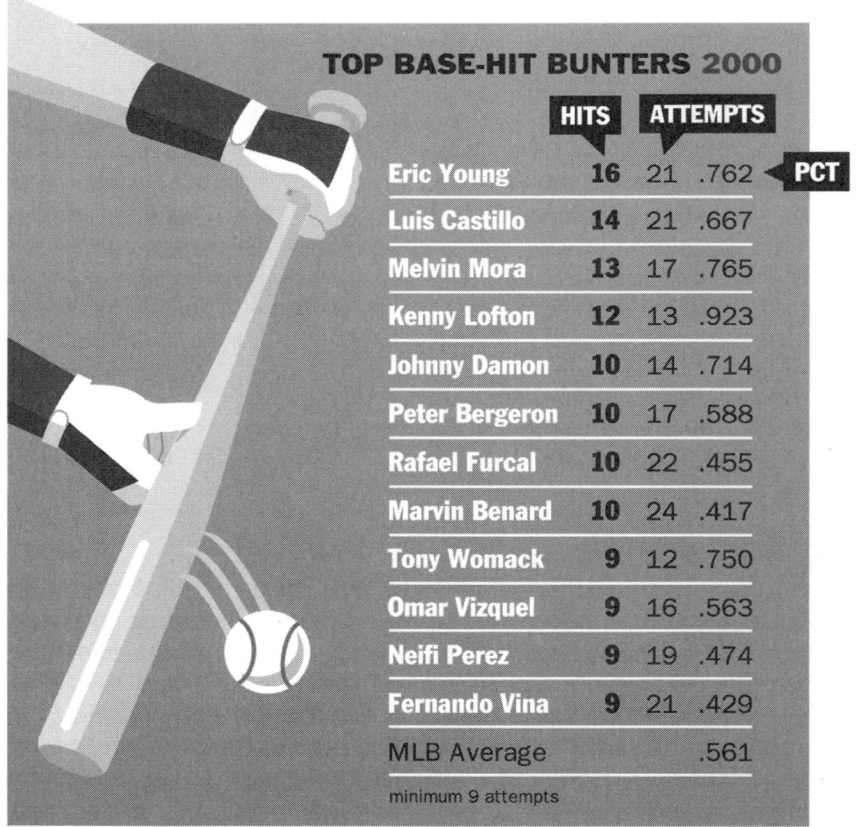

TOP BASE-HIT BUNTERS 2000

Player	HITS	ATTEMPTS	PCT
Eric Young	16	21	.762
Luis Castillo	14	21	.667
Melvin Mora	13	17	.765
Kenny Lofton	12	13	.923
Johnny Damon	10	14	.714
Peter Bergeron	10	17	.588
Rafael Furcal	10	22	.455
Marvin Benard	10	24	.417
Tony Womack	9	12	.750
Omar Vizquel	9	16	.563
Neifi Perez	9	19	.474
Fernando Vina	9	21	.429
MLB Average			.561

minimum 9 attempts

Vizquel snuck in nine base-hit bunts in 2000, though that total was 10 fewer than he dropped down in 1999. The Cubs' Eric Young paced the bigs with 16 such hits last year, but Vizquel's teammate, Kenny Lofton, boasted the best success rate.

Now that the numbers are in, let's do a quick breakdown of the five 2000 FlatBat finalists:

Eric Young. Young's legs were healthy last year for the first time in a couple of seasons, and the Cubs put his wheels to good use. Besides leading the majors in bunt hits, E.Y. also was a perfect 7-for-7 in sac bunt attempts.

Luis Castillo. Castillo had nearly as many bunt hits (14) last year as he did doubles (17). His bunt-hit percentage wasn't all that impressive, but he did successfully execute 9 of 10 sacrifice bunt attempts.

Melvin Mora. Mora logged just 414 at-bats last year between the Mets and Baltimore, but he showed enough promise to be a candidate for the O's starting lineup in 2001. His total of 13 bunt hits was impressive, but he finished with just four successful sac bunts.

Kenny Lofton. Lofton may have been coming back from shoulder surgery, but he proved that his legs were just fine. On top of his nearly-perfect bunt-hit percentage, he added six sac bunts in eight tries.

Johnny Damon. Damon had more extra-base hits than any of the other finalists, but he also used his speed to leg out 10 bunt hits. He was a perfect 8-for-8 when it came time for laying down a sacrifice.

Drumroll please. . .

For just the second time since 1992, the winner of the STATS FlatBat Award will *not* be Vizquel or Lofton. The crown for 2000 goes to Young, who was effective in all facets of the bunting game last season. The Cubs now hope that E.Y.'s wheels, which will be 34 in May, will allow him to defend his title in 2001. Besides, they already have some guy named Sosa to swing for the fences.

—Tony Nistler

A more complete listing for this category can be found on page 255.

Who Is the New Millennium's First Man on the Moon?

Ladies and gentlemen, we would like to introduce the newest member of the 500-foot club—Mr. Mike Piazza. On behalf of Mr. Piazza, we also would like to thank Randy Johnson, who proved that every action does have a tremendous reaction. On May 21, Piazza turned a Johnson fastball into a 500-foot shot into the left-field mezzanine at Shea Stadium. It was the longest home run in the majors last season.

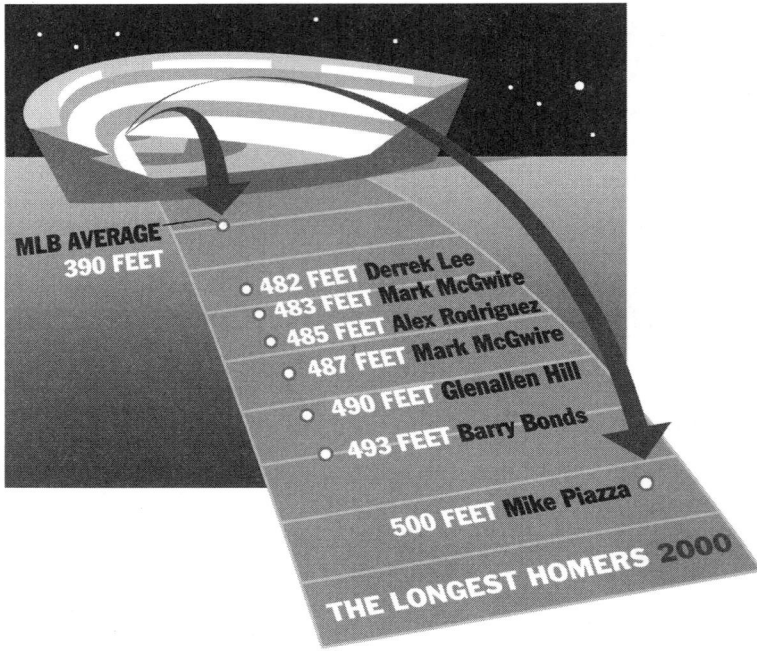

Piazza became the first Mets batsman to launch a baseball 500 feet since Darryl Strawberry reached the exact same distance on July 3, 1990, also at Shea. Piazza also became the first catcher, and just 11th player overall, to reach that distance since 1987.

After hitting an incredible 12 500-foot homers between 1997 and 1999, Mark McGwire failed to achieve the half-millennium plateau last season. However, Big Mac still showed his powerful flair in 2000 despite a bad knee, smacking a league-high nine home runs of more than 450 feet. Sammy Sosa and Barry Bonds were close behind, each reaching that distance six times in 2000. Piazza was next on the list with four shots of such magnitude.

Of course, we can't discuss this topic without making mention of the pitchers. On August 8 versus the Cubs, the Dodgers' Darren Dreifort was involved in two memorably long homers. Actually, he hit them. First, in the fourth inning, Dreifort stepped in against rookie pitcher Phil Norton and promptly belted a solo shot 440 feet into the Chavez Ravine night. While the fans at Dodger Stadium were quite satisfied with Dreifort's mammoth contribution to a four-homer fourth frame, Dreifort wasn't done making them cheer. The very next inning, Todd Van Poppel served up yet another home run to the Dodger pitcher—this one a 460-foot blast.

All the talk of Coors Field and Enron Field being two of the greatest hitters' parks is well deserved. While Coors Field surrendered 245 homers (3.02 a game), Enron Field eclipsed the light-air stadium by allowing an astounding 266 homers (3.28 a game). However, distance was another issue in 2000.

Most 450-Plus Foot Home Runs by Stadium—2000

Stadium	450+
Coors Field	17
Pro Player Stadium	9
Busch Stadium	8
Four Tied With	5
MLB Average	**3.1**

Ironically, only four of the 266 home runs hit at Enron Field traveled 450 feet. The mile-high altitude obviously lifted Coors to the top of this category, while McGwire certainly helped Busch stake its claim. Surprisingly, nine different players produced a 450-foot blast at Pro Player last season. Where's Shea, you ask? There were only three such moonshots in Flushing last season, all by that newest member of the 500-foot club, Mike Piazza.

—Sam Lubeck

A more complete listing for this category can be found on page 256.

Baseball Scoreboard

Who Are the Human Air Conditioners?

Chicago has long been known as the Windy City, but the city has gotten much breezier since Sammy Sosa came to town. He has failed to make contact more than any other major leaguer in six of the past eight seasons, swinging and missing 3,165 times over that span, or almost 400 times per year. The King of Swing (and Miss) defended his crown last season.

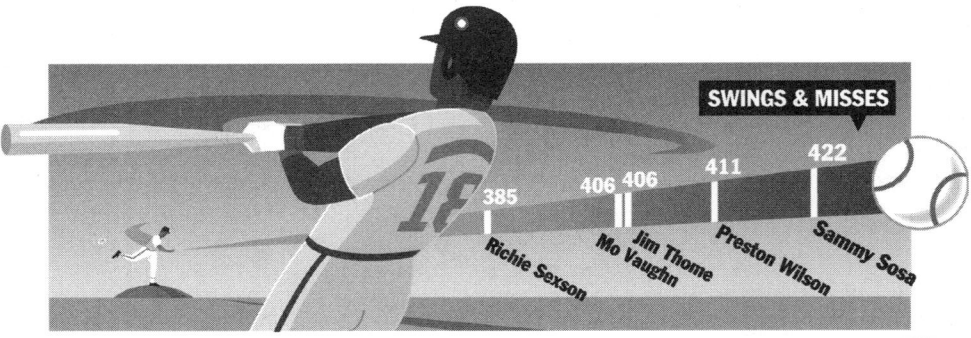

Sosa also led all of baseball by belting 50 home runs in 2000. Actually, he produced one bomb for every 8.4 swing-and-misses, which is quite a bit better than the major league mean of one home run for every 11.2 misses.

Each of the top five "swingers" from the above chart hit at least 30 homers, so there's some method to their swing-from-the-heels madness. Sixteen players hit 40-plus homers last season, and six of them actually made contact more often than the MLB average (19.8 percent). Todd Helton utilized the thin air of Coors to post the best ratio of the lot, pounding out 42 homers while grabbing air only 113 times, or less than 10 percent of his swings. Other power hitters who made above-average contact were notoriously patient guys like Frank Thomas (43 homers, 149 misses), Barry Bonds (49-144) and Gary Sheffield (43-159). So who hit nothing but air in the highest percentage of their swings in 2000?

Highest Percentage of Swings That Missed—2000

Player, Team	Swings	Misses	Pct
Ray Lankford, StL	936	336	35.9
Ruben Rivera, SD	903	303	33.6
Richie Sexson, Cle-Mil	1,173	385	32.8
Jim Thome, Cle	1,251	406	32.5
Preston Wilson, Fla	1,278	411	32.2
Sammy Sosa, ChC	1,326	422	31.8

Player, Team	Swings	Misses	Pct
Mo Vaughn, Ana	1,318	406	30.8
Chris Truby, Hou	524	161	30.7
Andres Galarraga, Atl	1,039	316	30.4
Jose Canseco, TB-NYY	694	211	30.4
MLB Average			**19.8**

(minimum 500 swings)

Ray Lankford would have had an even bigger lead had Tony La Russa not platooned him, as the lefthanded-hitting Lankford fanned in exactly half of his at-bats against lefties last season. The list features a mix of young players and established veterans. Ruben Rivera, who clearly proved his sixth tool is his ability to fan at pitches, Preston Wilson and Chris Truby are all 27 or younger, so they may have many freon-laden years ahead of them. If we expand the list to include hitters with fewer than 500 swings, the leader is young Russ Branyan. The 25-year-old flailed and missed 175 times in just 443 swings, or almost 40 percent of the time. Here is a potential whiffing superstar in the making.

What about the other guys, the slap hitters who can spoil good pitches until they see one that they like? As Tony Gwynn and Wade Boggs move closer to the walls of the Hall of Fame, it will be intriguing to see who will replace them as the masters of making contact.

Lowest Percentage of Swings That Missed—2000

Player, Team	Swings	Misses	Pct
Mark Loretta, Mil	664	46	6.9
Luis Sojo, Pit-NYY	533	40	7.5
Eric Young, ChC	984	75	7.6
Chuck Knoblauch, NYY	695	53	7.6
Luis Castillo, Fla	1,028	81	7.9

Two things jump out from this group: 1) all five players are, or have been in Mark Loretta's case, second basemen; 2) Chuck Knoblauch and his postseason replacement, Luis Sojo, both appear here. Joe Torre must want contact hitters to complement Derek Jeter. While Knoblauch is the only repeater from last year's top five, Loretta has proven that he can continue to make contact with increased playing time; those two would appear to be the conditional heirs to the Gwynn/Boggs legacy.

—Don Hartack

A more complete listing for this category can be found on page 257.

Can a Team Strike Out a Lot And Still Win?

Of all the records that are being set in this free-swinging era, the 2000 Cardinals came close to establishing one of the most dubious. The team that featured baseball's single-season home-run champ only two years earlier continued to swing for the fences. And yes, St. Louis continued to strike out at a spectacular rate, too.

The Cardinals fanned 1,253 times last year. Although that total surpassed the previous National League record, it did fall 15 shy of Detroit's major league mark of 1,268, set in 1996. Too bad Mark McGwire got hurt. If he hadn't, the Redbirds almost certainly would have shattered the Tigers' record. Last season Big Mac struck out roughly twice as often as Will Clark, who was McGwire's primary replacement down the stretch.

The thing is, all those strikeouts didn't hurt the Cardinals too much. After all, they wound up winning the NL Central and advanced to the National League Championship Series. It was much the same story over in the American League. The Oakland A's weren't quite as prolific as St. Louis, whiffing "only" 1,159 times. Nevertheless, that sum led the AL, though Oakland still managed to capture the American League West crown. Last year's experience might lead you to believe that leading the league in strikeouts isn't necessarily a recipe for disaster. But looking at the teams that have led their circuit in total strikeouts since the end of World War II, only 12 have wound up winning their league or division:

League/Division Winners Leading League in Strikeouts—1946-2000

Year	Team	Lg	SO	Pct	R/G	R/G Rank	Lg R/G
1948	Indians	AL	575	.626	5.38	3	4.73
1958	Yankees	AL	822	.597	4.90	1	4.17
1971	Athletics	AL	1,018	.627	4.29	3	3.87
1971	Giants	NL	1,042	.556	4.36	3	3.91
1976	Reds	NL	902	.630	5.29	1	3.98
1979	Orioles	AL	847	.642	4.76	6	4.67
1981	Athletics*	AL	647	.587	4.20	6	4.07
1983	White Sox	AL	888	.611	4.94	1	4.48
1984	Tigers	AL	941	.642	5.12	1	4.42
1989	Giants	NL	1,071	.568	4.31	2	3.94
2000	Athletics	AL	1,159	.565	5.88	2	5.29
2000	Cardinals	NL	1,253	.586	5.48	4	5.00

(*—based on overall record in 1981)

That's just 12 teams in 55 seasons. That may not seem like such a bad percentage, but remember, there were 186 league or division championships between 1946-2000 (excluding the 1994 strike year). Six of the 12 high-strikeout teams wound up advancing to the World Series, where four of them (1948 Indians, 1958 Yankees, 1976 Reds and 1984 Tigers) won the world championship. But no club setting the pace in strikeouts won a title of any kind in the decade between 1990-99.

The 12 teams on the previous chart were able to score runs despite their numerous strikeouts. All of them ranked in their league's upper half in terms of runs scored. But they're more the exception rather than the rule. In fact, of the last 10 teams to lead their league in strikeouts, most had difficulty plating tallies.

Teams Leading League in Strikeouts—1996-2000

Year	Team	Lg	SO	Pct	Place	R/G	R/G Rank	Lg R/G
1996	Tigers	AL	1,268	.327	5	4.83	11	5.39
1996	Dodgers	NL	1,190	.556	2	4.34	12	4.68
1997	Athletics	AL	1,181	.401	4	4.72	11	4.93
1997	Cardinals	NL	1,191	.451	4	4.25	11	4.60
1998	Blue Jays	AL	1,132	.543	3	5.01	8	5.01
1998	Diamondbacks	NL	1,239	.401	5	4.10	14	4.60
1999	Athletics	AL	1,129	.537	2	5.51	4	5.17
1999	Cardinals	NL	1,202	.466	4	5.02	10	5.00
2000	Athletics	AL	1,159	.565	1	5.88	2	5.29
2000	Cardinals	NL	1,253	.586	1	5.48	4	5.00

Excluding last year's squads, six of the previous eight strikeout leaders ranked 10th or lower in runs scored per game. A few of them really struggled to win, too. The 1996 Tigers, for instance, posted the most losses and worst winning percentage of any team since the 1979 Blue Jays. The 1997 A's and 1998 Diamondbacks both lost 97 games. Overall, the 110 league leaders since 1946 have combined for a winning percentage of just .469. Nearly two-thirds of those clubs, 72, suffered losing campaigns.

The A's and Cardinals may have bucked the odds last season by enjoying success while racking up loads of Ks. But history indicates their formula probably isn't the best one to follow when trying to build a winner.

—Jim Henzler

A more complete listing for this category can be found on page 259.

Are Hitters Taking More Pitches These Days?

Our parents reminded us that "Patience is a virtue." The French naturalist Comte de Buffon perhaps went further, stating "Genius is patience." Well, if that's the case, major league hitters may have gained moral strength and gotten smarter over the past several years, as the evidence indicates that hitters are demonstrating greater patience and looking at more pitches these days.

"Ten years ago, players got all over hitters who took a lot of pitches," Orel Hershiser told Peter Gammons in a 1999 interview. "Now the game is to wait, take, and get into hitters' counts and hit hitters' pitches. Ten years ago, hitters went up with the idea, 'If I put the ball in play, something good will happen.' Now, it's the opposite."

Let's consider the pitch count information that STATS has gathered over the past decade or so. STATS has been tracking pitch counts since 1987, and here is the number of pitches that hitters have averaged per plate appearance over that span, broken down by year:

Pitches Per Plate Appearance—1987-2000

Year	P/PA	Year	P/PA
1987	3.50	1994	3.71
1988	3.56	1995	3.71
1989	3.52	1996	3.75
1990	3.60	1997	3.71
1991	3.65	1998	3.71
1992	3.62	1999	3.74
1993	3.64	2000	3.74

As you can see, an increase in pitches per plate appearance (P/PA) has corresponded with the well-known increase in offense that we've witnessed over the past decade. The P/PA has remained fairly constant since 1994, peaking at 3.75 pitches per plate appearance in 1996. The past couple years have been just a tick behind, with P/PA rates of 3.74.

Compare the recent rates with the average in 1990. That year hitters saw 3.60 pitches per plate appearance. Now, 0.14 fewer P/PA may not seem like a lot. But when you realize that there were more than 190,000 plate appearances last season, the difference adds up to roughly 27,000 more pitches overall. That translates to about 11 more pitches per game, or just over one every inning.

The extra pitches theoretically mean pitchers have to work longer or the bullpen is called upon more often. Under the first scenario, working longer offers hitters a chance to face hurlers who are more tired than they would be without the extra pitches. Under the second, lineups get to face the soft underbelly of a club's pitching staff, its middle relievers, more often. Either case figures to be advantageous to the offense.

One of the main factors increasing the number of pitches thrown may be what hitters are doing with the first offering they see.

Pitches by Year—1987-2000

Year	Pct Pitches Taken (0-0)	Pct Strikes Taken (0-0)
1987	.683	.239
1988	.679	.247
1989	.677	.249
1990	.681	.247
1991	.694	.254
1992	.691	.257
1993	.692	.258
1994	.693	.256
1995	.691	.257
1996	.693	.263
1997	.695	.265
1998	.700	.271
1999	.708	.269
2000	.708	.272

Last year hitters took nearly 71 percent of the pitches they viewed on 0-0 counts. That rate gradually has risen almost every year since 1989. In addition, batters' fear of falling behind in the count apparently has declined. Just look at how often they're taking first-pitch strikes—27 percent last year. That's a significant increase since 1987, when less than 24 percent of first pitches were allowed to pass for strikes.

How important is forcing opponents to throw more pitches? You can get a sense when we look at the teams on the following page that saw the most pitches per plate appearance last season:

Pitches Per Plate Appearance—2000

Team	P/PA	Record	W-L Pct
Mariners	3.96	91-71	.562
Athletics	3.91	91-70	.565
Indians	3.88	90-72	.556
Phillies	3.87	65-97	.401
Dodgers	3.85	86-76	.531
Brewers	3.79	73-89	.451
Yankees	3.78	87-74	.540
Mets	3.77	94-68	.580
Marlins	3.77	79-82	.491
Cardinals	3.77	95-67	.586
Giants	3.76	97-65	.599
White Sox	3.76	95-67	.586
MLB Average	**3.74**		

Wow. Ten teams won at least 86 games last year, and all but one of them (the Braves) ranked among the top dozen teams in most pitches per plate appearance. As we know, success tends to breed imitation. If that occurs in this case, we probably would expect hitters to take even more pitches in the future, and for games to take even longer. The Athletics' organization, for one, has been emphasizing strike-zone judgment to its young hitters in recent seasons. That philosophy began paying off in 2000, when Oakland won the American League West.

Of course, umpires might call the strike zone differently in 2001, which could result in significantly different data this coming season. If more high strikes are called, hitters may not be able to remain as patient while looking for a fat offering. It'll be interesting to see if good things will continue to come to those who wait.

—Jim Henzler

A more complete listing for this category can be found on page 261.

Are Hitters More Patient in the Postseason?

This question comes courtesy of the always inquisitive Steven Schulman, the Runs Prevented guru. Steve sent this e-mail to me during last year's White Sox-Mariners Division Series:

You're probably at the ChiSox game right now, so this may be apropos, as Parque has thrown 45 pitches in two innings. The conventional wisdom is that the Braves don't win because deep starting pitching doesn't mean as much in the postseason. I think, though, that it may be that starters can't go as long because hitters are more deliberative, forcing pitchers to work deeper into the count, and therefore leave earlier with high pitch counts. Is there any evidence that pitches per at bat increase in the postseason?

Good question, especially for anyone who has sat through one of those eternally long postseason games of recent vintage. Is Steve onto something here? Let's look at the eight teams that qualified for postseason play last year. The chart lists their average total of pitches per plate appearance during the regular season, and then in the postseason:

Pitches Per Plate Appearance, Regular vs. Postseason—2000

Team	Regular Season	Postseason
White Sox	3.76	3.91
Yankees	3.78	3.80
Athletics	3.91	4.03
Mariners	3.96	4.03
Braves	3.63	3.79
Mets	3.77	3.77
Cardinals	3.77	3.66
Giants	3.76	3.80
AL Average	**3.75**	**3.90**
NL Average	**3.73**	**3.74**
MLB Average	**3.74**	**3.83**

Overall, six of the eight teams averaged more pitches per PA during the postseason than they did during the regular campaign, while only one, the Cardinals, saw their rate of P/PA go down. Overall, the rate of P/PA was 2.4 percent higher during the postseason. That would contribute a little to making the games longer, but it wouldn't knock a pitcher out of a game that much earlier. At the rate of 3.74 P/PA, a pitcher would reach the 120-pitch mark—the approximate upper limit for a starting pitcher these days—through his 32nd hitter. At a rate of 3.83 P/PA, he'd reach the 120-pitch mark one batter earlier. Even using the greater difference in P/PA for American League games doesn't amount to much. At a rate of 3.75 P/PA, a pitcher hits the 120-pitch mark in 32.0 hitters. At a rate of 3.90 P/PA, he gets to 120 pitches in 30.8 hitters.

Were last year's figures unusual? To find out, we went back to 1990 to give us 10 years' worth of regular-season and postseason data (there was no postseason in 1994, of course, so we did not include regular-season data from that year). Here's what we found:

Pitches Per Plate Appearance, Regular vs. Postseason—1990-2000

League	Regular Season	Postseason
AL	3.72	3.81
NL	3.65	3.72
MLB	3.69	3.77

(1994 regular-season data excluded)

Plate appearances *do* last longer in the postseason, though again the difference isn't huge, about 2.2 percent higher overall. The data is pretty consistent. Of the 64 teams that qualified for the postseason from 1990-2000, 44 of them had a higher rate of P/PA in postseason play than they did in the regular year, while only 18 had a lower rate (the 1996 Cardinals and 2000 Mets had exactly the same rate). The biggest single difference was posted by the 1997 Giants, who averaged 3.70 P/PA during the regular season, 4.10 in the postseason—a rate nearly 11 percent higher. The Giants' greater patience didn't help them much, as they were swept by the Marlins in three straight games.

One could speculate all day as to why postseason at-bats tend to run a little longer. It's quite possible that the pitchers, facing higher-caliber hitters, tend to nibble a little more. Maybe the hitters, understanding that each plate appearance could be crucial, lay off bad pitches a little bit more. Or maybe the umpires, consciously or not, squeeze the strike zone a little more in an effort to produce more scoring. Whatever the case, the difference isn't great enough to explain why a team with good starting pitching like the Braves hasn't been as dominant in the postseason as one would expect. But it does play a small part in contributing to the ever-increasing length of those postseason games. No wonder Major League Baseball wants the umpires to expand their strike zones.

—Don Zminda

Who Plays It Smart on the Bases?

It's one of baseball's fundamentals. Along with hitting the cutoff man and moving runners up, baseball analysts are fond of citing the importance of smart baserunning. So, who really does make mistakes on the bases? Which teams rarely get put out on the bases? And, which ones find all sorts of ways to make an out without a bat in their hands?

Surprisingly enough, there's not a lot of difference between teams in this area, especially if we look only at baserunning outs that most often can be classified as mistakes. After all, there are a number of different ways to be put out on the bases. Being on the front-end of a fielder's choice or a double play, for instance, are the most popular ways to register a baserunning out. But, those rarely are the result of some sort of gaffe. Being thrown out attempting to steal is another way to run yourself out of an inning. Again, this isn't something that normally qualifies as bad baserunning. Besides, the outs that result from these plays already are "credited" in the form of GDPs, caught stealings or hitless at-bats (for fielder's choices).

We want to look at all the hidden, or "unforced" outs—the ones that go untracked in the box scores and stat sheets. The unforced outs include all outs on bases that aren't scored as GDPs, ground into triple plays, fielder's choices or caught stealings—such things as pickoffs, foiled attempts to take an extra base, times doubled off on flyballs, etc.

"Unforced" Outs on Bases—2000

AL Team	Outs	NL Team	Outs
Detroit	45	Cincinnati	46
Seattle	47	Milwaukee	46
Texas	48	San Diego	51
Chicago	49	Arizona	53
Toronto	50	Pittsburgh	53
Tampa Bay	52	Philadelphia	54
New York	53	San Francisco	54
Baltimore	54	Los Angeles	55
Boston	59	Montreal	55
Oakland	59	Chicago	58
Kansas City	62	St. Louis	58
Minnesota	63	New York	59
Anaheim	64	Houston	61
Cleveland	78	Colorado	64
		Atlanta	65
		Florida	65

Baseball Scoreboard

See any pattern here? Veteran teams don't appear to commit any fewer baserunning errors than inexperienced ones. As far as the "good" teams go, the eight playoff clubs averaged 55.5 mistakes, as opposed to a major league average of 56. Maybe good teams aren't "smart baserunners"? Or, more likely, maybe this makes very little difference at all. The difference between the best team in the National League and the worst is only 19 outs all year. That's not a lot. By contrast, the difference between the NL's best batting average team in 2000 and its worst is more than 200 outs.

In the American League, the difference between the best teams and the worst is larger, thanks to the Indians. What's going on in Cleveland? They've got some speed, but perhaps they are a little too aggressive sometimes. Roberto Alomar led all Indians with 10 baserunning outs of this type. But, he did not lead the majors. Take a look at who did:

Most "Unforced" Outs on Bases—2000

Player, Team	Outs
Eric Young, ChC	14
Jason Giambi, Oak	13
Carlos Delgado, Tor	12
Delino DeShields, Bal	12
Adam Kennedy, Ana	12
Jay Bell, Ari	11
Randy Velarde, Oak	11
12 players tied with	10

It obviously doesn't hurt your MVP chances to commit a lot of baserunning outs. Just ask Jason Giambi and Carlos Delgado. Sure, it seems somewhat excusable for fast, aggressive baserunners like Eric Young or Roberto Alomar to run into a lot of outs, but what's Giambi's excuse? And maybe Delgado's league-leading total of 57 doubles came at some cost?

In fairness, we should note some of the more error-free baserunners of 2000, as well. The regulars with one baserunning miscue were Garrett Anderson, Steve Finley, Alex S. Gonzalez, Ray Lankford, Ruben Rivera, Matt Stairs, Lee Stevens and Bernie Williams. For true perfection, Rusty Greer and Butch Huskey take the cake. They are the only players with more than 300 at-bats who avoided a single unforced out on the bases. In this aspect of the game, they've got the fundamentals down to a science.

—John Sasman

A more complete listing for this category can be found on page 262.

III. QUESTIONS ON PITCHING

Who Are the Top 300-Win Candidates?

Four years ago, in the 1997 edition of this book, I introduced a method to estimate a pitcher's chances of winning 300 games in his career. Since we last looked at this issue in the 1999 *Scoreboard*, there are four things that have happened:

1. Greg Maddux essentially has pulled even with Roger Clemens as the top active candidates for 300 wins.

2. Some people have dropped off the list of semi-serious 300-win candidates.

3. Some other people have crawled onto the list, and

4. People have stopped saying that we're not going to have any more 300-game winners.

Taking those one at a time:

1. **Greg Maddux essentially has pulled even with Roger Clemens as the top active candidates for 300 wins.** Two years ago, Clemens' chance of winning 300 games was 60%, Maddux', 47%. Since then Clemens has crept up to 66%, on the basis of a couple of so-so years, while Maddux, with two more outstanding seasons, has pulled alongside him at 62%.

2. **Some people have dropped off the list of semi-serious 300-win candidates.** Actually, only three people who had any real shot at 300 wins two years ago have dropped from sight, which is kind of unusual. The three are John Smoltz (19% two years ago), David Cone (11%) and Scott Erickson (9%).

3. **Some other people have crawled onto the bottom of the list.** Replacing them on the list are Mike Hampton (12%), Chuck Finley (11%) and Andy Pettitte (8%).

The nature of the war for 300 wins, or any other career milestone, is that players take many short strides toward that goal, and then fall out of position very quickly. A pitcher doesn't go from a 0% chance at 300 wins to a 40% chance in one year; he goes from 0 to 1, 1 to 3, 3 to 6, 6 to 8, 8 to 11, etc. But it is real easy for a pitcher's 300-win chance to go from 40% to zero in one step. If Mike Hampton has another good year this year, he'll move from 11% to 14% or thereabouts. But if Tom Glavine has a David Cone year, he'll go from 42% to nothin'.

4. **People have stopped saying that we're not going to have any more 300-game winners.** Two years ago, certainly four years ago, a lot of people were saying that there weren't going to be any more 300-game winners. With Clemens and Maddux having 500 career wins between them, nobody is saying that anymore.

The following are the top active candidates for 300 career wins, as I see them:

Active Pitchers With Best Chance For 300 Wins

Pitcher	Age	Won-Lost	Chance
Roger Clemens	38	260-142	66%
Greg Maddux	35	240-135	62%
Tom Glavine	35	208-125	42%
Randy Johnson	37	179-95	33%
Pedro Martinez	29	125-56	33%
Mike Mussina	32	147-81	21%
Kevin Brown	36	170-114	20%
Mike Hampton	28	85-53	12%
Chuck Finley	38	181-151	11%
Andy Pettitte	29	100-55	8%

(age as of June 30, 2001)

Two other pitchers are also at 8%—David Wells, and Darryl Kile. Nobody else is close to being on the list. The long-shot candidates are Kevin Appier and Brad Radke (4%), Andy Benes and Aaron Sele (3%), Denny Neagle and Pat Hentgen (2%), and Al Leiter and Curt Schilling (1%).

—Bill James

What Might We Expect From Wells in 2001—And Beyond?

After posting double-digit wins in eight of 10 seasons leading up to the 2000 campaign—including a career-high 18 victories for the world champion Yankees in 1998—David Wells finally enjoyed a 20-win campaign last summer. It was a first for the lefthander known as Boomer, who was 37 years and four months old when he won his 20th against his former Yankee teammates on September 21.

That's quite old for a first-time 20-game winner, but amazingly, two pitchers were older than Wells when they secured their 20th victory for a first time.

Oldest First-Time 20-Game Winners—1876-2000

Pitcher	Age	Year	Record
George McConnell	37	1915	25-10
Allie Reynolds	37	1952	20-8
David Wells	**37**	**2000**	**20-8**
Preacher Roe	36	1951	22-3
Virgil Trucks	36	1953	20-10
Rip Sewell	36	1943	21-9
Spud Chandler	35	1943	20-4
Curt Davis	35	1939	22-16

George McConnell, a spitball pitcher, had struggled to go 12-28 for the New York Yankees and Chicago Cubs in the three years prior to his big 1915 season in the upstart Federal League. His emergence says a great deal about the quality of play in the short-lived circuit, which had nine 20-game winners in that final season. Pitching for the league champion Chicago Whales, McConnell led the league in victories, claiming his 20th just days shy of his 38th birthday. His career was over after going 4-12 for the Cubs in 1916, and he never won more than eight games in any of his five seasons in the American and National leagues.

On the other hand, Allie Reynolds was a hard-throwing righthander who averaged 16 wins a year for the Yankees and the Indians in the seven seasons before he finally won 20 in 1952. For a guy who didn't win his first major league game until he was 28, it's almost appropriate that Reynolds earned his 20th win for the first time at age 37 years and seven months.

With the 2000 season in the rearview mirror, the White Sox have to be wondering what they can expect from the aging Wells in 2001 and beyond.

The following chart involving those late-blooming 20-game winners suggests Wells may do just fine for a few more years:

Records After 20-Win Season, Oldest First-Time 20-Game Winners

Pitcher	Age	Yr 1	Age	Yr 2	Age	Yr 3	Age	Yr 4
George McConnell	37	25-10	38	4-12	—	—	—	—
Allie Reynolds	37	20-8	38	13-7	39	13-4	—	—
Preacher Roe	36	22-3	37	11-2	38	11-3	39	3-4
Virgil Trucks	36	20-10	37	19-12	38	13-8	39	6-5
Rip Sewell	36	21-9	37	21-12	38	11-9	39	8-12
Spud Chandler	35	20-4	36	0-0	37	2-1	38	20-8
Curt Davis	35	22-16	36	8-11	37	13-7	38	15-6

(Yr 1 is first 20-win season)

Collectively, this group was 266-179 (.589) in all remaining seasons after its members won 20 games. If you take away McConnell's 4-12 swan song—because he arguably wasn't as talented as the rest of these "old-timers" and posted his big season in an inferior league—that record improves to 262-167 (.611).

All seven pitchers still worked in their 38th year, which Wells will do in 2001, and collectively the 38-year-olds were 34 games over .500 at 87-53. Once again, if you take out McConnell's 4-12 mark at age 38, the others are an amazing 83-41 for a winning percentage of .669.

Expecting Wells to pitch at a .669 clip isn't realistic, but he may draw inspiration from the six pitchers who were remarkable performers in their twilight years:

Allie Reynolds. After winning 20 games in 1952, Reynolds became the Yankees' relief ace in '53 and worked effectively in the bullpen behind primary closer Johnny Sain in '54. He topped off a fine career by winning the World Series finales in relief in both '52 and '53.

Preacher Roe. Roe's 22-3 mark in 1951 produced an .880 winning percentage, a National League record among 20-game winners. Roe finished his career by going 25-9 after his 20-win season, and the Brooklyn southpaw beat the Yankees in the 1952 World Series. In a 1955 *Sports Illustrated* article after his retirement, Roe admitted he complemented his soft-tossing arsenal with an occasional spitter.

Virgil Trucks. His two no-hitters with Detroit during a frustrating 5-19 season in 1952 should have been an omen. Trucks reached the 20-win plateau for the first time with the White Sox in '53 after coming *this* close with a 19-11 mark in '49. He then went 19-12 for the Sox in 1954 and was 49-34 in the five seasons after his 20-win campaign.

Rip Sewell. After winning 21 games for the Pirates at age 36, Sewell repeated the feat in 1944, when he was 11 days older than Wells was upon winning No. 20 last September. By that time, Sewell was throwing his famous blooper pitch, tossing the ball 20-25 feet into the air en route to home plate. He pitched six seasons after winning 20 for the first time, accumulating an impressive 65-41 record with Pittsburgh, but his latter years probably are best remembered for serving up an All-Star game home run to Ted Williams in 1946—on his blooper pitch.

Spud Chandler. In 1943, as the ace of the Yankees' staff, Chandler led the American League in wins (20), complete games (20) and ERA (1.64). He also won the World Series clincher that year and secured the American League MVP Award shortly after his 36th birthday. Despite his age, Chandler lost most of the next two seasons to the military, but he returned to show his war-years MVP wasn't a fluke. He was 20-8 in 1946, winning his 20th game 17 days after his 39th birthday. A year later he won the AL ERA title with the Yankees, the only team for which he played.

Curt Davis. Before winning 22 games for the Cardinals in 1939, Davis' claim to fame might have been being traded by the Cubs to the Cards for Dizzy Dean. Like many Cubs trades, Chicago acquired a star player whose best days were behind him. Although Dean went 7-1 in 1938 and helped the Cubs win the NL flag, Davis won 22 for the Cardinals the next year. From 1940-45, he posted a 66-58 record with St. Louis and Brooklyn.

While STATS wouldn't advocate waiting until age 37 to win 20 games, pitchers who reached that plateau at that advanced age showed they weren't done yet, both in the regular season and in World Series play. Obviously White Sox general manager Ken Williams subscribes to the theory that Wells—who brings a lifetime 8-1 postseason record with him to Chicago—has plenty of juice left for the next couple of seasons.

Wells thinks so, too, even though going 55-22 over the last three seasons hasn't convinced everyone. When the 37-year-old southpaw was quizzed about concerns for his age and conditioning by the Chicago media recently, Wells quipped: "I'm fat and you're ugly. But I can diet."

—Thom Henninger

Has Any Pitcher Started Hotter Than Hudson?

As they entered the 1997 amateur draft, the Athletics needed pitching, so they focused on mound prospects. They spent three of their four first-round picks on college pitchers: West Virginia righthander Chris Enochs, Mississippi State lefthander Eric DuBose and Virginia Tech righty Denny Wagner.

Oakland took four more college pitchers with their next four selections. The A's grabbed Memphis righty Chad Harville in the second round, Long Beach State righty Marcus Jones in the third, Radford lefty Jason Anderson in the fourth and Wisconsin-Oshkosh righty Andy Kimball in the fifth.

The A's didn't stop there. In the sixth round, they took a two-way star who had led Auburn to the College World Series. Though Tim Hudson had batted .396-18-95, Oakland coveted his right arm more. He went 15-2, 2.97 with 165 strikeouts in 118 innings as a senior, but Hudson didn't go higher in the draft because he was of slight stature and lacked an overpowering fastball.

Hudson fared well initially as a pro, then stalled in Double-A in the second half of 1998. After he went 7-0, 1.75 in the upper minors at the beginning of 1999, Hudson arrived in the majors. To stay.

As a rookie, Hudson went 11-2, 3.23. In 2000, his first full season in the majors, he went 20-6, 4.14 to lead the American League in both victories and winning percentage (.769).

Hudson's 31 wins are the second-most ever by a pitcher in his first 39 decisions since the lively-ball era began.

Most Wins in First 39 Career Decisions—1920-2000

Pitcher	First 39 Decisions W-L	Pct	Afterward W-L	Pct
Howie Krist	33-6	.846	4-5	.444
Juan Guzman	31-8	.795	60-71	.458
Tim Hudson	**31-8**	**.795**	—	—
Roger Clemens	30-9	.769	230-133	.634
Jim Coates	30-9	.769	13-13	.500
Ron Guidry	30-9	.769	140-82	.631
Tex Hughson	30-9	.769	66-45	.595
Emil Yde	30-9	.769	19-16	.543
Johnny Allen	29-10	.744	113-65	.635

Pitcher	First 39 Decisions		Afterward	
	W-L	Pct	W-L	Pct
Joe Black	29-10	.744	1-2	.333
Boo Ferriss	29-10	.744	36-20	.643
Whitey Ford	29-10	.744	207-96	.683
Larry Jansen	29-10	.744	93-79	.541
Sal Maglie	29-10	.744	90-52	.634
Vic Raschi	29-10	.744	103-56	.648
Schoolboy Rowe	29-10	.744	129-91	.586

The only pitcher to win more games than Hudson in his first 39 decisions was Cardinals swingman Howie Krist, who excelled during the early years of World War II. Krist began his career by going 33-6, went 4-3 to finish out the 1943 season—and never won another big league game. He spent 1944 and 1945 in the U.S. Army and returned with arm problems. Krist went 0-2 in 15 games in 1946, his final year in the majors.

Juan Guzman, who matched Hudson's 31 wins, has been a sub-.500 pitcher since his hot start. He led the American League in ERA in 1996 and in losses two years later. He's nearing the end of the line at age 34, pitching in just one game for the Devil Rays last year before succumbing to a shoulder injury.

Other pitchers on the list also fizzled—Joe Black won just one more game after going 29-10—but for the most part these hurlers enjoyed solid careers. Roger Clemens and Ron Guidry would go on to win Cy Young Awards, while Whitey Ford set the career record for winning percentage (.690) en route to the Hall of Fame.

The worst record in a pitcher's first 39 decisions belongs to Anthony Young, who lost 27 consecutive decisions on his way to a 5-34 (.128) mark. Among pitchers enshrined in Cooperstown, Red Ruffing easily had the worst start. He began 12-27 (.308) for some bad Red Sox teams in the 1920s and was 39-96 when Boston traded him to the Yankees in 1930. Afterward, he went 234-129 (.645).

It took the A's eight tries before they finally found an ace in the 1997 draft. Of the pitchers they selected ahead of Hudson, only Harville remains a legitimate prospect.

—Jim Callis

A more complete listing for this category can be found on page 264.

Who Are the Game's Best "Stoppers"?

The question above is a bit loaded. To some people, "stopper" is synonymous with "closer," meaning the reliever counted on to protect slim leads in the late innings. To others, the term refers to a standout starting pitcher who has the ability to snuff out his team's losing streaks.

This book annually devotes several pages to analyzing relievers, so we're going to focus on the latter definition. STATS has a detailed database of day-by-day results for every major league game back to 1920, so we have complete information for the lively-ball era.

We'll begin by looking at the career leaders in stopper wins:

Most Wins Following a Team Loss, Career—1920-2000

Pitcher	Following Loss			Other		
	W	L	Pct	W	L	Pct
Phil Niekro	166	142	.539	152	132	.535
Warren Spahn	164	109	.601	199	136	.594
Tom Seaver	158	103	.605	153	102	.600
Nolan Ryan	156	155	.502	168	137	.551
Bert Blyleven	153	125	.550	134	125	.517
Gaylord Perry	153	123	.554	161	142	.531
Steve Carlton	151	117	.563	178	127	.584
Fergie Jenkins	143	103	.581	141	123	.534
Tommy John	141	106	.571	147	125	.540
Roger Clemens	139	60	.698	121	82	.596

These 10 pitchers have a few things in common. Seven of them already are in the Hall of Fame, with Roger Clemens certain to join them five years after he retires. Tommy John (288) and Bert Blyleven (287) have more wins than any pitchers not currently enshrined in Cooperstown. All 10 of these guys were big winners, with Clemens bringing up the rear with 260 victories, a total to which he's still adding.

What's most striking, however, is the difference of these pitchers' performances as stoppers compared to other times. Or rather, the lack of a difference. As a group, they had a .571 winning percentage following a team loss and a .558 winning percentage otherwise. Phil Niekro tops this list not because he rose to the occasion following his team's defeats, but rather because he pitched for a long time and for generally mediocre clubs.

Baseball Scoreboard

The only one of the 10 pitchers on the previous page who had a winning percentage increase of at least .050 as a stopper was Clemens, whose .698 mark is the fourth-highest ever.

Highest Winning Percentages Following a Team Loss, Career—1920-2000

Pitcher	Following Loss			Other		
	W	L	Pct	W	L	Pct
Vic Raschi	54	20	.730	78	46	.629
Gary Nolan	52	21	.712	58	49	.542
Don Gullett	44	18	.710	65	32	.670
Roger Clemens	139	60	.698	121	82	.596
Spud Chandler	41	18	.695	68	25	.731
Whitey Ford	81	36	.692	155	70	.689
Art Nehf	39	18	.684	145	102	.587
Andy Pettitte	45	21	.682	55	34	.618
Jimmy Key	85	40	.680	101	77	.567
Randy Johnson	98	48	.671	81	47	.633

(minimum 50 decisions following a team loss)

All of these guys had overall winning percentages of .605 or better, and they all were very good pitchers who consistently performed for good teams. In other words, they'd be expected to have a gaudy winning percentage in any situation.

But unlike the career victory leaders, the career percentage leaders did step it up when they made a start following a team loss. They combined for a .693 winning percentage in those situations, and a .622 in all others. Vic Raschi's .730 stopper winning percentage, the best ever, was 101 points better than he fared when he wasn't following a loss. Gary Nolan finished second in stopper winning percentage at .712—170 points higher than his mark otherwise.

Interestingly, the overall winning percentage leaders didn't fare much different than normal when they were stoppers. Spud Chandler, whose .717 mark is the best ever for pitchers with at least 100 decisions, actually dropped to .695 when he pitched after a Yankees defeat. Whitey Ford, the record-holder at .690 when the minimum is raised to 200 decisions, had a .692 winning percentage as a stopper.

There are some other items of note that don't show up on the chart. Mark Clark, who doesn't exactly come to mind as a formidable pitcher, is 43-26

(.623) as a stopper and 31-45 (.408) otherwise. By contrast, John Smoltz has a reputation as one of the best postseason pitchers in the game's history, but he's just 53-54 (.495) as a regular-season stopper compared to 104-59 (.638) otherwise.

Two Hall of Famers, Jesse Haines (74-76, .493) and Rube Marquard (30-34, .469) were sub-.500 stoppers. The all-time worst mark belongs to the eminently forgettable Jesse Jefferson, who went 13-44 (.228).

Now let's examine the best single-season performances:

Most Wins Following a Team Loss, Season—1920-2000

Pitcher, Team	Year	Following Loss			Other		
		W	L	Pct	W	L	Pct
Red Faber, CWS	1921	19	11	.633	6	4	.600
Steve Carlton, Phi	1972	18	9	.667	9	1	.900
Dazzy Vance, Bkn	1924	17	4	.810	11	2	.846
Howard Ehmke, BosA	1923	16	9	.640	4	8	.333
Bob Feller, Cle	1941	16	8	.667	9	5	.643
Hal Newhouser, Det	1945	16	1	.941	9	8	.529
Bob Feller, Cle	1946	16	9	.640	10	6	.625
Bobby Shantz, PhiA	1952	16	4	.800	8	3	.727
Jim Maloney, Cin	1963	16	4	.800	7	3	.700
Larry Jackson, ChC	1964	16	4	.800	8	7	.533
Sandy Koufax, LA	1966	16	4	.800	11	5	.688

Most of these pitchers were stars on mediocre teams. Hall of Famer Red Faber halted 19 losing streaks for the 1921 White Sox, who had been decimated by the Black Sox scandal and went 37-77 when he didn't get a decision. Fellow Cooperstown immortal Steve Carlton had 18 stopper wins in 1972, when he went 27-10 for a 59-97 club. Another Hall of Famer, Bob Feller, shows up twice for yeoman work on sub-.500 teams.

Three more Hall of Famers deserve special mention for their performances in the midst of pennant races. Hal Newhouser (16-1 as a stopper in 1945) and Sandy Koufax (16-4 in 1966) pitched their teams to the World Series. Both won pennants by one-and-a-half games and wouldn't have made it to the Fall Classic without their aces. Dazzy Vance nearly did the same for the 1924 Brooklyn Dodgers, who finished a game-and-a-half out of first place. Not surprisingly, Vance and Newhouser won league MVP awards. Koufax finished a close second to Roberto Clemente in 1966 but captured all the votes for the Cy Young Award at a time when it was jointly presented by both leagues. Clemens doesn't show up on the previous single-season list, but he leads all pitchers with eight years with 10 or more stopper victories. Blyleven, Gaylord Perry and Warren Spahn each had seven.

Only one pitcher has gone undefeated as a stopper in 10 or more tries in a season:

Highest Winning Percentages Following a Team Loss, Season—1920-2000

Pitcher, Team	Year	Following Loss			Other		
		W	L	Pct	W	L	Pct
Whitey Ford, NYY	1961	10	0	1.000	15	4	.789
Hal Newhouser, Det	1945	16	1	.941	9	8	.529
Roger Clemens, Bos	1986	14	1	.933	10	3	.769
Tex Hughson, BosA	1942	12	1	.923	10	5	.667
Vic Raschi, NYY	1950	12	1	.923	9	7	.563
Bob Purkey, Cin	1962	12	1	.923	11	4	.733
Roger Clemens, Bos	1987	12	1	.923	8	8	.500
Steve Avery, Atl	1993	12	1	.923	6	5	.545
Juan Marichal, SF	1964	11	1	.917	10	7	.588
Randy Johnson, Sea	1997	11	1	.917	9	3	.750

(minimum 10 decisions following a team loss)

Six of these nine guys pitched their clubs to the postseason, and only Clemens in 1987 couldn't at least keep his team in contention. Considering the pressure, the most impressive performances came from Newhouser (16-1 in 1945), Raschi (12-1 in 1950) and Steve Avery (12-1 in 1993)—all three of their clubs won their league or division by three games or less. When Ford went 10-0 in 1961, the Yankees took the American League flag by eight games.

More remarkable, Clemens went 26-2 as a stopper over two seasons from 1986-87. On the flip side, the worst single-year mark with a minimum of 10 total decisions was Tim Leary's 1-13 (.071) for the 1990 Yankees.

For a career, Clemens is our pick for the most impressive stopper of the lively-ball era. For a season, we'll go with Newhouser in 1945. But as we've also noted, there's evidence to suggest that the concept of the stopper may be overblown. That just might be a good question for a future edition of the *Baseball Scoreboard*.

—Jim Callis

A more complete listing for this category can be found on page 265.

Are Tall Pitchers Really Better?

Check out any source for top baseball prospects and it would be hard to overlook the relative absence of short pitchers on any of the lists. Take the *STATS Minor League Scouting Notebook 2001*, for example. There are 693 pitchers whom author John Sickels felt were worthy of write-ups in the book. Of those 693 hurlers, only 46, or 6.6 percent, are listed at less than six feet tall. There actually are more pitchers 6-foot-7 or taller (49) than 5-foot-11 or shorter. We haven't studied many demographic charts recently, but we have a strong suspicion that there are more adult males in the population who are under six feet in height than over 6-foot-6.

Clearly, there are valid reasons for pitchers skewing as tall as they do. Scouts are no dummies. They know that in most physical professions other than horse jockey, the bigger you are, the greater your chances for success. If that wasn't the case, 200-pound football linemen and six-foot basketball centers wouldn't be extinct species. Baseball is no different, though not to the degree of the other sports. Still, the taller you are, the greater your leverage and the harder you'll likely throw. And scouts love hard throwers.

Prospects eventually become major leaguers, so big league pitchers generally are tall fellows, too. But does height really make a difference? Are tall pitchers really more successful? As with the general population, baseball players gradually have gotten taller through the years. The short pitchers of today wouldn't have been considered "vertically-challenged" in the 1920s, when the average height of hurlers was just under six feet. So in order to obtain as large a population sample as possible, as well as one that tries to limit the bias caused by growth over time, we'll limit our study to the years since 1990.

Since then, there have been 1,532 pitchers that have worked in the big leagues. And here's their breakdown by height:

Pitchers by Height—1990-2000

Height	No.	Pct
5-8	1	0.1
5-9	16	1.0
5-10	26	1.7
5-11	65	4.2
6-0	183	11.9
6-1	238	15.5
6-2	317	20.7

Height	No.	Pct
6-3	282	18.4
6-4	190	12.4
6-5	121	7.9
6-6	52	3.4
6-7	30	2.0
6-8	8	0.5
6-9	1	0.1
6-10	2	0.1

As you can see, the median height of all the pitchers since 1990 has been 6-foot-2. Only one listed at less than 5-foot-9 has worked in the past 11 seasons—Dan Boone. Two other position players, John Cangelosi and Doug Dascenzo, also have seen limited action on the mound during that time, but we're considering true pitchers only. Meanwhile, there have been 11 pitchers who were 6-foot-8 or taller, with the tallest being Terry Bross (6-foot-9), Eric Hillman (6-foot-10) and Randy Johnson (6-foot-10).

When we total the stats for all 1,532 pitchers since 1990, here's what we find:

Combined Pitching Stats—1990-2000

Ht	BB/9	SO/9	W-L Pct	Sv Pct	Avg	OPS	ERA
5-8	2.79	1.86	—	—	.308	.834	2.79
5-9	4.46	7.06	.468	.750	.251	.726	4.21
5-10	3.41	6.10	.489	.743	.265	.739	4.02
5-11	3.74	7.18	.528	.730	.253	.724	4.05
6-0	3.40	5.97	.518	.606	.265	.746	4.30
6-1	3.36	6.05	.506	.644	.266	.748	4.28
6-2	3.55	6.18	.498	.689	.266	.754	4.41
6-3	3.47	6.13	.494	.660	.267	.751	4.40
6-4	3.45	6.32	.499	.705	.263	.738	4.28
6-5	3.50	6.23	.491	.750	.268	.756	4.43
6-6	3.74	6.71	.476	.709	.264	.751	4.40
6-7	3.46	5.65	.475	.538	.268	.755	4.50
6-8	4.11	7.04	.469	.600	.258	.742	4.37
6-9	3.00	4.50	—	—	.227	.678	3.00
6-10	3.65	10.55	.643	.667	.220	.650	3.25

Well, if tall people really do have an advantage as pitchers, it would be hard to prove based on the above figures. The second-highest winning percentage actually occurs for pitchers who are 5-foot-11. The percentage generally decreases as height increases from that point. The 6-foot-10 guys do have a winning percentage of .643. But that's due, of course, to Johnson (169-82). The Big Unit is the ultimate "outlier," to use a statistical term. The other guy that size, Hillman, was 4-14 (.222).

Likewise, three of the best four save conversion percentages occur between 5-foot-9 and 5-foot-11, a range that features the likes of Tom Gordon, John Franco and Billy Wagner. Only the 6-foot-5 group, which includes closers such as Rick Aguilera, Tom Henke and Robb Nen, was able to match the smaller guys.

Excluding heights of 6-foot-9 and taller, earned run average is lowest for the shorter pitchers, as well. It then remains within a range of 4.28-4.50 for most of the larger heights. Opposition batting average and OPS allowed follow similar trends. Even in a category where we might suspect tall pitchers would have a decided advantage, strikeouts, the 5-foot-11 group boasts the best rate per nine innings, at least if you exclude Johnson. Still, it is true that the whiff rate does generally rise from six feet upward. And the collection of 5-foot-11 guys benefits from the presence of a couple of strikeout artists in Wagner and Pedro Martinez.

That condition actually may explain a lot, since there are relatively fewer short pitchers. The Wagners and Martinezes of the world might therefore dominate their particular group's numbers, which would otherwise be more mediocre without them. Or it may be that short pitchers have to be demonstrably better than the "average" hurler in order to overcome the bias that passes as conventional wisdom. Under such a scenario, only the best short pitchers will establish themselves in the big leagues, while taller fellas who may be somewhat suspect still could receive the benefit of the doubt. How else would you explain guys like 6-foot-5 Mike Thurman and 6-foot-4 Kyle Farnsworth?

One last thing. The short bias seems especially prevalent among right-handed pitchers. The only 5-foot-8 pitcher on the above list was lefthanded. Ten of the 16 hurlers who were 5-foot-9 were southpaws, as were 16 of the 26 players in the 5-foot-10 group. At every other height excluding Johnson's 6-foot-10, righthanders outnumbered the lefties. Among pitchers 6-foot-2 or taller, southpaws were outnumbered by a factor of 3-1.

So it appears short righthanders have a double-whammy against them. In the world of baseball, some stereotypes have a way of lingering, whether they're correct or not.

—Jim Henzler

Which Pitchers Love Home Cookin'?

We tend to think of pitchers as being represented by their overall statistics. Last year, when Mike Hampton pitched in the playoffs, the announcers didn't always refer to his 11-4 record with a 2.05 ERA at home and his 4-6 mark with a 4.83 ERA on the road; they said he was a solid 15-10 with a 3.14 ERA, which didn't give the whole picture.

Like Hampton, many major league hurlers prefer pitching at home (unless they pitch in Coors or Enron, of course). Let's take a look at the pitchers with the biggest home-field preferences over the last three years:

Biggest Home-Road ERA Differentials—1998-2000

Pitcher	Home	Road	Diff
Shawn Estes	3.27	6.26	3.09
Ismael Valdes	3.04	5.80	2.76
David Cone	3.29	5.80	2.51
Brett Tomko	3.67	5.60	1.93
Brian Meadows	4.48	6.19	1.71
Willie Blair	4.68	6.38	1.70
Rick Reed	3.17	4.83	1.66
Russ Ortiz	3.80	5.33	1.53
Carlos Perez	4.16	5.68	1.52
Chan Ho Park	3.32	4.82	1.50
MLB Average	**4.55**	**4.99**	**0.44**

(minimum 450 IP)

What does this chart tell us? First, it's been really good to pitch in Dodger Stadium. Chan Ho Park has been an average pitcher on the road, but last year he had the third-best home ERA (2.34) in the National League, behind teammate Kevin Brown (1.79) and Hampton (2.05). Carlos Perez may not have a career without Dodger Stadium, and Ismael Valdes now gets to try the AL without his favorite park. By the way, Hampton (1.48 home-road difference) and Brown (1.44) just missed making the three-year top 10.

The Giants are credited for having a first-rate rotation. What they really have is a first-rate pitchers' park. Even though Shawn Estes *really* preferred 3Com Park, he still allowed over two runs a game more in 2000 away from Pac Bell. As a team, the Giants' ERA was 3.45 at home, the best in the majors, while on the road it was 4.99, right at the major league average. That 1.54 margin was second in the majors, behind the Cubs' 1.66—the wind must've been blowing in an awful lot in Wrigley last year.

What also jumps out on the previous chart is just how terrible the top guys have been on the road. Only two of the top 10 have road ERAs under 5.33, and three are well over 6.00. The question for David Cone this year is not how healthy his arm is, but whether he can win without Yankee Stadium. He wasn't even good *there* last year, with an ERA of 5.33, but on the road, he was a bullpen-exhausting 8.50. Brian Meadows has hung his hat in three parks the last three years, and as the old song goes, any place he hung his hat was home. It helped that he spent two years in Florida, a good pitchers' park, and half a year in San Diego, an even better pitchers' park.

Last year's top home-cookin' pitchers were an interesting mix of veterans and newcomers. Cone easily was the worst, with a home-road margin of 3.17. He was followed by a rookie, the A's Mark Mulder, with a 3.94 ERA at home and a 6.86 mark on the road. Two Mets pitchers came next, Bobby J. Jones (3.60, 6.44) and Hampton (2.05, 4.83)—you have to think they'll miss pitcher-friendly Shea Stadium. The Padres' Matt Clement (3.86, 6.48) was next; he'll have to learn to pitch on the road if he is going to develop into the ace they need.

What about the other side of the picture, the guys who live with their bags packed, hoping to get out of town fast? Well, most of them pitch in Colorado, including Pedro Astacio, Brian Bohanon and Rolando Arrojo. While Astacio's 7.05 ERA at Coors compared to his 4.11 on the road over the last three years is mind-boggling, we already know Colorado isn't helpful to pitchers. Let's look at the top 10 road warriors since 1998 who haven't pitched for the Rockies.

Biggest Road-Home ERA Differentials—1998-2000

Pitcher	Road	Home	Diff
James Baldwin	4.27	5.83	1.56
John Burkett	4.69	6.16	1.47
Pat Rapp	4.45	5.86	1.41
LaTroy Hawkins	4.86	5.95	1.09
Darren Dreifort	3.76	4.79	1.03
Pat Hentgen	4.50	5.32	0.82
Pete Harnisch	3.36	4.17	0.81
Steve Woodard	4.42	5.18	0.76
Denny Neagle	3.67	4.40	0.73
Rick Helling	4.28	4.94	0.66

What on earth is Darren Dreifort doing here? In each of the last three years, he actually has done better on the road than at Chavez Ravine. It's hard to believe he won't find a comfort zone at Dodger Stadium eventually, which just might enable him to earn the big money Los Angeles will be paying him.

On the other hand, Pat Rapp has pitched for three teams since the beginning of the '98 campaign, so home and road parks are temporary conditions for him. There's no reason why James Baldwin should hate Comiskey so much, but among non-Rockies pitchers, he was the worst last year—3.49 on the road, 6.08 at home.

Denny Neagle's top billing on the three-year road-home chart invites a comparison with Hampton, another starter who was brave enough to head for the mountains in 2001. Hampton is an extreme home-field pitcher, Neagle an extreme road pitcher. It will be interesting to see who will suffer the most from the Coors home-park effect. By the way, Bohanon was hurt the most by his home park last year, with a 6.65 home ERA wiping out his sterling 2.79 road mark. Will someone please get him out of there?

—Barry Rubinowitz

A more complete listing for this category can be found on page 267.

Who Are Baseball's Best-Hitting Pitchers?

Pitchers at the plate with a bat in their hands usually conjure up images of guys like Willie Blair and Vicente Palacios. Blair has an .075 career average with 88 strikeouts in 146 at-bats, while Palacios checks in at .045 with 43 whiffs in 88 at-bats. You can add all *three* of Palacios' hitting percentages and they total a less than robust .158.

All pitchers don't fit the Blair/Palacios mold, however. Some have followed in the footsteps of Don Drysdale (29 career homers) and Bob Gibson (.206-24-144), two modern-era hurlers who weren't one-dimensional. Let's take a look at the active major league pitchers with the best career batting averages:

ACTIVE PITCHERS WHO CAN HIT CAREER

	AVG	SLG
Allen Watson	.257	.343
Omar Olivares	.242	.344
Mike Hampton	.231	.277
Livan Hernandez	.227	.299
Javier Vazquez	.226	.277
MLB Average	.145	.182

minimum 150 career PA

The list is a reminder that the DH rule takes the bat out of so many pitchers' hands. Allen Watson and Omar Olivares held firm to the top two spots from last year's list, largely by virtue of playing in the American League. They had only one at-bat between them during the 2000 season. On the other hand, Livan Hernandez and Javier Vazquez are young National League hurlers who are showing they occasionally can help their clubs with both their arms and their lumber.

Do Hernandez and Vazquez represent a trend toward better-hitting pitchers? Probably not, but it's interesting that the best-hitting pitchers of 2000 include some of the best young arms in the game.

Baseball Scoreboard

Best-Hitting Pitchers in Baseball—2000

Pitcher, Team	Avg	OBP	Slg	AB	H	2B	HR	RBI	BB	SH
Adam Eaton, SD	.289	.400	.342	38	11	2	0	4	6	0
A.J. Burnett, Fla	.280	.357	.520	25	7	1	1	3	3	2
Mike Hampton, NYM	.274	.313	.274	73	20	0	0	8	5	4
Omar Daal, Ari-Phi	.267	.327	.400	45	12	3	1	6	4	5
Woody Williams, SD	.259	.308	.379	58	15	4	1	9	4	1
Rick Ankiel, StL	.250	.292	.382	68	17	1	2	9	4	1
Kerry Wood, ChC	.250	.286	.325	40	10	0	1	4	2	4
Terry Mulholland, Atl	.250	.250	.333	36	9	3	0	4	0	9
Livan Hernandez, SF	.236	.244	.303	89	21	3	1	9	1	9
Jesus Sanchez, Fla	.232	.246	.232	56	13	0	0	4	1	3

(minimum 30 PA)

It's remarkable that this list includes so many young hurlers, from young vets Hernandez and Kerry Wood to 2000 rookies Adam Eaton, A.J. Burnett and Rick Ankiel. It's not often that three of the most promising rookie arms in the majors also showed they could do it with the bat. Among major league hurlers with 30 plate appearances in 2000, Eaton led them all in batting average and on-base percentage, collecting 11 hits and six walks in just 44 trips to the plate. Ankiel stroked a double, a triple and a pair of homers last summer. And how about Burnett's .520 slugging percentage? He recorded a double, triple and homer in just 25 at-bats.

Not far behind this top 10 were Montreal's Vazquez (.231 and two doubles) and the Dodgers' Chan Ho Park (.214 with four doubles and two homers). Still, the small sample size and a more detailed look at pitchers' hitting in 2000 suggest the emergence of young hurlers who can hit is just an aberration. It's worth noting that the four *worst* batting averages among pitchers with 30 plate appearances in 2000 belong to Octavio Dotel (.031), Bruce Chen (.033), Tony Armas Jr. (.038) and Mike Thurman (.042).

That doesn't diminish the fact that Eaton, Burnett and Ankiel are athletic young pitchers who haven't given up on hitting. It will be interesting to see if they continue their success at the plate, and whether more young hurlers enjoy similar results in the batter's box in 2001. The discussion of up-and-coming pitchers who can hit could become a national phenomenon if Toe Nash, Tampa Bay's mystery prospect, reaches the majors as a fireballing righthander with power from either side of the plate.

—Thom Henninger

A more complete listing for this category can be found on page 268.

Who's Toughest to Pull?

In the three years that we've studied the pitchers who are toughest—and easiest—to pull, we've learned two things: 1) While velocity is an important factor, a pitcher doesn't have to be a hard thrower to rank high on the least-often-pulled list; and 2) Where the pitcher puts the ball in the strike zone is a huge factor in whether hitters are likely to pull his pitches.

In fact, the title of this piece is a bit of a misnomer: it's an essay on which pitchers are pulled most and least *often*, which is not always the same as being "tough" or "easy" to pull. To better understand this, look at the pitchers who were pulled least often last season:

TOUGHEST PITCHERS TO PULL 2000

	IN PLAY	PULLED	PCT
Kevin Millwood	647	188	29.1
Jim Parque	622	181	29.1
Tom Glavine	748	218	29.1
Ryan Rupe	319	95	29.8
Carl Pavano	291	87	29.9
Roger Clemens	583	185	31.7
Todd Stottlemyre	286	91	31.8
Russ Ortiz	562	180	32.0
Scott Williamson	271	87	32.1
John Snyder	422	137	32.5
MLB Average			38.0

minimum 400 batters faced; bunts and popups less than 70 feet excluded

As usual, there are plenty of hard throwers on the list: Kevin Millwood, Ryan Rupe, Roger Clemens and Scott Williamson, to name four. Those guys would be tough for any hitter to get around on. At the same time, you also find pitchers like Jim Parque, Tom Glavine and John Snyder... guys who rely heavily on finesse. The quintessential seldom-pulled finesse pitcher is Glavine, who is notorious for working the outside corner (like six inches outside, if he can get away with it). In the three seasons we've been studying this data, Glavine has ranked third, first and third on the least-pulled list. Based strictly on his velocity, Glavine probably is fairly easy for a hitter to get around on. But try to pull one of Glavine's outside offerings and you're most likely going to end up with a weak groundball to short or third. That, of course, is playing right into his hands.

Braves pitchers turn up so frequently on the toughest-to-pull list that it isn't shocking to discover that Atlanta's pitching staff was pulled least often from 1998-2000. Credit Atlanta's crafty pitching coach, Leo Mazzone, as much as the Braves' pitchers. Last season, however, the Braves ranked second to the Giants, whose staff primarily consists of finesse pitchers. Giants pitching coach Dave Righetti might soon rank with Mazzone when it comes to teaching his staff to paint that outside corner.

These are the pitchers who were pulled *most* often last season:

Pitchers Pulled Most Often—2000

Pitcher, Team	Th	Hit	Pull	Pct
Tim Wakefield, Bos	R	518	249	48.1
Gil Heredia, Oak	R	674	319	47.3
Jason Grimsley, NYY	R	323	152	47.1
Kenny Rogers, Tex	L	765	359	46.9
Dave Mlicki, Det	R	430	201	46.7
Al Leiter, NYM	L	557	260	46.7
Tim Hudson, Oak	R	572	265	46.3
Reid Cornelius, Fla	R	424	192	45.3
Jose Lima, Hou	R	676	306	45.3
Robert Person, Phi	R	460	208	45.2

No one on this list is going to hit triple digits on the radar gun. As usual, the most interesting name is Al Leiter, who has ranked among the most-pulled pitchers in each of the last three years. Even at 34, Leiter threw hard enough to fan 200 batters in 208 innings last year, ranking fifth in the NL in strikeouts. When it comes to location, however, Leiter is the opposite of Glavine: he works the *inside* corner repeatedly, especially with his splendid cut fastball. With that style, he's going to get pulled by hitters who are trying to hit the ball where it's pitched. Just like they do with Glavine.

—Don Zminda

A more complete listing for this category can be found on page 270.

Which Pitchers Scored the Highest?

The game score was developed by Bill James as a unique way to measure the dominance of an individual pitcher in a single game. It is calculated using the following method:

1. Start with 50.
2. Add one point for each out recorded.
3. Add two points for each inning completed after the fourth.
4. Add one point for each strikeout.
5. Subtract one point for each walk.
6. Subtract two points for each hit.
7. Subtract four points for each earned run.
8. Subtract two points for each unearned run.

The keys to this system are keeping men off base while recording a high number of strikeouts, two things that American League Cy Young Award winner Pedro Martinez certainly excels at. For the second straight season, Martinez recorded one of the top game scores in the majors. Actually, in 2000 he recorded *two* of the top scores.

Highest Game Scores—2000

Pitcher, Team	Date	Opp	W/L	IP	H	R	ER	BB	SO	Score
Pedro Martinez, Bos	5/12	@Bal	W	9.0	2	0	0	0	15	98
Mike Mussina, Bal	8/1	Min	W	9.0	1	0	0	2	15	98
Pedro Martinez, Bos	8/29	@TB	W	9.0	1	0	0	0	13	98
Bartolo Colon, Cle	9/18	@NYY	W	9.0	1	0	0	1	13	97
Chan Ho Park, LA	9/29	@SD	W	9.0	2	0	0	1	13	95
Tim Hudson, Oak	8/28	CWS	W	9.0	1	0	0	1	8	92
Ron Villone, Cin	9/29	@StL	W	9.0	2	1	0	5	16	92
Kevin Brown, LA	9/23	SD	W	9.0	2	1	1	1	13	91
Randy Johnson, Ari	4/9	Pit	W	9.0	5	0	0	0	13	90
Pedro Martinez, Bos	7/23	CWS	W	9.0	6	0	0	0	15	90
Pat Hentgen, StL	9/14	ChC	W	9.0	3	0	0	0	9	90

Martinez tied for league leadership in 1999 with a game score of 98, and he logged a pair of 98s in 2000. His win over Baltimore in May featured more strikeouts, but his outing against Tampa was more impressive. In the latter contest, Martinez took a no-hitter into the top of the ninth inning before John Flaherty's single to right ended the bid. Still, Martinez closed out the final frame to record the third complete-game one-hitter of his career.

On the subject of one-hitters, Mike Mussina tossed a one-hit gem against the Twins on August 1. His game score of 98 was the highest of his career, outdistancing the 95 he fashioned against the Indians in 1997. The Yankees hope he has a few more of those performances left in the tank to help justify the significant salary they will pay him over the next six years. Cleveland's Bartolo Colon and Oakland's Tim Hudson also scored well on the strength of one-hitters.

Besides measuring individual game performances, the game-score method also can highlight outstanding pitchers' duels. Not surprisingly, Martinez was right in the thick of the top two mano-a-mano battles in 2000.

Best Pitchers' Duels—2000

Pitcher, Team	Date	W/L	IP	H	R	ER	BB	SO	Score	Total
Steve Trachsel, TB	5/6	W	9.0	3	0	0	3	11	89	176
Pedro Martinez, Bos		L	9.0	6	1	1	1	17	87	
Pedro Martinez, Bos	5/28	W	9.0	4	0	0	1	9	87	169
Roger Clemens, NYY		L	9.0	5	2	2	0	13	82	

(minimum 80 Score for each starter)

The best pitcher in baseball took the hill three times and compiled a 1.64 ERA against the 69-92 Devil Rays last season, yet his efforts produced only a win, a loss and a no-decision. His loss came courtesy of Steve Trachsel's three-hit blanking of Boston—at Fenway, no less. Trachsel couldn't quite keep up in the strikeout department, but he held the Red Sox to an 0-for-4 mark with runners in scoring position.

However, the most intriguing matchup in 2000, especially when you consider the enormity of the storylines, was the Martinez-Roger Clemens grudge match at Yankee Stadium. In the first regular-season meeting between the past and present Boston legends, the pair fought to a 0-0 stalemate through eight frames before the Red Sox finally broke through on the strength of a two-out, two-run homer by Trot Nixon. Martinez hit two Yankees batters in the bottom of the inning, but he pitched out of a bases-loaded jam to take Round One from the Rocket. Round Two on June 14 was not the epic battle that the first meeting was, as Clemens left the game in the first inning with a strained groin. But with both hurlers currently under contract for at least the next couple of seasons, there should be at least one or two more duels to add to the Boston-New York scrapbook.

—Tony Nistler

A more complete listing for this category can be found on page 272.

What If a Staff Has Quality, But Not Quantity?

It's been said that the hardest thing to do in all of sports is to hit a small, round ball with a wooden bat. That theory may not be entirely true, however. Actually, the hardest thing to do in all of sports is to hit a small, round ball *thrown by Pedro Martinez* with a wooden bat. All Martinez did in 2000 was post an 18-6 record and stifle offenses to the tune of a 1.74 ERA, the lowest figure by an American League qualifier since Luis Tiant's 1.60 for Cleveland in 1968 (Ron Guidry finished with a 1.74 ERA for the '78 Yankees, but Martinez' figure was slightly lower before rounding).

Martinez also set the standard for quality last season. The Boston ace paced the majors in highest percentage of quality starts, or any start in which a pitcher works six or more innings while giving up three or fewer earned runs. Martinez failed to meet those requirements just four times in his 29 outings. As seen in the chart to the right, among hurlers with at least 25 total starts in 2000, his quality-start percentage of 86.2 was tops by a wide margin.

In 1999, Martinez finished second to Randy Johnson in this category. Martinez also made 29 starts that season, of which *just* 24 (82.8 percent) were of the quality variety. For his part, Johnson also continued to churn out quality outings in 2000, as did Kevin Brown, who was the only other member of the '99 top 10 to show up on this year's list. Returning to the top 10 after one-year absences were quality-control stalwarts Tom Glavine, Greg Maddux and Roger Clemens, while Javier Vazquez and Mike Sirotka made their first appear-

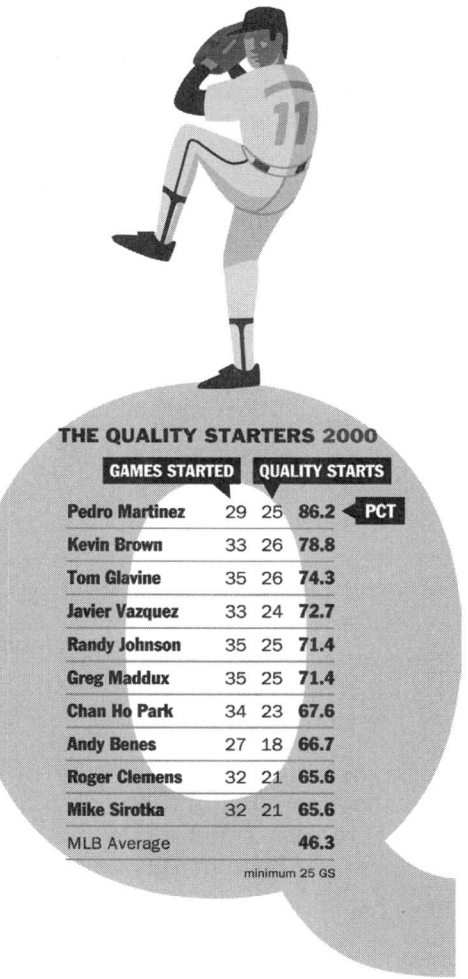

THE QUALITY STARTERS 2000

	GAMES STARTED	QUALITY STARTS	PCT
Pedro Martinez	29	25	86.2
Kevin Brown	33	26	78.8
Tom Glavine	35	26	74.3
Javier Vazquez	33	24	72.7
Randy Johnson	35	25	71.4
Greg Maddux	35	25	71.4
Chan Ho Park	34	23	67.6
Andy Benes	27	18	66.7
Roger Clemens	32	21	65.6
Mike Sirotka	32	21	65.6
MLB Average			46.3

minimum 25 GS

ances. The White Sox may be interested to note that David Wells, whom they traded Sirotka for in January, finished last year with fewer quality outings (19) than Sirotka despite logging three more starts.

As for the Red Sox, Boston may have had plenty of quality from Martinez, but it certainly didn't enjoy much in the way of quantity. Sans Martinez, the rest of the Boston staff turned in quality efforts just 31.6 percent of the time. In fact, no other Boston starter reached double digits in quality starts in 2000, and even with Martinez' Herculean contributions, the team finished near the bottom of the majors with 67 total quality starts. Not surprisingly, the Braves (93), Dodgers (87), Cardinals (85) and Diamondbacks (84) all finished near the top.

One of the teams that actually finished below the Red Sox in quality starts in 2000 was Colorado (66). However, the Rockies spent millions during the offseason in an effort to add a little quality for the 2001 campaign.

Highest Quality Start Percentages—1996-2000

Pitcher	GS	QS	Pct
Kevin Brown	168	132	78.6
Pedro Martinez	155	117	75.5
Greg Maddux	170	122	71.8
Randy Johnson	141	101	71.6
Tom Glavine	172	121	70.3
Curt Schilling	149	98	65.8
Denny Neagle	150	98	65.3
Roger Clemens	163	106	65.0
Al Leiter	151	98	64.9
Mike Hampton	160	102	63.8
MLB Average			**47.4**

(minimum 100 GS)

With the signings of both Mike Hampton and Denny Neagle, the Rockies welcomed a pair of aces who have combined for exactly 200 quality starts over the past five years. Colorado obviously is hoping to provide a little relief to a bullpen that got the call a major league-leading 480 times last season. If Hampton and Neagle can acclimate to their new surroundings, the Rockies might have quality *and* quantity in 2001.

—Tony Nistler

A more complete listing for this category can be found on page 273.

Who Gets the Red Barrett Trophy?

Efficiency, thy name is Greg Maddux. Last season, Atlanta's bi-speckled ace again led big league qualifiers in fewest pitches thrown per batter, averaging a mere 3.18 offerings to opposing hitters. It was the fourth time in the past five years that he has held the title. . . yet another gold star for his Hall of Fame report card.

Maddux also made a run in 2000 at another measure of pitching efficiency—the STATS Red Barrett Trophy. The RBT annually is awarded to the hurler who uses the fewest pitches in a nine-inning complete game. The story goes that Charles Henry "Red" Barrett once needed just 58 pitches to navigate nine innings back in 1944. While Maddux came close on more than one occasion last year, he couldn't quite secure top honors.

Fewest Pitches in a Nine-Inning Complete Game—2000

Pitcher, Team	Date	Score	Opp	W/L	IP	H	ER	BB	SO	Pit
John Halama, Sea	5/17	4-0	Min	W	9.0	4	0	0	2	87
Chris Carpenter, Tor	4/21	8-3	NYY	W	9.0	5	3	0	3	88
David Wells, Tor	4/8	4-0	@Tex	W	9.0	9	0	1	5	89
Greg Maddux, Atl	9/13	4-0	Fla	W	9.0	4	0	0	4	89
Greg Maddux, Atl	9/7	4-0	Ari	W	9.0	4	0	0	6	90
Darryl Kile, StL	9/2	2-1	NYM	W	9.0	5	1	0	2	94
Tim Hudson, Oak	9/9	10-0	TB	W	9.0	2	0	0	4	94
Shawn Estes, SF	8/6	7-1	Pit	W	9.0	10	0	1	4	95
Greg Maddux, Atl	6/24	1-2	Mil	L	9.0	6	2	1	5	96
Orlando Hernandez, NYY	9/16	6-3	Cle	W	9.0	4	3	0	6	98
Tom Glavine, Atl	9/25	6-0	@Mon	W	9.0	8	0	0	3	98
MLB Average										**116**

Congratulations to Seattle's John Halama, who captured top honors on the strength of his 87-pitch shutout of the Twins. Making the most of his only complete-game effort of 2000, Halama struck out just two Minnesota hitters. He did not walk a batter, however, and allowed only four hits en route to his second career shutout. Interestingly enough, his award-winning performance came just one start after he needed 84 pitches to get through *four* innings in a no-decision against Oakland. Still, Halama paced American League qualifiers in 2000 with an average of just 87 pitches per start.

Not far behind Halama on our list were Toronto teammates Chris Carpenter and David Wells, whose 88- and 89-pitch outings came just 13 days apart. Wells was the Red Barrett Trophy runner-up in 1999, and he again came tantalizingly close in 2000. After him, our list is a blur of Maddux and the Braves. Maddux went the distance six times last year, requiring more than 104 pitches in just one of those contests.

Of course, that was hardly news from the master of maximizing results while minimizing effort. To put his efficiency into some sort of context, consider a comparison with the other 300-win candidate: Roger Clemens. Since the start of the 1987 season—Maddux' first full campaign in the bigs—Maddux and Clemems have faced 13,325 and 13,110 batters, respectively. Despite having faced 215 more batsmen during that span, Maddux has thrown just 44,509 pitches to Clemens' 51,533. Efficiency may not break radar guns, but it nonetheless can break bats, spirits and records.

Then there are the guys who were in no danger of being mistaken for good ol' Red last year. Here are the leaders in arm-punishing outings in 2000:

Most Pitches in a Game—2000

Pitcher, Team	Date	Score	Opp	W/L	IP	H	ER	BB	SO	Pit
Ron Villone, Cin	9/29	8-1	@StL	W	9.0	2	0	5	16	148
Kevin Appier, Oak	7/3	3-8	@Tex	L	7.0	5	3	5	4	146
Randy Johnson, Ari	7/30	3-4	@Fla	ND	7.0	7	2	1	11	146
Livan Hernandez, SF	5/30	7-3	Phi	W	8.1	8	3	1	7	143
Doug Davis, Tex	8/20	6-2	@Bos	W	9.0	9	1	4	5	142
Garrett Stephenson, StL	7/25	7-3	Ari	W	8.0	5	3	4	2	141
Brian Bohanon, Col	9/13	11-0	@SD	W	9.0	9	0	3	3	140
Mike Mussina, Bal	4/29	3-1	Tex	W	9.0	9	1	1	6	138
Chris Holt, Hou	5/23	10-2	Phi	W	9.0	8	2	4	7	138
Four tied with										137

In what would be his final start in a Cincinnati uniform, Ron Villone threw 148 pitches in a complete-game victory over St. Louis. Six weeks after his gutsy, 16-strikeout performance, the Reds dealt him to Colorado, where he will join Brian Bohanon to give the Rockies a pair of bottom-of-the-rotation workhorses. Bohanon hit the vaunted 140-mark himself last year in a September whitewashing of the Padres. And speaking of the 140-mark, the venerable Randy Johnson reached that plateau for the 44th time in his career on July 30 against the Marlins. For his part, Maddux has just four 140-plus pitch outings to his credit. Then again, *you* try walking out to the mound and taking the ball out of the Big Unit's hands.

—Tony Nistler

A more complete listing for this category can be found on page 274.

Whose Heater Is Hottest?

On September 10 of last season, Arizona's Randy Johnson became a member of not one, but two elite power-pitching clubs. Johnson fanned 14 Florida hitters in a rather innocuous matchup against the Marlins, recording both his 300th strikeout of the 2000 campaign and the 3,000th whiff of his career. In doing so, he became just the third pitcher in history to set down 300 or more opponents in three consecutive seasons (joining Nolan Ryan and Amos Rusie), and just the 12th hurler to cross the 3,000 threshold. The Big Unit now has 1,040 Ks over the past three years, solidifying his place as the King of Heat over the past decade—if not all-time.

Johnson also topped our list of "hottest heaters" among starters in 2000, setting down opposing batsmen to the tune of 12.6 strikeouts per nine innings.

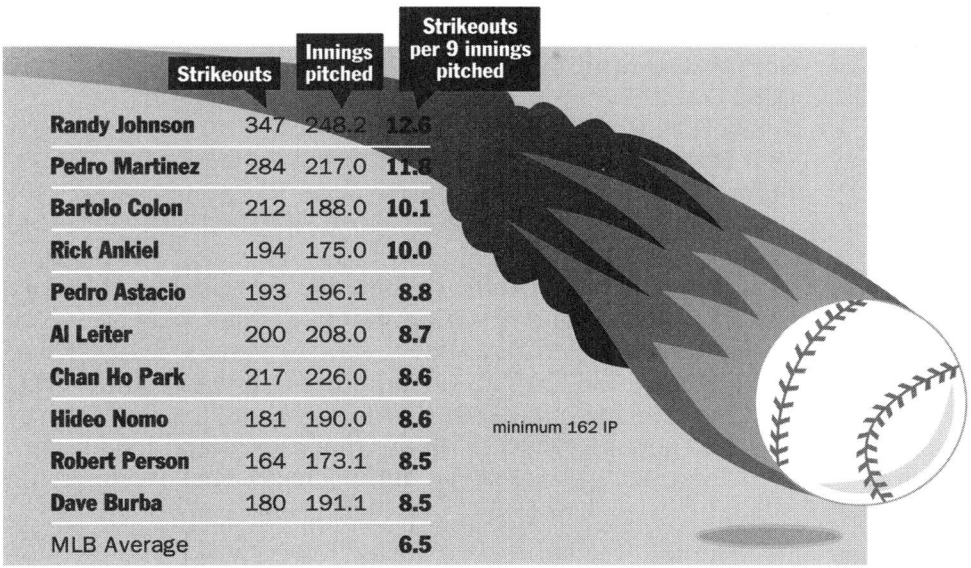

	Strikeouts	Innings pitched	Strikeouts per 9 innings pitched
Randy Johnson	347	248.2	12.6
Pedro Martinez	284	217.0	11.8
Bartolo Colon	212	188.0	10.1
Rick Ankiel	194	175.0	10.0
Pedro Astacio	193	196.1	8.8
Al Leiter	200	208.0	8.7
Chan Ho Park	217	226.0	8.6
Hideo Nomo	181	190.0	8.6
Robert Person	164	173.1	8.5
Dave Burba	180	191.1	8.5
MLB Average			6.5

minimum 162 IP

We always are quick to point out that the title for this essay can be a bit misleading, as this category isn't actually a measurement of velocity, and a screaming fastball isn't necessarily a requirement when it comes to striking out hitters. But a hot heater certainly doesn't hurt, and many of the names on this list post plenty of radar-gun readings that begin with the number "9."

Both Johnson and Pedro Martinez also topped this chart in 1999, though it was Martinez who occupied the No. 1 spot two years ago. Martinez could muster "only" 284 strikeouts last year, but that total still was good enough to pace the American League. Pedro Astacio and Hideo Nomo are the other two top-10 repeaters from '99, but the 2000 list also contains a couple of young guns in Bartolo Colon and Rick Ankiel, both of whom know a thing or two about burning holes in catchers' mitts. Speaking of burning mitts, relievers often are the ones who *really* can turn up the heat, as well as the numbers, in this category.

Most Strikeouts Per 9 Innings, Relievers—2000

Pitcher, Team	SO	IP	SO/9
Byung-Hyun Kim, Ari	111	70.2	14.1
John Rocker, Atl	77	53.0	13.1
Armando Benitez, NYM	106	76.0	12.6
Robb Nen, SF	92	66.0	12.5
Kazuhiro Sasaki, Sea	78	62.2	11.2
Scott Williamson, Cin	136	112.0	10.9
Doug Creek, TB	73	60.2	10.8
Trevor Hoffman, SD	85	72.1	10.6
Felix Rodriguez, SF	95	81.2	10.5
Arthur Rhodes, Sea	77	69.1	10.0

(minimum 50 relief IP and fewer than 162 IP overall)

Back in 1992, "Nasty Boy" Rob Dibble became the first pitcher in history to work at least 50 frames while reaching the 14.0 SO/9 plateau. Since then, that level has been eclipsed five times, with Arizona's Byung-Hyun Kim becoming the latest to do so. The sidearming Kim, who can reach 92 MPH despite his low arm angle, combined with Johnson to make it plenty hot inside Bank One Ballpark—even *with* the roof closed and the air conditioning on. Not surprisingly, Arizona hurlers paced the majors with 1,220 Ks in 2000.

As for the starter and reliever who averaged the fewest strikeouts per nine innings last season, those dubious distinctions go to the Giants' Kirk Rueter (3.5) and Anaheim's Mark Petkovsek (3.4), respectively. Rueter has averaged just 4.5 SO/9 in his eight years in the big leagues, yet he's managed to compile an 81-48 (.628) record. Hot heaters can make pitchers very rich, but there *are* other ways to burn opposing hitters.

—Tony Nistler

A more complete listing for this category can be found on page 275.

Has Anyone Ever Dominated Hitters Like Martinez Did in 2000?

It doesn't take a genius to figure out that Pedro Martinez had a terrific season in 2000. You probably already know many of the categories in which he led the majors. . . earned run average, shutouts, batting average allowed, slugging percentage allowed. . . those are the stats that are readily available to almost any fan. Other indicators of his brilliance may not be so handy, though. Such as allowing opponents to string more than two hits in an inning on only six occasions all year. Or surrendering one run or less in 17 of his 29 starts. Or permitting three runs or less in all but two.

But perhaps Martinez' excellence can be summed up best in two stats, or, more precisely, in the ratio between the two—284 strikeouts and 128 hits allowed. In other words, he struck out 2.2 batters for every hit he allowed. That ratio is breathtaking, if considered from an historical perspective.

A ratio of one strikeout for every hit allowed usually is considered outstanding. Furthermore, through the first 124 years of professional baseball, no pitcher who had worked at least 100 innings in a season had managed a ratio of 2-1. A mark of 2.00 seemed to be the equivalent of a 3:45 mile or a 30-foot long jump. Pitchers occasionally would come close to the seemingly invincible barrier, but would finish just short. The great Nolan Ryan threatened on occasion, falling only one strikeout shy of a 2-1 ratio in 1991. Rookie Kerry Wood also missed by one strikeout in 1998.

That's what makes Martinez' 2000 campaign so amazing. He didn't just squeak by the 2.00 mark, he bounded over it. Looking at the all-time list of strikeout-hit ratios, Martinez makes everyone else look almost mortal:

Best Strikeout-Hit Ratios, Season—1876-2000

Pitcher, Team	Year	SO	H	SO/H
Pedro Martinez, Bos	2000	284	128	2.22
Kerry Wood, ChC	1998	233	117	1.99
Nolan Ryan, Tex	1991	203	102	1.99
Nolan Ryan, Cal	1972	329	166	1.98
Randy Johnson, Sea	1997	291	147	1.98
Pedro Martinez, Bos	1999	313	160	1.96
Pedro Martinez, Mon	1997	305	158	1.93
Hideo Nomo, LA	1995	236	124	1.90
Nolan Ryan, Tex	1989	301	162	1.86
Randy Johnson, Sea	1995	294	159	1.85

(minimum 162 innings)

Baseball Scoreboard

Ryan and Randy Johnson are two of the hardest-throwing pitchers in history. Both could fire fastballs around 100 MPH, and not many hitters felt comfortable standing in the batter's box against them. Martinez may not throw quite that hard, but he's just as nasty from a hitter's perspective. He joins Ryan as the only pitchers with three seasons in the top 10. Johnson has two, while Wood and Hideo Nomo each generated one such campaign.

Nine of the 10 highest strikeout-hit seasons have occurred since 1989. That may be due partially to the characteristics of the current era. Even though batting averages gradually have increased over the past decade, strikeouts have risen about twice as fast. It also may be due to the pitchers themselves, as Martinez and Johnson are superior talents.

Martinez and the Big Unit ranked one-two in K/H last year, while 20-year-old Rick Ankiel finished third with a mark of 1.42. But before we anoint Ankiel as the logical successor to Martinez and Johnson, we better wait to make sure Ankiel steadies his control. Two other relatively young pitchers, Bartolo Colon and Chan Ho Park, round out last year's top five.

Highest Strikeout-Hit Ratio—2000

Pitcher, Team	SO	H	SO/H
Pedro Martinez, Bos	284	128	2.22
Randy Johnson, Ari	347	202	1.72
Rick Ankiel, StL	194	137	1.42
Bartolo Colon, Cle	212	163	1.30
Chan Ho Park, LA	217	173	1.25
Kevin Brown, LA	216	181	1.19
Robert Person, Phi	164	144	1.14
Al Leiter, NYM	200	176	1.14
Roger Clemens, NYY	188	184	1.02
Tim Hudson, Oak	169	169	1.00

(minimum 162 IP)

The importance of a good strikeout-hit ratio is demonstrated by the success of all the pitchers in last year's top 10. They combined to go 152-73, which translates to a .676 winning percentage. Clearly, K/H is a leading indicator of a hurler's dominance. And it's clear that few pitchers ever have been as dominant as Pedro Martinez was last year.

—Jim Henzler

A more complete listing for this category can be found on page 277.

Why Are Managers Using So Many Situational Relievers?

When discussing how to shorten games, the number and pace of pitching changes usually appear on the short list of complaints. Of course, it's not just the relief appearances themselves, but the events that accompany them that cause the clock to spin. Each new pitcher almost always is preceded by not one, but two strolls from the dugout to the mound and back, a leisurely discussion that lasts until broken up by the home-plate ump, the eventual trudge-in from the bullpen, another few words of encouragement, then eight more warm-up tosses...

Last season, major league teams averaged a total of fewer than eight complete games apiece. They used an average of two-and-a-half relief pitchers per game. Multiply that by two teams and toss in the starters and you get seven pitchers every contest. That's a lot of dead time.

It hasn't always been this way. At the turn of the century, it was quite rare to see any relief pitchers at all. In 1901, teams averaged a little more than 20 bullpen appearances all season. That year, the Boston Beaneaters used just five pitchers to complete a 140-game schedule (and that included one guy who appeared in just six games). Over the course of the last 100 years, the number of complete games has plummeted while concurrently, the number of relievers has risen steadily. This trend really has picked up momentum in the last quarter-century.

Pitching Staff Management—1901-2000

Year	CG/Tm	CG Pct	Pitchers/G
1901	119.6	86.2	2.3
1925	75.6	49.2	3.7
1950	62.4	40.3	4.2
1975	43.8	27.2	4.8
2000	7.8	4.8	7.1

It may not be a coincidence that Tony La Russa has been managing in the major leagues for most of those last 25 years. As much as anyone, La Russa has turned bullpen usage into an obsession. Since 1987, when STATS first began tracking in-game information, he has required 20 more relief appearances per season than the average manager. He also burned up one of his bullpen guys to face just one batter 13 percent more than his average fellow skipper did over that span.

Naturally, since La Russa has had so much success, others have decided to play along. Last year, Colorado's Buddy Bell went to his bullpen 480 times, the most in baseball, and he also used one of his relievers to face just one batter 57 times. Tied for second in both categories, ironically enough, were former White Sox manager Gene Lamont and current Sox skipper Jerry Manuel (466-44). When it came to changing pitchers in the middle of an inning, Texas' Johnny Oates led with 233, just beating out Detroit's Phil Garner (228).

What these guys were looking for with all the managerial chess maneuvers is the elusive platoon advantage. And what is that exactly? It's a measure of what kind of advantage teams gain by "bringing the lefthander in from the pen".

Platoon Splits, MLB—2000

Matchup	Avg	OBP	Slg	OPS
RHB vs. RHP	.266	.333	.429	.762
RHB vs. LHP	.276	.351	.442	.793
LHB vs. RHP	.275	.357	.449	.806
LHB vs. LHP	.262	.339	.408	.747

The chart helps to summarize why there are so many late-inning relief changes. For example, with runners on base and close games on the line, managers strive to gain 13 batting average points, not to mention the sizable drop in slugging percentage and OPS (on-base plus slugging), by bringing in a southpaw to face a lefthanded batter.

That's not the whole story, however, as the above splits include all pitchers, starters and relievers. A manager gains a bit of an advantage simply by bringing in a fresh arm out of the pen, and look what happens when he gets the exact matchup that he wants:

Opponents' Hitting vs. Pitchers in Different Roles, MLB—2000

Matchup	Avg	OBP	Slg	OPS
All Pitchers	.270	.345	.437	.782
Starters	.274	.344	.446	.790
Relievers	.264	.347	.418	.765
Relievers, 1-Batter App	.161	.248	.247	.495

Now we get to the crux of the matter. When relievers are brought in to face just one batter, they turn the other guy into a pitcher with a stick in his hand. This is exactly why guys like Jesse Orosco continue to find high-dollar employment well into their 40s. And it's also why the toughest part of the modern manager's job arguably is the handling of the bullpen. When a reliever's work consists of five pitches and a shower, it must be tempting to trot him out there night after night.

Relievers worked two days in a row 2,185 times last season, compiling an ERA of 4.44. Guys were able to go out there for a third straight night almost exactly one-sixth as many times (364 appearances), though the ones who could do it actually had a better ERA (3.77). Three straight days of work is about the max, as there were only 55 times that a reliever pitched four or more straight days in 2000. In those games, they collectively averaged just over two outs per outing.

The two guys who worked the most total innings on the second of two consecutive days both pitched for the Reds: Scott Sullivan and Danny Graves pitched 24 and 21 innings under those circumstances, respectively, compiling very respectable ERAs of 3.00 and 2.14. Sullivan was effective (2.08 ERA) in the five appearances he made on the third day in a row, while Graves seemed to hit the wall at that point (5.68). Robb Nen had the most innings (9.2) on the third day in a row, putting up a 0.93 ERA, while Sullivan and Todd Jones tied for the most innings (3.1) on the fourth day with no respite. This is where Sullivan lost steam, as his ERA jumped to a lofty 8.10.

As might be expected, closers dominate the list of hard-worked relievers. After all, a manager has to try to squeeze out a win whenever he can. Trevor Hoffman seems to get stronger, as he did not allow a single earned run in the 8.1 innings he pitched on the third or fourth day in a row. Rick Aguilera also had a 0.00 ERA when he came out of the bullpen for the second, third or fourth consecutive day. When he pitched with any rest at all, his ERA was 6.27. Another veteran closer, John Wetteland, was the opposite. He had a 6.27 ERA when trying to come back with no rest, while his ERA when rested was exactly three runs lower.

A pitcher worked five days in a row just four times last season, and ironically enough, half of those outings were logged by recent Cardinal acquisition Steve Kline. As La Russa is juggling his bullpen this coming season, he might note that Kline's ERA at the end of his second five-day stint (June 5) was a sterling 1.09. From that point through the end of the season, it was 5.11. At some point, even the most durable of relievers needs his proper rest.

—Don Hartack

Who Gets the Easy Saves—And Who Toughs It Out?

The Marlins' Antonio Alfonseca led the majors with 45 saves and finished second with a .918 save percentage in 2000. The White Sox' Keith Foulke had 34 saves and an .872 percentage, ranking ninth in both categories. So who had the better year?

The answer seems pretty obvious. And it is, if you know what numbers to look at.

Every year in the *Baseball Scoreboard*, we break down saves into three categories: easy, regular and tough. And we'll do that again, as soon as we refresh your memory as to the definitions.

An easy save opportunity occurs when a reliever pitches no more than one inning and doesn't enter the game with the tying run on base or at the plate. A tough save chance is any in which the reliever enters with the tying run on base. A regular save situation is any that doesn't fit into either of the other two categories.

Keith Foulke

All save opportunities aren't created equal. The average reliever converted 86 percent of his easy opportunities in 2000—hence the name—but those success rates plummeted to 64 percent for regular chances and just 32 percent in tough situations.

While Alfonseca had 45 saves, not once was he asked to close out a game with a tough opportunity. He cashed in on 31 of 32 (97 percent) easy chances and 14 of 17 (82 percent) regular situations, but an average closer would have converted 42 saves if he had been in Alfonseca's shoes.

Meanwhile, just nine of Foulke's 39 save chances were easy, and he converted all of those. He faced 21 regular opportunities and made good on 19 of them, a 90 percent success rate, well above the major league average. He also had six tough saves (ranking second only to the Cardinals' Dave Veres, who had eight), and Foulke's 67 percent tough-save success rate more than doubled the big league norm. An average closer faced with the same situations as Foulke would have had 24 saves, compared to Foulke's 34.

Though Alfonseca had 11 more saves and a better save percentage than Foulke, the in-depth look at the numbers reveals that the latter was more effective. Alfonseca came out three saves ahead of an average reliever, while Foulke was 10 saves ahead. Foulke's 25 non-easy saves also led all major leaguers.

Here's the complete breakdown for all pitchers with at least 30 saves in 2000:

Save Conversion Rates—2000

Pitcher, Team	Easy Sv/Opp	Pct	Regular Sv/Opp	Pct	Tough Sv/Opp	Pct	Overall Sv/Opp	Pct
Antonio Alfonseca, Fla	31/32	97	14/17	82	0/0	—	45/49	92
Trevor Hoffman, SD	25/28	89	16/19	84	2/3	67	43/50	86
Todd Jones, Det	27/30	90	11/12	92	4/4	100	42/46	91
Derek Lowe, Bos	20/20	100	20/25	80	2/2	100	42/47	89
Armando Benitez, NYM	20/20	100	18/21	86	3/5	60	41/46	89
Robb Nen, SF	31/33	94	10/12	83	0/1	0	41/46	89
Kazuhiro Sasaki, Sea	25/25	100	9/10	90	3/5	60	37/40	93
Mariano Rivera, NYY	16/17	94	17/18	94	3/6	50	36/41	88
Keith Foulke, CWS	9/9	100	19/21	90	6/9	67	34/39	87
John Wetteland, Tex	16/18	89	18/24	75	0/1	0	34/43	79
Billy Koch, Tor	14/15	93	18/22	82	1/1	100	33/38	87
J. Isringhausen, Oak	21/22	95	10/15	67	2/3	67	33/40	83
Roberto Hernandez, TB	19/21	90	12/17	71	1/2	50	32/40	80
Troy Percival, Ana	15/20	75	17/22	77	0/0	—	32/42	76
Danny Graves, Cin	11/11	100	15/18	83	4/6	67	30/35	86
Bob Wickman, Mil-Cle	20/23	87	9/11	82	1/3	33	30/37	81
MLB Average		86		64		32		65

(minimum 30 Sv, ranked by Sv)

Probably the biggest closer news in the offseason was the three-player trade in January between the Athletics, Devil Rays and Royals. Convinced

Baseball Scoreboard

that it would lose outfielder Johnny Damon as a free agent after the 2001 season, Kansas City sent him to Oakland for journeyman catcher A.J. Hinch and shortstop prospect Angel Berroa, who addressed two areas of weakness in the Royals' organization. The A's also shipped outfielder Ben Grieve to Tampa Bay, which sent righthander Cory Lidle to Oakland and closer Roberto Hernandez to Kansas City.

The Royals had made shoring up their bullpen their top offseason priority after their relievers ranked 28th in the major leagues with a 5.57 ERA in 2000. But Hernandez may not be that much of an upgrade on Ricky Bottalico, who converted 16 of 23 save attempts (10 of 12 easy, 4 of 8 regular, 2 of 3 tough) last season. Hernandez has become more hittable, especially against lefthanders, over the past two years. And plugging his success rates (90 percent easy, 71 percent regular, 50 percent tough) into Bottalico's chances, Hernandez would have had 19 saves, just three more than Bottalico had. Breaking down each reliever like we did with Alfonseca and Foulke shows that Hernandez came out two saves ahead of an average reliever, while Bottalico was dead even.

And Bottalico didn't cost Kansas City seven wins with his seven blown saves. He rallied to earn victories in three of those outings, and the Royals won another in which he had no decision. It's unlikely Hernandez will offset the loss of Damon, who hit .327 and topped the American League with 136 runs and 46 stolen bases, and Hernandez certainly won't fix the problems with the rest of the club's relief corps.

—Jim Callis

A more complete listing for this category can be found on page 279.

If You Hold the Fort, Will You Soon Be Closing the Gate?

Baseball clubs understand the importance of setup men who can shut down the opposition in the seventh and eighth innings. The middle-relief bridge to the closer wasn't always viewed as a key to success, but that's changed.

Over the winter, some of the game's best setup men were on the open market, and the dollars they received demonstrated their importance to the team concept. Jeff Nelson left the Yankees for Seattle by agreeing to a three-year, $10.65 million deal. The Mets re-signed their two setup men, righthander Turk Wendell and southpaw John Franco, to three-year contracts that will pay $3-3.5 million a season. And Rheal Cormier departed Boston for Philadelphia after receiving a three-year, $8.75 million deal.

Setup men often come into games in save situations. If they retire at least one batter and pass the save opportunity to another reliever, they receive a hold. So, let's look at the hold leaders from the 2000 season:

HOLDING THE FORT 2000 — HOLDS

Player	Holds
Felix Rodriguez	30
Paul Shuey	28
Buddy Groom	27
Kelly Wunsch	25
Arthur Rhodes	24
Mike Remlinger	23
Jason Christiansen	22
Scott Sullivan	22
Jim Mecir	21
Jeff Zimmerman	21

A year ago, both Derek Lowe and Keith Foulke made this list, and in 2000 they proved just as effective at protecting leads in the ninth inning as they had at maintaining leads in the seventh and eighth frames in 1999. Lowe took over for injured Boston closer Tom Gordon, saving 42 games to share the American League lead with Detroit's Todd Jones. Foulke swapped jobs with White Sox teammate Bob Howry in 2000, taking over as the team closer and saving 34 games after Howry struggled in April.

The list of 2000 leaders in holds features a potential closer in Felix Rodriguez, but it was the dominating duo of Rodriguez and San Francisco closer Robb Nen that was so critical to the Giants' success all season long. With Rodriguez leading all major leaguers in holds and Nen allowing just 37 hits in 66 innings and posting a big league-best 1.50 ERA among relievers, don't look for their roles to change in 2001.

Mike Remlinger, however, earned 12 saves last season in a supporting role to John Rocker. Remlinger started the season 5-for-5 in save opportunities with a 2.08 ERA in April and May while Rocker was preparing for the season after his suspension for flapping his mouth to *Sports Illustrated*. Remlinger may enjoy a similar role in 2001.

Remlinger is one of three pitchers to repeat from the 1999 list. The others are Buddy Groom and Jeff Zimmerman. Working for Oakland, Groom ranked second among major leaguers in holds in '99, and he placed third in 2000 with Baltimore. Zimmerman has been the holds leader for Texas in each of the last two seasons, but his baserunners allowed and ERA ballooned in 2000, when he wasn't nearly as effective as he was in 1999.

Otherwise, it's hard to envision anyone else among the game's top 10 in 2000 becoming a closer in 2001. Paul Shuey has been mentioned as a potential closer, but his control has kept him from taking the job when he's had chances. Jason Christiansen had been a closer in training, but he hasn't pitched as effectively since a dominating 1998 campaign with Pittsburgh.

Just as high hold totals don't always lead to closer jobs, impressive *team* hold totals don't translate into higher win totals. Only Cleveland (77) ranked higher than Baltimore (68) in holds last summer, but the Orioles finished 74-88 in the American League East. The winner of four of the last five World Series, the Yankees, ranked third from the bottom in the league with just 39 holds. They have finished near the bottom of the AL in holds for three straight seasons, but that doesn't keep them from winning. The truth is, holds are more of a function of how a manager uses his starters and bullpen, rather than how effective the bullpen actually is.

—Thom Henninger

A more complete listing for this category can be found on page 280.

Who Knows How to Handle His Inheritance?

For Curtis Leskanic, 635 feet must have felt like the top of the world last season. Leskanic was traded to the Brewers following the 1999 campaign after spending the first seven years of his career toiling in the Rockies' bullpen. The trade gave Leskanic a fresh start after several mediocre seasons with Colorado. More importantly, it dropped the elevation of the pitching mound in his home games from 5,280 feet at Coors Field to a much less hitter-friendly 635 ticks above sea level at County Stadium.

The results were impressive: a 9-3 record, 2.56 ERA and 12 saves in 13 chances. He excelled as the primary righthanded setup man for the Brewers during the first half of the season, and he continued to roll along once he became the stopper after the team traded Bob Wickman. Leskanic's effectiveness while wearing a variety of hats also helped him top the list in best inherited runners scoring percentages in 2000.

Best Inherited Runners Scoring Percentages—2000

Pitcher, Team	IR	Scored	Pct
Curtis Leskanic, Mil	31	3	9.7
Mike Myers, Col	64	9	14.1
Rob Ramsay, Sea	34	5	14.7
Turk Wendell, NYM	40	6	15.0
Vic Darensbourg, Fla	44	7	15.9
Al Levine, Ana	31	5	16.1
Steve Reed, Cle	36	6	16.7
Mike Holtz, Ana	59	10	16.9
Rick White, TB-NYM	44	8	18.2
LaTroy Hawkins, Min	33	6	18.2
MLB Average			**34.2**

(minimum 30 IR)

Of the 31 ducks on the pond when Leskanic entered the game last season, all but three remained stranded when he left. It was a marked improvement over a '99 effort with Colorado that saw him allow 39.6 percent (19 of 48) of inherited runners to score. His performance was so encouraging that the Brewers wrapped him up with an incentive-laden three-year deal in November, and manager Davey Lopes handed him the closer's job for 2001.

Also cracking the top 10 were a handful of situational lefthanders, including the man whom the Brewers gave up to acquire Leskanic, Mike Myers.

In a Seinfeld-like, bizarro-world twist, the two players swapped addresses while enjoying similar results. Myers saw his ERA drop from 5.23 with the Brewers in 1999 to 1.99 for the Rockies last season. Still, Myers finished third in this category in 1999 and has *stranded* a staggering 121 runners over the past two campaigns. Rob Ramsay, Vic Darensbourg and Mike Holtz also fit the situational lefty profile and excelled in their roles.

While righthanded setup men and situational lefties may be prevalent on the previous list, true closers rarely make the minimum of inheriting 30 or more baserunners over the course of a single season these days. Both Leskanic and LaTroy Hawkins did spend the last part of the 2000 campaign as the stopper for their clubs, but they finished with just 12 and 14 saves, respectively. As for the guys who regularly shut the door last year, here are the top firemen at preventing inherited runners from scoring:

Best Inherited Runners Scoring Percentages, Closers—2000

Pitcher, Team	IR	Scored	Pct
John Rocker, Atl	17	2	11.8
Keith Foulke, CWS	23	4	17.4
Kazuhiro Sasaki, Sea	25	5	20.0
Trevor Hoffman, SD	20	4	20.0
Billy Koch, Tor	18	4	22.2
Todd Jones, Det	28	7	25.0
Robb Nen, SF	18	5	27.8
Dave Veres, StL	45	15	33.3
Mike Williams, Pit	15	5	33.3
Danny Graves, Cin	47	17	36.2

(minimum 20 Sv and 15 IR)

John Rocker did a remarkable job of shutting out the distractions once he stepped between the white lines last season. Yes, he inherited just 17 runners, but he allowed only two of those opponents to score and converted 24 of 27 save opportunities. American League Rookie of the Year Kazuhiro Sasaki proved that he more than belonged on this side of the pond, keeping pace with 1999's top stopper in this category, Trevor Hoffman. If Sasaki's new Japanese teammate in Seattle, Ichiro Suzuki, has as much success clearing the bases as Sasaki did at keeping them full, the Mariners just might start printing their media guides in two languages.

—Tony Nistler

A more complete listing for this category can be found on page 281.

Which Relievers Prevent the Most Runs?

Open the *STATS Major League Handbook 2001*, to pages 344-345 and you'll find a whole host of names in the relief pitching leader boards. But among the five pitchers listed in each of the 23 relief categories for each league—230 entries in all—how can you tell who really are the most valuable relievers?

Antonio Alfonseca led the National League in saves and save percentage, but Robb Nen finished first in ERA and second in opponent batting average, while Curtis Leskanic allowed only 9.7 percent of inherited runners to score. In the American League, Anaheim's Mike Fyhrie led relievers in ERA, and Mariner Rob Ramsay stranded 85.3 percent of inherited runners. What's a fan to think?

Runs prevented, a statistic introduced in the 1997 *Scoreboard*, combines many of these other measures, leveling the playing field for every reliever, whether he's a closer, setup man or long reliever. How does runs prevented do it? In short, runs prevented accounts for the runners a reliever inherits, the runs that score while he's in the game, and the men he leaves behind.

The foundation of runs prevented is run expectation, shorthand for "how many runs do we expect to score the remainder of the inning given the outs and runners on base?" The following chart answers the question:

MLB Run Expectation—1996-2000

Runners	Number of Outs		
	0	1	2
None	.56	.30	.12
1st	.95	.57	.25
2nd	1.19	.72	.34
3rd	1.45	.99	.39
1st & 2nd	1.57	.98	.47
1st & 3rd	1.87	1.21	.54
2nd & 3rd	2.04	1.43	.60
Bases Loaded	2.38	1.64	.79

Runs prevented is just a short hop from run expectation. First, we take the run expectation when a reliever enters the game. If he leaves before the inning ends, we then subtract from the initial run expectation the run expectation when he hits the showers and any runs that scored while he was on the mound, and then total it up. If he finishes an inning (with a run expectation of zero, by definition), we account for that inning, and start anew the next inning.

A quick example: Dan Plesac enters the game with a runner on third and nobody out. He surrenders a sacrifice fly to the first lefty, strikes out the next one, and then out trots Buck Martinez when a righty approaches the plate. Plesac started with a run expectation of 1.45, allowed one (1.0) run to score, and left with two outs and nobody on (0.12). His inning (and game) total would be 0.33 runs prevented (1.45 - 1.0 - 0.12 = 0.33). In other words, he prevented one-third of a run more than we expected.

At season's end, we total each reliever's runs prevented, with the average score coming out to around zero. After all, the average pitcher should prevent exactly as many runs as we expect. The better pitchers have positive runs prevented, and the guys who make you cringe when the bullpen door swings open find themselves with negative scores. (If you'd like a more detailed explanation, see the Glossary.)

So, who were the best relievers at preventing runs last season?

Most Runs Prevented—2000

Pitcher, Team	Relief IP	RP
Robb Nen, SF	66.0	28.2
Jeff Tam, Oak	85.2	27.2
Jim Mecir, TB-Oak	85.0	25.8
Scott Sullivan, Cin	106.1	25.6
Derek Lowe, Bos	91.1	24.5
Curtis Leskanic, Mil	77.1	24.3
Turk Wendell, NYM	82.2	23.2
Matt Herges, LA	87.2	23.0
Keith Foulke, CWS	88.0	22.8
Danny Graves, Cin	91.1	22.4

You certainly didn't need runs prevented, or any other new statistic for that matter, to tell you that Robb Nen was the best reliever in baseball last year. While the more traditional statistics sometimes aren't helpful, they aren't entirely useless, either, particularly when you see a 1.50 ERA and 41 saves. Throw in Nen's unbelievable .471 opposition on-base plus slugging percentage (OPS) and the fact that he stranded 13 of 18 inherited runners, and you have a pretty good run preventer by any measure.

But who, aside from Athletics general manager Billy Beane, would have listed Jeff Tam and Jim Mecir as two of the best relievers in baseball? The pair combined for 170.2 innings—just 31.2 frames fewer than staff ace Tim Hudson—and allowed only 27 of 108 inherited runners to score. They deserve much of the credit for leading Oakland to the postseason. Mecir's performance should not be any great shock, however, as he finished seventh in runs prevented in 1998 before missing most of 1999 with an injury.

Another amazing duo was Cincinnati's Scott Sullivan and Danny Graves, who both repeated their top 10 appearances from 1999. On these very pages last year we doubted that these two (and fellow Cincy reliever Scott Williamson) would be able to replicate their performances, as it is a rare feat for relievers to bounce back from seasons of 90-plus innings. Well, Sullivan and Graves proved us wrong, and they kept pace when Williamson headed to the rotation. In fact, Williamson worked 56.2 innings out of the bullpen and totaled 8.1 runs prevented in 2000 to combine with Sullivan and Graves to form the best relief trio in baseball aside from Oakland's Tam, Mecir and Jason Isringhausen.

Keith Foulke and Derek Lowe, who finished first and third in runs prevented in 1999, repeated their strong performances to make the list again in 2000. Foulke leveraged his strong 1999 campaign to capture the job as the White Sox' closer last season. He was joined in the Chicago bullpen by five other relievers who placed in the top 100 in runs prevented—only the Dodgers had as many relievers place so high. Lowe also anchored a very strong bullpen that prevented nearly 70 runs, which allowed Boston to become the first team to lead the American League in ERA while finishing last in starters' innings pitched.

Finishing just behind Lowe, Leskanic finally escaped the pitchers' purgatory that is Coors Field and broke out for a surprisingly strong campaign in Milwaukee. His performance allowed the Brewers to trade Bob Wickman (12.7 runs prevented, 38th) to Cleveland for slugger Richie Sexson. While Leskanic was hopeless in Colorado, Gabe White, Mike Myers and Jose Jimenez somehow managed to overcome the Coors effect and finish in the top 40 in runs prevented. Perhaps Mike Hampton and Denny Neagle were attracted by more than just Colorado's mile-high mountains of money.

There is one glaring omission from the Top 10 this year. For the first time since we started tracking runs prevented in 1996, the Yankees' Mariano Rivera did not finish among the league leaders. Last season, Rivera placed 28th with 15.1 runs prevented, just ahead of Arizona's Greg Swindell and just behind Montreal's Anthony Telford.

New York fans no doubt will protest, but they should spend their time worrying about the Yankees' bullpen in 2001. The team's best run preventer in 2000, Jeff Nelson (21.1 runs prevented, 11th place), now makes his home in Seattle. And one other item: Joe Torre was right to go with essentially a three-man bullpen in the postseason, as Doc Gooden was the only New York reliever to compile positive runs prevented in 2000 aside from the favored trio of Nelson, Rivera and Mike Stanton.

Other fans who maybe should worry? Kansas City doesn't need any more bad news, but incoming closer Roberto Hernandez placed 73rd in baseball with 7.9 runs prevented in 2000, down from 16.5 runs prevented in 1999. OK, a bit of a dropoff. But who finished 74th in runs prevented in 2000? None other than erstwhile Royals reliever Ricky Bottalico—and it wouldn't have cost Johnny Damon to keep him.

And what of the relievers found in the *STATS Major League Handbook* leader boards? While Nen, Lowe and Foulke all are featured prominently on those pages, some of their neighbors simply are not in their run-preventing class. American League relief ERA leader Mike Fyhrie finished the season 37th in runs prevented. Cleveland's Paul Shuey was first in the AL with 28 holds, but he managed only a tie for 60th in the majors in runs prevented, primarily because he allowed 16 of his 40 inherited runners to score.

How about NL saves leader Antonio Alfonseca? The Florida closer placed 111th in runs prevented, perhaps that's not surprising given his 4.24 ERA and the fact that he inherited only five runners all season, one of which scored. Seattle's Rob Ramsay posted the AL's lowest percentage of inherited runners scored, but he prevented only 2.6 runs, good for 152nd in the majors. There's no simple explanation for Ramsay's finish, but that's the beauty of runs prevented—it often shows you what you can't otherwise see, even if you stare long and hard at those leader boards.

—Steven Schulman

Steven Schulman, the creator of runs prevented and author of this essay, is a SABR member and an attorney practicing in Washington, D.C.

A more complete listing for this category can be found on page 282.

IV. QUESTIONS ON DEFENSE

Which Catchers Catch Thieves?

The King is dead. Long live the King.

Well, he isn't really dead, but after leading all major league catchers in caught-stealing percentage for five straight seasons, Ivan Rodriguez has been dethroned as the king of this category.

To be fair to the game's premier backstop, Rodriguez' 2000 campaign ended in late July with a fractured thumb. While Rodriguez was healthy, opponents smartly avoided running on him. The miniscule total of 34 attempted steals demonstrates how his mere presence on the field deters the running game. He allowed just .24 stolen bases per nine innings in 2000, far and away the lowest number of steals per nine among all catchers who caught at least 700 innings last summer.

Using the same minimum, here are the best of 2000 at catching thieves:

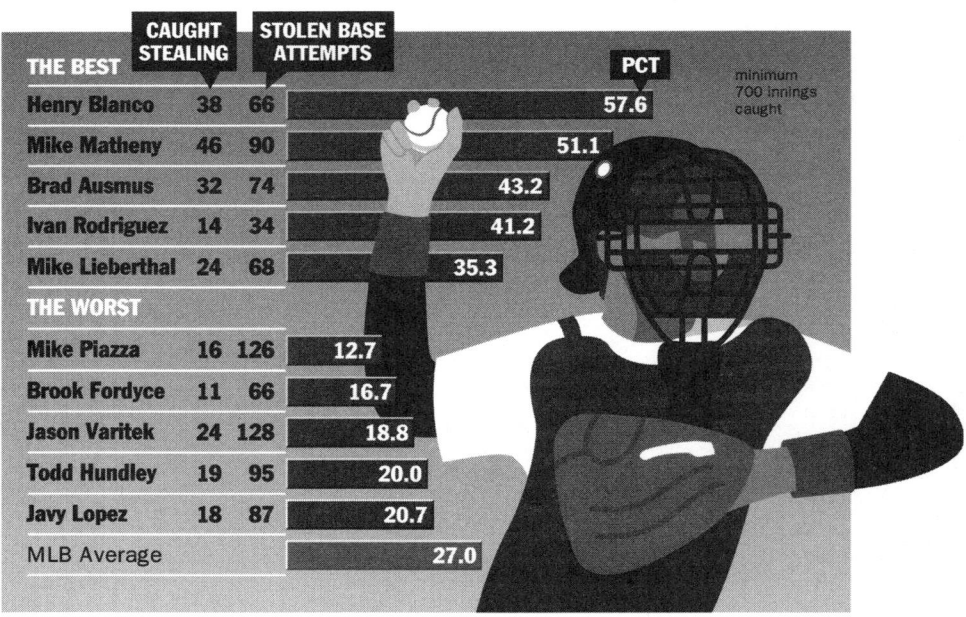

THE BEST	CAUGHT STEALING	STOLEN BASE ATTEMPTS	PCT
Henry Blanco	38	66	57.6
Mike Matheny	46	90	51.1
Brad Ausmus	32	74	43.2
Ivan Rodriguez	14	34	41.2
Mike Lieberthal	24	68	35.3
THE WORST			
Mike Piazza	16	126	12.7
Brook Fordyce	11	66	16.7
Jason Varitek	24	128	18.8
Todd Hundley	19	95	20.0
Javy Lopez	18	87	20.7
MLB Average			27.0

minimum 700 innings caught

The new caught-stealing king in 2000 was Milwaukee's Henry Blanco, who took over a majority of the Brewers' catching duties after he arrived from Colorado in the four-team Vinny Castilla trade a year ago. Blanco gave the Brewers the defensive component they were looking for in a catcher. He posted a solid .991 fielding percentage and threw out 57.6 percent of all baserunners trying to steal.

Interestingly, the runnerup to Blanco also changed teams prior to the 2000 season. Mike Matheny moved from Toronto to St. Louis via free agency, and reached career highs in games played, hits, doubles, RBI, walks and the three hitting percentages. He topped his career year with a stellar .994 fielding percentage and a 51.1 percent success rate in nailing opposing baserunners.

Other than Pudge Rodriguez, Brad Ausmus is the only other catcher to return to the top five in this category from the 1999 season. Ausmus boosted his caught-stealing percentage from 35.2 percent in '99 to 43.2 percent last summer. While Blanco and Matheny played on new teams in 2000, Ausmus makes his move this offseason. In December, he was dealt from Detroit to Houston in a six-player trade that shipped young backstop Mitch Meluskey to the Tigers.

When it comes to stopping the running game, the Astros win out by dealing for Ausmus. Meluskey's caught-stealing percentage in 2000 was below the league average at 22 percent, and he allowed a very high .74 stolen bases per nine innings. Ausmus, on the other hand, ranked second behind I-Rod by giving up just .31 steals per nine.

Now that we've come back to Pudge, look for a healthy Rodriguez to return to the top of the pack in catching basestealers during the 2001 campaign. After all, in the five seasons prior to 2000, his league-leading caught-stealing percentage inched upward each year to a career high 52.8 percent in 1999. He retired more than half of all baserunners attempting to steal against him in the three years prior to last season, and in both '98 and '99, his lead over the second-best catcher at nailing basestealers was more than 14 percentage points.

So, to Henry Blanco, who suffered a rotator cuff injury late in 2000 that remains a concern this spring, we say, "Long live the King."

—Thom Henninger

A more complete listing for this category can be found on page 283.

Who's Best in the Infield Zone?

A year ago, *STATS Baseball Scoreboard* celebrated the New York Mets' infield as one of the best defensive foursomes of all time. The quartet of John Olerud, Edgardo Alfonzo, Rey Ordonez and Robin Ventura committed just 33 errors in all of 1999, the fewest number recorded by a starting infield in the history of the game. Plus, all four ranked among the top five major leaguers at their position in infield zone rating.

That infield unit seemed to be compromised when Olerud signed with Seattle and the Mets countered by inking third baseman-catcher Todd Zeile to play first base. Zeile arrived with a mediocre .983 fielding percentage in 76 career games at first, but he responded with arguably his best defensive performance in 2000 while tackling a new position. Zeile committed just 10 errors last summer—just one more than Olerud made in 1999—and he ranked first among all first basemen in zone rating:

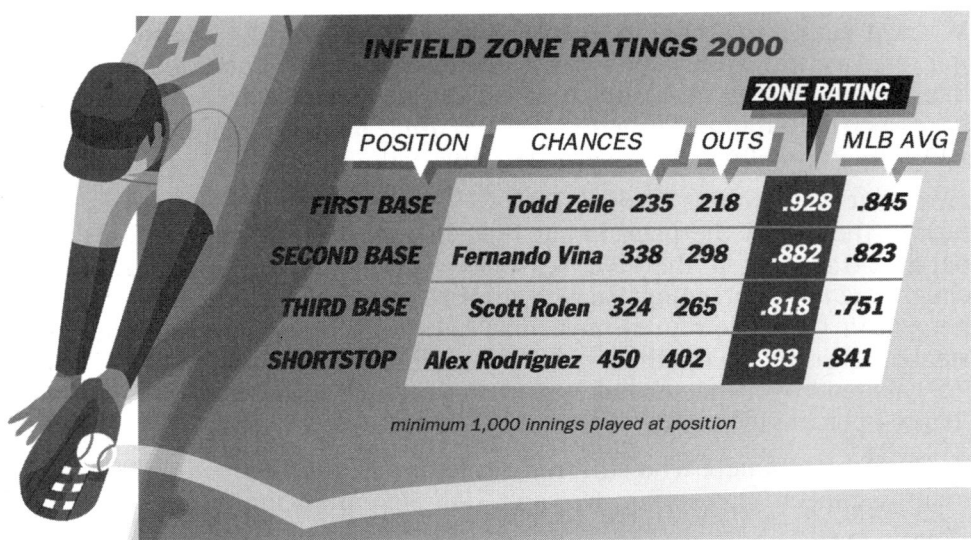

INFIELD ZONE RATINGS 2000

POSITION	CHANCES		OUTS	ZONE RATING	MLB AVG
FIRST BASE	Todd Zeile	235	218	.928	.845
SECOND BASE	Fernando Vina	338	298	.882	.823
THIRD BASE	Scott Rolen	324	265	.818	.751
SHORTSTOP	Alex Rodriguez	450	402	.893	.841

minimum 1,000 innings played at position

By charting the distance and direction of every batted ball, STATS reporters covering major league games document how many groundballs are hit into the designated zone of each defensive player on the field. Each infielder gets a zone rating based on the number of grounders he converts into outs. Popups and flyballs are ignored for infielders. Last February, zone-rating calculations were revamped, with infielders no longer getting credit for two outs when they start a double play. Thus, our new zone ratings are slightly lower than our old ones.

Let's break down the 2000 leaders in zone rating at each position:

Highest Zone Ratings, First Basemen—2000

Player, Team	Rtg
Todd Zeile, NYM	.928
Tino Martinez, NYY	.889
Mark Grace, ChC	.885
Jason Giambi, Oak	.882
John Olerud, Sea	.872
Lowest	
Mo Vaughn, Ana	.774
MLB Average	**.845**

(minimum 1,000 innings)

Tino Martinez, Mark Grace and Olerud return from the 1999 list, with Olerud taking his fine defensive game to Seattle. The real surprise, though, is Zeile. While all four Met infielders ranked among the best in zone rating in '99, Zeile is the *only* Met to make the top five at his position in 2000.

Highest Zone Ratings, Second Basemen—2000

Player, Team	Rtg
Fernando Vina, StL	.882
Pokey Reese, Cin	.874
Luis Castillo, Fla	.849
Mark Grudzielanek, LA	.849
Eric Young, ChC	.849
Lowest	
Jay Bell, Ari	.794
MLB Average	**.823**

(minimum 1,000 innings)

Fernando Vina returned from an injury-riddled 1999 season to have a stellar year defensively. He made just seven errors in 122 games at second, led the National League in fielding percentage and ranked first in the majors in zone rating and double-play conversion. He finished ahead of Pokey Reese in zone rating, who easily was the best in '99 after moving from short to second base. Mark Grudzielanek made the same move in 2000, replacing Eric Young, who moved to the Cubs.

Highest Zone Ratings, Third Basemen—2000

Player, Team	Rtg
Scott Rolen, Phi	.818
Adrian Beltre, LA	.804
Bill Mueller, SF	.792
Corey Koskie, Min	.782
Tony Batista, Tor	.779
Lowest	
Mike Lamb, Tex	.707
MLB Average	**.751**

(minimum 1,000 innings)

Scott Rolen recorded his lowest full-season error total and career-best fielding percentage in 2000, and he took over the top spot in zone rating from Robin Ventura, who ranked first the two previous seasons.

Highest Zone Ratings, Shortstops—2000

Player, Team	Rtg
Alex Rodriguez, Sea	.893
Rey Sanchez, KC	.878
Miguel Tejada, Oak	.867
Nomar Garciaparra, Bos	.862
Royce Clayton, Tex	.858
Lowest	
Desi Relaford, Phi-SD	.789
MLB Average	**.841**

(minimum 1,000 innings)

The broken forearm suffered by Mets shortstop Rey Ordonez in May opened the door to a new top dog. Rey Sanchez finished second in zone rating once again, this time behind Alex Rodriguez.

Here's a look at the leaders over the last three seasons:

Highest Infield Zone Ratings—1998-2000

First Basemen	Rtg
John Olerud	.879
Tino Martinez	.875
Mark Grace	.872
Lee Stevens	.868
Tony Clark	.864

Lowest

Andres Galarraga	.796
MLB Average	**.845**

Second Basemen	Rtg
Pokey Reese	.888
Edgardo Alfonzo	.849
Eric Young	.845
Luis Castillo	.843
Craig Biggio	.842
Lowest	
Todd Walker	.753
MLB Average	**.823**

Third Basemen	Rtg
Scott Rolen	.812
Robin Ventura	.798
Adrian Beltre	.791
Scott Brosius	.783
Bill Mueller	.783
Lowest	
Russ Davis	.672
MLB Average	**.748**

Shortstops	Rtg
Rey Sanchez	.888
Alex Rodriguez	.867
Barry Larkin	.866
Mike Bordick	.866
Orlando Cabrera	.862
Lowest	
Cristian Guzman	.795
MLB Average	**.840**

(minimum 2,000 innings)

Sanchez finally wins out here for his consistency over three seasons. Steady, consistent play is synonymous with most of these guys, many of whom have been among the best at their positions throughout their careers.

—Thom Henninger

A more complete listing for this category can be found on page 284.

Who Can Turn the Pivot?

Fernando Vina, the second baseman for the Cardinals, battled through nagging rib and hamstring injuries last summer. He missed nearly 40 games because of these ailments, but nothing kept him from finishing first in fielding percentage among National League second basemen.

Detroit second sacker Damion Easley suffered through a ribcage injury early in the 2000 season. Then he went down with a hairline fracture of his right wrist in mid-May, and was lost to the Tigers for three weeks. Still, he led all American League second basemen in fielding percentage.

Vina and Easley have more in common than their surehandedness, their injury troubles in 2000 and their league-leading fielding percentages. Both were born in 1969, making them 31 years old heading into the 2001 campaign. And no second baseman in the game last season completed a higher percentage of double-play opportunities than Vina and Easley.

Best Pivot Men—2000

Player, Team	DP	Opp	Pct
Fernando Vina, StL	45	59	.763
Damion Easley, Det	54	71	.761
Luis Castillo, Fla	48	66	.727
Pokey Reese, Cin	50	69	.725
Homer Bush, Tor	44	61	.721
Randy Velarde, Oak	55	78	.705
Jose Vidro, Mon	59	86	.686
Mark Grudzielanek, LA	54	80	.675
Ray Durham, CWS	69	105	.657
Miguel Cairo, TB	45	69	.652
MLB Average			**.615**

(minimum 50 Opp)

STATS defines a double-play opportunity as any situation with a runner on first and less than two outs in which the second baseman records a putout at second base. With a double play on the line, the better pivot men at second will complete the twin killing more than 60 percent of the time.

Vina has been known as one of the game's premier pivot men for a long time. He ranked first in double-play conversion in 1995, '96 and '98, outdistancing his peers by a wide margin in two of those years. He dropped off the radar in '97 and '99 when serious injuries sidelined him.

Easley claimed top honors in double-play conversion in 1997 while Vina was missing half the season with a fractured ankle. Easley has ranked among the top 10 each year since '97.

The list also includes a couple of newcomers. One-time utility man Jose Vidro has settled in well at second base for Montreal, his impressive bat complemented by improved range and a quicker double-play pivot. Mark Grudzielanek has made a smooth transition from shortstop to second with the Dodgers, showing he's able to handle double-play duties from either side of the diamond.

No one on the list, however, has been as consistently solid at the double-play pivot over the last five seasons than Vina and Easley.

Best Pivot Men—1996-2000

Player	DP	Opp	Pct
Fernando Vina	236	324	.728
Damion Easley	238	344	.692
Edgardo Alfonzo	135	205	.659
Randy Velarde	172	269	.639
Luis Castillo	149	233	.639
Ray Durham	305	484	.630
Ron Belliard	113	180	.628
Miguel Cairo	161	257	.626
Mark McLemore	248	411	.603
Jeff Kent	205	341	.601
MLB Average			**.591**

(minimum 180 Opp)

While Vina easily outdistanced the pack in double-play conversion, Ray Durham far exceeded his peers in total double plays the last five seasons. Yet, Durham's *overall* game at second has him under consideration for a move to center field with the White Sox.

Durham clearly has more job security than Miguel Cairo, who, despite his place among the best pivot men in the game, has disappointed the Devil Rays with his work on routine plays and at the plate. The Rays released Cairo, who is just 26. He takes his speed, flash and success at the pivot to Oakland, thanks to a minor league deal, but he's not guaranteed to play.

—Thom Henninger

A more complete listing for this category can be found on page 286.

Which Outfielders Know How to Hold 'Em?

About the only part of Barry Bonds' game that can be dubbed "below average" is his throwing arm. Mentioning Bonds' arm can't help but induce images of Sid Bream plodding around third base and scoring the series-clinching run at the close of the 1992 National League Championship Series. Atlanta's lumbering first baseman slid safely into home just ahead of a weak throw from Bonds in left field.

Amazingly, nearly 10 years later, Bonds ranked first in 2000 among left fielders in lowest percentage of baserunners taking an extra base on him.

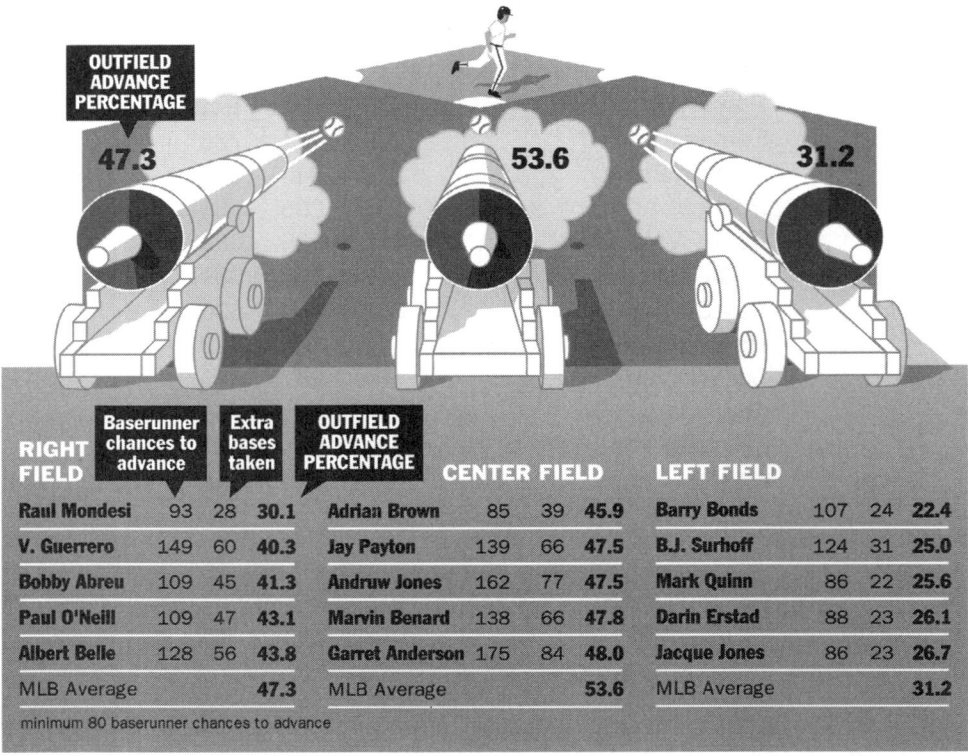

RIGHT FIELD	Baserunner chances to advance	Extra bases taken	OUTFIELD ADVANCE PERCENTAGE	CENTER FIELD				LEFT FIELD			
Raul Mondesi	93	28	30.1	Adrian Brown	85	39	45.9	Barry Bonds	107	24	22.4
V. Guerrero	149	60	40.3	Jay Payton	139	66	47.5	B.J. Surhoff	124	31	25.0
Bobby Abreu	109	45	41.3	Andruw Jones	162	77	47.5	Mark Quinn	86	22	25.6
Paul O'Neill	109	47	43.1	Marvin Benard	138	66	47.8	Darin Erstad	88	23	26.1
Albert Belle	128	56	43.8	Garret Anderson	175	84	48.0	Jacque Jones	86	23	26.7
MLB Average			47.3	MLB Average			53.6	MLB Average			31.2

minimum 80 baserunner chances to advance

Bonds' presence at the top of the left-field list may be a surprise, but the San Francisco outfielder has been one of the game's best defensive players and he's always had an accurate arm. He finished ahead of B.J. Surhoff, who is a perennial leader among left fielders in keeping runners from taking the extra base.

Others who regularly rank among the best in outfield advance percentage include Andruw Jones, Garret Anderson and Raul Mondesi. These guys have reputations for cutting down runners with their strong arms, and baserunners are less likely to test them.

An advance is charged against an outfielder whenever a runner takes an extra base on a ball hit to him. For example, if a batter singles to center with a runner on first base, the center fielder is tagged with an advance if the baserunner moves to third.

Center fielders often have the poorest outfield advance percentages. They cover more ground than the corner outfielders, which means they are more likely to have their arms tested and must throw the longest distances. Conversely, left fielders make some of the shortest throws and usually have the best outfield advance percentages.

The annual leaders in outfield assists aren't always the guys with the best arms, as they are likely to be challenged less often because of their reputations. On the other hand, outfield advance percentage may be more revealing in documenting an outfielder's success against baserunners. It records the real effects as well as the perceived threat of his arm.

To bridge the gap between perceived threat and real results, let's take a look at the leaders in outfield assists during the 2000 season:

Most Outfield Assists—2000

Right Field		Center Field		Left Field	
Dave Martinez, 4 Tms	15	Peter Bergeron, Mon	15	Bobby Higginson, Det	19
Bobby Abreu, Phi	13	Torii Hunter, Min	12	Geoff Jenkins, Mil	12
Mark Kotsay, Fla	13	Carl Everett, Bos	11	Carlos Lee, CWS	10
Jeromy Burnitz, Mil	12	Steve Finley, Ari	10	Darin Erstad, Ana	9
Vladimir Guerrero, Mon	12	Ken Griffey Jr., Cin	10	Troy O'Leary, Bos	9
Magglio Ordonez, CWS	12	Ruben Rivera, SD	10		
Tim Salmon, Ana	12				

Dante Bichette had led all left fielders in assists in 1998 and '99. Like Bichette, Bobby Higginson leads the category in 2000 primarily because of the large number of advances tried against him. Only Shannon Stewart faced more attempts, and Higginson's outfield advance percentage is just a tad better than the league average for left fielders.

Higginson wasn't the only assist leader who lacks a big-time reputation for cutting down runners. Montreal's Peter Bergeron was a rookie, and Dave

Martinez bounced between four teams as a role player. Both ranked well below the league average at their position in outfield advance percentage.

The same is true for Torii Hunter, Geoff Jenkins and Carlos Lee, but they are young and should improve defensively. Hunter is an impressive outfielder with a strong arm, and he should develop a reputation as someone to not take chances against on the bases.

Bobby Abreu is the stud on the previous list. He always ranks among the leaders in outfield advance percentage, yet he still posts impressive assist totals. Vladimir Guerrero has a budding reputation as a gunner. He's finished among right-field assist leaders two years in a row, and he ranked among leaders in outfield advance percentage for the first time in 2000.

So much for the young guns. Let's take a look at the guys who have produced the best outfield advance percentages over the last three seasons:

Highest Outfield Advance Percentages—1998-2000

Right Field		Center Field		Left Field	
Raul Mondesi	36.3	Andruw Jones	42.6	B.J. Surhoff	26.5
Bobby Abreu	36.8	Garret Anderson	47.6	Darin Erstad	26.8
Manny Ramirez	41.4	Chris Singleton	48.7	Greg Vaughn	28.1
Jose Guillen	43.9	Ken Griffey Jr.	49.3	Ron Gant	30.4
Vladimir Guerrero	44.0	Brian L. Hunter	49.6	Barry Bonds	30.5
Worst		**Worst**		**Worst**	
Matt Stairs	56.4	Devon White	60.2	Henry Rodriguez	39.5
MLB Average	**47.4**	**MLB Average**	**54.2**	**MLB Average**	**32.0**

(minimum 200 baserunner chances to advance)

Jones and Surhoff held on to the top spot in the three-year ranking for a second straight season—and now they patrol the same outfield in Atlanta. While the Braves were looking for more firepower offensively when they acquired Surhoff, he also strengthens the club's defense.

The two fielders listed just below Jones and Surhoff make up two-thirds of the Angels' outfield. But the combined throwing prowess of Garret Anderson and Darin Erstad may be broken up in 2001. With Mo Vaughn out indefinitely with an arm injury, Erstad may spend some time at first base. Losing Vaughn not only compromises Anaheim's offensive attack, it may open the door to more running against the Angels' outfielders.

—Thom Henninger

A more complete listing for this category can be found on page 287.

Who's Best in the Outfield Zone?

When Geoff Jenkins arrived in Milwaukee in 1998, the Brewers were anxious to get his bat into the lineup, but his defensive play simply made them anxious. Jenkins was no more than an average outfielder, his defensive game compromised by knee and shoulder surgeries as a minor leaguer.

While it isn't a surprise that Jenkins hit a career-high 34 homers in his third major league season, his emergence as one of the National League's better defensive left fielders is. Jenkins has decent speed and plays aggressively, which allows him to reach an impressive percentage of balls hit in his direction.

As we do with infielders, STATS measures an outfielder's zone rating by comparing the number of outs recorded by a player to the number of balls that are hit into his defensive area. Dividing the outs recorded by the balls hit into an outfielder's zone gives us his zone rating, and zone rating gives us an idea which outfielders cover the most ground. Our zone ratings were revamped a year ago, adding popups to an outfielder's responsibility, increasing his zone for flyballs and decreasing it for liners. The new, improved outfield zone ratings are considerably higher than the ratings we ran prior to the 2000 edition of the *Baseball Scoreboard*.

For those outfielders who played at least 1,000 innings at a particular position in 2000, here are the leaders in zone ratings, beginning with left field:

Highest Zone Ratings, Left Fielders—2000

Player, Team	Rtg
Geoff Jenkins, Mil	.947
Luis Gonzalez, Ari	.902
Bobby Higginson, Det	.901
Barry Bonds, SF	.899
Shannon Stewart, Tor	.898
Lowest	
Carlos Lee, CWS	.820
MLB Average	**.875**

(minimum 1,000 innings)

Shannon Stewart is the only speed demon on the list, which suggests that other defensive assets—from accurate reads and quick jumps to soft hands—are just as critical in the outfield. The others have decent speed, including Jenkins and Luis Gonzalez, who were among last year's zone-rating leaders in left field. Now for the center fielders:

Highest Zone Ratings, Center Fielders—2000

Player, Team	Rtg
Kenny Lofton, Cle	.929
Ken Griffey Jr., Cin	.926
Ruben Rivera, SD	.924
Terrence Long, Oak	.917
Juan Encarnacion, Det	.901
Lowest	
Gerald Williams, TB	.860
MLB Average	**.888**

(minimum 1,000 innings)

The center-field group features more raw speed, and plenty of offensive production as well. Kenny Lofton and Ken Griffey Jr. are top all-around performers, and two 25-year-olds, Terrence Long and Juan Encarnacion, are starting to show that they can excel both at the plate and in the field. Finally, the men who man right:

Highest Zone Ratings, Right Fielders—2000

Player, Team	Rtg
Brian Jordan, Atl	.928
Vladimir Guerrero, Mon	.922
Jermaine Dye, KC	.918
Jeromy Burnitz, Mil	.916
Mark Kotsay, Fla	.911
Lowest	
Magglio Ordonez, CWS	.872
MLB Average	**.894**

(minimum 1,000 innings)

In 2000, Brian Jordan played with a partially torn rotator cuff in his right shoulder and a host of other injuries involving his left shoulder, ribcage, left elbow, right knee, both ankles and groin. Consequently, his offensive numbers were down a bit from 1999, but he repeated as the everyday right fielder with the best zone rating in the major leagues.

If Jordan ranked first in right-field zone rating while enduring his most injury-riddled summer, it should come as no surprise that he also ranks first among right fielders over the last three seasons.

Highest Outfield Zone Ratings—1998-2000

Left Fielders	Rtg
Darin Erstad	.945
Geoff Jenkins	.932
Ron Gant	.918
Luis Gonzalez	.895
Greg Vaughn	.894
Lowest	
Dante Bichette	.789
MLB Average	**.874**

Center Fielders	Rtg
Ruben Rivera	.914
Carlos Beltran	.909
Kenny Lofton	.905
Mike Cameron	.904
Andruw Jones	.902
Lowest	
Marvin Benard	.846
MLB Average	**.884**

Right Fielders	Rtg
Brian Jordan	.917
Jermaine Dye	.913
Jeromy Burnitz	.908
Paul O'Neill	.906
Raul Mondesi	.904
Lowest	
Albert Belle	.805
MLB Average	**.882**

(minimum 2,000 innings)

Jenkins isn't the only young player who has emerged both offensively and defensively. Darin Erstad, Jermaine Dye, Andruw Jones and Mike Cameron all produce at the plate and cover lots of ground in the outfield. While the Padres have been waiting patiently for Ruben Rivera's bat to come around for the last three seasons—which might put him in the same class as Dye or Cameron—at least the San Diego center fielder has managed to rank first in zone rating over all of his major league peers.

—Thom Henninger

A more complete listing for this category can be found on page 288.

Which Fielders Have the Best Defensive Batting Averages?

Defense is no doubt one of the toughest aspects of the game to evaluate. We can isolate parts of a player's defensive skills, but it's no easy task putting a number on the whole package. That's where Defensive Batting Average comes in. Created by STATS founder John Dewan, DBA combines several defensive measures into one single number that is similar to a regular batting average. The formula uses standard deviations of a variety of defensive statistics, including zone rating, fielding percentage, pivot percentage and outfield advance percentage.

DBA Statistics and Weighting

Pos	Statistics (Weighting)
1B	Zone Rating (75%), Fielding Percentage (25%)
2B	Zone Rating (60%), Pivot Pct. (25%), Fielding Pct. (15%)
3B	Zone Rating (60%), Fielding Percentage (40%)
SS	Zone Rating (80%), Fielding Percentage (20%)
LF	Zone Rating (65%), OF Advance Pct. (20%), Fielding Pct. (15%)
CF	Zone Rating (55%), OF Advance Pct. (30%), Fielding Pct. (15%)
RF	Zone Rating (50%), OF Advance Pct. (35%), Fielding Pct. (15%)

Let's examine each position and list the five best and single worst defensive batting averages from 2000 (minimum 1,000 innings at a position):

Highest Defensive Batting Averages, First Basemen—2000

Player, Team	Zone	FPct	DBA
Todd Zeile, NYM	.348	.271	.329
Mark Grace, ChC	.312	.315	.313
Tino Martinez, NYY	.315	.292	.310
Jason Giambi, Oak	.309	.299	.306
John Olerud, Sea	.301	.313	.304
Lowest			
Mo Vaughn, Ana	.217	.243	.223

(minimum 1,000 innings)

With the possible exception of catcher, first base probably is the most difficult position to pin down. We have yet to devise a way to track how many hits a good first sacker robs each season by digging throws out of the dirt. While it's tough to make a case for Todd Zeile as the best glove man at this position, the numbers show that he got to many more balls in his zone than his counterparts. As for big Mo Vaughn, he exhibited little range and also made 14 errors, tied for second most at the position.

Highest Defensive Batting Averages, Second Basemen—2000

Player, Team	Zone	Pivot	FPct	DBA
Fernando Vina, StL	.335	.334	.314	.332
Pokey Reese, Cin	.329	.320	.274	.318
Luis Castillo, Fla	.307	.321	.290	.308
Mark Grudzielanek, LA	.307	.302	.257	.298
Mickey Morandini, Phi-Tor	.305	.269	.316	.298
Lowest				
Warren Morris, Pit	.266	.230	.270	.258

(minimum 1,000 innings)

Fernando Vina has been an underrated second baseman for years, and he made just seven errors in 2000. Pokey Reese, last year's DBA leader at second, has so much range that he functions as a second shortstop for the Reds. Farther down the list was nine-time Gold Glove winner Roberto Alomar (.270), while at the bottom were Todd Walker (.220) and Chuck Knoblauch (.225)—two Tom Kelly exiles—though neither logged 1,000 innings at the keystone. If Warren Morris does not pick it up with the glove and the bat next season, he may be facing exile as well.

Highest Defensive Batting Averages, Third Basemen—2000

Player, Team	Zone	FPct	DBA
Scott Rolen, Phi	.331	.312	.323
Bill Mueller, SF	.309	.317	.312
Corey Koskie, Min	.300	.303	.301
Adrian Beltre, LA	.319	.268	.299
Tony Batista, Tor	.297	.298	.298
Lowest			
Mike Lamb, Tex	.235	.218	.228

(minimum 1,000 innings)

It's hard to argue with any of these names. Scott Rolen can flat-out pick it, and he should get even better now that Philadelphia has replaced the ConcreteTurf. Adrian Beltre made 23 errors last season, but he covers a lot of ground and won't turn 22 until just after Opening Day. On the other end, it was hard for anyone to compete with Mike Lamb's 33 errors.

Highest Defensive Batting Averages, Shortstops—2000

Player, Team	Zone	FPct	DBA
Alex Rodriguez, Sea	.344	.318	.339
Rey Sanchez, KC	.325	.338	.328
Miguel Tejada, Oak	.311	.286	.306
Nomar Garciaparra, Bos	.305	.284	.301
Royce Clayton, Tex	.301	.297	.300
Lowest			
Desi Relaford, Phi-SD	.216	.217	.216

(minimum 1,000 innings)

The concept of DBA seems to work very well at the skill positions, and there are some smooth operators at the top of the list of shortstops. Alex Rodriguez led all qualifiers in 2000; if this kid ever learns to hit, he might just make it in the big leagues. A-Rod actually placed second behind another lesser-known Alex, Cora of the Dodgers (.340), but Cora played just 828.1 innings at short. Desi Relaford hit .215 and fielded .216 last year, making him the classic bad-glove, no-stick infielder.

Highest Defensive Batting Averages, Left Fielders—2000

Player, Team	Zone	Adv	FPct	DBA
Geoff Jenkins, Mil	.344	.265	.264	.316
Barry Bonds, SF	.302	.340	.300	.309
Luis Gonzalez, Ari	.304	.299	.303	.303
Shannon Stewart, Tor	.301	.269	.312	.296
B.J. Surhoff, Bal-Atl	.284	.323	.302	.294
Lowest				
Carlos Lee, CWS	.232	.256	.302	.247

(minimum 1,000 innings)

It gets a little tricky in the outfield. Darin Erstad (.336) is head-and-shoulders above everyone else listed here. In fact, he is so good that he played enough center field to keep his innings down in left. Last year's second-place finisher, Geoff Jenkins, is willing to sacrifice his body to get to a lot of balls. Barry Bonds won eight Gold Gloves in the '90s, and when he comes to play, he's as good as anyone out there. There is little argument about Carlos Lee's lack of defensive prowess, but he was ahead of Cliff Floyd (.215), who was injured last season and did not log enough innings.

Highest Defensive Batting Averages, Center Fielders—2000

Player, Team	Zone	Adv	FPct	DBA
Kenny Lofton, Cle	.340	.276	.290	.313
Ruben Rivera, SD	.333	.284	.271	.309
Ken Griffey Jr., Cin	.336	.253	.283	.303
Andruw Jones, Atl	.272	.333	.319	.297
Richard Hidalgo, Hou	.294	.306	.276	.294
Lowest				
Gerald Williams, TB	.238	.223	.267	.238

(minimum 1,000 innings)

Ken Griffey Jr., Kenny Lofton and Andruw Jones own 17 Gold Gloves between them. Johnny Damon (.318) actually had a higher DBA than anyone in center, but he split his time between center and left. Gerald Williams was quite a bit behind the next-lowest qualifier, and it probably is a stretch to ask him to play this position full-time at this point in his career.

Highest Defensive Batting Averages, Right Fielders—2000

Player, Team	Zone	Adv	FPct	DBA
Bobby Abreu, Phi	.297	.308	.299	.301
Vladimir Guerrero, Mon	.307	.308	.242	.298
Brian Jordan, Atl	.313	.272	.303	.297
Jermaine Dye, KC	.304	.294	.263	.295
Paul O'Neill, NYY	.282	.303	.312	.294
Lowest				
Sammy Sosa, ChC	.294	.227	.244	.263

(minimum 1,000 innings)

Bobby Abreu tops the right-field list for the second straight year, but he was behind a few guys who did not garner enough playing time. J.D. Drew was tops (.319) and Raul Mondesi (.311) was not far back. Only 12 players managed to post 1,000-plus innings in right. Still, the position is well represented. While his defense has been maligned over the last couple of years, Sammy Sosa ended up at the bottom almost by default. Albert Belle had the lowest DBA of all right fielders (.247), but his degenerative hip kept him on the bench for much of the second half of the season.

—Don Hartack

A more complete listing for this category can be found on page 289.

V. GENERAL QUESTIONS

What's Been the Role of Parks in Increasing Offense in the Years 1990-2000?

Wow. Well, I guess that's why you do research. . .

In 1990 the average major league team scored 689 runs. In 2000, after a decade of almost constant increases in offense, the average was 832 runs. Why?

Obviously, the parks play some role in the increase. I wrote many years ago that the primary factor in shaping how baseball is played in any generation is the parks in which it is played. Throughout the '90s, I have continued to believe and I have continued to say that this was true—that most of the increase in scoring was attributable to the parks. When Colorado came into the league, I argued, this added a few points to the batting average of every hitter in the league. Look at the other recent parks—the new park in Texas, Jacobs Field in Cleveland, the BOB in Arizona, Camden Yards, Enron Field. . . all of these are adding runs to the league. Even the parks which are the same, I would say, often have been remodeled to increase offense, like Royals Stadium and Busch Stadium. If you look at runs scored in the parks which haven't changed, they've increased somewhat, but not all that much.

This argument was based on piecemeal and sometimes subjective analysis of the park changes. For this year's *Scoreboard*, I decided to do a systematic study of the issue, attempting to pin down exactly how much of the increase in offense was attributable to parks. In all candor, I was going to use this to advance the argument that I had been making all along, to "demonstrate" that this was true. I was going to do this by studying each park change, and estimating as accurately as I could how many runs each specific change had added to the league. I was confident that, when I did this, the runs added to the league by park changes would account for 70 or 80% of the overall increase.

Well, guess what. I was wrong. I was dead wrong; I was completely wrong. Not to put too fine a point on it, I didn't know what the hell I was talking about. Let's start with Coors Field. . . how many runs did the addition of Coors Field in 1995 add to the National League?

Since I am contrasting here the 1990 season to the 2000 season, Mile High Stadium has nothing to do with the issue, and I am going to ignore the fact that it ever existed. The Rockies in 1995 scored and allowed 975 runs at home in 1995, whereas they scored and allowed only 593 runs on the road. We could estimate, then, that the characteristics of Coors Field had added

382 runs to the league—975, minus the 593 the Rockies could have been expected to score and allow in a park and at an altitude which was like the rest of the league.

This first estimate fails to consider at least two factors. It is better to look at multiyear data, rather than one-year data. The 1995 season was strike-shortened to 144 games, rather than the normal 162. Looking at the multi-year data, I get a raw park factor for Coors Field of 1.567, meaning a 57% increase in runs scored per game in that park. Since the National League average at that time was about 728 runs per team per season, my estimate is that the addition of Coors Field added about 413 runs to the NL.

OK, so let's enter Coors Field at +413. The overall increase in runs scored in the major leagues between the years 1990 and 2000 was about 4,295 runs (143 runs per team, times 30 teams). Coors Field, by itself, accounts for about 10% of that increase.

In 1990 the Houston Astros played in the Astrodome, one of the best pitchers' parks of all time. The raw Park Factor for the Astrodome, based on data from 1999 and immediately previous seasons, was about .8977. In 2000 they moved to Enron Field, which was quickly nicknamed 10-run field. The Park Factor for Enron, based on one year's data, appears to be about 1.1460. Since the National League average is about 810 runs per season and there is a park differential of .2483, we can estimate that the addition of Enron Field to the National League, in place of the Astrodome, added about 201 runs to the league.

When we begin to look at all of the park changes systematically, however, the picture begins to shift. Now, I should say this: there are judgment calls that have to be made interpreting the data. These are not perfect estimates. The data is never entirely clean, and the "before" and "after" situations which must be contrasted to estimate the effects of the park are never perfectly parallel; there are always other factors which should be considered, but cannot. These estimates are based on three components: a "before" park estimate, an "after" park estimate, and a "context", and it is never 100% clear which number should be used for any of these components.

Second, I did tend to be conservative in making any judgment calls, because I did not want to prejudice the data toward my thesis, which was that the parks were largely responsible for the changes in levels of run scoring. In so doing, I may, at times, have slightly prejudiced the data against that conclusion, and thus underestimated the impact of parks in changing offense. The impact could be very slightly larger than I have estimated it to be.

Still, let's list the cases. In 1992 the Baltimore Orioles moved from Memorial Stadium, a pitchers' park, to Camden Yards. This added about 69 runs to the American League. I will list this in the chart below as:

1992 Camden Yards in Baltimore   +69

These are the 18 park changes which have occurred in the major leagues over the span of 1990 to 2000:

Major League Park Changes—1990-2000	
1991 New Comiskey in Chicago	-14
1992 Camden Yards in Baltimore	+69
1994 The Ballpark in Arlington	+13
1994 Jacobs Field in Cleveland	-27
1994 Pro Player Stadium (Fla) remodeled	-44
1995 Kauffman in KC remodeled	+9
1995 Coors Field	+413
1996 Busch Stadium in St.L (remodeled)	+5
1996 Qualcomm Stadium in SD (remodeled)	-52
1996 Oakland Coliseum remodeled	+143
1997 Turner Field in Atlanta	-104
1998 Edison (remodeling) in Anaheim	-13
1998 Tropicana in Tampa Bay	+24
1998 BankOne Ballpark in Arizona	+1
1999 Safeco in Seattle	-125
2000 Enron Field in Houston	+201
2000 Pac Bell Park in San Francisco	-41
2000 Comerica Park in Detroit	-77
Total	**+381**

All of the park changes in the major leagues in the last 10 years have added about 381 runs per season to the major leagues. Coors Field by itself has added 413 runs, but the other 17 changes are, on balance, neutral, having subtracted about 32 runs from each major league season.

Thus, of the 4,295-run increase between the 1990 and 2000 seasons, only about 381 runs, or 9%, can be confidently attributed to changes in parks. The actual figure could be slightly higher if less conservative estimates were used.

Some of the new parks, particularly Jacobs Field and the Ballpark in Arlington, are perceived as hitters' parks—not because they are hitters' parks, but because... well, it seems like lots of runs are scored there. But lots of runs are scored there because that's the way baseball is played in the modern era: there are lots of runs.

This conclusion also can be reached by looking at the remaining data, the runs scored in the 12 parks which have not been substantially changed in the last 10 years, except that the names may have been changed to promote the guilty. Those 12 parks are:

> Fenway Park in Boston
> Yankee Stadium in New York
> The Metrodome in Minnesota
> The Skydome in Toronto
>
> County Stadium in Milwaukee
> Wrigley Field in Chicago
> Cinergy Field (Riverfront) in Cincinnati
> Shea Stadium in New York
>
> Olympic Stadium in Montreal
> Veterans Stadium in Philadelphia
> Three Rivers Stadium in Pittsburgh
> Dodger Stadium in Los Angeles

More runs were scored in the year 2000 than in 1990 in every one of these parks except Wrigley Field, where there was an 8% decline. But overall, there was a 16% increase in runs scored in these 12 parks which were (essentially) unchanged during the 1990s. The overall increase in runs scored in the years 1990-2000 was 21%; in the parks which haven't changed substantially, the increase was 16%. While one could interpret this data to attribute as much as 26% of the increase in offense to park changes, this nonetheless makes it very clear that it has not been stadium architecture which has been driving the changes in baseball over the last 10 years.

—Bill James

Is It Easier to Win in a Pitchers' Park?

Alex Rodriguez started the argument. Last fall, when he still was talking to the Mariners about re-signing, A-Rod suggested on his official website that the M's should move in the fences at Safeco Field. Mariners general manager Pat Gillick was quick to respond. "No, we want to win," said Gillick. "One player does not dictate policy." Peter Gammons quickly joined the fray. Writing that "Gillick understands the price of a World Series ring," Gammons added that "Gillick and the Mariners aren't moving in the fences because they know that pitching wins, and it's a lot easier to develop pitching in a pitchers' park." For a few weeks, at least, A-Rod was labeled a selfish ballplayer, a guy who'd rather pad his stats in a hitters' park than play in a stadium more conducive to winning.

But are Gillick and Gammons correct in saying that it's easier to win in a pitchers' park? Let's look at some data, using the park indexes compiled annually in the *STATS Major League Handbook*. The full definition of the term is in the glossary, but all you really need to know for the purposes of this essay is that a park index of 100 equals a neutral park, one that favors neither pitchers nor hitters. The more over 100 the index, the more it's conducive to offense, while an index well under 100 indicates a park that favors the pitcher.

The first thing to get out of the way is that A-Rod is right about Safeco Field: based on the average number of runs scored per game since the park opened in midseason of 1999, Safeco ranked as the best pitchers' park in the American League for the 1998-2000 period with an index of 84.

Five of the other seven teams that made the playoffs last year had park indexes of 95 or lower for the period from '98 through 2000 (when applicable). Pac Bell Park in San Francisco matched Seattle's index of 84, Network Associates Coliseum in Oakland had an index of 88, the Mets' Shea Stadium came in with a 92, Yankee Stadium had a 93 and Atlanta's Turner Field had an index of 94. Meanwhile only one playoff team played in a park with an index of 105 or higher: the Cardinals, whose Busch Stadium had an index of exactly 105.

That sounds like a ringing endorsement for the Gillick/Gammons point of view, but was the 2000 data typical? Let's go back to the major league expansion of 1961 and define a pitchers' park as one with a park index for runs scored of 95 or under. If a park had an index of 105 or higher, we'll consider it a hitters' park. All other parks would be considered neutral, ones favoring neither the hitter nor the pitcher.

Let's first look at all teams during that span. Here is the overall won-lost percentages by each group of parks:

Won-Lost Records by Park Type—1961-2000

Park Type	W	L	Pct
Pitchers'	28,200	27,369	.507
Neutral	24,629	24,120	.505
Hitters'	25,986	27,326	.487

Teams playing in pitchers' parks had the best overall winning percentage. They didn't have a significant edge over teams playing in neutral parks, but there appeared to be a significant *disadvantage* to playing in a park that favors hitting. Looking at the winning percentages of the three groups in each of the 40 seasons from 1961-2000, we find that teams playing in pitchers' parks had the best overall won-lost percentages in 20 seasons, compared to 14 seasons for teams playing in neutral parks and only six seasons for teams that played in hitters' parks. Gillick and Gammons seem to be onto something here.

These differences are more extreme if we only go back to 1993, when the current era of big hitting really began. In the eight seasons from 1993-2000, teams playing in pitchers' parks posted a won-lost percentage of .516 (6,419-6,019), compared with a .494 (6,231-6,391) winning percentage for teams playing in neutral parks and a .488 (5,050-5,290) percentage for teams that played in hitters' parks. In seven of the eight seasons since 1993, the pitchers' park group has posted the best winning percentage.

That's looking at teams overall—but how about the teams that actually finished first? Since 1961, there have been a total of 158 first-place teams (we'll leave out the 12 wild-card teams from 1995-2000 for simplicity's sake). Here's how those clubs sorted out by park index:

First-Place Teams by Park Type—1961-2000

Park Type	No. of Teams	Pct of Total
Pitchers'	66	41.8
Neutral	55	34.8
Hitters'	37	23.4

More than 40 percent of the first-place teams played in parks that favored pitchers, while only 23 percent played in hitters' parks. If you go further and define an extreme hitters' park as one with an index of 110 or higher

Baseball Scoreboard

and an extreme pitchers' park as one with an index of 90 or lower, we find that only 20 of the 158 first-place clubs played in extreme hitters' parks, while 40—twice as many as the extreme hitters' park group and one-fourth of the total number of first-place clubs—played their home games in extreme pitchers' parks.

These differences hold up if we confine the study to the most recent period of major league history (1993-2000). Over those eight seasons, 18 of the 46 first-place teams (39.1 percent) played in pitchers' parks, compared to 16 teams (34.8) in neutral parks and 12 teams (26.1) in hitters' parks. Only four of the 46 teams played in parks with an index of 110 or higher (the extreme hitters' parks), compared to 12 teams which played in parks with an index of 90 or lower (the extreme pitchers' park).

Overall, it's hard to avoid the conclusion that if winning is the goal, there's some advantage to playing in a pitchers' park, and a definite disadvantage to playing in a hitters' park. Why would this be so? Bill James once speculated that teams playing in extreme hitters' parks have more difficulty developing teamwork, since they don't have as much need to piece together a string of singles, walks, sacrifices, etc., in order to produce a run.

Another factor might be that teams playing in hitters' parks tend to overrate their own hitters, who often are nothing special when forced to play on the road. Gammons' take is that "it's a lot easier to win in a big park; ask Oakland. It's a lot easier to lose in a hitters' park; ask the Orioles or Astros." Peter is dead-wrong here about the Orioles, who play in a park that has favored the pitcher in recent years. But we get his point.

As for A-Rod, he's moving from the best *pitchers'* park in the American League, Safeco Field, to The Ballpark in Arlington, the AL's best *hitters'* park for 1998-2000 with a runs per game index of 112. Since 1961, only 15 of the 158 first-place clubs have had a park index of 112 or higher. In the last 20 years, only one team with a runs scored index of 110 or higher has won a World Series: the 1988 Dodgers. And that index probably was a fluke, as Dodger Stadium usually favors pitchers. All in all, playing in The Ballpark at Arlington figures to help pad A-Rod's stats. But if he wants to win, he probably made the wrong career move.

—Don Zminda

A more complete listing for this category can be found on page 291.

Was Getting Swept a Bad Omen For the White Sox?

For White Sox fans used to playing second fiddle to the Cubs, the 2000 regular season was the best of times: an exciting young club came out of nowhere to win the Central Division title with 95 victories, most in the American League. But in the postseason, it was the worst of times: the Sox were swept by the Mariners in the Division Series, three games to none. By the time that series ended with a frustrating 2-1 loss at Safeco Field on October 6, Sox fans weren't quite sure *how* to feel. Should they be happy about their young team's performance during the regular season, or apprehensive over whether the club would be able to recover from its postseason debacle?

A check of the history books revealed that only 14 other teams since 1900 have posted the best record in their respective league during the regular season, only to fail to win a postseason game. Here's the list of teams, along with their won-lost records the year following the postseason sweep:

League's Best Record, Then Swept in First Round of Postseason—1900-2000

Team	Lg	Year	Record	Pct	Next Yr	Pct
Tigers	AL	1907	92-58	.613	90-63	.588
Athletics	AL	1914	99-53	.651	43-109	.283
Yankees	AL	1922	94-60	.610	98-54	.645
Pirates	NL	1927	94-60	.610	85-67	.559
Cardinals	NL	1928	95-59	.617	78-74	.513
Cubs	NL	1932	90-64	.584	86-68	.558
Cubs	NL	1938	89-63	.586	84-70	.545
Reds	NL	1939	97-57	.630	100-53	.654
Phillies	NL	1950	91-63	.591	73-81	.474
Indians	AL	1954	111-43	.721	93-61	.604
Yankees	AL	1963	104-57	.646	99-63	.611
Dodgers	NL	1966	95-67	.586	73-89	.451
Athletics	AL	1975	98-64	.605	87-74	.540
Yankees	AL	1980	103-59	.636	59-48	.551
White Sox	**AL**	**2000**	**95-67**	**.586**	—	—
Totals			1,447-894	.618	1,148-974	.541

(1904 and 1994 excluded)

Two of these teams weren't actually swept in the postseason. The 1907 Tigers and 1922 Yankees each played a World Series game that ended in a tie. But since neither team *won* a postseason game, we thought it made sense to include them. Overall, the clubs suffered a pretty substantial decline in the season following the sweep, with their cumulative winning percentage dropping from .618 (about 100 wins in a 162-game schedule) to .541 (approximately 88 victories).

However, one of the teams was the 1914 Philadelphia Athletics, who were dismantled by Connie Mack after the '14 season because competition from the new Federal League resulted in a bidding war for top players. Rather than try to compete with the Feds, Mack sold or traded off most of his stars, and the A's plunged to last place in 1915 with 109 losses. Eliminate the A's from the study, and the overall winning percentage drops from .616 to .561, only about nine fewer wins over 162 games. Since the normal statistical pattern for teams with winning records is to regress toward .500 in the following season, there's no real evidence that these teams were suffering any major ill effects from the sweep.

In fact, five of the 14 teams returned to postseason play the very next year: the 1907 Tigers, 1922 Yankees, 1939 Reds, 1963 Yankees and 1980 Yankees. Two of them, the 1923 Yanks and 1940 Reds, won the World Series the year after being swept. Two more teams barely missed returning to the postseason—the Indians finished only three games behind the pennant-winning Yankees in 1955, and the Oakland A's of 1976 missed repeating as division champs by only two-and-a-half games.

Apart from the 1915 A's, two teams posted losing records the year after getting swept: the 1951 Phillies and 1967 Dodgers. The Dodgers easily are explainable, as Sandy Koufax' retirement following the '66 season sent the team into temporary decline. The '51 Phillies appeared to show some effects from getting swept by the Yankees in the 1950 World Series, as they dropped from 91 victories to 73. In truth, the Phils were a bit lucky to even have reached the Series in '50, as they barely held off the Dodgers at the wire. The Phils had some good players, but they hardly were in Brooklyn's class, and their 1950 pennant probably can be considered a fluke.

All in all, getting swept in the postseason does not seem like any sort of dark omen for the future of the White Sox. The club had to feel let down by the sweep after posting a great record during the regular season, but when it was over, the Sox rolled up their sleeves and spent the winter trying to get better. They're hoping that if they make it to the playoffs again this year, the addition of David Wells (8-1 lifetime postseason record) will help make them, at the very least, "sweep-proof." It figures to be another interesting season on the South Side of Chicago.

—Don Zminda

Which Teams Were 2000's Biggest Overachievers And Underachievers?

It's no secret that scoring and preventing runs correlates directly to winning. Years ago, Bill James developed what he called the Pythagorean theorem, that a team's winning percentage usually parallels the square of its runs scored, divided by the sum of the squares of its runs and its opponents' runs.

The Diamondbacks were a perfect example—and we do mean perfect—last season. Arizona scored 792 runs and allowed 754, which projects to a .525 winning percentage. That's exactly what the Diamondbacks achieved.

Not every club got what it deserved. For example, the Astros didn't catch many breaks last year. Craig Biggio, Shane Reynolds and Billy Wagner went down with the first major injuries of their careers. Ken Caminiti got hurt yet again and Jose Lima had an allergic reaction to Enron Field. Under those conditions, it wasn't surprising that Houston's streaks of three straight National League Central titles and eight consecutive .500 seasons ended.

But the club's run differential of 938-944 theoretically should have produced a .497 winning percentage. Instead the Astros went 72-90 (.444), thanks in large part to a fluky 15-31 record in one-run games, the worst such mark in the majors. They finished with 8.5 fewer wins than their Pythagorean projection, making them the unluckiest club in the game in 2000.

Unluckiest Teams—2000

Team	W-L	Pct	Pythag W	Pythag Pct	+/-
Astros	72-90	.444	80.5	.497	-8.5
Rockies	82-80	.506	87.2	.538	-5.2
Phillies	65-97	.401	68.2	.421	-3.2
Indians	90-72	.556	93.2	.575	-3.2
Pirates	69-93	.426	71.9	.444	-2.9

As badly as Houston underperformed, Cleveland has every right to be more disappointed. Though the Indians' Pythagorean winning percentage of .5754 edged the Mariners' mark of .5748 for fourth-best in the American League, Seattle beat out Cleveland for the wild-card berth by one game.

A similar situation existed with the National League wild-card race. The Dodgers ranked fourth in Pythagorean winning percentage at .5451, just

Baseball Scoreboard

ahead of the Mets at .5446. But while Los Angeles won 2.3 fewer games than expected, New York overperformed by 5.8 wins to grab the wild-card and eventually reached the World Series. Only the Blue Jays were luckier last season.

Luckiest Teams—2000

Team	W-L	Pct	Pythag W	Pythag Pct	+/-
Blue Jays	83-79	.512	76.7	.473	6.3
Mets	94-68	.580	88.2	.545	5.8
Marlins	79-82	.491	73.6	.457	5.4
Orioles	74-88	.457	69.8	.431	4.2
Braves	95-67	.586	91.2	.563	3.8

When he created the Pythagorean formula, James also discovered that teams that diverge significantly from their expected winning percentage did so mostly by chance. Those clubs didn't continue to overachieve and underachieve in future seasons, which is good news for the Astros and bad news for the Blue Jays.

However, there are exceptions. The Phillies have appeared on the unlucky list for two straight seasons, which contributed to the firing of manager Terry Francona. The Braves have shown up on the lucky list the last two years, though they would have made the playoffs without the good fortune both times. Atlanta is proof that while it may be better to be good than it is to be lucky, it's best to be both.

—Jim Callis

A more complete listing for this category can be found on page 292.

Have Hall of Fame Standards For Pitchers Gotten Too Strict?

The baseball writers have cast their Hall of Fame ballots for 2001, and it was another frustrating election year for Tommy John, Bert Blyleven and Jim Kaat. John (288 lifetime victories) and Blyleven (287) are the winningest pitchers not yet elected to the Hall, with Kaat (283 wins) ranking next among 20th century pitchers.

None of them are making much progress toward election to the Hall, either. In the voting for 2001, John was listed on only 28 percent of the ballots, Kaat on 27 percent and Blyleven 24 percent—far short of the 75 percent needed for election. None of the three ever has received more than 30 percent of the vote in any election. Have the Hall of Fame voters changed their standards for electing pitchers? Are John and company being held to unreasonable standards that weren't applied to pitchers of the past?

Let's look at the 25 pitchers who did the bulk of their work after 1920, and who also won more than 250 games in their major league careers. We'll divide them into three groups: those with 300 or more wins, those with 270-299 wins and those with 251-269 wins. For each group we'll list their career won-lost record and ERA, the number of Cy Young and MVP Awards they won, their total of 20-win seasons, the number of strikeout and ERA titles they won, and how many years they spent on the Hall of Fame ballot before being elected by the writers—if they did. A few pitchers on the list were named to the Hall of Fame by the Veterans Committee, and of course John and company still are waiting.

Since the Cy Young Award didn't begin until 1956, and since there was only one award for both leagues for a number of years thereafter, we are including the retroactive Cy Young Awards that were listed in the *STATS All-Time Baseball Sourcebook*. If a pitcher won both the MVP and Cy Young Award in the same year, he gets double credit. The idea is to highlight pitchers who truly were dominant during their prime.

At any rate, here are the 300-game winners:

Pitchers With 300 or More Victories

Pitcher	W-L	ERA	Cy/MVP	20	SO	ERA	Elected
Warren Spahn	363-245	3.09	5	13	4	3	1st Yr
Steve Carlton	329-244	3.22	4	6	5	1	1st Yr
Nolan Ryan	324-292	3.19	0	2	11	2	1st Yr
Don Sutton	324-256	3.26	0	1	0	1	5th Yr
Phil Niekro	318-274	3.35	0	3	1	1	5th Yr

Pitcher	W-L	ERA	Cy/MVP	20	SO	ERA	Elected
Gaylord Perry	314-265	3.11	2	5	0	0	3rd Yr
Tom Seaver	311-205	2.86	3	5	5	3	1st Yr
Lefty Grove	300-141	3.06	8	8	7	9	4th Yr
Early Wynn	300-244	3.54	1	5	2	1	4th Yr

Every 300-game winner to date has been elected to the Hall of Fame. But the road was easier for some than others. Warren Spahn, Steve Carlton, Nolan Ryan and Tom Seaver sailed in the first year they were eligible; others needed as many as five tries. While it may seem like a recent development for the voters to hesitate before deciding a 300-game winner was worthy of the Hall of Fame, it really isn't.

As absurd as it might seem, Lefty Grove was on the ballot four times before he finally won Hall of Fame election. Early Wynn also needed four elections before he finally was selected in 1972. The Grove case had more to do with Hall of Fame politics than anything, but Wynn had the same problem that later delayed the election of Gaylord Perry, Phil Niekro and Don Sutton: many voters did not consider them dominant pitchers during their heyday. The lack of "black ink"—awards and league-leading performances—was particularly a problem for Sutton and Niekro.

Pitchers With 270-299 Victories

Pitcher	W-L	ERA	Cy/MVP	20	SO	ERA	Elected
Tommy John	288-231	3.34	0	3	0	0	—
Bert Blyleven	287-250	3.31	0	1	1	0	—
Robin Roberts	286-245	3.41	2	6	2	0	4th Yr
Fergie Jenkins	284-226	3.34	1	7	1	0	3rd Yr
Jim Kaat	283-237	3.45	1	3	0	0	—
Red Ruffing	273-225	3.80	1	4	1	0	15th Yr
Burleigh Grimes	270-212	3.53	1	5	1	0	Vets

Call this the John/Blyleven/Kaat group. We gave Jim Kaat a retroactive Cy Young Award for 1966, as there was only one award for both leagues back then. Had there been a real award back then, it might have helped his Hall of Fame candidacy a little. But he'd probably still have a tough time getting in.

Of the four pitchers in this group who eventually made the Hall of Fame, none had a particularly easy time. Fergie Jenkins, who showed plenty of dominance with seven 20-win seasons along with a Cy Young Award, needed three seasons to win election. Robin Roberts, a six-time 20-game winner and the dominant pitcher in the National League from 1950-55 (we felt he would have won the Cy Young Award in 1952 and 1955), didn't make it until his fourth year of eligibility. Red Ruffing, a major star for the Yankees in the 1930s and a 273-game winner despite pitching for a number of seasons with miserable Boston Red Sox teams, made the Hall of Fame in his 15th and final try on the writers' ballot. Burleigh Grimes, the last legal spitballer and a five-time 20-game winner, never got more than 34 percent of the vote in the writers' balloting; he was named to the Hall by the Veterans Committee.

The lesson? The problems of John, Blyleven and Kaat are nothing new. Since their peak seasons lack the dominance shown by Roberts and Jenkins, they may never get in unless it's through the Veterans Committee.

Pitchers With 250-269 Victories

Pitcher	W-L	ERA	Cy/MVP	20	SO	ERA	Elected
Jim Palmer	268-152	2.86	3	8	0	2	1st Yr
Bob Feller	266-162	3.25	4	6	7	1	1st Yr
Eppa Rixey	266-251	3.15	1	4	0	0	Vets
Roger Clemens*	260-142	3.07	6	5	5	6	—
Ted Lyons	260-230	3.67	0	3	0	1	10th Yr
Red Faber	254-213	3.15	1	4	0	2	Vets
Jack Morris	254-186	3.90	0	3	1	0	—
Carl Hubbell	253-154	2.98	4	5	1	3	3rd Yr
Bob Gibson	251-174	2.91	3	5	1	1	1st Yr

(* active in 2000)

The pitchers on this list won fewer career games than the John/Blyleven/Kaat group, but overall they were a lot more dominant. Jim Palmer won three Cy Young Awards and had eight 20-win seasons. Bob Feller was the strikeout king of his day and would have won several Cy Young Awards, had the honor existed when he was in his prime. Carl Hubbell won two MVP Awards (and two retroactive Cy Young Awards for the same seasons). And Bob Gibson won two Cy Young Awards and an MVP Award while winning 20 games five times. All those guys except Hubbell (who, like Grove, had to wait his turn for a couple of seasons) made the Hall of Fame the first year they were eligible. Roger Clemens also will be a first-ballot Hall of Famer, once he's eligible.

The pitchers whom John, Blyleven and Kaat most resemble are Eppa Rixey, Ted Lyons and Red Faber. Rixey and Faber needed the Veterans Committee to get in. Lyons eventually was voted in by the writers, but he needed 10 tries. Were John and company demonstrably better pitchers than Rixey, Lyons and Faber? In their prime they probably weren't, but you have to give them some credit for winning 20-30 additional games. On the other hand, saying a pitcher should be a Hall of Famer because he was a little better than Eppa Rixey isn't going to sway a lot of voters.

All in all, we can't avoid concluding that the baseball writers *haven't* raised their standards for electing pitchers to the Hall of Fame. This is not to say that the system isn't maddening and often arbitrary, especially when it comes to the selections made by the Veterans Committee. Give the Vets a chance, and they'll almost certainly elect John, Blyleven and Kaat at some point down the road. The writers, though, generally have had higher standards, and that's why John, Blyleven and Kaat still are on the outside, looking in.

—Don Zminda

VI. AWARDS

Which Players Cleaned Up at the Awards Banquet?

The STATS awards banquet highlights the standout performers and performances that you may have missed last year. You won't find another rundown of Cy Young winners or MVPs. You *will* find the recipients of our unique set of annual honors, including the esteemed STATS FlatBat (best bunter), the coveted Slidin' Billy Trophy (best leadoff man), the GARBI (go-ahead RBI), the Hottest Heater Award (most strikeouts per nine innings) and the Red Barrett Trophy (fewest pitches in a nine-inning complete game). We'll also hand out another set of STATS Gold Gloves.

STATS FlatBat

The STATS FlatBat goes to the game's best all-around bunter. We give credit to those who either can bunt over a runner or beat one out for a base hit. Here are the annual winners:

Year	Player	Year	Player
1989	Brett Butler	1995	Otis Nixon
1990	Brett Butler	1996	Kenny Lofton
1991	Steve Finley	1997	Omar Vizquel
1992	Brett Butler	1998	Omar Vizquel
1993	Omar Vizquel	1999	Omar Vizquel
1994	Kenny Lofton	2000	Eric Young

E.Y. breaks a four-year stranglehold by Cleveland's Omar Vizquel and Kenny Lofton. Young led the majors with 16 bunt hits in 2000, and he successfully converted all seven of his sacrifice bunt attempts. For his part, Lofton was 12 of 13 when trying to bunt for a base hit in 2000.

Slidin' Billy Trophy

In honor of Billy Hamilton, who owns the record of 192 runs scored in a single season, the Slidin' Billy Trophy goes to the top leadoff hitter:

Year	Player	Year	Player
1989	Rickey Henderson	1995	Chuck Knoblauch
1990	Rickey Henderson	1996	Chuck Knoblauch
1991	Paul Molitor	1997	Craig Biggio
1992	Brady Anderson	1998	Craig Biggio
1993	Lenny Dykstra	1999	Craig Biggio
1994	Kenny Lofton	2000	Darin Erstad

Craig Biggio fell short in his bid for a Slidin' Billy four-peat. Though Biggio was derailed by a season-ending knee injury on August 1, that should take nothing away from Darin Erstad, who walked away with the hardware in this category on the strength of 239 hits while hitting No. 1 in the Anaheim lineup. The fact that Erstad also scored 121 times and drove in 100 runs gave him the nod over Kansas City's Johnny Damon.

Go-Ahead RBI Leaders

Some RBI are more important than others. The go-ahead RBI (GARBI) is a measure of the number of times a player drove in a run that gave his team the lead at any point during a game, even if his team failed to hold that advantage. Here are the players who have led the majors in GARBI:

Year	Player	GARBI	Year	Player	GARBI
1989	Pedro Guerrero	40	1995	Barry Bonds	38
1990	Joe Carter	36	1996	Dante Bichette	35
1991	Fred McGriff	37	1997	Jeff Bagwell	46
1992	Carlos Baerga	42	1998	Sammy Sosa	43
1993	Albert Belle	36	1999	Manny Ramirez	41
1994	Jeff Bagwell	36	2000	Mike Sweeney	37

It helps to be proficient with runners in scoring position in this category, and the Royals' Mike Sweeney hit .385 under such conditions last season. Right behind Sweeney were San Francisco's Barry Bonds and Florida's Preston Wilson, who each racked up 35 GARBI. Bonds outdid MVP teammate Jeff Kent, who accounted for a *mere* 29 go-ahead RBI in 2000.

RBI Percentage Leaders

The leaders in RBI percentage are the players who drive in the highest percentage of their available RBI (i.e., if they homered in every at-bat). No one was more efficient with their opportunities last year than the AL MVP:

Year	Player	Pct
1994	Jeff Bagwell	17.2
1995	Mark McGwire	16.4
1996	Mark McGwire	16.1
1997	Ken Griffey Jr.	14.7
1998	Mark McGwire	18.0
1999	Mark McGwire	17.2
2000	Jason Giambi	15.8

Giambi took the mantle held by former Oakland first baseman Mark McGwire. Giambi set a new career mark with 137 RBI, taking full advantage of his 869 RBI available. Big Mac would have walked away with another title had he made our minimum of 80 total RBI—McGwire finished with 73 ribbies and an RBI percentage of 17.8 in 2000.

Hottest Heater

The winner of each year's Hottest Heater Award is the pitcher with the highest strikeout rate per nine innings. Though we acknowledge that this award isn't actually a measurement of velocity, we think you'll agree that our winners can pack some heat:

Year	Pitcher	SO/9	Year	Pitcher	SO/9
1989	Rob Dibble	12.8	1995	Roberto Hernandez	12.7
1990	Rob Dibble	12.5	1996	Randy Johnson	12.5
1991	Rob Dibble	13.6	1997	Billy Wagner	14.4
1992	Rob Dibble	14.1	1998	Billy Wagner	14.6
1993	Duane Ward	12.2	1999	Billy Wagner	15.0
1994	Bobby Ayala	12.1	2000	Byung-Hyun Kim	14.1

Arizona's Byung-Hyun Kim relies as much on his funky motion—a sidearm, almost underhand delivery—as he does on velocity, but he still can hit 92 MPH. He struck out 111 batters in just 70.2 innings last season. Teammate Randy Johnson, who knows a thing or two about throwing fastballs, led all starters with 12.6 strikeouts per nine innings in 2000.

Red Barrett Trophy

In 1944, Red Barrett threw a complete game using only 58 pitches, or so the legend goes. Amazing, especially when you consider that 58 pitches may buy you only a complete *inning* at Coors Field. In honor of Barrett's achievement, we dole out the award for the pitcher who throws the fewest pitches in a nine-inning complete game each season:

Year	Pitcher	Pitches	Year	Pitcher	Pitches
1989	Frank Viola	85	1995	Greg Maddux	88
1990	Bob Tewksbury	76	1996	Bob Wolcott	79
1991	Chris Bosio	82	1997	Greg Maddux	78
1992	John Smiley	80	1998	Andy Ashby	75
1993	Tom Glavine	79	1999	David Cone	88
1994	Bobby Munoz	80	2000	John Halama	87

Seattle's John Halama earned his second career shutout on May 17 with an 87-pitch blanking of the Twins. He did not walk a batter and gave up just four hits in what turned out to be his only complete game of the season. For his part, former Trophy winner Greg Maddux fashioned six complete games in 2000, with four of those efforts requiring fewer than 100 pitches.

Hold Leaders

The hold was invented to measure how well each middle man succeeds at his most important function—protecting the leads he's given. Not surprisingly, many of the past leaders in this category moved on to closer roles:

Year	Pitcher	Holds	Year	Pitcher	Holds
1989	Rick Honeycutt	24	1996	Mariano Rivera	27
1990	Barry Jones	30	1997	Stan Belinda	28
1991	Mark Eichhorn	25		Bob Wickman	28
1992	Duane Ward	25	1998	Dan Plesac	27
	Todd Worrell	25		Paul Quantrill	27
1993	Mike Jackson	34	1999	John Johnstone	28
1994	Mel Rojas	19	2000	Felix Rodriguez	30
1995	Troy Percival	29			

After years of shuffling teams, Felix Rodriguez seems to have found a home in San Francisco. The converted catcher became the majors' first 30-holds man since Mike Jackson in 1993. Rodriguez combined with Robb Nen last year to give the Giants one of the most effective late-inning duos in the bigs, and expect them to protect plenty of leads again in 2001.

Best-Throwing Catchers

As we said in the essay on this topic in the defensive section of the *Scoreboard*, "The King is dead. Long live the King." For the first time since 1994, someone other than Ivan Rodriguez was the majors' best-throwing catcher over the course of a season:

Year	Catcher	CS%	Year	Catcher	CS%
1989	Damon Berryhill	44.6	1995	Ivan Rodriguez	43.7
1990	Ron Karkovice	50.0	1996	Ivan Rodriguez	48.9
1991	Gil Reyes	50.6	1997	Ivan Rodriguez	51.9
1992	Ivan Rodriguez	49.0	1998	Ivan Rodriguez	52.5
1993	Steve Lake	54.5	1999	Ivan Rodriguez	52.8
1994	Tom Pagnozzi	46.8	2000	Henry Blanco	57.6

Baseball Scoreboard

A relative unknown prior to the 2000 campaign, Milwaukee's Henry Blanco nabbed 38 of 66 would-be thieves and finished with a .991 fielding percentage. In his defense, Rodriguez caught just 87 games last year before breaking his thumb, so a return to health could mean a return to the throne—especially if the rotator cuff injury Blanco suffered at the end of 2000 haunts the Brewers' backstop in 2001.

STATS Gold Gloves

Sure, there are those "other" Gold Gloves, but when it comes to picking the game's best defensive players, there's enough room for differences of opinion. We like jaw-dropping stops as much as the next guy, but range, reliability and a host of other factors merit consideration, too.

Catcher

Year	American	National	Year	American	National
1997	Ivan Rodriguez	Charles Johnson	1999	Ivan Rodriguez	Mike Lieberthal
1998	Ivan Rodriguez	Charles Johnson	2000	Ivan Rodriguez	Mike Matheny

While Brad Ausmus was the first American League catcher in years to generate a better caught-stealing percentage than Ivan Rodriguez, Pudge edges out Ausmus by committing just two errors in 87 games and posting the best fielding percentage among AL backstops (.996). He was on pace to allow fewer stolen bases than anyone else before a fractured thumb ended his season in July. The National League winner is Mike Matheny, who ranked second among his NL peers in fielding percentage (.994) and caught-stealing percentage (51.1 percent).

First Base

Year	American	National	Year	American	National
1989	Don Mattingly	Will Clark	1995	Wally Joyner	Jeff Bagwell
1990	Mark McGwire	Sid Bream	1996	Rafael Palmeiro	Mark Grace
1991	Don Mattingly	Mark Grace	1997	Jeff King	Wally Joyner
1992	Wally Joyner	Mark Grace	1998	David Segui	John Olerud
1993	Don Mattingly	Mark Grace	1999	Tino Martinez	Mark Grace
1994	Don Mattingly	Jeff Bagwell	2000	John Olerud	Mark Grace

In a close AL race, the winner is John Olerud, who ranked second in the league in chances, but committed just five errors for an AL-best .996 fielding percentage. In our first deviation from the MLB awards, the STATS Gold Glove goes to Mark Grace for a second straight year. He had a better blend of defensive numbers than Todd Zeile, who posted the best defensive batting average but was at the league average in fielding percentage.

Second Base

Year	American	National	Year	American	National
1989	Harold Reynolds	Ryne Sandberg	1995	Carlos Baerga	Jody Reed
1990	Billy Ripken	Ryne Sandberg	1996	Fernando Vina	Bret Boone
1991	Mike Gallego	Ryne Sandberg	1997	Chuck Knoblauch	Bret Boone
1992	Carlos Baerga	Ryne Sandberg	1998	Roberto Alomar	Fernando Vina
1993	Harold Reynolds	Robby Thompson	1999	Roberto Alomar	Pokey Reese
1994	Jody Reed	Mickey Morandini	2000	Mark McLemore	Fernando Vina

It's a no-brainer in the National League, where Fernando Vina led his peers in zone rating, fielding percentage and double-play conversion. The AL winner is Mark McLemore, who ranked among the best AL second sackers in zone rating and fielding percentage.

Third Base

Year	American	National	Year	American	National
1989	Gary Gaetti	Tim Wallach	1995	Travis Fryman	Charlie Hayes
1990	Gary Gaetti	Charlie Hayes	1996	Robin Ventura	Ken Caminiti
1991	Wade Boggs	Steve Buechele	1997	Jeff Cirillo	Edgardo Alfonzo
1992	Robin Ventura	Terry Pendleton	1998	Robin Ventura	Jeff Cirillo
1993	Robin Ventura	Matt Williams	1999	Scott Brosius	Robin Ventura
1994	Wade Boggs	Matt Williams	2000	Corey Koskie	Scott Rolen

In just his second full season, Corey Koskie committed just 12 errors and posted the best defensive batting average among his AL peers. In the NL, Scott Rolen edges out Bill Mueller by virtue of his superior zone rating.

Shortstop

Year	American	National	Year	American	National
1989	Ozzie Guillen	Ozzie Smith	1995	Gary DiSarcina	Kevin Stocker
1990	Ozzie Guillen	Ozzie Smith	1996	Omar Vizquel	Greg Gagne
1991	Cal Ripken	Ozzie Smith	1997	Omar Vizquel	Rey Ordonez
1992	Cal Ripken	Ozzie Smith	1998	Omar Vizquel	Barry Larkin
1993	Ozzie Guillen	Ozzie Smith	1999	Rey Sanchez	Rey Ordonez
1994	Gary DiSarcina	Barry Larkin	2000	Rey Sanchez	Ricky Gutierrez

Omar Vizquel committed just three errors in 156 games for a .995 fielding percentage that no shortstop could top. But Omar's zone coverage has slipped, and Rey Sanchez' four errors in 26 more chances and superior zone rating earn him a second straight STATS Gold Glove in a squeaker over Alex Rodriguez. The best clearly were in the AL in 2000, but the NL award goes to Ricky Gutierrez, the league leader among shortstops in zone rating and fielding percentage.

Left Field

Year	American	National	Year	American	National
1989	Rickey Henderson	Barry Bonds	1995	Garret Anderson	Luis Gonzalez
1990	Rickey Henderson	Barry Bonds	1996	Tony Phillips	Bernard Gilkey
1991	Dan Gladden	Bernard Gilkey	1997	B.J. Surhoff	Barry Bonds
1992	Greg Vaughn	Barry Bonds	1998	B.J. Surhoff	Barry Bonds
1993	Greg Vaughn	Barry Bonds	1999	B.J. Surhoff	Ron Gant
1994	Tony Phillips	Moises Alou	2000	Darin Erstad	Barry Bonds

The NL winner for the third time in four years is Barry Bonds, who ranked second among left fielders in defensive batting average but posted better than .300 marks in each of its three components. The AL Gold Glove goes to Darin Erstad, who easily finished first among his peers in DBA, but fell just short of the DBA title because his solid "D" often was used in center.

Center Field

Year	American	National	Year	American	National
1989	Devon White	Eric Davis	1995	Jim Edmonds	Marquis Grissom
1990	Gary Pettis	Lenny Dykstra	1996	Kenny Lofton	Steve Finley
1991	Devon White	Brett Butler	1997	Jim Edmonds	Steve Finley
1992	Devon White	Darrin Jackson	1998	Brian Hunter	Andruw Jones
1993	Kenny Lofton	Darren Lewis	1999	Chris Singleton	Andruw Jones
1994	Devon White	Marquis Grissom	2000	Kenny Lofton	Andruw Jones

The best DBA among all center-field qualifiers belonged to Kenny Lofton, our AL Gold Glove winner. While Andruw Jones' zone rating dropped off in 2000, he won a third straight STATS Gold Glove with just two errors in 161 games for a .996 fielding percentage.

Right Field

Year	American	National	Year	American	National
1989	Jesse Barfield	Andre Dawson	1995	Tim Salmon	Reggie Sanders
1990	Jesse Barfield	Tony Gwynn	1996	Paul O'Neill	Sammy Sosa
1991	Joe Carter	Larry Walker	1997	Tim Salmon	Sammy Sosa
1992	Mark Whiten	Larry Walker	1998	Paul O'Neill	Derek Bell
1993	Paul O'Neill	Tony Gwynn	1999	Magglio Ordonez	Bobby Abreu
1994	Paul O'Neill	Reggie Sanders	2000	Paul O'Neill	Bobby Abreu

In the NL, Vladimir Guerrero had a slight edge over Bobby Abreu in zone rating and keeping runners from advancing, but Guerrero's 10 errors cost him the Gold Glove. Despite his age, Paul O'Neill still has a good glove and solid arm, which earned him the AL award over Jermaine Dye.

—Tony Nistler, Thom Henninger

Appendix

Each Appendix has two pieces of information to help reference it to its corresponding essay: the title which matches the title in the Table of Contents, and the page number of the corresponding essay.

In some appendices, we couldn't include every team for players who played with more than one club in 2000. In those cases, the player is listed with the number of teams he played for. The team abbreviations for current franchises:

American League Teams		National League Teams	
Ana	Anaheim Angels	Ari	Arizona Diamondbacks
Bal	Baltimore Orioles	Atl	Atlanta Braves
Bos	Boston Red Sox	ChC	Chicago Cubs
CWS	Chicago White Sox	Cin	Cincinnati Reds
Cle	Cleveland Indians	Col	Colorado Rockies
Det	Detroit Tigers	Fla	Florida Marlins
KC	Kansas City Royals	Hou	Houston Astros
Min	Minnesota Twins	LA	Los Angeles Dodgers
NYY	New York Yankees	Mil	Milwaukee Brewers
Oak	Oakland Athletics	Mon	Montreal Expos
Sea	Seattle Mariners	NYM	New York Mets
TB	Tampa Bay Devil Rays	Phi	Philadelphia Phillies
Tex	Texas Rangers	Pit	Pittsburgh Pirates
Tor	Toronto Blue Jays	StL	St. Louis Cardinals
		SD	San Diego Padres
		SF	San Francisco Giants

Baseball Scoreboard

Anaheim Angels: How Impressive Was Erstad's Improvement? (p. 4)

Biggest Single-Season Hit Improvements—1876-2000
(minimum 500 AB in Yr1)

Player	Years	Yr1 H	Yr2 H	Yr2-Yr1	Yr3 H	Yr1 Avg	Yr2 Avg	Yr3 Avg
Darin Erstad	1999-01	148	240	92	—	.253	.355	—
Paul Molitor	1995-97	142	225	83	164	.270	.341	.305
George Sisler	1919-21	180	257	77	216	.352	.407	.371
Omar Moreno	1978-80	121	196	75	168	.235	.282	.249
Keith Hernandez	1978-80	138	210	72	191	.255	.344	.321
Lenny Dykstra	1989-91	121	192	71	73	.237	.325	.297
Billy Shindle	1888-90	107	178	71	189	.208	.314	.324
Al Simmons	1924-26	183	253	70	199	.308	.387	.341
Earl Averill	1935-37	162	232	70	182	.288	.378	.299
Pete Rose	1964-66	139	209	70	205	.269	.312	.313
Dave May	1972-74	119	189	70	108	.238	.303	.226
Harry Heilmann	1920-22	168	237	69	162	.309	.394	.356
Milt Stock	1924-26	136	202	66	0	.242	.328	.000
Marquis Grissom	1995-97	142	207	65	146	.258	.308	.262
Heinie Manush	1927-29	177	241	64	204	.298	.378	.355
Jimmie Foxx	1931-33	150	213	63	204	.291	.364	.356
George Brett	1978-80	150	212	62	175	.294	.329	.390
Mickey Vernon	1952-54	143	205	62	173	.251	.337	.290
Al Kaline	1954-56	139	200	61	194	.276	.340	.314
Jim Bottomley	1924-26	167	227	60	180	.316	.367	.299
Cal Ripken Jr.	1990-92	150	210	60	160	.250	.323	.251
Luis Gonzalez	1998-00	146	206	60	192	.267	.336	.311
Freddy Lindstrom	1927-29	172	231	59	175	.306	.358	.319
Eddie Collins	1919-21	165	224	59	177	.319	.372	.337
Austin McHenry	1920-22	142	201	59	72	.282	.350	.303
Lou Brock	1963-65	141	200	59	182	.258	.315	.288
Brian McRae	1992-94	119	177	58	119	.223	.282	.273
Jerry Priddy	1947-49	108	166	58	158	.214	.296	.290
Paul Waner	1926-28	180	237	57	223	.336	.380	.370
Freddy Lindstrom	1929-31	175	231	56	91	.319	.379	.300
Ed Delahanty	1898-00	183	238	55	174	.334	.410	.323
Frankie Frisch	1922-24	168	223	55	198	.327	.348	.328
Tris Speaker	1911-13	167	222	55	189	.334	.383	.363
Rogers Hornsby	1919-21	163	218	55	235	.318	.370	.397
Buddy Myer	1934-36	160	215	55	42	.305	.349	.269
Bobby Lowe	1893-95	157	212	55	122	.298	.346	.296
Thurman Munson	1974-76	135	190	55	186	.261	.318	.302
Luis Aparicio	1965-67	127	182	55	127	.225	.276	.233
Emmett Seery	1888-90	110	165	55	88	.220	.314	.223
Ty Cobb	1910-12	194	248	54	227	.383	.420	.410
Lou Gehrig	1929-31	166	220	54	211	.300	.379	.341
Mickey Rivers	1979-81	156	210	54	114	.293	.333	.286
Ray Powell	1920-22	137	191	54	163	.225	.306	.296
Matt Williams	1998-00	136	190	54	102	.267	.303	.275
Willie Davis	1963-65	126	180	54	133	.245	.294	.238
Cy Seymour	1904-06	166	219	53	165	.313	.377	.286
Felipe Alou	1965-67	165	218	53	157	.297	.327	.274
Cal Ripken Jr.	1982-84	158	211	53	195	.264	.318	.304
Felipe Alou	1967-69	157	210	53	134	.274	.317	.282
Tito Fuentes	1976-78	137	190	53	6	.263	.309	.140
Jim Busby	1952-54	130	183	53	187	.236	.312	.298
Tommy Harper	1969-71	126	179	53	151	.235	.296	.258
Ralph Kiner	1946-48	124	177	53	147	.247	.313	.265

Baltimore Orioles: Did the O's Need to Sign Segui? (p. 6)

Rookie And Sophomore Seasons—1876-2000, Listed Alphabetically
(minimum seasonal age 26, 200 AB, 10 HR, .500 Slg in rookie season)

Name	Age	Year	AB	H	2B	HR	RBI	Avg	OBP	Slg	AB/HR
Benny Agbayani	27	1999	276	79	18	14	42	.286	.363	.525	19.71
	28	2000	350	101	20	15	60	.289	.391	.480	23.33
Dale Alexander	26	1929	626	215	43	25	137	.343	.397	.580	25.04
	27	1930	602	196	33	20	135	.326	.372	.507	30.10
Buzz Arlett	32	1931	418	131	26	18	72	.313	.387	.538	23.22
Earl Averill	27	1929	597	198	43	18	96	.332	.398	.538	33.17
	28	1930	534	181	33	19	119	.339	.404	.537	28.11
Del Bissonette	28	1928	587	188	30	25	106	.320	.396	.543	23.48
	29	1929	431	121	28	12	75	.281	.351	.476	35.92
Hal Breeden	29	1973	258	71	10	15	43	.275	.353	.535	17.20
	30	1974	190	47	13	2	20	.247	.330	.347	95.00
Mandy Brooks	27	1925	349	98	25	14	72	.281	.322	.513	24.93
	28	1926	48	9	1	1	6	.188	.278	.271	48.00
Ron Coomer	29	1996	233	69	12	12	41	.296	.340	.511	19.42
	30	1997	523	156	30	13	85	.298	.324	.438	40.23
Brian Daubach	27	1999	381	112	33	21	73	.294	.360	.562	18.14
	28	2000	495	123	32	21	76	.248	.315	.448	23.57
Walt Dropo	27	1950	559	180	28	34	144	.322	.378	.583	16.44
	28	1951	360	86	14	11	57	.239	.312	.369	32.73
Johnny Frederick	27	1929	628	206	52	24	75	.328	.372	.545	26.17
	28	1930	616	206	44	17	76	.334	.383	.524	36.24
Buck Freeman	27	1899	588	187	19	25	122	.318	.362	.563	23.52
	28	1900	418	126	19	6	65	.301	.355	.452	69.67
Jim Gentile	26	1960	384	112	17	21	98	.292	.403	.500	18.29
	27	1961	486	147	25	46	141	.302	.423	.646	10.57
Bob Hamelin	26	1994	312	88	25	24	65	.282	.388	.599	13.00
	27	1995	208	35	7	7	25	.168	.278	.313	29.71
Bob Johnson	26	1933	535	155	44	21	93	.290	.387	.505	25.48
	27	1934	547	168	26	34	92	.307	.375	.563	16.09
Duke Kenworthy	27	1914	545	173	40	15	91	.317	.372	.525	36.33
	28	1915	396	118	30	3	52	.298	.355	.432	132.00
Dale Long	29	1955	419	122	19	16	79	.291	.362	.513	26.19
	30	1956	517	136	20	27	91	.263	.326	.485	19.15
Hack Miller	28	1922	466	164	28	12	78	.352	.389	.511	38.83
	29	1923	485	146	24	20	88	.301	.343	.482	24.25
Minnie Minoso	28	1951	530	173	34	10	76	.326	.422	.500	53.00
	29	1952	569	160	24	13	61	.281	.375	.424	43.77
Jim Morrison	26	1979	240	66	14	14	35	.275	.324	.508	17.14
	27	1980	604	171	40	15	57	.283	.329	.424	40.27
Ben Paschal	29	1925	247	89	16	12	56	.360	.417	.611	20.58
	30	1926	258	74	12	7	32	.287	.354	.438	36.86
Curtis Pride	27	1996	267	80	17	10	31	.300	.372	.513	26.70
	28	1997	164	35	4	3	20	.213	.316	.341	54.67
Chris Richard	26	2000	215	57	14	14	37	.265	.326	.544	15.36
Al Rosen	26	1950	554	159	23	37	116	.287	.405	.543	14.97
	27	1951	573	152	30	24	102	.265	.362	.447	23.88
Bill Salkeld	28	1945	267	83	16	15	52	.311	.420	.547	17.80
	29	1946	160	47	8	3	19	.294	.432	.400	53.33
George Watkins	30	1930	391	146	32	17	87	.373	.415	.621	23.00
	31	1931	503	145	30	13	51	.288	.336	.477	38.69
Earl Webb	29	1927	332	100	18	14	52	.301	.391	.506	23.71
	30	1928	140	35	7	3	23	.250	.318	.407	46.67

Boston Red Sox: How Unusual Are Martinez' Control "Lapses"? (p. 9)

Highest HB/BB Ratios, Season—1900-2000 (minimum 150 IP)

Pitcher, Team	Year	IP	HB	BB	HB/BB
Bill Wolfe, NYA-Was	1904	160.1	13	26	.500
Kevin Brown, Fla	1996	233.0	16	33	.485
Jesse Tannehill, Bos	1904	281.2	15	33	.455
Danny Darwin, Pit-Hou	1996	164.2	12	27	.444
Pedro Martinez, Bos	2000	217.0	14	32	.438
Jesse Tannehill, Pit	1902	231.0	10	25	.400
Jesse Tannehill, Pit	1900	234.0	17	43	.395
Chief Bender, Phi	1903	270.0	25	65	.385
Nick Maddox, Pit	1909	203.1	15	39	.385
Don Drysdale, LA	1966	273.2	17	45	.378
Jake Weimer, Cin	1907	209.0	23	63	.365
Ed Summers, Det	1908	301.0	20	55	.364
Joe McGinnity, Bro	1900	343.0	41	113	.363
Eddie Plank, Phi	1903	336.0	23	65	.354
Jim Bunning, Phi	1966	314.0	19	55	.345
Win Mercer, NYG	1900	242.2	20	58	.345
Jack Warhop, NYA	1911	209.2	15	44	.341
Clark Griffith, CWS	1902	213.0	16	47	.340
Tom Walker, Cin	1904	217.0	18	53	.340
Walter Johnson, Was	1915	336.2	19	56	.339
Jack Chesbro, Pit	1902	286.1	21	62	.339
Cy Young, Bos	1905	320.2	10	30	.333
Hank Robinson, Pit	1912	175.0	10	30	.333
Barney Pelty, StL	1906	260.2	19	59	.322
Jack Warhop, NYA	1909	243.1	26	81	.321
Eddie Plank, Phi	1905	346.2	24	75	.320
Cy Young, Bos	1906	287.2	8	25	.320
Gerry Staley, StL	1953	230.0	17	54	.315
Clark Griffith, ChN	1900	248.0	16	51	.314
Bert Blyleven, Min	1988	207.1	16	51	.314
Bryn Smith, Mon	1988	198.0	10	32	.313
Mark Leiter, SF	1995	195.2	17	55	.309
Don Cardwell, Pit	1963	213.2	16	52	.308
Bret Saberhagen, NYM	1994	177.1	4	13	.308
Frank Lary, Det	1960	274.1	19	62	.306
Tom Murphy, Cal	1969	215.2	21	69	.304
Jim Bunning, Phi	1964	284.1	14	46	.304
Jeff Weaver, Det	1999	163.2	17	56	.304
Bret Saberhagen, NYM-Col	1995	153.0	10	33	.303
Bob Tewksbury, StL	1993	213.2	6	20	.300
Greg Maddux, Atl	1997	232.2	6	20	.300
Nixey Callahan, ChN	1900	285.1	22	74	.297
Barney Pelty, StL	1907	273.0	19	64	.297
Eddie Plank, Phi	1902	300.0	18	61	.295
Eddie Plank, Phi	1906	211.2	15	51	.294
Jesse Tannehill, NYA	1903	239.2	10	34	.294

Pitcher, Team	Year	IP	HB	BB	HB/BB
Rolando Arrojo, TB	1998	202.0	19	65	.292
George Suggs, Cin	1910	266.0	14	48	.292
Roy Patterson, CWS	1904	165.0	7	24	.292
John Tsitouris, Cin	1963	191.0	11	38	.289
Wade Blasingame, Hou	1971	158.1	13	45	.289
Jeff Weaver, Det	2000	200.0	15	52	.288
Ned Garvin, ChN	1900	246.1	18	63	.286
Willie Mitchell, Det	1917	185.1	13	46	.283
Otto Hess, Cle	1906	333.2	24	85	.282
Ed Doheny, NYG-Pit	1901	150.2	11	39	.282
Frank Corridon, Phi	1905	212.0	16	57	.281
Patsy Flaherty, CWS	1903	293.2	14	50	.280
Jesse Tannehill, Pit	1901	252.1	10	36	.278
Milt Pappas, ChC	1972	195.0	8	29	.276
Bill Sherdel, StL	1920	170.0	11	40	.275
John Burkett, SF	1993	231.2	11	40	.275
Walter Johnson, Was	1923	261.0	20	73	.274
Harry Moran, New	1915	205.2	18	66	.273
Willie Mitchell, Cle	1910	183.2	15	55	.273
Archie Stimmel, Cin	1901	153.1	12	44	.273
Bob Shaw, Mil	1962	225.0	12	44	.273
Steve Woodard, Mil	1998	165.2	9	33	.273
Jack Warhop, NYA	1912	258.0	16	59	.271
Addie Joss, Cle	1903	283.2	10	37	.270
Luther Taylor, Cle-NYG	1902	234.2	17	63	.270
Jeff Pfeffer, Bro	1916	328.2	17	63	.270
Jack Chesbro, Pit	1901	287.2	14	52	.269
Bill Burns, Was-CWS	1909	197.1	11	41	.268
Babe Adams, Pit	1922	171.1	4	15	.267
Harry Krause, Phi	1909	213.0	13	49	.265
Deacon Phillippe, Pit	1901	296.0	10	38	.263
Jack Cronin, Det	1901	219.2	11	42	.262
Addie Joss, Cle	1905	286.0	12	46	.261
Dennis Martinez, Cle	1995	187.0	12	46	.261
Barney Pelty, StL	1904	301.0	20	77	.260
Joe McGinnity, NYG	1907	310.1	15	58	.259
Sam Leever, Pit	1902	222.0	8	31	.258
David Wells, Tor	2000	229.2	8	31	.258
Doc White, CWS	1911	214.1	9	35	.257
Jesse Tannehill, Bos	1906	196.1	10	39	.256
Long Tom Hughes, Was	1907	211.0	12	47	.255
David Cone, NYY	1998	207.2	15	59	.254
Casey Patten, Was	1904	357.2	20	79	.253
Weldon Henley, Phi	1904	295.2	19	76	.250
Rube Benton, Cin-NYG	1915	237.0	19	76	.250
Doc White, Phi	1901	236.2	14	56	.250
Snake Wiltse, Pit-Phi	1901	210.1	12	48	.250
Jack Warhop, NYY	1914	216.2	11	44	.250
Pete Donohue, Cin	1924	222.1	9	36	.250
Al Orth, Phi	1901	281.2	8	32	.250

Baseball Scoreboard

Detroit Tigers: Is Comerica Park the New Astrodome? (p. 16)

Lowest Home-Run Indexes—1987-2000
(based on HR per AB)

Year	Team	Hm HR	Hm AB	Hm Rate	Rd HR	Rd AB	Rd Rate	Index
1991	Indians	63	5,593	.011	126	5,500	.023	49.2
1991	Astros	71	5,500	.013	137	5,458	.025	51.4
1989	Royals	64	5,413	.012	123	5,570	.022	53.5
1992	Royals	65	5,501	.012	116	5,502	.021	56.0
1987	Astros	97	5,488	.018	166	5,449	.030	58.0
1990	Astros	82	5,414	.015	142	5,446	.026	58.1
2000	Tigers	122	5,017	.024	200	5,003	.040	60.8
1992	Dodgers	59	5,404	.011	95	5,421	.018	62.3
1991	Cardinals	73	5,547	.013	109	5,183	.021	62.6
1991	Royals	87	5,694	.015	135	5,530	.024	62.6
1988	Astros	83	5,418	.015	136	5,597	.024	63.0
1989	Cardinals	63	5,510	.011	94	5,450	.017	66.3
1995	Astros	89	5,019	.018	138	5,171	.027	66.4
1999	Astros	110	5,116	.022	157	4,899	.032	67.1
1990	Royals	88	5,553	.016	128	5,427	.024	67.2
1995	Expos	98	4,871	.020	148	4,944	.030	67.2
1991	Expos	68	4,535	.015	138	6,222	.022	67.6
1989	White Sox	94	5,363	.018	144	5,618	.026	68.4
2000	Red Sox	125	5,018	.025	181	4,973	.036	68.4
1999	Marlins	109	4,944	.022	158	4,913	.032	68.6
1988	Royals	92	5,490	.017	131	5,453	.024	69.8
1996	Dodgers	111	5,426	.020	164	5,638	.029	70.3
1988	Cardinals	68	5,572	.012	94	5,458	.017	70.9
1994	Rangers	130	4,412	.029	151	3,658	.041	71.4
1993	Royals	99	5,618	.018	131	5,340	.025	71.8
2000	Brewers	137	5,158	.027	181	4,922	.037	72.2
1992	Astros	90	5,576	.016	120	5,406	.022	72.7
1998	Expos	116	4,931	.024	157	4,876	.032	73.1
1995	Dodgers	110	4,827	.023	155	5,003	.031	73.6
1993	Brewers	118	5,556	.021	160	5,546	.029	73.6
1987	Dodgers	108	5,517	.020	147	5,553	.026	73.9
1992	Brewers	86	5,327	.016	123	5,645	.022	74.1
1992	Pirates	88	5,510	.016	119	5,566	.021	74.7
1988	Athletics	114	5,481	.021	158	5,689	.028	74.9
1990	Athletics	121	5,335	.023	166	5,507	.030	75.2
1995	White Sox	132	4,976	.027	178	5,075	.035	75.6
1996	Astros	123	5,567	.022	160	5,564	.029	76.8
1988	White Sox	119	5,549	.021	151	5,420	.028	77.0
1993	Red Sox	107	5,590	.019	134	5,389	.025	77.0
1995	Red Sox	133	5,030	.026	169	4,966	.034	77.7
1994	Royals	89	4,066	.022	106	3,764	.028	77.7
1987	Royals	130	5,471	.024	166	5,476	.030	78.4
1997	Astros	104	4,845	.021	141	5,158	.027	78.5
1997	Blue Jays	122	4,862	.025	164	5,134	.032	78.6

Kansas City Royals: How Common Is the Sophomore Slump? (p. 19)

Largest Decreases in Runs Created For Rookies of the Year—1947-99 (minimum -10 Diff)

Player, Team	Year	Lg	RC	RC-2	Diff	RC-3
Walt Dropo, Bos	1950	AL	120	40	-80	80
Carlos Beltran, KC	1999	AL	111	39	-72	—
Joe Charboneau, Cle	1980	AL	71	11	-60	6
Sandy Alomar Jr., Cle	1990	AL	62	4	-58	26
Willie Mays, NYG	1951	NL	75	18	-57	—
Todd Hollandsworth, LA	1996	NL	82	30	-52	26
Bob Hamelin, KC	1994	AL	67	15	-52	43
Albie Pearson, Was	1958	AL	69	18	-51	11
Al Bumbry, Bal	1973	AL	68	24	-44	47
Roy Sievers, StL	1949	AL	85	44	-41	8
Benito Santiago, SD	1987	NL	73	32	-41	48
Pat Listach, Mil	1992	AL	78	39	-39	5
Tommie Agee, CWS	1966	AL	96	62	-34	25
Tim Salmon, Cal	1993	AL	101	70	-31	132
Fred Lynn, Bos	1975	AL	117	87	-30	71
Chris Sabo, Cin	1988	NL	67	39	-28	86
Pete Rose, Cin	1963	NL	79	53	-26	113
Bake McBride, StL	1974	NL	83	59	-24	46
Ted Sizemore, LA	1969	NL	68	44	-24	50
Ben Grieve, Oak	1998	AL	107	84	-23	101
Ron Kittle, CWS	1983	AL	84	61	-23	53
Rod Carew, Min	1967	AL	71	49	-22	81
Jerome Walton, ChC	1989	NL	69	47	-22	20
Ron Hansen, Bal	1960	AL	79	58	-21	13
Frank Howard, LA	1960	NL	64	43	-21	93
Mike Piazza, LA	1993	NL	101	81	-20	91
Carlton Fisk, Bos	1972	AL	87	68	-19	39
Al Dark, Bos	1948	MLB	78	59	-19	86
Alfredo Griffin, Tor	1979	AL	76	57	-19	23
Walt Weiss, Oak	1988	AL	45	26	-19	46
Mark McGwire, Oak	1987	AL	125	107	-18	84
Dick Allen, Phi	1964	NL	130	113	-17	124
Harvey Kuenn, Det	1953	AL	92	76	-16	96
Thurman Munson, NYY	1970	AL	73	57	-16	58
Wally Moon, StL	1954	NL	103	88	-15	92
Gil McDougald, NYY	1951	AL	82	67	-15	84
Alvin Davis, Sea	1984	AL	110	96	-14	78
Jim Gilliam, Bro	1953	NL	103	89	-14	69
Tommy Helms, Cin	1966	NL	63	50	-13	53
Ken Hubbs, ChC	1962	NL	59	46	-13	—
Curt Blefary, Bal	1965	AL	90	78	-12	82
Vince Coleman, StL	1985	NL	83	71	-12	105
Ozzie Guillen, CWS	1985	AL	54	43	-11	61

Oakland Athletics: Are Chavez And Tejada the Best Young SS/3B Combo Ever? (p. 28)

Highest Combined OPS, Primary SS & 3B (Age 25 or Younger)—1876-2000 (minimum 400 PA and 80 G at position; age as of June 30)

Player, Team	Pos	Age	Year	OBP	Slg	OPS	Comb OPS
John McGraw, Bal	3B	21	1894	.451	.436	0.887	
Hughie Jennings, Bal	SS	25	1894	.411	.479	0.890	1.777
Jumbo Davis, Bal	3B	25	1887	.353	.485	0.838	
Oyster Burns, Bal	SS	22	1887	.414	.519	0.933	1.770
Fernando Tatis, StL	3B	24	1999	.404	.553	0.957	
Edgar Renteria, StL	SS	23	1999	.334	.400	0.734	1.691
Eric Chavez, Oak	3B	22	2000	.355	.495	0.850	
Miguel Tejada, Oak	SS	24	2000	.349	.479	0.828	1.678
Freddy Lindstrom, NYG	3B	23	1929	.354	.464	0.819	
Travis Jackson, NYG	SS	25	1929	.367	.490	0.857	1.676
Freddy Lindstrom, NYG	3B	22	1928	.383	.511	0.894	
Travis Jackson, NYG	SS	24	1928	.339	.436	0.775	1.669
Bill Brubaker, Pit	3B	25	1936	.352	.384	0.736	
Arky Vaughan, Pit	SS	24	1936	.453	.474	0.927	1.663
Pie Traynor, Pit	3B	25	1925	.377	.464	0.840	
Glenn Wright, Pit	SS	24	1925	.341	.480	0.822	1.662
Mike Higgins, Phi	3B	24	1933	.383	.485	0.868	
Dib Williams, Phi	SS	23	1933	.342	.444	0.786	1.654
Freddy Lindstrom, NYG	3B	21	1927	.354	.436	0.790	
Travis Jackson, NYG	SS	23	1927	.363	.486	0.849	1.639
Denny Lyons, Phi	3B	21	1887	.421	.523	0.943	
Chippy McGarr, Phi	SS	24	1887	.326	.366	0.692	1.635
Mike Higgins, Phi	3B	25	1934	.392	.508	0.901	
Eric McNair, Phi	SS	25	1934	.321	.412	0.734	1.634
Harlond Clift, StL	3B	24	1937	.413	.546	0.960	
Bill Knickerbocker, StL	SS	25	1937	.303	.365	0.668	1.628
Freddy Lindstrom, NYG	3B	20	1926	.351	.420	0.771	
Travis Jackson, NYG	SS	22	1926	.362	.494	0.856	1.626
Buddy Lewis, Was	3B	20	1937	.367	.425	0.792	
Cecil Travis, Was	SS	23	1937	.395	.439	0.834	1.626
Buddy Lewis, Was	3B	22	1939	.402	.478	0.879	
Cecil Travis, Was	SS	25	1939	.342	.403	0.745	1.624
Buddy Lewis, Was	3B	21	1938	.354	.431	0.785	
Cecil Travis, Was	SS	24	1938	.401	.432	0.833	1.618
Bob Horner, Atl	3B	25	1983	.383	.528	0.911	
Rafael Ramirez, Atl	SS	25	1983	.337	.368	0.705	1.616
Rube Lutzke, Cle	3B	25	1923	.338	.337	0.675	
Joe Sewell, Cle	SS	24	1923	.456	.479	0.935	1.610

Player, Team	Pos	Age	Year	OBP	Slg	OPS	Comb OPS
George Davis, NYG	3B	22	1893	.410	.554	0.964	
Shorty Fuller, NYG	SS	25	1893	.325	.300	0.624	1.588
Ben Chapman, NYY	3B	21	1930	.370	.474	0.844	
Lyn Lary, NYY	SS	24	1930	.357	.386	0.743	1.586
Ken Keltner, Cle	3B	24	1941	.330	.485	0.815	
Lou Boudreau, Cle	SS	23	1941	.355	.415	0.770	1.585
Jimmy Dykes, Phi	3B	25	1922	.359	.421	0.780	
Chick Galloway, Phi	SS	25	1922	.368	.433	0.801	1.581
Wade Boggs, Bos	3B	25	1983	.444	.486	0.931	
Glenn Hoffman, Bos	SS	24	1983	.306	.340	0.646	1.577
Home Run Baker, Phi	3B	25	1911	.379	.508	0.887	
Jack Barry, Phi	SS	24	1911	.333	.344	0.677	1.564
Brooks Robinson, Bal	3B	25	1962	.342	.486	0.828	
Jerry Adair, Bal	SS	25	1962	.319	.414	0.734	1.562
Bob Bailey, Pit	3B	23	1966	.360	.447	0.807	
Gene Alley, Pit	SS	25	1966	.334	.418	0.752	1.559
Scott Rolen, Phi	3B	23	1998	.391	.532	0.923	
Desi Relaford, Phi	SS	24	1998	.293	.338	0.631	1.554
George Kell, Det	3B	25	1948	.369	.402	0.772	
Johnny Lipon, Det	SS	25	1948	.384	.397	0.782	1.553
Ken Keltner, Cle	3B	23	1940	.322	.418	0.740	
Lou Boudreau, Cle	SS	22	1940	.370	.443	0.814	1.553
Brooks Robinson, Bal	3B	23	1960	.329	.440	0.769	
Ron Hansen, Bal	SS	22	1960	.342	.440	0.781	1.551
Bob Horner, Atl	3B	24	1982	.350	.501	0.851	
Rafael Ramirez, Atl	SS	24	1982	.319	.379	0.698	1.548
Clete Boyer, NYY	3B	25	1962	.331	.413	0.745	
Tom Tresh, NYY	SS	24	1962	.359	.441	0.800	1.545
Doug Baird, Pit-StL	3B	25	1917	.316	.357	0.673	
Rogers Hornsby, StL	SS	21	1917	.385	.484	0.868	1.541
Pete Ward, CWS	3B	23	1963	.353	.482	0.835	
Ron Hansen, CWS	SS	25	1963	.330	.351	0.681	1.516
Patsy Tebeau, Cle	3B	24	1889	.332	.390	0.722	
Ed McKean, Cle	SS	25	1889	.375	.418	0.793	1.515
Eric Chavez, Oak	3B	21	1999	.333	.427	0.760	
Miguel Tejada, Oak	SS	23	1999	.325	.427	0.751	1.512
Rich Rollins, Min	3B	25	1963	.359	.444	0.803	
Zoilo Versalles, Min	SS	23	1963	.303	.401	0.704	1.508
Les Bell, StL	3B	24	1926	.383	.518	0.901	
Tommy Thevenow, StL	SS	22	1926	.291	.311	0.602	1.503
Joe Foy, Bos	3B	24	1967	.325	.426	0.751	
Rico Petrocelli, Bos	SS	24	1967	.330	.420	0.750	1.501
Pie Traynor, Pit	3B	24	1924	.340	.417	0.756	
Glenn Wright, Pit	SS	23	1924	.318	.425	0.744	1.500

Baseball Scoreboard

Seattle Mariners: Is Martinez an Overshadowed Legend? (p. 31)

Longest Streaks With 20-Plus Home Runs And .320-Plus Batting Average—1876-2000

Player	Years	Span	Player	Years	Span
Lou Gehrig	1930-37	8	Rogers Hornsby	1924-25	2
Ted Williams	1939-42, 1946-49	8	Lou Gehrig	1927-28	2
Babe Ruth	1926-32	7	Dale Alexander	1929-30	2
Stan Musial	1948-54	7	Jimmie Foxx	1929-30	2
Joe DiMaggio	1936-41	6	Babe Herman	1929-30	2
Edgar Martinez	1995-00	6	Lefty O'Doul	1929-30	2
Chuck Klein	1929-33	5	Mel Ott	1929-30	2
Jimmie Foxx	1932-36	5	Hack Wilson	1929-30	2
Ted Williams	1954-58	5	Hank Greenberg	1934-35	2
Al Simmons	1929-32	4	Bill Dickey	1936-37	2
Hank Aaron	1956-59	4	Joe Medwick	1937-38	2
Don Mattingly	1984-87	4	Jimmie Foxx	1938-39	2
Mike Piazza	1995-98	4	Duke Snider	1953-54	2
Babe Ruth	1919-21	3	Mickey Mantle	1956-57	2
Ken Williams	1921-23	3	Willie Mays	1957-58	2
Jack Fournier	1923-25	3	Hank Aaron	1961-62	2
Rogers Hornsby	1927-29	3	Frank Robinson	1961-62	2
Chick Hafey	1928-30	3	Tony Oliva	1970-71	2
Mel Ott	1934-36	3	Joe Torre	1970-71	2
Johnny Mize	1937-39	3	Cesar Cedeno	1972-73	2
Kirby Puckett	1986-88	3	Dave Parker	1977-78	2
Larry Walker	1997-99	3	George Brett	1979-80	2
Bernie Williams	1997-99	3	Jeff Bagwell	1993-94	2
Nomar Garciaparra	1998-00	3	Frank Thomas	1996-97	2
Ivan Rodriguez	1998-00	3	Todd Helton	1999-00	2
Rogers Hornsby	1921-22	2	Manny Ramirez	1999-00	2
Babe Ruth	1923-24	2	Mike Sweeney	1999-00	2

Tampa Bay Devil Rays: How Critical Is Up-The-Middle Offense? (p. 34)

Worst Up-the-Middle OPS—2000

Team	W-L	Pct	Place/Tms	OBP	Slg	OPS
Phillies	65-97	.401	5/5	.317	.360	.677
Devil Rays	69-92	.429	5/5	.309	.368	.677
Twins	69-93	.426	5/5	.308	.385	.694
Padres	76-86	.469	5/5	.323	.374	.698
Brewers	73-89	.451	3/6	.324	.383	.706
Blue Jays	83-79	.512	3/5	.315	.396	.711
Royals	77-85	.475	4/5	.338	.377	.715
Cubs	65-97	.401	6/6	.340	.375	.716
Marlins	79-82	.491	3/5	.336	.381	.716
Angels	82-80	.506	3/4	.309	.412	.722
Expos	67-95	.414	4/5	.317	.413	.729
Dodgers	86-76	.531	2/5	.339	.399	.737
Tigers	79-83	.488	3/5	.338	.410	.748
Rockies	82-80	.506	4/5	.347	.415	.761
White Sox	95-67	.586	1/5	.340	.429	.769
Diamondbacks	85-77	.525	3/5	.334	.437	.771
Athletics	91-70	.565	1/4	.340	.432	.772
Orioles	74-88	.457	4/5	.342	.431	.773
Pirates	69-93	.426	5/6	.355	.419	.774
Indians	90-72	.556	2/5	.360	.414	.774
Reds	85-77	.525	2/6	.345	.438	.783
Braves	95-67	.586	1/5	.362	.434	.797
Rangers	71-91	.438	4/4	.344	.453	.797
Red Sox	85-77	.525	2/5	.357	.452	.809
Mariners	91-71	.562	2/4	.361	.454	.815
Cardinals	95-67	.586	1/6	.365	.454	.819
Giants	97-65	.599	1/5	.359	.462	.822
Astros	72-90	.444	4/6	.367	.455	.822
Mets	94-68	.580	2/5	.360	.468	.828
Yankees	87-74	.540	1/5	.378	.473	.850
MLB Average		.500		.341	.418	.760

Teams Finishing Last in Up-the-Middle OPS—1987-2000

Year	Team	Lg	W-L	Pct	Place/Tms	OBP	Slg	OPS
1987	Angels	AL	75-87	.463	6/7	.302	.322	.624
1987	Expos	NL	91-71	.562	3/6	.310	.366	.675
1988	Royals	AL	84-77	.522	3/7	.296	.348	.644
1988	Phillies	NL	65-96	.404	6/6	.303	.335	.638
1989	Angels	AL	91-71	.562	3/7	.295	.344	.639
1989	Pirates	NL	74-88	.457	5/6	.292	.319	.611
1990	Yankees	AL	67-95	.414	7/7	.295	.341	.636
1990	Astros	NL	75-87	.463	4/6	.323	.322	.645
1991	Angels	AL	81-81	.500	7/7	.306	.326	.632
1991	Phillies	NL	78-84	.481	3/6	.305	.329	.633
1992	Red Sox	AL	73-89	.451	7/7	.306	.322	.628
1992	Mets	NL	72-90	.444	5/6	.302	.319	.621
1993	Brewers	AL	69-93	.426	7/7	.315	.338	.654
1993	Padres	NL	61-101	.377	7/7	.309	.354	.663
1994	Angels	AL	47-68	.409	4/4	.305	.351	.656
1994	Giants	NL	55-60	.478	2/4	.312	.332	.644
1995	Royals	AL	70-74	.486	2/5	.315	.358	.673
1995	Cardinals	NL	62-81	.434	4/5	.304	.365	.669
1996	Blue Jays	AL	74-88	.457	4/5	.318	.350	.667
1996	Giants	NL	68-94	.420	4/4	.320	.348	.668
1997	Blue Jays	AL	76-86	.469	5/5	.300	.338	.638
1997	Cubs	NL	68-94	.420	5/5	.313	.382	.696
1998	Devil Rays	AL	63-99	.389	5/5	.304	.359	.663
1998	Phillies	NL	75-87	.463	3/5	.308	.358	.667
1999	Angels	AL	70-92	.432	4/4	.309	.358	.666
1999	Cardinals	NL	75-86	.466	4/6	.325	.389	.714
2000	Devil Rays	AL	69-92	.429	5/5	.309	.368	.677
2000	Phillies	NL	65-97	.401	5/5	.317	.360	.677
	Average (28 teams)			.453		.308	.347	.655

222 *Baseball Scoreboard*

Texas Rangers: Can A-Rod Create Enough Runs to Justify the Funds?
(p. 36)

Most Runs Created Through Seasonal Age 24
(age as of June 30)

Player	RC	1	2	3	4	5	6	7	8	9	10	Total
Ty Cobb	763	148	99	80	154	123	144	90	100	81	120	1,139
Mel Ott	756	143	130	140	120	134	107	105	110	124	71	1,184
Jimmie Foxx	713	166	144	139	152	119	172	142	115	97	33	1,279
Mickey Mantle	700	155	138	110	118	157	114	46	116	65	69	1,088
George Davis	689	105	133	85	82	80	87	98	1	80	87	838
Joe Kelley	650	127	98	122	102	88	75	77	77	46	49	861
Alex Rodriguez	627	—	—	—	—	—	—	—	—	—	—	0
Ted Williams	622	—	—	166	161	160	174	98	144	4	34	941
Ken Griffey Jr.	603	45	132	148	135	140	108	—	—	—	—	708
Jimmy Sheckard	592	58	78	85	74	55	79	79	115	86	30	739
Al Kaline	590	82	116	83	102	93	79	101	99	60	72	887
Buddy Lewis	590	—	—	—	53	84	53	—	33	—	—	223
Mike Tiernan	582	88	118	83	129	136	120	80	16	—	—	770
Arky Vaughan	577	84	109	99	117	72	70	100	—	—	—	651
Eddie Mathews	574	117	88	131	124	120	104	108	78	88	66	1,024
Freddy Lindstrom	570	46	75	80	50	40	9	—	—	—	—	300
Vada Pinson	561	91	108	92	96	59	52	81	62	56	48	745
Joe DiMaggio	559	128	146	121	—	—	—	91	109	137	74	806
John McGraw	555	136	134	90	75	32	2	2	0	0	—	471
Frank Robinson	543	127	152	88	124	113	141	108	75	117	95	1,140
Cesar Cedeno	536	95	87	31	62	84	35	63	38	51	46	592
Joe Jackson	532	81	115	99	14	110	138	—	—	—	—	557
Orlando Cepeda	531	111	97	2	79	115	67	84	104	34	13	706
Hank Aaron	522	143	117	125	134	146	114	117	115	124	95	1,230
Sherry Magee	521	132	83	84	84	106	84	53	50	62	19	757
Joe Medwick	503	163	105	103	88	93	79	55	83	35	13	817
Hal Trosky	493	120	104	108	54	—	—	63	—	31	—	480
Denny Lyons	492	127	74	119	60	23	89	21	—	—	—	513
Jake Beckley	482	119	128	113	71	93	80	111	110	86	89	1,000
Oyster Burns	477	109	90	121	74	124	33	—	—	—	—	551
Tris Speaker	475	116	123	107	136	111	82	87	146	116	110	1,134
Rickey Henderson	471	102	135	108	83	109	105	122	93	85	102	1,044
Sam Crawford	468	96	87	117	104	105	90	136	108	105	106	1,054
Bill Dahlen	465	89	134	66	105	92	83	69	74	80	78	870
Willie Keeler	464	153	109	127	113	100	83	82	87	81	80	1,015
Hugh Duffy	461	131	147	204	139	99	135	103	92	33	50	1,133
Robin Yount	454	55	136	109	101	75	91	118	113	124	84	1,006
Roberto Alomar	453	118	61	79	128	77	85	142	102	—	—	792
Johnny Bench	452	83	111	99	65	85	61	76	56	29	44	709
Lou Bierbauer	452	46	81	86	87	58	34	2	0	—	—	394
Rogers Hornsby	447	152	179	106	162	158	97	139	135	178	17	1,323
Fred Carroll	445	99	53	—	—	—	—	—	—	—	—	152
Bobby Doerr	442	85	103	—	89	73	109	99	111	72	—	741
Vladimir Guerrero	440	—	—	—	—	—	—	—	—	—	—	0

Baseball Scoreboard

Toronto Blue Jays: Is Batista the Littlest Big Bopper? (p. 38)

40-Plus HR Seasons Sorted by Weight—1876-2000
(all players <190 lbs.)

Player, Team	Year	HR	Ht	Wt	Player, Team	Year	HR	Ht	Wt
Ben Oglivie, Mil	1980	41	6'2"	160	Hank Aaron, Atl	1960	40	6'0"	180
Mel Ott, SF	1929	42	5'9"	170	Hank Aaron, Atl	1962	45	6'0"	180
Willie Mays, SF	1954	41	5'10"	170	Hank Aaron, Atl	1963	44	6'0"	180
Willie Mays, SF	1955	51	5'10"	170	Hank Aaron, Atl	1966	44	6'0"	180
Willie Mays, SF	1961	40	5'10"	170	Hank Aaron, Atl	1969	44	6'0"	180
Willie Mays, SF	1962	49	5'10"	170	Hank Aaron, Atl	1971	47	6'0"	180
Willie Mays, SF	1964	47	5'10"	170	Hank Aaron, Atl	1973	40	6'0"	180
Willie Mays, SF	1965	52	5'10"	170	Ernie Banks, ChC	1955	44	6'1"	180
Dave Johnson, Atl	1973	43	6'1"	170	Ernie Banks, ChC	1957	43	6'1"	180
Rogers Hornsby, StL	1922	42	5'11"	175	Ernie Banks, ChC	1958	47	6'1"	180
C. Yastrzemski, Bos	1967	44	5'11"	175	Ernie Banks, ChC	1959	45	6'1"	180
C. Yastrzemski, Bos	1969	40	5'11"	175	Ernie Banks, ChC	1960	41	6'1"	180
C. Yastrzemski, Bos	1970	40	5'11"	175	George Foster, Cin	1977	52	6'1"	180
Rico Petrocelli, Bos	1969	40	6'0"	175	George Foster, Cin	1978	40	6'1"	180
Billy Williams, ChC	1970	42	6'1"	175	Cy Williams, Phi	1923	41	6'2"	180
Tony Perez, Cin	1970	40	6'2"	175	Frank Robinson, Bal	1966	49	6'1"	183
Duke Snider, LA	1953	42	6'0"	179	Tony Batista, Tor	2000	41	6'0"	185
Duke Snider, LA	1954	40	6'0"	179	Norm Cash, Det	1961	41	6'0"	185
Duke Snider, LA	1955	42	6'0"	179	Chuck Klein, Phi	1929	43	6'0"	185
Duke Snider, LA	1956	43	6'0"	179	Chuck Klein, Phi	1930	40	6'0"	185
Duke Snider, LA	1957	40	6'0"	179	Dick Allen, Phi	1966	40	5'11"	187
Al Rosen, Cle	1953	43	5'10"	180	Willie Stargell, Pit	1971	48	6'2"	188
Hank Aaron, Atl	1957	44	6'0"	180	Willie Stargell, Pit	1973	44	6'2"	188

Arizona Diamondbacks: Is Finley's Post-30 Power Surge Unprecedented? (p. 40)

Highest Percentages of Career Home Runs (Through Seasonal Age 35)
Hit Between Ages 31-35—1876-2000
(minimum 150 HR through seasonal age 35; age as of June 30)

Player	HR 31-35	HR thru 35	HR Pct	Player	HR 31-35	HR thru 35	HR Pct
Hank Sauer	165	172	.96	Frank Howard	172	370	.46
Ken Williams	135	151	.89	Joe Carter	152	327	.46
Steve Finley	141	188	.75	Ron Cey	117	252	.46
Edgar Martinez	125	174	.72	Deron Johnson	103	226	.46
Ken Caminiti	139	196	.71	Babe Ruth	256	565	.45
Brady Anderson	126	182	.69	Cecil Cooper	101	223	.45
Sid Gordon	126	183	.69	Jay Buhner	139	308	.45
Mike Stanley	104	154	.68	Joe Adcock	127	283	.45
Brian Downing	110	166	.66	Sam Chapman	80	180	.44
B.J. Surhoff	103	160	.64	Greg Vaughn	141	320	.44
Dante Bichette	153	239	.64	Bobby Grich	89	202	.44
Jim Hickman	94	154	.61	Dwight Evans	143	325	.44
Dolph Camilli	133	231	.58	Joe Gordon	111	253	.44
Andres Galarraga	141	247	.57	Fred Lynn	114	264	.43
Carl Furillo	99	174	.57	Chili Davis	114	270	.42
Mickey Tettleton	137	242	.57	Jack Clark	141	335	.42
Bob Elliott	89	161	.55	Ron Fairly	74	176	.42
Jeff King	85	154	.55	David Justice	116	276	.42
Mark McGwire	284	522	.54	Chris Chambliss	75	180	.42
Jim Lemon	89	164	.54	Bob Watson	71	171	.42
Cliff Johnson	82	152	.54	Stan Musial	146	352	.41
Jay Bell	97	180	.54	Joe Morgan	88	213	.41
Al Smith	83	158	.53	Craig Biggio	66	160	.41
Glenallen Hill	97	185	.52	George Brett	105	255	.41
Earl Averill	110	211	.52	Willie Mays	223	542	.41
Ellis Burks	148	285	.52	Gorman Thomas	110	268	.41
Ben Oglivie	114	220	.52	Eddie Robinson	70	171	.41
Roy Campanella	125	242	.52	Barry Bonds	202	494	.41
Doug DeCinces	114	221	.52	Andre Dawson	141	346	.41
Rafael Palmeiro	206	400	.52	Paul Molitor	65	160	.41
Charlie Gehringer	79	154	.51	Kirby Puckett	84	207	.41
Donn Clendenon	79	155	.51	Dave Parker	99	247	.40
Joe Cronin	80	160	.50	Gus Zernial	92	230	.40
Ray Boone	74	150	.49	Ron Gant	116	292	.40
Barry Larkin	81	168	.48	Billy Williams	148	376	.39
Paul O'Neill	107	223	.48	Lou Gehrig	194	493	.39
Lou Whitaker	100	209	.48	Tommy Henrich	60	153	.39
Ken Singleton	106	222	.48	Norm Cash	116	297	.39
Roberto Clemente	103	217	.47	Rickey Henderson	88	226	.39
Bob Johnson	119	252	.47	Moises Alou	68	175	.39
Graig Nettles	132	280	.47	Harry Heilmann	71	183	.39
Todd Zeile	96	205	.47	George Scott	105	271	.39
Willie Stargell	172	368	.47	Devon White	68	176	.39
Roy Sievers	136	291	.47	Dave Winfield	128	332	.39
Andre Thornton	110	236	.47	Gil Hodges	133	345	.39

Atlanta Braves: How Extraordinary Was Furcal's First Season? (p. 42)

Highest Batting Averages, Teenagers—1876-2000
(minimum 300 PA; age as of June 30)

Player, Team	Year	Age	Avg	OBP	SB	RC
Mel Ott, NYG	1928	19	.322	.397	3	85
Ty Cobb, Det	1906	19	.316	.355	23	56
Cesar Cedeno, Hou	1970	19	.310	.340	17	55
Rafael Furcal, Atl	2000	19	.295	.394	40	73
Buddy Lewis, Was	1936	19	.291	.347	6	87
Tony Conigliaro, Bos	1964	19	.290	.354	2	67
Chubby Dean, Phi	1936	19	.287	.337	3	45
Freddy Lindstrom, NYG	1925	19	.287	.332	5	48
Monte Ward, Prv	1879	19	.286	.299	—	59
Sherry Magee, Phi	1904	19	.277	.308	11	50
Jimmy Sheckard, Bro	1898	19	.277	.349	8	69
Johnny Lush, Phi	1904	18	.276	.336	12	52
Al Kaline, Det	1954	19	.276	.305	9	45
Travis Jackson, NYG	1923	19	.275	.321	3	42
Phil Cavarretta, ChC	1935	18	.275	.322	4	81
Phil Cavarretta, ChC	1936	19	.273	.306	8	53
Joe Quinn, STL	1884	19	.270	.285	—	69
John McGraw, Bal	1892	19	.269	.355	15	46
Robin Yount, Mil	1975	19	.267	.307	12	65
Mickey Mantle, NYY	1951	19	.267	.349	8	57
George Davis, Cle	1890	19	.264	.336	22	90
Ken Griffey Jr., Sea	1989	19	.264	.329	16	67
Ed Kranepool, NYM	1964	19	.257	.310	0	53
Milt Scott, Det-Pit	1885	19	.254	.272	—	43
Les Mann, Bos	1913	19	.253	.291	7	47
Bob Kennedy, CWS	1940	19	.252	.301	3	56
Sibby Sisti, Bos	1940	19	.251	.311	4	55
Robin Yount, Mil	1974	18	.250	.276	7	32
Milt Scott, Det	1884	18	.247	.262	—	57
Cass Michaels, CWS	1945	19	.245	.307	8	42
Doggie Miller, Pit	1884	19	.225	.257	—	38
Rusty Staub, Hou	1963	19	.224	.309	0	52
Bobby Del Greco, Pit	1952	19	.217	.301	6	27
Ted Kazanski, Phi	1953	19	.217	.275	1	30
Jose Oquendo, NYM	1983	19	.213	.260	8	15
Will Smalley, Cle	1890	19	.213	.303	10	56
Jack Glasscock, Cle	1879	19	.209	.224	—	30
Mike Slattery, Bos	1884	17	.208	.216	—	45
John Knight, Phi	1905	19	.203	.227	4	19
Ben Conroy, Phi	1890	19	.171	.262	17	40

Chicago Cubs: Can Sosa Keep Swinging Away And Still Hit .300? (p. 44)

Most Strikeouts While Batting .300 or Better, Season—1876-2000 (minimum 110 SO)

Player, Team	Year	H	AB	SO	Avg	Next Yr Avg
Bobby Bonds, SF	1970	200	663	189	.302	.288
Sammy Sosa, ChC	1998	198	643	171	.308	.288
Sammy Sosa, ChC	2000	193	604	168	.320	—
Andres Galarraga, Col	1996	190	626	157	.304	.318
Mo Vaughn, Bos	1996	207	635	154	.326	.315
Mo Vaughn, Bos	1997	166	527	154	.315	.337
Andres Galarraga, Mon	1988	184	609	153	.302	.257
Greg Luzinski, Phi	1975	179	596	151	.300	.304
Dick Allen, Phi	1965	187	619	150	.302	.317
Mo Vaughn, Bos	1995	165	550	150	.300	.326
Andres Galarraga, Atl	1998	169	555	146	.305	—
Mo Vaughn, Bos	1998	205	609	144	.337	.281
Cito Gaston, SD	1970	186	584	142	.318	.228
Andres Galarraga, Col	1997	191	600	141	.318	.305
Dale Murphy, Atl	1985	185	616	141	.300	.265
Jim Thome, Cle	1996	157	505	141	.311	.286
Greg Luzinski, Phi	1977	171	554	140	.309	.265
Dick Allen, Phi	1964	201	632	138	.318	.302
Dick Allen, Phi	1966	166	524	136	.317	.307
Danny Tartabull, KC	1987	180	582	136	.309	.274
Geoff Jenkins, Mil	2000	155	512	135	.303	—
Phil Bradley, Sea	1986	163	526	134	.310	.297
Mike Easler, Bos	1984	188	601	134	.313	.262
Tony Perez, Cin	1970	186	587	134	.317	.269
Bobby Abreu, Phi	1998	155	497	133	.312	.335
Manny Ramirez, Cle	1999	174	522	131	.333	.351
Phil Bradley, Sea	1985	192	641	129	.300	.310
Jose Canseco, Oak	1988	187	610	128	.307	.269
Donn Clendenon, Pit	1965	184	612	128	.301	.299
Travis Fryman, Det	1993	182	607	128	.300	.263
Jeff Bagwell, Hou	1999	171	562	127	.304	.310
Lou Brock, ChC-StL	1964	200	634	127	.315	.288
Andres Galarraga, Mon	1987	168	551	127	.305	.302
Dick Allen, CWS	1972	156	506	126	.308	.316
Derek Bell, Hou	1998	198	630	126	.314	.236
Andres Galarraga, Atl	2000	149	494	126	.302	—
Juan Gonzalez, Tex	1998	193	606	126	.318	.326
Jim Rice, Bos	1978	213	677	126	.315	.325
Bernard Gilkey, NYM	1996	181	571	125	.317	.249
Jeffrey Leonard, SF	1984	155	514	123	.302	.241
Jay Bell, Pit	1993	187	604	122	.310	.276
Reggie Jackson, NYY	1980	154	514	122	.300	.237
Jim Rice, Bos	1975	174	564	122	.309	.282
Reggie Sanders, Cin	1995	148	484	122	.306	.251

Player, Team	Year	H	AB	SO	Avg	Next Yr Avg
Ken Griffey Jr., Sea	1997	185	608	121	.304	.284
Ron LeFlore, Det	1977	212	652	121	.325	.297
Phil Nevin, SD	2000	163	538	121	.303	—
Alex Rodriguez, Sea	1998	213	686	121	.310	.285
Alex Rodriguez, Sea	2000	175	554	121	.316	—
Dick Stuart, Pit	1961	160	532	121	.301	.228
Danny Tartabull, KC	1991	153	484	121	.316	.266
Mickey Mantle, NYY	1958	158	519	120	.304	.285
Jim Rice, Bos	1977	206	644	120	.320	.315
Willie Stargell, Pit	1969	160	522	120	.307	.264
Jimmie Foxx, Bos	1936	198	585	119	.338	.285
Derek Jeter, NYY	1998	203	626	119	.324	.349
Eric Karros, LA	1999	176	578	119	.304	.250
George Scott, Bos	1967	171	565	119	.303	.171
John Jaha, Mil	1996	163	543	118	.300	.247
Dick Allen, Phi	1967	142	463	117	.307	.263
Shawn Green, Tor	1999	190	614	117	.309	.269
Tony Perez, Cin	1973	177	564	117	.314	.265
Manny Ramirez, Cle	2000	154	439	117	.351	—
Bobby Abreu, Phi	2000	182	576	116	.316	—
Jeff Bagwell, Hou	2000	183	590	116	.310	—
Derek Jeter, NYY	1999	219	627	116	.349	.339
Al Martin, Pit	1996	189	630	116	.300	.291
Manny Ramirez, Cle	1997	184	561	115	.328	.294
Jeff Bagwell, Hou	1996	179	568	114	.315	.286
Ellis Burks, Col	1996	211	613	114	.344	.290
Jim Edmonds, Ana	1998	184	599	114	.307	.250
Bobby Abreu, Phi	1999	183	546	113	.335	.316
Craig Biggio, Hou	1998	210	646	113	.325	.294
Carl Everett, Bos	2000	149	496	113	.300	—
Felix Jose, StL	1991	173	568	113	.305	.295
Henry Rodriguez, ChC	1999	136	447	113	.304	.256
Jim Thome, Cle	1995	142	452	113	.314	.311
Mickey Mantle, NYY	1961	163	514	112	.317	.321
Mark McGwire, Oak	1996	132	423	112	.312	.274
Manny Ramirez, Cle	1995	149	484	112	.308	.309
Benito Santiago, SD	1987	164	546	112	.300	.248
Frank Thomas, CWS	1991	178	559	112	.318	.323
Mo Vaughn, Bos	1994	122	394	112	.310	.300
Travis Fryman, Cle	2000	184	574	111	.321	—
Ron LeFlore, Det	1976	172	544	111	.316	.325
Mickey Mantle, NYY	1952	171	549	111	.311	.295
Tim Salmon, Cal	1995	177	537	111	.330	.286
Cecil Cooper, Mil	1977	193	643	110	.300	.312
Richard Hidalgo, Hou	2000	175	558	110	.314	—
Ray Lankford, StL	1999	129	422	110	.306	.253
Dale Murphy, Atl	1983	178	589	110	.302	.290

Florida Marlins: Is Castillo the New Enzo Hernandez? (p. 52)

Highest AB/RBI Rates, Season —1876-2000
(minimum 500 AB)

Player, Team	Year	AB	RBI	AB/RBI	Avg
Enzo Hernandez, SD	1971	549	12	45.8	.222
Billy Sunday, Pit	1888	505	15	33.7	.236
Clyde Milan, Was	1910	531	16	33.2	.279
Luis Castillo, Fla	2000	539	17	31.7	.334
Morrie Rath, CWS	1912	591	19	31.1	.272
Ivy Olson, Bro	1918	506	17	29.8	.239
Richie Ashburn, Phi	1959	564	20	28.2	.266
Doc Casey, Bro	1907	527	19	27.7	.231
Greasy Neale, Cin	1916	530	20	26.5	.262
Larry Bowa, Phi	1971	650	25	26.0	.249
Sparky Adams, StL-Cin	1933	568	22	25.8	.257
Don Blasingame, StL	1959	615	24	25.6	.289
John Farrell, StL	1904	509	20	25.5	.255
Harry Bay, Cle	1905	552	22	25.1	.301
Patsy Dougherty, Bos-NYA	1904	647	26	24.9	.280
Charles Moran, Was-StL	1904	515	21	24.5	.196
Sandy Alomar, Cal	1972	610	25	24.4	.239
Donie Bush, Det	1917	581	24	24.2	.281
Jigger Statz, Bro	1927	507	21	24.1	.274
Burt Shotton, Was	1918	505	21	24.0	.261
Sonny Jackson, Hou	1966	596	25	23.8	.292
Beals Becker, Bos	1909	562	24	23.4	.246
Lloyd Waner, Pit	1927	629	27	23.3	.355
Alan Wiggins, SD	1983	503	22	22.9	.276
Donie Bush, Det	1918	500	22	22.7	.234
John Farrell, StL	1902	565	25	22.6	.250
Frank Taveras, NYM	1980	562	25	22.5	.279
Horace Clarke, NYY	1968	579	26	22.3	.230
Larry Kopf, Cin	1917	573	26	22.0	.255
Julio Cruz, Sea	1978	550	25	22.0	.235

Highest Career AB/RBI Rates
(minimum 1,500 AB; only seasons with RBI available are considered)

Player	AB	RBI	AB/RBI	Avg
Luis Castillo	1,606	71	22.6	.289
Morrie Rath	2,048	92	22.3	.254
Al Burch	2,185	103	21.2	.254
Enzo Hernandez	2,327	113	20.6	.224
Alan Wiggins	2,247	118	19.0	.259
Frank Taveras	4,043	214	18.9	.255
Sonny Jackson	3,055	162	18.9	.251
Harry Bay	2,640	141	18.7	.273
Bobby Young	2,447	137	17.9	.249
Bud Harrelson	4,744	267	17.8	.236
Roy Thomas	5,296	299	17.7	.290
Miller Huggins	5,558	318	17.5	.265
Wayne Tolleson	2,322	133	17.5	.241
Jose Tartabull	1,857	107	17.4	.261
Bob Ganley	2,129	123	17.3	.254
Don Blasingame	5,296	308	17.2	.258
Burt Shotton	4,945	290	17.1	.271
Bob Lillis	2,328	137	17.0	.236
Bill North	3,900	230	17.0	.261

Baseball Scoreboard

Milwaukee Brewers: Is Hammonds An Upgrade Over Grissom? (p. 61)

OPS—2000, Listed Alphabetically
(minimum 502 PA)

Player, Team	OBP	Slg	OPS	Player, Team	OBP	Slg	OPS
Abreu, Phi	.416	.554	.970	DeShields, Bal	.369	.444	.813
Alfonzo, NYM	.425	.542	.967	Durham, CWS	.361	.450	.810
Alicea, Tex	.365	.404	.769	Dye, KC	.390	.561	.951
Alomar, Cle	.378	.475	.853	Easley, Det	.350	.416	.766
Alou, Hou	.416	.623	1.039	Edmonds, StL	.411	.583	.994
Anderson B, Bal	.375	.421	.796	Encarnacion, Det	.330	.433	.764
Anderson G, Ana	.307	.519	.827	Erstad, Ana	.409	.541	.951
Aurilia, SF	.339	.444	.783	Everett, Bos	.373	.587	.959
Ausmus, Det	.357	.365	.722	Finley, Ari	.361	.544	.904
Bagwell, Hou	.424	.615	1.039	Fryman, Cle	.392	.516	.908
Batista, Tor	.307	.519	.827	Fullmer, Tor	.340	.558	.898
Bell D, Sea	.316	.381	.697	Furcal, Atl	.394	.382	.776
Bell D, NYM	.348	.425	.773	Galarraga, Atl	.369	.526	.895
Bell J, Ari	.348	.437	.786	Garciaparra, Bos	.434	.599	1.033
Belle, Bal	.342	.474	.817	Giambi J, Oak	.476	.647	1.123
Belliard, Mil	.354	.389	.743	Giles, Pit	.432	.594	1.026
Beltre, LA	.360	.475	.835	Glanville, Phi	.307	.374	.681
Benard, SF	.342	.396	.739	Glaus, Ana	.404	.604	1.008
Bergeron, Mon	.320	.349	.669	Gonzalez A, Tor	.313	.404	.717
Bichette, Cin-Bos	.350	.477	.826	Gonzalez L, Ari	.392	.544	.935
Bonds, SF	.440	.688	1.127	Goodwin, Col-LA	.346	.352	.698
Boone B, SD	.326	.421	.747	Grace, ChC	.394	.429	.824
Bordick, Bal-NYM	.341	.443	.783	Green S, LA	.367	.472	.839
Brosius, NYY	.299	.374	.673	Grieve, Oak	.359	.487	.845
Buford, ChC	.324	.390	.714	Griffey Jr., Cin	.387	.556	.942
Burnitz, Mil	.356	.456	.811	Grissom, Mil	.288	.351	.640
Cameron, Sea	.365	.438	.803	Grudzielanek, LA	.335	.389	.724
Casey, Cin	.385	.517	.902	Guerrero V, Mon	.410	.664	1.074
Castillo L, Fla	.418	.388	.806	Gutierrez, ChC	.375	.401	.775
Chavez E, Oak	.355	.495	.850	Guzman, Min	.299	.388	.687
Cirillo, Col	.392	.477	.869	Hammonds, Col	.395	.529	.924
Clark W, Bal-StL	.418	.546	.964	Helton, Col	.463	.698	1.162
Clayton, Tex	.301	.384	.685	Henderson, NYM-Sea	.368	.305	.673
Coomer, Min	.317	.415	.733	Hidalgo, Hou	.391	.636	1.028
Cordero, Pit-Cle	.328	.464	.792	Higginson, Det	.377	.538	.915
Cruz D, Det	.318	.449	.767	Jackson, SD	.345	.377	.721
Cruz J, Tor	.323	.466	.789	Jenkins, Mil	.360	.588	.948
Damon, KC	.382	.495	.877	Jeter, NYY	.416	.481	.896
Daubach, Bos	.315	.448	.764	Jones A, Atl	.366	.541	.907
Delgado C, Tor	.470	.664	1.134	Jones C, Atl	.404	.566	.970

Player, Team	OBP	Slg	OPS	Player, Team	OBP	Slg	OPS
Jones J, Min	.319	.463	.781	Piazza, NYM	.398	.614	1.012
Jordan B, Atl	.320	.421	.742	Posada, NYY	.417	.527	.943
Justice, Cle-NYY	.377	.584	.961	Quinn, KC	.342	.488	.830
Karros, LA	.321	.459	.780	Ramirez M, Cle	.457	.697	1.154
Kendall, Pit	.412	.470	.882	Randa, KC	.343	.438	.781
Kennedy, Ana	.300	.403	.703	Reese, Cin	.319	.386	.705
Kent, SF	.424	.596	1.021	Relaford, Phi-SD	.351	.300	.651
Klesko, SD	.393	.516	.909	Renteria, StL	.346	.423	.770
Konerko, CWS	.363	.481	.844	Rodriguez A, Sea	.420	.606	1.026
Koskie, Min	.400	.441	.841	Rolen, Phi	.370	.551	.920
Kotsay, Fla	.347	.443	.791	Salmon, Ana	.404	.540	.945
Lamb M, Tex	.328	.373	.702	Sanchez, KC	.314	.322	.637
Lansing, Col-Bos	.292	.365	.657	Segui, Tex-Cle	.388	.510	.898
Lawton, Min	.405	.460	.865	Sexson, Cle-Mil	.349	.499	.848
Ledee, NYY-Cle-Tex	.322	.381	.703	Sheffield, LA	.438	.643	1.081
Lee C, CWS	.345	.484	.829	Singleton, CWS	.301	.382	.683
Lee D, Fla	.368	.507	.875	Snow, SF	.365	.459	.824
Lofton, Cle	.369	.422	.791	Sosa, ChC	.406	.634	1.040
Long, Oak	.336	.452	.788	Stairs, Oak	.333	.414	.747
Lopez J, Atl	.337	.484	.822	Stewart, Tor	.363	.518	.882
Lowell, Fla	.344	.474	.818	Surhoff, Bal-Atl	.344	.443	.787
Martin, SD-Sea	.338	.452	.791	Sweeney M, KC	.407	.523	.930
Martinez D, 4Tm	.346	.370	.716	Tejada, Oak	.349	.479	.828
Martinez E, Sea	.423	.579	1.002	Thomas, CWS	.436	.625	1.061
Martinez T, NYY	.328	.422	.749	Thome, Cle	.398	.531	.929
McGriff, TB	.373	.452	.826	Valentin J, CWS	.343	.491	.835
McLemore, Sea	.353	.316	.669	Varitek, Bos	.342	.388	.730
Meares, Pit	.305	.381	.685	Vaughn G, TB	.365	.499	.864
Molina, Ana	.318	.421	.739	Vaughn M, Ana	.365	.498	.864
Morris W, Pit	.341	.343	.684	Velarde, Oak	.354	.400	.754
Mueller, SF	.333	.388	.721	Ventura, NYM	.338	.439	.777
Nevin, SD	.374	.543	.916	Vidro, Mon	.379	.540	.918
Nixon, Bos	.368	.461	.830	Vina, StL	.380	.398	.779
O'Leary, Bos	.320	.411	.731	Vizquel, Cle	.377	.375	.753
O'Neill, NYY	.336	.424	.760	Williams B, NYY	.391	.566	.957
Offerman, Bos	.354	.359	.713	Williams G, TB	.312	.427	.739
Olerud, Sea	.392	.439	.831	Wilson P, Fla	.331	.486	.817
Ordonez M, CWS	.371	.546	.917	Womack, Ari	.307	.384	.692
Owens, SD	.346	.381	.727	Young D, Cin	.346	.491	.837
Palmeiro R, Tex	.397	.558	.954	Young E, ChC	.367	.399	.766
Palmer, Det	.338	.471	.809	Young K, Pit	.311	.433	.744
Payton, NYM	.331	.447	.778	Zeile, NYM	.356	.467	.823
Perez N, Col	.314	.427	.741	**MLB Average**	**.345**	**.437**	**.782**

Montreal Expos: Is Guerrero's Combination of Power And Discipline Unmatched? (p. 63)

Lowest SO/PA Ratios, Players With 40-Plus Home Runs in Consecutive Years—1961-2000, Listed Alphabetically

Player	Years	HR	SO	PA	SO/PA
Hank Aaron	1962-1963	89	167	1,381	.121
Jeff Bagwell	1999-2000	89	243	1,448	.168
Albert Belle	1995-1996	98	167	1,346	.124
Barry Bonds	1996-1997	82	163	1,365	.119
Jay Buhner	1995-1996	84	279	1,206	.231
Jay Buhner	1996-1997	84	334	1,332	.251
Vinny Castilla	1996-1997	80	196	1,341	.146
Vinny Castilla	1997-1998	86	197	1,365	.144
Carlos Delgado	1999-2000	85	245	1,392	.176
Cecil Fielder	1990-1991	95	333	1,385	.240
George Foster	1977-1978	92	245	1,376	.178
Andres Galarraga	1996-1997	88	298	1,365	.218
Andres Galarraga	1997-1998	85	287	1,322	.217
Juan Gonzalez	1992-1993	89	242	1,219	.199
Juan Gonzalez	1996-1997	89	189	1,171	.161
Juan Gonzalez	1997-1998	87	233	1,248	.187
Ken Griffey Jr.	1993-1994	85	164	1,184	.139
Ken Griffey Jr.	1996-1997	105	225	1,342	.168
Ken Griffey Jr.	1997-1998	112	242	1,424	.170
Ken Griffey Jr.	1998-1999	104	229	1,426	.161
Ken Griffey Jr.	1999-2000	88	225	1,337	.168
Vladimir Guerrero	1999-2000	86	136	1,315	.103
Frank Howard	1968-1969	92	237	1,365	.174
Frank Howard	1969-1970	92	221	1,408	.157
Harmon Killebrew	1961-1962	94	251	1,322	.190
Harmon Killebrew	1962-1963	93	247	1,262	.196
Harmon Killebrew	1963-1964	94	240	1,278	.188
Harmon Killebrew	1969-1970	90	168	1,374	.122
Mickey Mantle	1960-1961	94	237	1,290	.184
Willie Mays	1961-1962	89	162	1,365	.119
Willie Mays	1964-1965	99	143	1,303	.110
Mark McGwire	1996-1997	110	271	1,205	.225
Mark McGwire	1997-1998	128	314	1,338	.235
Mark McGwire	1998-1999	135	296	1,342	.221
Rafael Palmeiro	1998-1999	90	160	1,383	.116
Manny Ramirez	1998-1999	89	252	1,303	.193
Alex Rodriguez	1998-1999	84	230	1,320	.174
Alex Rodriguez	1999-2000	83	230	1,244	.185
Mike Schmidt	1979-1980	93	234	1,327	.176
Sammy Sosa	1998-1999	129	342	1,434	.238
Sammy Sosa	1999-2000	113	339	1,417	.239
Frank Thomas	1995-1996	80	144	1,296	.111
Greg Vaughn	1998-1999	95	258	1,304	.198
Carl Yastrzemski	1969-1970	80	157	1,405	.112
Average (44 players)		**94**	**231**	**1,331**	**.174**

Philadelphia Phillies: How Damaging Are Poor Starts? (p. 68)

Worst Run Differentials After First Inning—2000

Team	Own	Opp	Diff	Trail	W-L	Pct	Lead	W-L	Pct	Tied	W-L	Pct	Overall	Pct
Phillies	69	120	-51	49	12-37	.245	31	18-13	.581	82	35-47	.427	65-97	.401
Rangers	112	154	-42	51	15-36	.294	39	26-13	.667	72	30-42	.417	71-91	.438
Dodgers	103	135	-32	56	23-33	.411	41	29-12	.707	65	34-31	.523	86-76	.531
Brewers	88	110	-22	43	11-31	.262	38	22-16	.579	82	40-42	.488	73-89	.451
Angels	99	119	-20	46	14-32	.304	35	26-9	.743	81	42-39	.519	82-80	.506
Cubs	91	111	-20	43	13-30	.302	34	21-13	.618	85	31-54	.365	65-97	.401
Astros	114	132	-18	51	19-32	.373	35	22-13	.629	76	31-45	.408	72-90	.444
Red Sox	87	103	-16	41	19-22	.463	35	29-6	.829	86	37-49	.430	85-77	.525
Twins	87	102	-15	42	8-34	.190	38	24-14	.632	82	37-45	.451	69-93	.426
Expos	100	115	-15	40	10-30	.250	37	20-17	.541	85	37-48	.435	67-95	.414
Braves	94	108	-14	39	17-22	.436	46	32-14	.696	77	46-31	.597	95-67	.586
Devil Rays	76	88	-12	34	7-27	.206	32	20-12	.625	95	42-53	.442	69-92	.429
Royals	93	104	-11	39	10-29	.256	40	24-16	.600	83	43-40	.518	77-85	.475
Padres	109	112	-3	46	15-31	.326	41	23-18	.561	75	38-37	.507	76-86	.469
Yankees	91	92	-1	38	11-27	.289	39	29-10	.744	84	47-37	.560	87-74	.540
Reds	113	110	3	51	22-29	.431	51	31-19	.620	61	32-29	.525	85-77	.525
Blue Jays	118	115	3	41	14-27	.341	46	28-18	.609	75	41-34	.547	83-79	.512
Marlins	116	110	6	45	14-31	.311	50	33-17	.660	66	32-34	.485	79-82	.491
Rockies	130	120	10	49	18-31	.367	45	32-13	.711	68	32-36	.471	82-80	.506
Pirates	126	116	10	42	11-31	.262	46	24-22	.522	74	34-40	.459	69-93	.426
Indians	111	98	13	40	14-26	.350	46	31-15	.674	76	45-31	.592	90-72	.556
Athletics	129	113	16	48	20-28	.417	42	29-13	.690	71	42-29	.592	91-70	.565
Orioles	101	85	16	37	12-25	.324	38	25-13	.658	87	37-50	.425	74-88	.457
Mets	89	73	16	34	18-16	.529	41	30-11	.732	87	46-41	.529	94-68	.580
Giants	131	112	19	36	13-23	.361	48	35-13	.729	78	49-29	.628	97-65	.599
D-Backs	99	79	20	33	11-22	.333	35	25-10	.714	94	49-45	.521	85-77	.525
Mariners	127	98	29	40	10-30	.250	45	32-13	.711	77	49-28	.636	91-71	.562
White Sox	131	97	34	35	16-19	.457	53	42-11	.792	74	37-37	.500	95-67	.586
Tigers	106	66	40	31	10-21	.323	44	29-15	.659	87	40-47	.460	79-83	.488
Cardinals	147	90	57	32	11-21	.344	61	42-19	.689	69	42-27	.609	95-67	.586
MLB Avg						.334			.666			.500		.500

Baseball Scoreboard

Pittsburgh Pirates: Is Kendall Better Suited to Bat Leadoff Than Any Catcher Ever? (p. 70)

Best Leadoff Skills, Catchers—1876-2000, Sorted by OBP
(minimum 500 G, 50 percent of G at catcher and .310 OBP)

Player	OBP	R/162G	SB/162G	Player	OBP	R/162G	SB/162G
Mickey Cochrane	.419	114	7	Shanty Hogan	.348	47	1
Johnny Bassler	.416	50	3	Ted Simmons	.348	71	1
Jason Kendall	.402	97	23	Yogi Berra	.348	90	2
Wally Schang	.393	68	11	Larry Woodall	.347	48	5
Mike Piazza	.392	102	2	Jack Clements	.347	87	8
Dick Dietz	.390	57	1	Tony Eusebio	.347	49	0
Gene Tenace	.388	68	4	Andy Seminick	.347	61	3
Roger Bresnahan	.386	76	24	Thurman Munson	.346	79	5
Bill Dickey	.382	84	3	Jim Pagliaroni	.344	51	1
Rick Ferrell	.378	59	2	Mike Scioscia	.344	45	3
Pat Collins	.378	44	1	Phil Masi	.344	55	6
Aaron Robinson	.375	55	0	Geno Petralli	.344	37	2
Earl Smith	.374	42	3	Frankie Hayes	.343	65	4
Mike Grady	.374	86	20	Hal Wagner	.343	43	2
Bubbles Hargrave	.372	60	6	Hank Severeid	.342	48	4
Fred Carroll	.370	117	29	Heinie Peitz	.342	70	12
Gabby Hartnett	.370	71	2	Johnny Gooch	.342	46	2
Mike Stanley	.370	69	1	Johnny Bench	.342	82	5
Spud Davis	.369	43	1	Ron Hodges	.342	29	2
Mickey Tettleton	.369	78	3	Birdie Tebbetts	.341	50	4
Chief Meyers	.367	45	7	John Stearns	.341	67	18
Chris Hoiles	.366	75	1	Jocko Milligan	.341	92	9
Muddy Ruel	.365	54	7	Carlton Fisk	.341	83	8
Babe Phelps	.362	53	2	Deacon McGuire	.341	70	11
Smoky Burgess	.362	46	1	Charlie Bennett	.340	84	6
Butch Henline	.361	56	4	Ivan Rodriguez	.340	92	8
Roy Campanella	.360	84	3	Ray Schalk	.340	53	16
Bob O'Farrell	.360	56	4	Brent Mayne	.340	45	2
Ernie Lombardi	.358	53	1	Jack Lapp	.340	48	5
Joe Ferguson	.358	65	4	Duke Sims	.340	51	1
Darren Daulton	.357	71	7	Ron Hassey	.340	47	2
Art Wilson	.357	47	10	Bill Freehan	.340	64	2
Sherm Lollar	.357	58	2	Tom Haller	.340	58	2
Wes Westrum	.356	53	2	Pinky Hargrave	.339	44	4
Ellie Rodriguez	.356	46	4	Chief Zimmer	.339	78	19
Harry McCurdy	.355	44	4	Clint Courtney	.339	45	1
Frankie Pytlak	.355	64	11	Biff Pocoroba	.339	36	2
Ed Bailey	.355	58	2	Grover Hartley	.339	38	8
John Romano	.354	64	1	Ken O'Dea	.338	51	1
Joe Garagiola	.354	47	1	Red Wilson	.338	56	7
Darrell Porter	.354	70	4	Ted Easterly	.338	49	10
Tommy Clarke	.351	39	10	Brad Ausmus	.338	70	13
Stan Lopata	.351	71	3	Duke Farrell	.338	86	16
Mike LaValliere	.351	34	1	Don Slaught	.338	51	2
Hank Gowdy	.351	42	9	Javy Lopez	.338	70	1
Earl Battey	.349	56	2	Bob Stinson	.337	41	2
Steve O'Neill	.349	46	3	Tim McCarver	.337	50	5
Butch Wynegar	.348	62	1	Joe Nolan	.336	41	2

Player	OBP	R/162G	SB/162G	Player	OBP	R/162G	SB/162G
Jimmie Wilson	.336	62	9	Elston Howard	.322	62	1
Mike Tresh	.335	51	3	Gus Triandos	.322	52	0
Ed McFarland	.335	73	12	Hank Foiles	.321	46	1
Bruce Edwards	.335	52	2	Mike Fitzgerald	.321	42	6
Gary Carter	.335	72	3	Bill Rariden	.320	45	8
Chad Kreuter	.334	51	1	Hobie Landrith	.320	38	1
Joe Astroth	.334	49	2	Bruce Benedict	.320	35	2
Glenn Myatt	.334	56	3	Alan Ashby	.320	47	1
Bill Carrigan	.334	45	8	Charlie Moore	.319	55	6
Jeff Reed	.334	41	1	Chris Cannizzaro	.319	29	1
Val Picinich	.334	47	5	Johnny Kling	.319	61	16
Charles Johnson	.333	66	1	Rick Dempsey	.319	48	2
Johnny Peacock	.333	46	4	Cy Perkins	.319	46	2
Rick Wilkins	.333	63	2	Joe Sugden	.319	59	9
Les Moss	.333	41	0	Joe Girardi	.318	61	6
Joe Ginsberg	.332	39	2	Milt May	.318	43	1
Walker Cooper	.332	63	2	Charlie Lau	.318	32	1
Al Evans	.332	43	3	Nig Clarke	.318	50	5
Les Nunamaker	.332	44	8	Lew McCarty	.318	34	6
Eddie Taubensee	.331	59	2	Clyde Kluttz	.318	42	1
Mike Lieberthal	.331	76	2	Earl Williams	.318	66	0
Ray Hayworth	.331	51	0	Mickey Owen	.318	45	5
Earl Grace	.331	44	0	John Wathan	.318	57	20
Patsy Gharrity	.331	57	8	Hal Smith	.317	50	1
Harry Danning	.330	66	2	Bob Scheffing	.316	33	2
Carl Sawatski	.330	34	1	Jerry Grote	.316	40	2
Bob Brenly	.330	60	8	Wilbert Robinson	.316	75	23
Bennie Tate	.330	41	1	Jack Boyle	.315	100	19
Jake Early	.330	47	2	Gene Desautels	.315	48	3
Buddy Rosar	.330	55	3	Bob Boone	.315	49	3
Matt Batts	.329	48	2	Sandy Alomar Jr.	.315	68	4
Pop Schriver	.329	74	9	Dave Valle	.314	52	1
Brian Harper	.329	55	1	Mike Gonzalez	.314	44	8
Gus Mancuso	.328	43	1	Con Daily	.314	72	24
Don Pavletich	.328	49	2	Clyde McCullough	.314	45	4
Jim Essian	.327	44	2	Jim Keenan	.314	79	13
Jim Sundberg	.327	51	2	Ray Mueller	.314	46	2
Al Lopez	.326	51	4	Terry Kennedy	.314	52	1
Terry Steinbach	.326	67	2	Dan Wilson	.313	58	4
John Roseboro	.326	52	7	Frank Snyder	.313	39	4
Manny Sanguillen	.326	63	4	Lance Parrish	.313	70	2
Dave Rader	.326	49	2	Bob Swift	.312	34	2
Darrin Fletcher	.326	51	0	Del Crandall	.312	60	3
Ed Phelps	.325	48	8	Del Rice	.312	42	0
Todd Hundley	.325	69	2	Kirt Manwaring	.311	40	2
Ozzie Virgil	.324	57	1	Ed Ott	.311	56	4
Ernie Whitt	.324	55	3	Johnny Edwards	.311	47	2
Lenny Webster	.324	43	0	Rollie Hemsley	.311	57	3
Hank DeBerry	.323	43	3	Mickey Livingston	.310	37	2
Luke Sewell	.323	65	6	Jeff Sweeney	.310	44	16
Ed Fitz Gerald	.323	40	2	Boileryard Clarke	.310	67	9
Charlie Berry	.322	45	3	Ed Herrmann	.310	43	1
Mike Macfarlane	.322	64	2	Russ Nixon	.310	38	0
Clay Dalrymple	.322	36	0	Alex Trevino	.310	42	3
Tom Lampkin	.322	45	5				

Baseball Scoreboard

St. Louis Cardinals: Can Ankiel Overcome His Control Difficulties?
(p. 72)

Pitchers Who Averaged 4.00 BB/9 in One Season And 8.00 BB/9 in a Subsequent Season—1900-2000, Listed Alphabetically (minimum 20 IP in both seasons)

Pitcher	Career	BB/9 Prior	Year	BB/9	BB/9 Thereafter
Lloyd Allen	1969-75	4.89	1974	9.31	10.13
Frank Biscan	1942-48	3.67	1946	8.74	6.48
Steve Blass	1964-74	3.03	1973	8.53	12.60
George Boehler	1912-26	5.49	1923	8.26	5.97
Bernie Boland	1915-21	3.51	1921	9.33	—
Pedro Borbon	1992-00	4.22	2000	8.21	—
Marshall Bridges	1959-65	4.76	1963	8.18	4.33
Ernie Broglio	1959-66	3.70	1965	8.17	5.49
Joe Coleman	1942-55	4.08	1950	8.33	4.61
Harry Coveleski	1907-18	3.11	1910	9.61	2.37
Joe Decker	1969-79	4.15	1975	12.30	6.86
Rob Dibble	1988-95	3.30	1993	9.07	15.72
Paul Erickson	1941-48	4.56	1948	9.38	—
Jason Grimsley	1989-00	5.40	1995	8.47	4.65
Dave Hamilton	1972-80	3.86	1980	8.40	—
Dennis Higgins	1966-72	4.67	1972	8.74	—
Tommy Hughes	1941-48	3.87	1948	8.00	—
Michael Mimbs	1995-97	4.42	1997	8.48	—
Gary Neibauer	1969-73	4.81	1973	8.02	—
Bill Parsons	1971-74	3.16	1973	10.11	13.50
Ewald Pyle	1939-45	4.60	1945	9.90	—
Dick Radatz	1962-69	3.62	1967	8.89	3.88
Ken Reynolds	1970-76	4.38	1976	8.07	—
Elmer Riddle	1939-49	3.53	1945	8.19	4.78
Dave Righetti	1979-95	3.74	1994	8.41	3.28
Charley Schanz	1944-50	4.59	1950	9.53	—
Bill Scherrer	1982-88	3.54	1986	9.43	4.33
Ferdie Schupp	1913-22	3.66	1922	8.03	—
Mark Wohlers	1991-00	4.06	1998	14.61	7.22

San Diego Padres: Is There Hope For Rivera? (p. 75)

Lowest Batting Averages, Outfielders Through Age 26—1867-2000
(minimum 1,000 AB and 50 percent of G as outfielder; age as of June 30)

Player	AB	H	Avg	Player	AB	H	Avg
Ruben Rivera	1,115	234	.210	Phil Plantier	1,531	378	.247
Dave Nicholson	1,394	296	.212	Jay Buhner	1,056	261	.247
Joe Lahoud	1,142	244	.214	Cory Snyder	1,993	493	.247
Ken Williams	1,055	227	.215	Curtis Goodwin	1,014	251	.248
Bob Coluccio	1,095	241	.220	Pete Incaviglia	2,449	607	.248
Pat Seerey	1,815	406	.224	Bob Bescher	1,149	285	.248
Heity Cruz	1,404	316	.225	Marvell Wynne	1,644	408	.248
Ed Kirkpatrick	1,960	442	.226	Luis Melendez	1,474	366	.248
Eric Anthony	1,606	363	.226	Darren Lewis	1,550	385	.248
Rob Deer	1,126	255	.226	Gene Stephens	1,207	300	.249
Jim Gosger	1,314	298	.227	Mike Lum	1,540	383	.249
Harry Wheeler	1,122	256	.228	Larry Hisle	1,519	378	.249
Harry Lyons	1,526	350	.229	Mack Jones	1,169	291	.249
Paul Radford	2,271	522	.230	Gerald Young	1,679	418	.249
Cap Peterson	1,170	269	.230	George Wright	1,937	484	.250
Melvin Nieves	1,228	284	.231	Ruppert Jones	2,467	617	.250
Jake Evans	1,441	337	.234	Tommie Agee	2,163	541	.250
Greg Vaughn	1,538	360	.234	Tom Brunansky	3,297	825	.250
Ron Kittle	1,015	239	.235	Don Demeter	1,059	265	.250
Howard Shanks	2,682	632	.236	Nemo Leibold	1,919	481	.251
Charlie Jamieson	1,026	243	.237	Mike Anderson	1,380	346	.251
Herm Winningham	1,074	255	.237	Stan Javier	1,288	323	.251
Bill Hinchman	1,540	366	.238	Lu Clinton	1,733	435	.251
Paul Householder	1,236	295	.239	Gary Thomasson	1,947	489	.251
Vince DiMaggio	1,047	250	.239	Jack Graney	1,245	313	.251
Curt Blefary	2,697	645	.239	Bob Allison	1,662	418	.252
Daryl Boston	1,350	323	.239	Gary Geiger	2,139	538	.252
Mike Mansell	1,471	352	.239	Mark Whiten	1,565	394	.252
Milt Cuyler	1,270	304	.239	John Briggs	1,922	484	.252
Ed Daily	1,941	466	.240	Jud Birchall	1,007	254	.252
Norm Miller	1,312	315	.240	Pat Kelly	1,118	282	.252
Mike Cameron	1,366	328	.240	Mike Hershberger	2,442	616	.252
Bris Lord	1,580	380	.241	Ned Hanlon	1,795	453	.252
Cliff Carroll	1,590	384	.242	Rick Bosetti	1,462	369	.252
Dan Pasqua	1,168	283	.242	Gary Roenicke	1,040	263	.253
Ron Swoboda	2,212	536	.242	Roy Foster	1,016	257	.253
Chet Ross	1,155	281	.243	Dave Henderson	1,786	452	.253
Charlie Spikes	1,882	459	.244	Kevin Bass	1,098	278	.253
Bo Jackson	1,432	350	.244	Oddibe McDowell	2,341	593	.253
Darryl Motley	1,325	324	.245	Chuck Carr	1,369	347	.253
Jimmy McAleer	1,353	331	.245	Hugh Nicol	1,104	280	.254
Billy Sunday	1,530	375	.245	Tony Armas	1,514	384	.254
Jay Johnstone	2,108	517	.245	Joe Birmingham	2,086	530	.254
Mickey Stanley	1,871	459	.245	Cesar Geronimo	1,180	300	.254
Jose Cruz	1,699	417	.245	Devon White	1,788	455	.254
Emmett Seery	1,601	393	.245	Bill Sharp	1,104	281	.255
Ken Berry	1,443	355	.246	Adolfo Phillips	1,406	358	.255
Jack McGeachey	2,085	513	.246	Tommy Harper	2,312	589	.255
Jim Fogarty	2,880	709	.246	Leron Lee	1,506	384	.255
Jose Cruz	1,208	298	.247	Carmelo Martinez	1,782	455	.255

San Francisco Giants: How Good Was Kent's Season For a Second Baseman? (p. 77)

Highest Season OPS, Second Basemen—1901-2000
(minimum 3.1 PA per team G and 50 percent of G at second base)

Player, Team	Year	OBP	Slg	OPS
Rogers Hornsby, StL	1925	.489	.756	1.245
Rogers Hornsby, StL	1924	.507	.696	1.203
Rogers Hornsby, StL	1922	.459	.722	1.181
Rogers Hornsby, ChC	1929	.459	.679	1.139
Rogers Hornsby, Bos	1928	.498	.632	1.130
Nap Lajoie, Phi	1901	.463	.643	1.106
Rogers Hornsby, StL	1921	.458	.639	1.097
Rogers Hornsby, StL	1923	.459	.627	1.086
Rogers Hornsby, NYG	1927	.448	.586	1.035
Jeff Kent, SF	2000	.424	.596	1.021
Joe Morgan, Cin	1976	.444	.576	1.020
Tony Lazzeri, NYY	1929	.429	.561	.991
Rogers Hornsby, StL	1920	.431	.559	.990
Charlie Gehringer, Det	1936	.431	.555	.987
Charlie Gehringer, Det	1937	.458	.520	.978
Joe Morgan, Cin	1975	.466	.508	.974
Charlie Gehringer, Det	1939	.423	.544	.967
Charlie Gehringer, Det	1934	.450	.517	.967
Edgardo Alfonzo, NYM	2000	.425	.542	.967
Chuck Knoblauch, Min	1996	.448	.517	.965
Jackie Robinson, Bro	1949	.432	.528	.960
Nap Lajoie, Cle	1910	.445	.514	.960
Nap Lajoie, Cle	1904	.413	.546	.959
Jackie Robinson, Bro	1951	.429	.527	.957
Roberto Alomar, Cle	1999	.422	.533	.955
George Grantham, Pit	1930	.413	.534	.947
Charlie Gehringer, Det	1930	.404	.534	.938
Roberto Alomar, Bal	1996	.411	.527	.938
Charlie Gehringer, Det	1929	.405	.532	.936
Eddie Collins, CWS	1920	.438	.493	.932
Eddie Collins, Phi	1911	.451	.481	.932
Jay Bell, Ari	1999	.374	.557	.931
Frankie Frisch, StL	1930	.407	.520	.927
Bobby Doerr, Bos	1944	.399	.528	.927
Larry Doyle, NYG	1911	.397	.527	.924
Jackie Robinson, Bro	1950	.423	.500	.923
Bobby Grich, Cal	1981	.378	.543	.921
Joe Morgan, Cin	1974	.427	.494	.921
Rod Carew, Min	1975	.421	.497	.919
Buddy Myer, Was	1938	.454	.465	.918
Jose Vidro, Mon	2000	.379	.540	.918
Craig Biggio, Hou	1997	.415	.501	.916
Dave Johnson, Atl	1973	.370	.546	.916
Jeff Kent, SF	1998	.359	.555	.914
Ryne Sandberg, ChC	1990	.354	.559	.913

Who Hits the Most Late-Inning Clutch Home Runs? (p. 83)

Most Late-Inning Clutch Home Runs—1998-2000
(7th Inning or later, tying or lead run at bat or on base; sorted by HR)

Player	AB	HR	AB/HR	Player	AB	HR	AB/HR
Mark McGwire	123	15	8.20	Eddie Taubensee	126	7	18.00
Greg Vaughn	168	15	11.20	Ben Grieve	128	7	18.29
Sammy Sosa	187	15	12.47	Albert Belle	140	7	20.00
Mike Piazza	146	13	11.23	Ray Durham	140	7	20.00
Scott Rolen	151	13	11.62	Mike Lieberthal	146	7	20.86
Jeromy Burnitz	161	13	12.38	Andruw Jones	148	7	21.14
Jeff Bagwell	172	13	13.23	Derrek Lee	149	7	21.29
Eric Karros	174	12	14.50	Troy O'Leary	152	7	21.71
Bernie Williams	119	11	10.82	Todd Zeile	157	7	22.43
Carlos Delgado	135	11	12.27	Jeff Kent	166	7	23.71
Rafael Palmeiro	138	11	12.55	Dante Bichette	188	7	26.86
Matt Stairs	139	11	12.64	Dave Hansen	45	6	7.50
Cliff Floyd	149	11	13.55	Andres Galarraga	62	6	10.33
Todd Helton	158	11	14.36	Bubba Trammell	71	6	11.83
Alex Rodriguez	122	10	12.20	Brian Daubach	89	6	14.83
Tony Batista	136	10	13.60	Will Clark	104	6	17.33
Raul Mondesi	142	10	14.20	Larry Walker	107	6	17.83
Darin Erstad	157	10	15.70	Paul Konerko	111	6	18.50
Mo Vaughn	164	10	16.40	Tim Salmon	114	6	19.00
Jorge Posada	118	9	13.11	Scott Brosius	115	6	19.17
Henry Rodriguez	124	9	13.78	David Bell	120	6	20.00
Barry Bonds	133	9	14.78	Ron Gant	127	6	21.17
Chipper Jones	143	9	15.89	Robin Ventura	136	6	22.67
Matt Williams	147	9	16.33	Manny Ramirez	136	6	22.67
Ken Griffey Jr.	148	9	16.44	Mike Bordick	140	6	23.33
Brian Jordan	158	9	17.56	Todd Walker	141	6	23.50
Jay Bell	161	9	17.89	Carl Everett	156	6	26.00
Fred McGriff	167	9	18.56	Luis Gonzalez	161	6	26.83
Mike Lowell	91	8	11.38	Derek Bell	171	6	28.50
Moises Alou	107	8	13.38	Shawn Green	179	6	29.83
Miguel Tejada	114	8	14.25	Marquis Grissom	185	6	30.83
Tony Clark	120	8	15.00	Bret Boone	197	6	32.83
Juan Gonzalez	127	8	15.88	Jim Leyritz	66	5	13.20
Ivan Rodriguez	127	8	15.88	Kurt Abbott	67	5	13.40
Jim Thome	131	8	16.38	Jay Buhner	75	5	15.00
Richie Sexson	139	8	17.38	Kelly Stinnett	76	5	15.20
Rich Aurilia	145	8	18.13	Eric Davis	89	5	17.80
Bobby Higginson	146	8	18.25	Ken Caminiti	92	5	18.40
Nomar Garciaparra	154	8	19.25	Jeffrey Hammonds	93	5	18.60
David Justice	156	8	19.50	Harold Baines	99	5	19.80
Damion Easley	157	8	19.63	Tony Gwynn	109	5	21.80
Vinny Castilla	158	8	19.75	Darrin Fletcher	109	5	21.80
Edgardo Alfonzo	162	8	20.25	Alex S. Gonzalez	109	5	21.80
Steve Finley	178	8	22.25	Willie Greene	117	5	23.40
Todd Hundley	82	7	11.71	Glenallen Hill	118	5	23.60
Ruben Rivera	99	7	14.14	Preston Wilson	127	5	25.40
Troy Glaus	122	7	17.43	Phil Nevin	134	5	26.80

Baseball Scoreboard

Player	AB	HR	AB/HR	Player	AB	HR	AB/HR
Ed Sprague	136	5	27.20	Bobby Abreu	175	4	43.75
Gary Sheffield	138	5	27.60	Mark Kotsay	176	4	44.00
Brad Ausmus	142	5	28.40	Mark Grace	178	4	44.50
Travis Fryman	145	5	29.00	Jeff Cirillo	183	4	45.75
Charles Johnson	145	5	29.00	Neifi Perez	185	4	46.25
John Olerud	146	5	29.20	Alex Ramirez	26	3	8.67
Bill Mueller	158	5	31.60	Angel Echevarria	40	3	13.33
Rico Brogna	159	5	31.80	Mike Blowers	45	3	15.00
Ray Lankford	162	5	32.40	Tony Phillips	52	3	17.33
Matt Lawton	164	5	32.80	Kevin Elster	52	3	17.33
Vladimir Guerrero	169	5	33.80	Jay Payton	53	3	17.67
Kevin Young	172	5	34.40	Brian Johnson	59	3	19.67
Dmitri Young	172	5	34.40	Mark Quinn	65	3	21.67
Bob Hamelin	37	4	9.25	Terry Shumpert	66	3	22.00
Olmedo Saenz	42	4	10.50	Dave Nilsson	66	3	22.00
Armando Rios	52	4	13.00	Kevin Millar	67	3	22.33
Brian Hunter	54	4	13.50	Midre Cummings	70	3	23.33
Matt Mieske	58	4	14.50	Gabe Kapler	71	3	23.67
Herbert Perry	62	4	15.50	Rob Ducey	74	3	24.67
Gary Gaetti	76	4	19.00	Sean Berry	75	3	25.00
Carlos Hernandez	78	4	19.50	Danny Bautista	78	3	26.00
Carlos Lee	79	4	19.75	Shawon Dunston	80	3	26.67
Brant Brown	84	4	21.00	Chris Stynes	83	3	27.67
Michael Tucker	92	4	23.00	Chad Curtis	93	3	31.00
Aaron Boone	92	4	23.00	Tyler Houston	94	3	31.33
Jeff Reed	95	4	23.75	Scott Spiezio	95	3	31.67
John Flaherty	104	4	26.00	Darren Lewis	97	3	32.33
Russ Davis	106	4	26.50	Alex Ochoa	98	3	32.67
Lee Stevens	107	4	26.75	Randy Velarde	99	3	33.00
Jim Edmonds	110	4	27.50	Damon Buford	105	3	35.00
Javy Lopez	111	4	27.75	Wil Cordero	109	3	36.33
Ellis Burks	112	4	28.00	Mike Stanley	112	3	37.33
Charlie Hayes	113	4	28.25	Mike Cameron	116	3	38.67
Geoff Jenkins	116	4	29.00	Reggie Sanders	117	3	39.00
Chris Widger	122	4	30.50	Cal Ripken Jr.	118	3	39.33
Jose Vidro	122	4	30.50	Rondell White	118	3	39.33
Edgar Martinez	125	4	31.25	Jose Canseco	123	3	41.00
Tino Martinez	129	4	32.25	Pokey Reese	130	3	43.33
Travis Lee	131	4	32.75	Ryan Klesko	131	3	43.67
Jason Varitek	133	4	33.25	Pat Meares	132	3	44.00
Dean Palmer	137	4	34.25	Deivi Cruz	132	3	44.00
Derek Jeter	137	4	34.25	Jason Giambi	134	3	44.67
Fernando Tatis	137	4	34.25	Roberto Alomar	136	3	45.33
Brian Giles	139	4	34.75	Paul O'Neill	142	3	47.33
Magglio Ordonez	141	4	35.25	Sean Casey	143	3	47.67
J.T. Snow	142	4	35.50	Gerald Williams	148	3	49.33
Jason Kendall	142	4	35.50	Omar Vizquel	149	3	49.67
Jermaine Dye	146	4	36.50	Joe Randa	164	3	54.67
Jose Hernandez	157	4	39.25	Ron Coomer	168	3	56.00
Eric Young	158	4	39.50	Mark Grudzielanek	188	3	62.67
B.J. Surhoff	159	4	39.75	**MLB Average**			**34.70**

Are Veteran Hitters Better Than "Youngsters" in the Clutch? (p. 86)

Batting Averages, Close-And-Late—2000, Listed Alphabetically
(minimum 50 Close-And-Late PA)

Player, Team	AB	H	Avg	Player, Team	AB	H	Avg
Bobby Abreu, Phi	89	27	.303	Orlando Cabrera, Mon	58	10	.172
Benny Agbayani, NYM	61	16	.262	Miguel Cairo, TB	67	19	.284
Edgardo Alfonzo, NYM	70	25	.357	Mike Cameron, Sea	62	18	.290
Luis Alicea, Tex	83	22	.265	Raul Casanova, Mil	51	13	.255
Roberto Alomar, Cle	74	19	.257	Sean Casey, Cin	81	24	.296
Moises Alou, Hou	60	14	.233	Vinny Castilla, TB	56	12	.214
Brady Anderson, Bal	56	8	.143	Luis Castillo, Fla	72	22	.306
Garret Anderson, Ana	103	22	.214	Frank Catalanotto, Tex	46	10	.217
Rich Aurilia, SF	65	21	.323	Eric Chavez, Oak	65	10	.154
Brad Ausmus, Det	68	18	.265	Jeff Cirillo, Col	87	22	.253
Jeff Bagwell, Hou	90	24	.267	Royce Clayton, Tex	81	24	.296
Michael Barrett, Mon	47	12	.255	Greg Colbrunn, Ari	59	15	.254
Tony Batista, Tor	83	29	.349	Jeff Conine, Bal	64	15	.234
Danny Bautista, Fla-Ari	43	17	.395	Ron Coomer, Min	78	20	.256
David Bell, Sea	61	13	.213	Alex Cora, LA	46	16	.348
Derek Bell, NYM	76	17	.224	Wil Cordero, Pit-Cle	60	13	.217
Jay Bell, Ari	75	23	.307	Steve Cox, TB	51	15	.294
Albert Belle, Bal	78	18	.231	Deivi Cruz, Det	85	21	.247
Ron Belliard, Mil	97	24	.247	Jose Cruz, Tor	76	19	.250
Carlos Beltran, KC	73	17	.233	Chad Curtis, Tex	55	15	.273
Adrian Beltre, LA	89	16	.180	Johnny Damon, KC	89	25	.281
Marvin Benard, SF	61	15	.246	Brian Daubach, Bos	81	18	.222
Dave Berg, Fla	41	9	.220	Carlos Delgado, Tor	70	18	.257
Peter Bergeron, Mon	62	13	.210	Delino DeShields, Bal	76	21	.276
Lance Berkman, Hou	54	19	.352	J.D. Drew, StL	48	12	.250
Dante Bichette, Cin-Bos	76	23	.303	Ray Durham, CWS	72	15	.208
Craig Biggio, Hou	50	8	.160	Jermaine Dye, KC	101	27	.267
Henry Blanco, Mil	50	12	.240	Damion Easley, Det	63	15	.238
Geoff Blum, Mon	63	15	.238	Jim Edmonds, StL	63	20	.317
Barry Bonds, SF	68	17	.250	Juan Encarnacion, Det	64	20	.313
Aaron Boone, Cin	55	17	.309	Darin Erstad, Ana	101	31	.307
Bret Boone, SD	82	26	.317	Carl Everett, Bos	75	21	.280
Mike Bordick, Bal-NYM	52	21	.404	Carlos Febles, KC	50	12	.240
Scott Brosius, NYY	65	12	.185	Steve Finley, Ari	84	22	.262
Adrian Brown, Pit	64	18	.281	John Flaherty, TB	66	14	.212
Damon Buford, ChC	98	17	.173	Darrin Fletcher, Tor	68	19	.279
Jay Buhner, Sea	42	8	.190	Cliff Floyd, Fla	73	25	.342
Ellis Burks, SF	50	16	.320	Travis Fryman, Cle	77	21	.273
Jeromy Burnitz, Mil	87	14	.161	Brad Fullmer, Tor	64	16	.250
Pat Burrell, Phi	66	16	.242	Rafael Furcal, Atl	58	18	.310

Baseball Scoreboard

Player, Team	AB	H	Avg	Player, Team	AB	H	Avg
Andres Galarraga, Atl	63	23	.365	Charles Johnson, Bal-CWS	48	12	.250
Ron Gant, Phi-Ana	67	19	.284	Andruw Jones, Atl	86	28	.326
Nomar Garciaparra, Bos	81	30	.370	Chipper Jones, Atl	67	20	.299
Jason Giambi, Oak	58	20	.345	Jacque Jones, Min	77	24	.312
Jeremy Giambi, Oak	49	12	.245	Brian Jordan, Atl	63	16	.254
Brian Giles, Pit	86	24	.279	Kevin Jordan, Phi	78	11	.141
Joe Girardi, ChC	68	17	.250	Wally Joyner, Atl	44	10	.227
Doug Glanville, Phi	105	24	.229	Gabe Kapler, Tex	63	18	.286
Troy Glaus, Ana	98	31	.316	Eric Karros, LA	91	20	.220
Alex Gonzalez, Fla	54	5	.093	Jason Kendall, Pit	88	31	.352
Alex S. Gonzalez, Tor	65	17	.262	Adam Kennedy, Ana	97	27	.278
Juan Gonzalez, Det	61	16	.262	Jeff Kent, SF	82	22	.268
Luis Gonzalez, Ari	85	30	.353	Ryan Klesko, SD	92	20	.217
Wiki Gonzalez, SD	54	10	.185	Chuck Knoblauch, NYY	43	12	.279
Mark Grace, ChC	89	19	.213	Paul Konerko, CWS	72	19	.264
Shawn Green, LA	97	29	.299	Corey Koskie, Min	63	11	.175
Willie Greene, ChC	62	9	.145	Mark Kotsay, Fla	86	24	.279
Rusty Greer, Tex	54	16	.296	Mike Lamb, Tex	83	20	.241
Ben Grieve, Oak	79	21	.266	Ray Lankford, StL	58	12	.207
Ken Griffey Jr., Cin	92	24	.261	Mike Lansing, Col-Bos	54	15	.278
Marquis Grissom, Mil	98	22	.224	Barry Larkin, Cin	64	16	.250
Mark Grudzielanek, LA	93	21	.226	Matt Lawton, Min	93	35	.376
Vladimir Guerrero, Mon	80	27	.338	Carlos Lee, CWS	68	21	.309
Wilton Guerrero, Mon	52	13	.250	Derrek Lee, Fla	82	30	.366
Jose Guillen, TB	54	11	.204	Mike Lieberthal, Phi	70	17	.243
Ricky Gutierrez, ChC	79	11	.139	Kenny Lofton, Cle	56	20	.357
Cristian Guzman, Min	78	23	.295	Terrence Long, Oak	69	17	.246
Jeffrey Hammonds, Col	73	25	.342	Javy Lopez, Atl	68	17	.250
Scott Hatteberg, Bos	51	18	.353	Luis Lopez, Mil	42	16	.381
Charlie Hayes, Mil	74	19	.257	Mark Loretta, Mil	47	14	.298
Todd Helton, Col	84	33	.393	Mike Lowell, Fla	84	19	.226
Jose Hernandez, Mil	82	23	.280	Julio Lugo, Hou	50	15	.300
Ramon Hernandez, Oak	56	19	.339	Dave Magadan, SD	40	12	.300
Richard Hidalgo, Hou	72	15	.208	Al Martin, SD-Sea	47	13	.277
Bobby Higginson, Det	81	27	.333	Edgar Martinez, Sea	68	22	.324
Denny Hocking, Min	71	18	.254	Felix Martinez, TB	43	11	.256
Todd Hollandsworth, LA-Col	49	9	.184	Tino Martinez, NYY	68	20	.294
Tyler Houston, Mil	54	6	.111	Mike Matheny, StL	48	9	.188
Todd Hundley, LA	48	10	.208	Brent Mayne, Col	59	18	.305
Torii Hunter, Min	51	16	.314	Dave McCarty, KC	58	15	.259
Damian Jackson, SD	68	22	.324	Fred McGriff, TB	90	25	.278
Stan Javier, Sea	52	12	.231	Mark McLemore, Sea	61	16	.262
Geoff Jenkins, Mil	86	21	.244	Pat Meares, Pit	72	23	.319
Derek Jeter, NYY	66	23	.348	Mitch Meluskey, Hou	50	15	.300

Player, Team	AB	H	Avg	Player, Team	AB	H	Avg
Kevin Millar, Fla	54	16	.296	Richie Sexson, Cle-Mil	97	30	.309
Damian Miller, Ari	51	14	.275	Gary Sheffield, LA	70	16	.229
Ben Molina, Ana	86	31	.360	Terry Shumpert, Col	47	13	.277
Melvin Mora, NYM-Bal	43	8	.186	Chris Singleton, CWS	65	15	.231
Mickey Morandini, Phi-Tor	49	9	.184	Mark Smith, Fla	50	14	.280
Warren Morris, Pit	95	27	.284	J.T. Snow, SF	70	18	.257
Bill Mueller, SF	76	23	.303	Sammy Sosa, ChC	102	28	.275
Phil Nevin, SD	98	23	.235	Bill Spiers, Hou	68	22	.324
Trot Nixon, Bos	68	23	.338	Scott Spiezio, Ana	62	17	.274
Troy O'Leary, Bos	75	19	.253	Matt Stairs, Oak	63	16	.254
Paul O'Neill, NYY	66	16	.242	Lee Stevens, Mon	60	13	.217
Alex Ochoa, Cin	54	15	.278	Shannon Stewart, Tor	69	23	.333
Jose Offerman, Bos	54	16	.296	Kevin Stocker, TB-Ana	44	10	.227
John Olerud, Sea	64	16	.250	Chris Stynes, Cin	57	15	.263
Magglio Ordonez, CWS	77	25	.325	B.J. Surhoff, Bal-Atl	61	13	.213
David Ortiz, Min	65	19	.292	Mike Sweeney, KC	108	38	.352
Eric Owens, SD	100	24	.240	Miguel Tejada, Oak	66	24	.364
Orlando Palmeiro, Ana	42	11	.262	Frank Thomas, CWS	71	19	.268
Rafael Palmeiro, Tex	67	20	.299	Jim Thome, Cle	67	16	.239
Dean Palmer, Det	66	14	.212	Michael Tucker, Cin	54	12	.222
Craig Paquette, StL	57	13	.228	Jose Valentin, CWS	67	18	.269
Jay Payton, NYM	82	17	.207	John Vander Wal, Pit	79	18	.228
Neifi Perez, Col	96	26	.271	Jason Varitek, Bos	87	20	.230
Herbert Perry, TB-CWS	50	12	.240	Greg Vaughn, TB	77	25	.325
Mike Piazza, NYM	75	27	.360	Mo Vaughn, Ana	93	27	.290
Placido Polanco, StL	55	12	.218	Randy Velarde, Oak	54	15	.278
Jorge Posada, NYY	67	23	.343	Robin Ventura, NYM	77	14	.182
Mark Quinn, KC	86	23	.267	Quilvio Veras, Atl	39	11	.282
Manny Ramirez, Cle	54	24	.444	Jose Vidro, Mon	76	27	.355
Joe Randa, KC	92	36	.391	Fernando Vina, StL	46	10	.217
Jeff Reed, ChC	50	10	.200	Omar Vizquel, Cle	70	14	.200
Pokey Reese, Cin	93	24	.258	Daryle Ward, Hou	55	10	.182
Desi Relaford, Phi-SD	45	9	.200	Chris Widger, Mon-Sea	47	14	.298
Edgar Renteria, StL	72	15	.208	Bernie Williams, NYY	68	25	.368
Armando Rios, SF	42	13	.310	Gerald Williams, TB	104	25	.240
Ruben Rivera, SD	73	15	.205	Matt Williams, Ari	61	19	.311
Alex Rodriguez, Sea	59	12	.203	Preston Wilson, Fla	103	23	.223
Henry Rodriguez, ChC-Fla	46	11	.239	Tony Womack, Ari	76	23	.303
Scott Rolen, Phi	73	28	.384	Dmitri Young, Cin	96	30	.313
Tim Salmon, Ana	85	24	.282	Eric Young, ChC	100	21	.210
Rey Sanchez, KC	78	23	.295	Kevin Young, Pit	86	16	.186
Reggie Sanders, Atl	47	13	.277	Gregg Zaun, KC	45	18	.400
Benito Santiago, Cin	47	10	.213	Todd Zeile, NYM	90	28	.311
David Segui, Tex-Cle	52	18	.346	**MLB Average**			**.258**

Are Aaron's Records Safer? (p. 88)

Chances of Reaching Milestones
(age as of June 30, 2000)

Player	Age	Current H	Current HR	Current RBI	Home Runs 500	Home Runs 600	Home Runs 700	Home Runs 756	Home Runs 800	Hits 3000	Hits 4000	Hits 4257	RBI 2000	RBI 2298
Mark McGwire	36	1570	554	1350	8/5/99	97%	51%	23%	10%	—	—	—	1%	—
Barry Bonds	35	2157	494	1405	100%	89%	21%	6%	—	5%	—	—	9%	—
Ken Griffey Jr.	30	1883	438	1270	96%	90%	54%	36%	25%	35%	—	—	55%	25%
Sammy Sosa	31	1606	386	1079	94%	89%	50%	35%	26%	25%	—	—	35%	14%
Jose Canseco	35	1811	446	1358	94%	10%	—	—	—	—	—	—	—	—
Rafael Palmeiro	35	2321	400	1347	93%	24%	—	—	—	39%	—	—	19%	—
Juan Gonzalez	30	1554	362	1142	87%	29%	6%	—	—	16%	—	—	22%	3%
Albert Belle	33	1726	381	1239	71%	16%	—	—	—	11%	—	—	18%	—
Alex Rodriguez	24	966	189	595	70%	41%	23%	16%	11%	26%	1%	—	29%	15%
Jeff Bagwell	32	1630	310	1093	64%	24%	5%	—	—	14%	—	—	20%	2%
Manny Ramirez	28	1086	236	804	59%	29%	12%	5%	1%	10%	—	—	32%	16%
Vladimir Guerrero	24	695	136	404	55%	32%	18%	11%	7%	27%	4%	—	20%	9%
Frank Thomas	32	1755	344	1183	53%	13%	—	—	—	19%	—	—	21%	2%
Fred McGriff	36	2103	417	1298	49%	—	—	—	—	3%	—	—	—	—
Carlos Delgado	28	818	190	604	44%	21%	7%	1%	—	6%	—	—	16%	5%
Gary Sheffield	31	1508	279	916	41%	13%	—	—	—	8%	—	—	2%	—
Mo Vaughn	32	1479	299	977	39%	9%	—	—	—	5%	—	—	6%	—
Chipper Jones	28	1051	189	635	37%	16%	3%	—	—	15%	—	—	6%	—
Jim Thome	29	1033	233	685	34%	11%	—	—	—	—	—	—	1%	—
Greg Vaughn	34	1314	320	956	33%	3%	—	—	—	—	—	—	—	—
Troy Glaus	23	328	77	204	29%	14%	4%	—	—	—	—	—	—	—
Andruw Jones	23	635	116	361	29%	12%	2%	—	—	22%	1%	—	5%	—
Dean Palmer	31	1169	264	803	27%	4%	—	—	—	—	—	—	—	—
Todd Helton	26	594	107	368	25%	10%	—	—	—	16%	—	—	12%	3%
Richard Hidalgo	24	345	68	219	19%	6%	—	—	—	—	—	—	—	—
Jason Giambi	29	870	149	555	19%	3%	—	—	—	3%	—	—	8%	—
Tony Batista	26	496	100	298	18%	4%	—	—	—	—	—	—	—	—
Shawn Green	27	882	143	475	17%	2%	—	—	—	12%	—	—	3%	—
Mike Piazza	31	1356	278	881	15%	—	—	—	—	—	—	—	—	—
Eric Karros	32	1363	242	840	9%	—	—	—	—	—	—	—	—	—
Raul Mondesi	29	1109	187	585	8%	—	—	—	—	—	—	—	—	—
Scott Rolen	25	623	108	386	8%	—	—	—	—	—	—	—	—	—
Jim Edmonds	30	923	163	516	6%	—	—	—	—	—	—	—	—	—
Brian Giles	29	583	113	395	6%	—	—	—	—	—	—	—	—	—
Ben Grieve	24	492	76	303	5%	—	—	—	—	5%	—	—	1%	—
Matt Williams	34	1677	346	1097	5%	—	—	—	—	—	—	—	—	—
David Justice	34	1373	276	917	5%	—	—	—	—	—	—	—	—	—
Tim Salmon	31	1180	230	757	5%	—	—	—	—	—	—	—	—	—
Magglio Ordonez	26	546	80	319	4%	—	—	—	—	9%	—	—	4%	—
Richie Sexson	25	325	72	242	4%	—	—	—	—	—	—	—	—	—
Nomar Garciaparra	26	812	117	436	3%	—	—	—	—	21%	—	—	3%	—

		Current			Home Runs					Hits			RBI	
Player	Age	H	HR	RBI	500	600	700	756	800	3000	4000	4257	2000	2298
Jeromy Burnitz	31	711	154	504	2%	—	—	—	—	—	—	—	—	—
Jermaine Dye	26	566	84	319	1%	—	—	—	—	4%	—	—	—	—
Cal Ripken Jr.	39	3070	417	1627	—	—	—	—	—	4/15/00	—	—	—	—
Tony Gwynn	40	3108	134	1121	—	—	—	—	—	8/6/99	—	—	—	—
Rickey Henderson	41	2914	282	1052	—	—	—	—	—	80%	—	—	—	—
Roberto Alomar	32	2196	170	918	—	—	—	—	—	64%	1%	—	—	—
Derek Jeter	26	1008	78	414	—	—	—	—	—	33%	5%	1%	—	—
Johnny Damon	26	894	65	352	—	—	—	—	—	25%	1%	—	—	—
Darin Erstad	26	767	77	332	—	—	—	—	—	20%	—	—	—	—
Neifi Perez	25	655	36	234	—	—	—	—	—	18%	—	—	—	—
John Olerud	31	1595	186	865	—	—	—	—	—	17%	—	—	—	—
Edgardo Alfonzo	26	874	87	433	—	—	—	—	—	17%	—	—	—	—
Garret Anderson	28	1043	107	510	—	—	—	—	—	16%	—	—	—	—
Bernie Williams	31	1463	181	802	—	—	—	—	—	14%	—	—	3%	—
Edgar Renteria	24	767	39	253	—	—	—	—	—	13%	—	—	—	—
Mark Grace	36	2201	148	1004	—	—	—	—	—	11%	—	—	—	—
Jeff Cirillo	30	1059	77	487	—	—	—	—	—	11%	—	—	—	—
Ray Durham	28	980	77	371	—	—	—	—	—	11%	—	—	—	—
Luis Gonzalez	32	1434	164	775	—	—	—	—	—	10%	—	—	—	—
Shannon Stewart	26	574	44	216	—	—	—	—	—	9%	—	—	—	—
Bobby Abreu	26	572	65	273	—	—	—	—	—	9%	—	—	—	—
Mike Sweeney	26	569	70	336	—	—	—	—	—	8%	—	—	4%	—
Omar Vizquel	33	1605	41	515	—	—	—	—	—	8%	—	—	—	—
Chuck Knoblauch	31	1646	83	549	—	—	—	—	—	8%	—	—	—	—
Craig Biggio	34	1969	160	741	—	—	—	—	—	7%	—	—	—	—
Travis Fryman	31	1602	209	929	—	—	—	—	—	7%	—	—	—	—
Deivi Cruz	24	546	30	225	—	—	—	—	—	7%	—	—	—	—
B.J. Surhoff	35	1895	160	961	—	—	—	—	—	5%	—	—	—	—
Doug Glanville	29	730	32	219	—	—	—	—	—	4%	—	—	—	—
Jay Bell	34	1828	180	800	—	—	—	—	—	3%	—	—	—	—
Mark Kotsay	24	463	31	179	—	—	—	—	—	3%	—	—	—	—
Marquis Grissom	33	1695	145	663	—	—	—	—	—	2%	—	—	—	—
Jose Vidro	25	437	38	191	—	—	—	—	—	2%	—	—	—	—
Ivan Rodriguez	28	1459	171	704	—	—	—	—	—	1%	—	—	—	—
Luis Castillo	24	464	4	71	—	—	—	—	—	1%	—	—	—	—
Miguel Tejada	24	421	64	254	—	—	—	—	—	1%	—	—	—	—
Sean Casey	25	432	52	237	—	—	—	—	—	1%	—	—	—	—
Adrian Beltre	21	338	42	174	—	—	—	—	—	1%	—	—	—	—

Note: A date in place of a percentage indicates the date on which the player achieved the specific milestone.

Who Bagged the Most Runs Created? (p. 91)

Runs Created—2000, Listed Alphabetically
(minimum 350 PA)

Player, Team	RC	OWP	Player, Team	RC	OWP	Player, Team	RC	OWP
Abreu, Phi	119	.702	Castillo L, Fla	81	.541	Gonzalez A, Tor	64	.363
Agbayani, NYM	63	.624	Chavez E, Oak	82	.546	Gonzalez J, Det	64	.470
Alfonzo, NYM	129	.761	Cirillo, Col	122	.690	Gonzalez L, Ari	132	.708
Alicea, Tex	79	.486	Clark W, Bal-StL	92	.710	Goodwin, Col-LA	80	.518
Alomar, Cle	102	.556	Clayton, Tex	53	.278	Grace, ChC	89	.606
Alomar Jr., Cle	47	.433	Conine, Bal	54	.431	Green S, LA	106	.590
Alou, Hou	104	.746	Coomer, Min	71	.414	Greer, Tex	72	.601
Anderson B, Bal	80	.504	Cora, LA	33	.281	Grieve, Oak	101	.547
Anderson G, Ana	91	.460	Cordero, Pit-Cle	71	.493	Griffey Jr., Cin	108	.680
Aurilia, SF	77	.522	Cruz D, Det	76	.421	Grissom, Mil	61	.323
Ausmus, Det	61	.357	Cruz J, Tor	89	.470	Grudzielanek, LA	73	.412
Bagwell, Hou	143	.754	Damon, KC	134	.669	Guerrero V, Mon	133	.759
Batista, Tor	91	.480	Daubach, Bos	70	.461	Gutierrez, ChC	73	.547
Bautista, Fla-Ari	57	.557	Delgado C, Tor	161	.813	Guzman, Min	74	.358
Bell D, Sea	52	.341	DeShields, Bal	102	.587	Hammonds, Col	95	.708
Bell D, NYM	81	.513	Drew, StL	83	.681	Hayes, Mil	47	.423
Bell J, Ari	90	.553	Durham, CWS	100	.525	Helton, Col	173	.851
Belle, Bal	88	.516	Dye, KC	113	.642	Henderson, 2Tm	57	.409
Belliard, Mil	87	.520	Easley, Det	65	.449	Hernandez J, Mil	52	.377
Beltran, KC	39	.305	Edmonds, StL	122	.742	Hernandez R, Oak	57	.408
Beltre, LA	91	.615	Encarnacion, Det	77	.468	Hidalgo, Hou	117	.701
Benard, SF	76	.477	Erstad, Ana	140	.705	Higginson, Det	126	.686
Bergeron, Mon	54	.319	Everett, Bos	105	.685	Hocking, Min	61	.547
Berkman, Hou	67	.652	Finley, Ari	101	.632	Hollandsworth, 2Tm	51	.410
Bichette, Cin-Bos	85	.516	Flaherty, TB	44	.346	Jackson, SD	62	.449
Biggio, Hou	65	.576	Fletcher, Tor	63	.538	Jenkins, Mil	97	.664
Bonds, SF	129	.798	Floyd, Fla	86	.690	Jeter, NYY	114	.658
Boone B, SD	71	.517	Fryman, Cle	112	.650	Johnson C, 2Tm	87	.675
Bordick, Bal-NYM	79	.453	Fullmer, Tor	88	.603	Jones A, Atl	120	.644
Brosius, NYY	51	.311	Furcal, Atl	73	.560	Jones C, Atl	120	.692
Buford, ChC	59	.396	Galarraga, Atl	84	.603	Jones J, Min	71	.450
Buhner, Sea	76	.642	Gant, Phi-Ana	52	.402	Jordan B, Atl	70	.496
Burks, SF	90	.753	Garciaparra, Bos	122	.758	Justice, Cle-NYY	107	.657
Burnitz, Mil	91	.533	Giambi J, Oak	162	.840	Kapler, Tex	66	.504
Burrell, Phi	72	.611	Giles, Pit	132	.753	Karros, LA	82	.467
Cabrera O, Mon	48	.360	Girardi, ChC	46	.433	Kendall, Pit	110	.660
Cairo, TB	53	.441	Glanville, Phi	71	.368	Kennedy, Ana	73	.383
Cameron, Sea	90	.531	Glaus, Ana	117	.655	Kent, SF	136	.746
Casey, Cin	94	.674	Gonzalez A, Fla	31	.210	Klesko, SD	105	.694

Player, Team	RC	OWP	Player, Team	RC	OWP	Player, Team	RC	OWP
Knoblauch, NYY	57	.475	Nevin, SD	100	.648	Snow, SF	83	.529
Konerko, CWS	87	.554	Nixon, Bos	73	.554	Sosa, ChC	138	.744
Koskie, Min	83	.589	O'Leary, Bos	67	.421	Spiers, Hou	62	.614
Kotsay, Fla	66	.435	O'Neill, NYY	82	.467	Stairs, Oak	69	.452
Lamb M, Tex	54	.347	Offerman, Bos	52	.351	Stevens, Mon	64	.503
Lankford, StL	60	.518	Olerud, Sea	100	.575	Stewart, Tor	94	.563
Lansing, Col-Bos	53	.317	Ordonez M, CWS	116	.630	Stynes, Cin	65	.633
Larkin, Cin	65	.592	Ortiz D, Min	60	.478	Surhoff, Bal-Atl	76	.490
Lawton, Min	113	.658	Owens, SD	78	.469	Sweeney M, KC	140	.719
Ledee, NYY-Cle-Tex	68	.446	Palmeiro R, Tex	120	.672	Tejada, Oak	104	.568
Lee C, CWS	88	.521	Palmer, Det	88	.540	Thomas, CWS	164	.800
Lee D, Fla	74	.547	Paquette, StL	51	.447	Thome, Cle	109	.633
Lee T, Ari-Phi	44	.348	Payton, NYM	63	.450	Valentin J, CWS	105	.590
Lieberthal, Phi	60	.543	Perez N, Col	80	.428	Vander Wal, Pit	93	.760
Lofton, Cle	94	.557	Perry H, TB-CWS	70	.571	Varitek, Bos	54	.367
Long, Oak	97	.558	Piazza, NYM	105	.728	Vaughn G, TB	89	.614
Lopez J, Atl	73	.532	Posada, NYY	109	.681	Vaughn M, Ana	109	.583
Loretta, Mil	53	.519	Quinn, KC	81	.548	Velarde, Oak	63	.423
Lowell, Fla	87	.595	Ramirez M, Cle	129	.826	Ventura, NYM	70	.490
Lugo, Hou	56	.465	Randa, KC	97	.533	Vidro, Mon	111	.655
Martin, SD-Sea	60	.439	Reese, Cin	60	.388	Vina, StL	77	.573
Martinez D, 4Tm	52	.358	Relaford, Phi-SD	61	.486	Vizquel, Cle	88	.471
Martinez E, Sea	134	.745	Renteria, StL	75	.440	White R, Mon-ChC	66	.659
Martinez T, NYY	79	.450	Rivera, SD	51	.381	Williams B, NYY	114	.681
Matheny, StL	43	.329	Rodriguez A, Sea	136	.744	Williams G, TB	87	.447
McGriff, TB	98	.568	Rodriguez H, 2Tm	58	.548	Williams M, Ari	41	.374
McLemore, Sea	62	.376	Rodriguez I, Tex	75	.672	Wilson P, Fla	92	.519
Meares, Pit	51	.352	Rolen, Phi	89	.656	Womack, Ari	82	.464
Molina, Ana	53	.347	Salmon, Ana	114	.652	Young D, Cin	86	.563
Mondesi, Tor	63	.530	Sanchez, KC	48	.265	Young E, ChC	90	.527
Mora, NYM-Bal	56	.447	Segui, Tex-Cle	101	.609	Young K, Pit	61	.413
Morandini, Phi-Tor	44	.336	Sexson, Cle-Mil	93	.584	Zeile, NYM	85	.542
Morris W, Pit	59	.364	Sheffield, LA	132	.792	**MLB Average**		.500
Mueller, SF	63	.371	Singleton, CWS	67	.406			

Who's Second to None? (p. 93)

Secondary Averages—2000, Listed Alphabetically
(minimum 400 PA)

Player, Team	Sec	Player, Team	Sec	Player, Team	Sec	Player, Team	Sec
Abreu, Phi	.446	Dye, KC	.353	Justice, Cle-NYY	.447	Perez N, Col	.181
Agbayani, NYM	.346	Easley, Det	.295	Kapler, Tex	.275	Perry H, TB-CWS	.231
Alfonzo, NYM	.395	Edmonds, StL	.497	Karros, LA	.318	Piazza, NYM	.415
Alicea, Tex	.215	Encarnacion, Det	.219	Kendall, Pit	.304	Posada, NYY	.451
Alomar, Cle	.328	Erstad, Ana	.311	Kennedy, Ana	.207	Quinn, KC	.270
Alou, Hou	.383	Everett, Bos	.405	Kent, SF	.421	Ramirez M, Cle	.542
Anderson B, Bal	.360	Finley, Ari	.395	Klesko, SD	.449	Randa, KC	.198
Anderson G, Ana	.272	Flaherty, TB	.165	Knoblauch, NYY	.238	Reese, Cin	.268
Aurilia, SF	.277	Fletcher, Tor	.245	Konerko, CWS	.275	Relaford, Phi-SD	.300
Ausmus, Det	.243	Floyd, Fla	.398	Koskie, Min	.306	Renteria, StL	.272
Bagwell, Hou	.492	Fryman, Cle	.322	Kotsay, Fla	.243	Rivera, SD	.305
Batista, Tor	.315	Fullmer, Tor	.330	Lamb M, Tex	.160	Rodriguez A, Sea	.491
Bell D, Sea	.225	Furcal, Atl	.305	Lankford, StL	.431	Rodriguez H, 2Tm	.322
Bell D, NYM	.286	Galarraga, Atl	.294	Lansing, Col-Bos	.212	Rolen, Phi	.373
Bell J, Ari	.301	Gant, Phi-Ana	.374	Larkin, Cin	.316	Salmon, Ana	.430
Belle, Bal	.277	Garciaparra, Bos	.348	Lawton, Min	.346	Sanchez, KC	.112
Belliard, Mil	.273	Giambi J, Oak	.586	Ledee, 3Tm	.287	Segui, Tex-Cle	.267
Beltran, KC	.247	Giles, Pit	.494	Lee C, CWS	.266	Sexson, Cle-Mil	.341
Beltre, LA	.308	Girardi, ChC	.187	Lee D, Fla	.352	Sheffield, LA	.515
Benard, SF	.273	Glanville, Phi	.184	Lee T, Ari-Phi	.309	Singleton, CWS	.225
Bergeron, Mon	.212	Glaus, Ana	.524	Lieberthal, Phi	.301	Snow, SF	.295
Berkman, Hou	.433	Gonzalez A, Fla	.169	Lofton, Cle	.331	Sosa, ChC	.470
Bichette, Cin-Bos	.273	Gonzalez A, Tor	.233	Long, Oak	.247	Spiers, Hou	.237
Biggio, Hou	.313	Gonzalez J, Det	.284	Lopez J, Atl	.270	Stairs, Oak	.357
Bonds, SF	.642	Gonzalez L, Ari	.356	Lowell, Fla	.319	Stevens, Mon	.323
Boone B, SD	.287	Goodwin, Col-LA	.303	Lugo, Hou	.267	Stewart, Tor	.288
Bordick, Bal-NYM	.247	Grace, ChC	.333	Martin, SD-Sea	.244	Stocker, TB-Ana	.236
Brosius, NYY	.234	Green S, LA	.382	Martinez D, 4Tm	.208	Stynes, Cin	.255
Buford, ChC	.230	Greer, Tex	.299	Martinez E, Sea	.433	Surhoff, Bal-Atl	.243
Buhner, Sea	.426	Grieve, Oak	.335	Martinez T, NYY	.260	Sweeney M, KC	.312
Burks, SF	.415	Griffey Jr., Cin	.469	Matheny, StL	.177	Tejada, Oak	.323
Burnitz, Mil	.402	Grissom, Mil	.190	McGriff, TB	.339	Thomas, CWS	.486
Burrell, Phi	.358	Grudzielanek, LA	.198	McLemore, Sea	.272	Thome, Cle	.476
Cabrera O, Mon	.216	Guerrero V, Mon	.419	Meares, Pit	.221	Valentin J, CWS	.352
Cairo, TB	.200	Gutierrez, ChC	.285	Meluskey, Hou	.353	Vander Wal, Pit	.474
Cameron, Sea	.346	Guzman, Min	.242	Molina, Ana	.190	Varitek, Bos	.275
Canseco, TB-NYY	.392	Hammonds, Col	.306	Mondesi, Tor	.376	Vaughn G, TB	.434
Casey, Cin	.313	Hayes, Mil	.273	Mora, NYM-Bal	.222	Vaughn M, Ana	.358
Castillo L, Fla	.273	Helton, Col	.507	Morandini, Phi-Tor	.154	Velarde, Oak	.245
Chavez E, Oak	.341	Henderson, 2Tm	.340	Morris W, Pit	.201	Ventura, NYM	.362
Cirillo, Col	.261	Hernandez J, Mil	.211	Mueller, SF	.216	Vidro, Mon	.292
Clark W, Bal-StL	.396	Hernandez R, Oak	.239	Nevin, SD	.353	Vina, StL	.177
Clayton, Tex	.232	Hidalgo, Hou	.435	Nixon, Bos	.349	Vizquel, Cle	.250
Conine, Bal	.244	Higginson, Det	.382	O'Leary, Bos	.232	Williams B, NYY	.406
Coomer, Min	.215	Hocking, Min	.252	O'Neill, NYY	.240	Williams G, TB	.207
Cordero, Pit-Cle	.250	Hollandsw'th, 2Tm	.301	Offerman, Bos	.242	Wilson P, Fla	.349
Cruz D, Det	.165	Jackson, SD	.300	Olerud, Sea	.331	Womack, Ari	.217
Cruz J, Tor	.358	Jenkins, Mil	.369	Ordonez M, CWS	.357	Young D, Cin	.248
Damon, KC	.324	Jeter, NYY	.287	Ortiz D, Min	.304	Young E, ChC	.283
Daubach, Bos	.289	Johnson C, 2Tm	.406	Owens, SD	.190	Young K, Pit	.250
Delgado C, Tor	.534	Jones A, Atl	.351	Palmeiro R, Tex	.453	Zeile, NYM	.333
DeShields, Bal	.319	Jones C, Atl	.432	Palmer, Det	.345	**MLB Average**	**.285**
Drew, StL	.369	Jones J, Min	.231	Paquette, StL	.263		
Durham, CWS	.311	Jordan B, Atl	.252	Payton, NYM	.205		

Who Puts 'Em Ahead? (p. 96)

Go-Ahead RBI Percentages—2000, Listed Alphabetically
(minimum 75 total RBI)

Player, Team	Tot RBI	GA RBI	GA Opp	Pct	Player, Team	Tot RBI	GA RBI	GA Opp	Pct
Abreu, Phi	79	17	45	.378	Jones J, Min	76	18	34	.529
Alfonzo, NYM	94	26	53	.491	Jordan B, Atl	77	12	42	.286
Alomar, Cle	89	15	42	.357	Justice, Cle-NYY	118	27	55	.491
Alou, Hou	114	23	48	.479	Karros, LA	106	26	68	.382
Anderson G, Ana	117	21	54	.389	Kent, SF	125	29	65	.446
Aurilia, SF	79	16	36	.444	Klesko, SD	92	26	51	.510
Bagwell, Hou	132	32	61	.525	Konerko, CWS	97	20	39	.513
Batista, Tor	114	20	45	.444	Lawton, Min	88	22	49	.449
Belle, Bal	103	25	52	.481	Ledee, NYY-Cle-Tex	77	12	35	.343
Beltre, LA	85	16	34	.471	Lee C, CWS	92	15	25	.600
Bichette, Cin-Bos	90	19	45	.422	Long, Oak	80	14	24	.583
Bonds, SF	106	35	58	.603	Lopez J, Atl	89	16	30	.533
Bordick, Bal-NYM	80	15	37	.405	Lowell, Fla	91	16	42	.381
Buhner, Sea	82	10	22	.455	Martinez E, Sea	145	24	50	.480
Burks, SF	96	18	45	.400	Martinez T, NYY	91	14	39	.359
Burnitz, Mil	98	28	56	.500	McGriff, TB	106	29	67	.433
Burrell, Phi	79	13	41	.317	Nevin, SD	107	28	64	.438
Cameron, Sea	78	16	38	.421	O'Neill, NYY	100	21	54	.389
Casey, Cin	85	11	26	.423	Olerud, Sea	103	24	49	.490
Chavez E, Oak	86	12	26	.462	Ordonez M, CWS	126	26	58	.448
Cirillo, Col	115	22	49	.449	Palmeiro R, Tex	120	29	58	.500
Coomer, Min	82	16	51	.314	Palmer, Det	102	16	38	.421
Cruz D, Det	82	16	48	.333	Piazza, NYM	113	29	61	.475
Cruz J, Tor	76	12	35	.343	Posada, NYY	86	17	33	.515
Damon, KC	88	14	35	.400	Quinn, KC	78	18	36	.500
Daubach, Bos	76	12	39	.308	Ramirez M, Cle	122	25	50	.500
Delgado C, Tor	137	27	57	.474	Randa, KC	106	11	34	.324
DeShields, Bal	86	29	53	.547	Renteria, StL	76	15	35	.429
Durham, CWS	75	17	30	.567	Rodriguez A, Sea	132	29	47	.617
Dye, KC	118	27	58	.466	Rodriguez I, Tex	83	22	35	.629
Edmonds, StL	108	31	57	.544	Rolen, Phi	89	17	66	.258
Erstad, Ana	100	20	35	.571	Salmon, Ana	97	23	55	.418
Everett, Bos	108	16	41	.390	Segui, Tex-Cle	103	23	54	.426
Finley, Ari	96	21	50	.420	Sexson, Cle-Mil	91	17	36	.472
Floyd, Fla	91	30	54	.556	Sheffield, LA	109	30	49	.612
Fryman, Cle	106	17	46	.370	Snow, SF	96	19	45	.422
Fullmer, Tor	104	14	39	.359	Sosa, ChC	138	25	55	.455
Galarraga, Atl	100	30	60	.500	Stairs, Oak	81	16	42	.381
Garciaparra, Bos	96	27	49	.551	Stevens, Mon	75	17	47	.362
Giambi J, Oak	137	19	34	.559	Sweeney M, KC	144	37	59	.627
Giles, Pit	123	34	70	.486	Tejada, Oak	115	17	37	.459
Glaus, Ana	102	17	41	.415	Thomas, CWS	143	25	47	.532
Gonzalez L, Ari	114	28	55	.509	Thome, Cle	106	21	50	.420
Grace, ChC	82	16	48	.333	Valentin J, CWS	92	19	29	.655
Green S, LA	99	21	51	.412	Vander Wal, Pit	94	20	38	.526
Grieve, Oak	104	15	47	.319	Vaughn M, Ana	117	24	57	.421
Griffey Jr., Cin	118	29	55	.527	Ventura, NYM	84	16	43	.372
Guerrero V, Mon	123	33	64	.516	Vidro, Mon	97	20	41	.488
Hammonds, Col	106	19	47	.404	Williams B, NYY	121	27	62	.435
Helton, Col	147	29	51	.569	Williams G, TB	89	18	40	.450
Hidalgo, Hou	122	30	60	.500	Wilson P, Fla	121	35	65	.538
Higginson, Det	102	22	51	.431	Young D, Cin	88	15	38	.395
Jenkins, Mil	94	13	34	.382	Young K, Pit	88	19	50	.380
Johnson C, Bal-CWS	91	17	30	.567	Zeile, NYM	79	16	46	.348
Jones A, Atl	104	29	61	.475	**MLB Average**				**.397**
Jones C, Atl	111	27	60	.450					

Baseball Scoreboard

Who Are the Real RBI Kings? (p. 98)

RBI Percentages—2000, Listed Alphabetically
(minimum 500 RBI Avail)

Player, Team	RBI	Avail	Pct	Player, Team	RBI	Avail	Pct
Abreu, Phi	79	885	8.9	Cairo, TB	34	585	5.8
Agbayani, NYM	60	593	10.1	Cameron, Sea	78	914	8.5
Alfonzo, NYM	94	886	10.6	Canizaro, Min	40	538	7.4
Alicea, Tex	63	873	7.2	Canseco, TB-NYY	49	566	8.7
Alomar, Cle	89	1,047	8.5	Casey, Cin	85	813	10.5
Alomar Jr., Cle	42	601	7.0	Castilla, TB	42	563	7.5
Alou, Hou	114	816	14.0	Castillo L, Fla	17	775	2.2
Anderson B, Bal	50	757	6.6	Chavez E, Oak	86	848	10.1
Anderson G, Ana	117	1,136	10.3	Cirillo, Col	115	1,029	11.2
Aurilia, SF	79	894	8.8	Clark W, Bal-StL	70	702	10.0
Ausmus, Det	51	846	6.0	Clayton, Tex	54	884	6.1
Bagwell, Hou	132	985	13.4	Colbrunn, Ari	57	553	10.3
Batista, Tor	114	1,059	10.8	Conine, Bal	46	674	6.8
Bautista, Fla-Ari	59	589	10.0	Coomer, Min	82	930	8.8
Bell D, Sea	47	784	6.0	Cora, LA	32	594	5.4
Bell D, NYM	69	843	8.2	Cordero, Pit-Cle	68	847	8.0
Bell J, Ari	68	880	7.7	Cox, TB	35	502	7.0
Belle, Bal	103	939	11.0	Cruz D, Det	82	1,015	8.1
Belliard, Mil	54	855	6.3	Cruz J, Tor	76	948	8.0
Beltran, KC	44	649	6.8	Curtis, Tex	48	589	8.1
Beltre, LA	85	879	9.7	Damon, KC	88	1,026	8.6
Benard, SF	55	826	6.7	Daubach, Bos	76	819	9.3
Bergeron, Mon	31	744	4.2	Delgado C, Tor	137	969	14.1
Berkman, Hou	67	611	11.0	DeShields, Bal	86	932	9.2
Bichette, Cin-Bos	90	975	9.2	Drew, StL	57	655	8.7
Biggio, Hou	35	574	6.1	Durham, CWS	75	967	7.8
Blum, Mon	45	562	8.0	Dye, KC	118	1,044	11.3
Bogar, Hou	33	507	6.5	Easley, Det	58	759	7.6
Bonds, SF	106	761	13.9	Edmonds, StL	108	909	11.9
Boone A, Cin	43	501	8.6	Encarnacion, Det	72	892	8.1
Boone B, SD	74	784	9.4	Erstad, Ana	100	1,001	10.0
Bordick, Bal-NYM	80	960	8.3	Estalella, SF	53	513	10.3
Brosius, NYY	64	827	7.7	Everett, Bos	108	851	12.7
Buford, ChC	48	770	6.2	Febles, KC	29	583	5.0
Buhner, Sea	82	653	12.6	Finley, Ari	96	930	10.3
Burks, SF	96	741	13.0	Flaherty, TB	39	638	6.1
Burnitz, Mil	98	934	10.5	Fletcher, Tor	58	654	8.9
Burrell, Phi	79	704	11.2	Floyd, Fla	91	715	12.7
Cabrera O, Mon	55	684	8.0	Fordyce, CWS-Bal	49	505	9.7

Player, Team	RBI	Avail	Pct	Player, Team	RBI	Avail	Pct
Frye, Bos-Col	16	509	3.1	Jackson, SD	37	729	5.1
Fryman, Cle	106	1,012	10.5	Javier, Sea	40	563	7.1
Fullmer, Tor	104	844	12.3	Jenkins, Mil	94	828	11.4
Furcal, Atl	37	730	5.1	Jeter, NYY	73	930	7.8
Galarraga, Atl	100	852	11.7	Johnson C, Bal-CWS	91	730	12.5
Gant, Phi-Ana	54	677	8.0	Jones A, Atl	104	1,068	9.7
Garciaparra, Bos	96	887	10.8	Jones C, Atl	111	992	11.2
Giambi J, Oak	137	869	15.8	Jones J, Min	76	857	8.9
Gil, Ana	23	501	4.6	Jordan B, Atl	77	838	9.2
Giles, Pit	123	987	12.5	Jordan K, Phi	36	595	6.1
Girardi, ChC	40	589	6.8	Justice, Cle-NYY	118	897	13.2
Glanville, Phi	52	985	5.3	Kapler, Tex	66	791	8.3
Glaus, Ana	102	914	11.2	Karros, LA	106	1,040	10.2
Gonzalez A, Fla	42	629	6.7	Kendall, Pit	58	890	6.5
Gonzalez A, Tor	69	888	7.8	Kennedy, Ana	72	993	7.3
Gonzalez J, Det	67	799	8.4	Kent, SF	125	1,036	12.1
Gonzalez L, Ari	114	1,015	11.2	Klesko, SD	92	824	11.2
Goodwin, Col-LA	58	797	7.3	Knoblauch, NYY	26	586	4.4
Grace, ChC	82	865	9.5	Konerko, CWS	97	914	10.6
Green S, LA	99	1,039	9.5	Koskie, Min	65	798	8.1
Greer, Tex	65	657	9.9	Kotsay, Fla	57	847	6.7
Grieve, Oak	104	1,055	9.9	Lamb M, Tex	47	796	5.9
Griffey Jr., Cin	118	888	13.3	Lankford, StL	65	682	9.5
Grissom, Mil	62	929	6.7	Lansing, Col-Bos	60	813	7.4
Grudzielanek, LA	49	934	5.2	Larkin, Cin	41	623	6.6
Guerrero V, Mon	123	937	13.1	Lawton, Min	88	924	9.5
Guillen J, TB	41	517	7.9	Ledee, NYY-Cle-Tex	77	836	9.2
Gutierrez, ChC	56	756	7.4	Lee C, CWS	92	978	9.4
Guzman, Min	54	1,002	5.4	Lee D, Fla	70	769	9.1
Hammonds, Col	106	843	12.6	Lee T, Ari-Phi	54	708	7.6
Hayes, Mil	46	623	7.4	Lieberthal, Phi	71	667	10.6
Helton, Col	147	1,000	14.7	Lofton, Cle	73	854	8.5
Henderson, NYM-Sea	32	658	4.9	Long, Oak	80	892	9.0
Hernandez J, Mil	59	760	7.8	Lopez J, Atl	89	835	10.7
Hernandez R, Oak	62	718	8.6	Loretta, Mil	40	553	7.2
Hidalgo, Hou	122	989	12.3	Lowell, Fla	91	836	10.9
Higginson, Det	102	995	10.3	Lugo, Hou	40	674	5.9
Hill, ChC-NYY	58	510	11.4	Martin, SD-Sea	36	715	5.0
Hocking, Min	47	593	7.9	Martinez D, 4Tm	47	743	6.3
Hollandsworth, LA-Col	47	671	7.0	Martinez E, Sea	145	1,005	14.4
Hundley, LA	70	519	13.5	Martinez T, NYY	91	980	9.3
Hunter T, Min	44	568	7.7	Matheny, StL	47	708	6.6
Huskey, Min-Col	45	534	8.4	Mayne, Col	64	595	10.8

Player, Team	RBI	Avail	Pct	Player, Team	RBI	Avail	Pct
McGriff, TB	106	977	10.8	Sanchez, KC	38	838	4.5
McLemore, Sea	46	779	5.9	Sanders R, Atl	37	543	6.8
Meares, Pit	47	736	6.4	Segui, Tex-Cle	103	1,009	10.2
Meluskey, Hou	69	592	11.7	Sexson, Cle-Mil	91	879	10.4
Miller, Ari	44	539	8.2	Sheffield, LA	109	826	13.2
Molina, Ana	71	843	8.4	Singleton, CWS	62	849	7.3
Mondesi, Tor	67	644	10.4	Snow, SF	96	950	10.1
Mora, NYM-Bal	47	663	7.1	Sojo, Pit-NYY	37	503	7.4
Morandini, Phi-Tor	29	646	4.5	Sosa, ChC	138	1,029	13.4
Morris W, Pit	43	820	5.2	Spiers, Hou	43	551	7.8
Mueller, SF	55	911	6.0	Stairs, Oak	81	852	9.5
Nevin, SD	107	899	11.9	Stanley, Bos-Oak	46	501	9.2
Nixon, Bos	60	691	8.7	Stevens, Mon	75	761	9.9
O'Leary, Bos	70	888	7.9	Stewart, Tor	69	888	7.8
O'Neill, NYY	100	999	10.0	Stocker, TB-Ana	24	561	4.3
Offerman, Bos	41	689	6.0	Stynes, Cin	40	582	6.9
Olerud, Sea	103	1,007	10.2	Surhoff, Bal-Atl	68	887	7.7
Ordonez M, CWS	126	1,058	11.9	Sweeney M, KC	144	1,100	13.1
Ortiz D, Min	63	716	8.8	Tatis, StL	64	568	11.3
Owens, SD	51	893	5.7	Tejada, Oak	115	1,034	11.1
Palmeiro R, Tex	120	951	12.6	Thomas, CWS	143	968	14.8
Palmer, Det	102	906	11.3	Thome, Cle	106	981	10.8
Paquette, StL	61	687	8.9	Valentin J, CWS	92	944	9.7
Payton, NYM	62	833	7.4	Vander Wal, Pit	94	670	14.0
Perez N, Col	71	1,094	6.5	Varitek, Bos	65	775	8.4
Perry H, TB-CWS	62	687	9.0	Vaughn G, TB	74	733	10.1
Piazza, NYM	113	855	13.2	Vaughn M, Ana	117	1,029	11.4
Polanco, StL	39	527	7.4	Velarde, Oak	41	749	5.5
Polonia, Det-NYY	30	536	5.6	Ventura, NYM	84	796	10.6
Posada, NYY	86	829	10.4	Vidro, Mon	97	966	10.0
Quinn, KC	78	863	9.0	Vina, StL	31	699	4.4
Ramirez M, Cle	122	779	15.7	Vizquel, Cle	66	1,002	6.6
Randa, KC	106	1,063	10.0	White R, Mon-ChC	61	588	10.4
Reese, Cin	46	797	5.8	Williams B, NYY	121	927	13.1
Relaford, Phi-SD	46	663	6.9	Williams G, TB	89	1,014	8.8
Renteria, StL	76	959	7.9	Williams M, Ari	47	627	7.5
Ripken Jr., Bal	56	509	11.0	Wilson P, Fla	121	1,037	11.7
Rivera, SD	57	651	8.8	Womack, Ari	57	931	6.1
Rodriguez A, Sea	132	936	14.1	Young D, Cin	88	924	9.5
Rodriguez H, ChC-Fla	61	595	10.3	Young E, ChC	47	909	5.2
Rodriguez I, Tex	83	614	13.5	Young K, Pit	88	883	10.0
Rolen, Phi	89	821	10.8	Zeile, NYM	79	909	8.7
Salmon, Ana	97	940	10.3	**MLB Average**			**8.5**

Can a Change of Scenery Be Good For the Heart? (p. 101)

American League, Sorted by Most RBI—2000

Team	Avg	HR	RBI	Slg	Main 3-4-5 Hitters
Mariners	.300	95	394	.522	Rodriguez A, Martinez E, Olerud
White Sox	.305	98	376	.529	Thomas, Ordonez M, Konerko
Indians	.303	111	374	.551	Alomar, Ramirez M, Thome
Royals	.302	76	373	.484	Sweeney M, Dye, Randa
Blue Jays	.298	107	368	.544	Mondesi, Delgado C, Fullmer
Rangers	.311	89	362	.528	Rodriguez I, Palmeiro R, Segui
Yankees	.286	89	362	.489	O'Neill, Williams B, Martinez T
Athletics	.283	98	357	.505	Giambi J, Grieve, Stairs
Angels	.279	108	338	.511	Vaughn M, Salmon, Anderson G
Red Sox	.293	76	328	.490	Everett, Garciaparra, O'Leary
Tigers	.278	81	301	.473	Higginson, Gonzalez J, Palmer
Orioles	.279	56	290	.438	DeShields, Belle, Conine
Devil Rays	.261	75	285	.441	Vaughn G, McGriff, Canseco
Twins	.276	39	248	.413	Lawton, Coomer, Ortiz D

National League, Sorted by Most RBI—2000

Team	Avg	HR	RBI	Slg	Main 3-4-5 Hitters
Astros	.322	139	427	.620	Bagwell, Caminiti, Alou
Rockies	.334	85	394	.561	Walker L, Helton, Hammonds
Giants	.319	112	385	.585	Bonds, Kent, Snow
Cardinals	.283	126	364	.548	Edmonds, McGwire, Lankford
Pirates	.288	84	362	.501	Giles, Young K, Vander Wal
Reds	.287	92	354	.502	Griffey Jr., Bichette, Casey
Mets	.289	101	347	.521	Alfonzo, Piazza, Ventura
Marlins	.275	91	345	.491	Floyd, Wilson P, Lowell
Braves	.300	94	342	.508	Jones C, Galarraga, Jordan B
Cubs	.282	97	338	.502	Sosa, Grace, Rodriguez H
Expos	.297	97	330	.526	White R, Guerrero V, Stevens
Dodgers	.271	101	330	.499	Sheffield, Green S, Karros
Padres	.279	86	321	.486	Klesko, Nevin, Boone B
Diamondbacks	.293	95	319	.519	Gonzalez L, Williams M, Finley
Brewers	.258	91	297	.466	Jenkins, Sexson, Burnitz
Phillies	.277	71	290	.481	Abreu, Rolen, Burrell
MLB Average	**.290**	**92**	**343**	**.508**	

Who Gets the Slidin' Billy Trophy? (p. 103)

Leadoff Men—2000, Listed Alphabetically
(minimum 125 leadoff PA)

Player, Team	OBP	AB	R	H	BB	HBP	SB
Agbayani, NYM	.365	106	20	27	18	1	2
Alicea, Tex	.363	442	73	129	51	2	0
Anderson B, Bal	.374	504	88	130	90	8	16
Becker, Oak-Det	.397	142	28	34	36	1	2
Belliard, Mil	.343	367	56	93	52	1	6
Benard, SF	.341	530	98	138	60	6	20
Bergeron, Mon	.321	433	64	109	45	0	10
Biggio, Hou	.413	159	31	39	38	8	5
Brown A, Pit	.368	237	49	73	23	0	8
Canizaro, Min	.302	117	15	29	9	0	2
Castillo L, Fla	.419	538	100	180	78	0	62
Cedeno, Hou	.388	155	34	46	23	0	16
Cruz J, Tor	.357	112	19	32	13	0	3
Damon, KC	.381	655	136	214	64	1	46
Durham, CWS	.361	611	121	172	74	7	24
Easley, Det	.373	184	34	51	26	2	6
Erstad, Ana	.409	675	121	239	64	1	28
Furcal, Atl	.401	334	65	98	59	2	30
Glanville, Phi	.312	491	69	136	25	2	23
Goodwin, Col-LA	.347	511	91	137	64	0	53
Grissom, Mil	.288	208	29	52	11	0	6
Guzman, Min	.301	262	42	69	15	0	8
Henderson, NYM-Sea	.368	420	73	98	88	4	36
Hocking, Min	.373	125	18	37	16	0	2
Hollandsworth, LA-Col	.335	203	37	52	24	0	8
Hunter B, Col-Cin	.337	161	30	41	19	1	14
Jackson, SD	.368	129	19	39	13	1	8
Knoblauch, NYY	.367	399	74	113	46	8	15
Lofton, Cle	.357	501	98	135	69	3	27
Long, Oak	.333	517	94	146	40	1	5
Lugo, Hou	.376	197	43	59	21	3	11
Martin, SD-Sea	.371	178	37	56	12	4	4
McLemore, Sea	.292	143	20	25	23	1	9
Mora, NYM-Bal	.310	118	23	32	8	0	3
Morris W, Pit	.327	237	36	63	22	0	3
Murray, SF	.345	143	23	34	21	3	9
Nixon, Bos	.398	138	21	40	26	0	2
Offerman, Bos	.336	356	51	88	48	1	0
Owens, SD	.332	389	57	106	34	2	14
Pierre, Col	.347	187	25	56	13	1	7
Polonia, Det-NYY	.339	279	40	79	25	1	10
Reese, Cin	.345	378	63	104	38	4	26
Spiers, Hou	.399	128	15	40	18	1	1
Stewart, Tor	.363	583	107	186	37	6	20
Stynes, Cin	.400	212	43	75	16	1	3
Veras Q, Atl	.404	270	46	81	47	3	22
Vina, StL	.382	483	81	146	35	28	10
White D, LA	.306	138	21	36	8	1	3
Williams G, TB	.303	573	80	153	28	3	11
Womack, Ari	.306	616	94	166	30	5	44
Young E, ChC	.370	603	96	180	63	8	54
MLB Average Team	**.349**	**684**	**116**	**189**	**74**	**6**	**29**

Who's the Best Bunter? (p. 105)

Sacrifice Hits And Bunt Hits—2000, Listed Alphabetically
(minimum 12 bunts in play)

Player, Team	SH	Fail	Pct	H	Fail	Pct	Player, Team	SH	Fail	Pct	H	Fail	Pct
Alicea, Tex	7	2	.778	3	1	.750	Johnson M, CWS	10	2	.833	3	0	1.000
Alomar, Cle	11	5	.688	6	3	.667	Kennedy, Ana	8	0	1.000	2	3	.400
Ashby, Phi-Atl	9	3	.750	0	0	—	Leiter, NYM	9	6	.600	0	0	—
Bell J, Ari	6	4	.600	2	0	1.000	Lewis D, Bos	8	0	1.000	2	4	.333
Benard, SF	2	1	.667	10	14	.417	Lofton, Cle	6	2	.750	12	1	.923
Benson, Pit	9	4	.692	0	0	—	Loretta, Mil	8	0	1.000	4	2	.667
Bergeron, Mon	14	5	.737	10	7	.588	Martinez F, TB	12	1	.923	2	4	.333
Bohanon, Col	11	3	.786	0	0	—	McEwing, NYM	8	1	.889	1	2	.333
Brown, LA	14	4	.778	1	0	1.000	McLemore, Sea	11	2	.846	2	3	.400
Buford, ChC	4	3	.571	3	2	.600	Millwood, Atl	14	3	.824	0	0	—
Cairo, TB	6	1	.857	3	4	.429	Mora, NYM-Bal	4	1	.800	13	4	.765
Cameron, Sea	7	2	.778	3	4	.429	Morandini, Phi-Tor	7	0	1.000	5	1	.833
Castillo L, Fla	9	1	.900	14	7	.667	Mouton J, Mil	4	1	.800	5	2	.714
Cirillo, Col	1	1	.500	6	4	.600	Palmeiro O, Ana	10	3	.769	2	2	.500
Clayton, Tex	12	3	.800	2	0	1.000	Perez C, LA	7	2	.778	0	3	.000
Cora, LA	6	1	.857	1	5	.167	Perez N, Col	7	1	.875	9	10	.474
D'Amico J, Mil	6	6	.500	0	0	—	Polonia, Det-NYY	3	1	.750	6	6	.500
Damon, KC	8	0	1.000	10	4	.714	Reed R, NYM	14	1	.933	0	1	.000
Dotel, Hou	7	5	.583	0	0	—	Reynoso, Ari	7	4	.636	1	0	1.000
Durham, CWS	5	1	.833	1	5	.167	Sanchez, KC	11	4	.733	5	5	.500
Estes, SF	11	1	.917	0	1	.000	Schilling, Phi-Ari	9	7	.563	0	0	—
Febles, KC	13	3	.813	5	5	.500	Singleton, CWS	12	1	.923	6	4	.600
Furcal, Atl	9	1	.900	10	12	.455	Stephenson, StL	13	1	.929	0	0	—
Gil, Ana	5	4	.556	2	6	.250	Stocker, TB-Ana	10	2	.833	2	7	.222
Glanville, Phi	12	1	.923	3	3	.500	Tapani, ChC	9	5	.643	0	0	—
Glavine, Atl	14	5	.737	0	0	—	Tyner, NYM-TB	8	1	.889	2	4	.333
Gonzalez A, Tor	16	5	.762	3	4	.429	Valentin J, CWS	13	4	.765	8	2	.800
Goodwin, Col-LA	5	1	.833	5	7	.417	Vazquez, Mon	13	1	.929	0	0	—
Green S, Tex	5	1	.833	5	4	.556	Veras Q, Atl	6	2	.750	1	3	.250
Guerrero W, Mon	6	2	.750	5	2	.714	Vina, StL	2	0	1.000	9	12	.429
Guillen C, Sea	7	1	.875	2	4	.333	Vizquel, Cle	7	2	.778	9	7	.563
Gutierrez, ChC	16	2	.889	1	0	1.000	Williams G, TB	9	3	.750	3	4	.429
Guzman, Min	7	3	.700	5	9	.357	Wolf, Phi	10	2	.833	0	0	—
Halter, Det	10	1	.909	4	2	.667	Womack, Ari	2	3	.400	9	3	.750
Hentgen, StL	8	4	.667	0	0	—	Yoshii, Col	12	2	.857	0	0	—
Hernandez R, Oak	10	2	.833	1	0	1.000	Young E, ChC	7	0	1.000	16	5	.762
Javier, Sea	4	0	1.000	5	3	.625	**MLB Average**			**.769**			**.561**

Who Is the New Millennium's First Man on the Moon? (p. 108)

Longest Home Runs—2000

Dis	Batter, Team	Pitcher, Team	Date	Site
500	Piazza, NYM	Johnson R, Ari	5/21	NYM
493	Bonds, SF	Etherton, Ana	6/6	Ana
490	Hill, ChC	Woodard, Mil	5/11	ChC
487	McGwire, StL	Perez C, LA	5/14	StL
485	Rodriguez A, Sea	Lee S, Bos	9/3	Bos
483	McGwire, StL	Hershiser, LA	6/24	StL
482	Lee D, Fla	Quevedo, ChC	6/25	Fla
479	Thome, Cle	Miller W, Hou	7/17	Cle
475	McGwire, StL	Estes, SF	6/22	StL
475	Griffey Jr., Cin	Tavarez, Col	7/13	Col
473	McGwire, StL	Villone, Cin	5/5	Cin
470	Canseco, TB	Ortiz R, Ana	4/22	TB
470	Canseco, TB	Martinez R, Bos	5/5	Bos
470	Buhner, Sea	Timlin, Bal	5/23	Bal
470	Sosa, ChC	Brock, Phi	7/19	ChC
466	Griffey Jr., Cin	White G, Col	4/11	Col
465	Glaus, Ana	Karl, Col	7/7	Ana
465	Thome, Cle	Trachsel, Tor	9/29	Cle
463	McGwire, StL	Karl, Col	4/23	StL
462	Vaughn G, TB	Burba, Cle	4/8	TB
462	Huskey, Min	Oliver, Tex	5/26	Min
461	McGwire, StL	Cordova, Pit	5/4	StL
461	Hammonds, Col	Farnsworth, ChC	5/24	Col
460	Sweeney M, KC	Miller T, Min	4/7	KC
460	Durazo, Ari	Williams W, SD	4/10	SD
460	Piazza, NYM	Tapani, ChC	4/23	NYM
460	Canseco, TB	Wells D, Tor	5/14	TB
460	McGwire, StL	Ritchie, Pit	5/21	Pit
460	Branyan, Cle	Sparks S, Det	6/24	Cle
460	Delgado C, Tor	Trachsel, TB	7/20	Tor
460	Vander Wal, Pit	Byrd, Phi	7/21	Pit
460	Dreifort, LA	Van Poppel, ChC	8/8	LA
460	Burrell, Phi	Walker K, SD	8/8	Phi
460	Sosa, ChC	Elarton, Hou	8/21	Hou
460	Grieve, Oak	Lopez A, TB	9/9	Oak
460	Bonds, SF	Miller W, Hou	9/13	Hou
459	Edmonds, StL	Cornelius, Fla	5/25	StL
458	Rodriguez A, Sea	Barcelo, CWS	8/8	CWS
457	Bonds, SF	Astacio, Col	5/13	Col
457	Glaus, Ana	Johnson R, Ari	6/9	Ari
456	Hidalgo, Hou	Kile, StL	7/2	StL
455	Galarraga, Atl	Quevedo, ChC	5/30	ChC
455	Rodriguez A, Sea	Cooper, Ana	7/5	Ana
455	Piazza, NYM	Benes A, StL	7/29	NYM
455	Berkman, Hou	Van Poppel, ChC	9/9	ChC
454	Klesko, SD	Benes A, StL	4/18	StL
454	Burnitz, Mil	Maddux G, Atl	6/24	Atl
453	Sosa, ChC	Milton, Min	7/14	Min
453	Glaus, Ana	Choate, NYY	8/11	Ana
452	Lowery, SF	Karl, Col	5/14	Col
452	Ramirez M, Cle	Frascatore, Tor	10/1	Cle
451	McGwire, StL	Clement, SD	6/12	SD
451	Jones C, Atl	Vazquez, Mon	7/5	Atl
451	Helton, Col	Kim, Ari	9/26	Col
390	**MLB Average**			

Who Are the Human Air Conditioners? (p. 110)

Percentages of Swings That Missed—2000, Listed Alphabetically
(minimum 500 swings)

Player, Team	Sw	Miss	Pct	Player, Team	Sw	Miss	Pct	Player, Team	Sw	Miss	Pct
Abreu, Phi	1,029	194	19	Cairo, TB	644	62	10	Galarraga, Atl	1,039	316	30
Agbayani, NYM	685	144	21	Cameron, Sea	1,073	250	23	Gant, Phi-Ana	809	196	24
Alfonzo, NYM	1,057	155	15	Canizaro, Min	578	98	17	Garciaparra, Bos	968	163	17
Alicea, Tex	979	130	13	Canseco, 2Tm	694	211	30	Giambi Je, Oak	527	100	19
Alomar, Cle	1,234	157	13	Casey, Cin	893	150	17	Giambi Ja, Oak	976	170	17
Alomar Jr., Cle	663	103	16	Castilla, TB	631	164	26	Gil, Ana	612	165	27
Alou, Hou	904	161	18	Castillo L, Fla	1,028	81	8	Giles, Pit	1,032	120	12
Anderson B, Bal	1,023	178	17	Catalanotto, Tex	566	73	13	Girardi, ChC	666	125	19
Anderson G, Ana	1,251	214	17	Chavez E, Oak	994	201	20	Glanville, Phi	1,162	164	14
Aurilia, SF	963	162	17	Cirillo, Col	1,095	145	13	Glaus, Ana	1,101	294	27
Ausmus, Det	984	137	14	Clark W, Bal-StL	828	155	19	Gonzalez A, Tor	1,019	254	25
Bagwell, Hou	1,235	294	24	Clayton, Tex	1,081	196	18	Gonzalez A, Fla	783	176	22
Baines, Bal-CWS	530	102	19	Colbrunn, Ari	712	129	18	Gonzalez J, Det	868	204	24
Batista, Tor	1,313	289	22	Conine, Bal	749	114	15	Gonzalez L, Ari	1,152	185	16
Bautista, Fla-Ari	622	118	19	Coomer, Min	981	147	15	Gonzalez W, SD	501	93	19
Becker, Oak-Det	512	110	21	Cora, LA	681	93	14	Goodwin, Col-LA	889	182	20
Bell D, NYM	1,059	240	23	Cordero, Pit-Cle	980	183	19	Grace, ChC	833	69	8
Bell D, Sea	871	122	14	Cox, TB	598	116	19	Green S, LA	1,222	281	23
Bell J, Ari	1,150	205	18	Cruz D, Det	1,025	123	12	Greene W, ChC	555	151	27
Belle, Bal	1,055	140	13	Cruz J, Tor	1,107	281	25	Greer, Tex	711	112	16
Belliard, Mil	1,031	157	15	Curtis, Tex	613	129	21	Grieve, Oak	1,026	216	21
Beltran, KC	680	131	19	Damon, KC	1,152	127	11	Griffey Jr., Cin	1,114	232	21
Beltre, LA	1,031	214	21	Daubach, Bos	1,028	263	26	Grissom, Mil	1,088	196	18
Benard, SF	1,116	190	17	Delgado C, Tor	1,100	237	22	Grudzielanek, LA	1,097	133	12
Bergeron, Mon	964	145	15	DeShields, Bal	1,015	179	18	Guerrero V, Mon	1,192	275	23
Berkman, Hou	728	170	23	Drew, StL	835	205	25	Guerrero W, Mon	549	92	17
Bichette, Cin-Bos	1,240	255	21	Durham, CWS	1,119	185	17	Guillen C, Sea	581	99	17
Biggio, Hou	744	152	20	Dye, KC	1,181	197	17	Guillen J, TB	639	149	23
Blanco, Mil	521	91	17	Easley, Det	793	142	18	Gutierrez, ChC	813	121	15
Blum, Mon	684	105	15	Edmonds, StL	1054	260	25	Guzman, Min	1,110	169	15
Bogar, Hou	613	105	17	Encarnacion, Det	1,088	230	21	Hammonds, Col	908	200	22
Bonds, SF	909	144	16	Erstad, Ana	1,206	172	14	Hayes, Mil	754	169	22
Boone A, Cin	563	115	20	Estalella, SF	667	202	30	Helton, Col	1,147	113	10
Boone B, SD	899	202	22	Everett, Bos	1,041	300	29	Henderson, 2Tm	783	97	12
Bordick, 2Tm	1,090	178	16	Febles, KC	630	94	15	Hernandez J, Mil	890	250	28
Brosius, NYY	848	156	18	Finley, Ari	1,010	180	18	Hernandez, Oak	776	131	17
Brown A, Pit	504	45	9	Flaherty, TB	761	135	18	Hidalgo, Hou	1,087	187	17
Buford, ChC	993	211	21	Fletcher, Tor	792	106	13	Higginson, Det	1,107	163	15
Buhner, Sea	682	193	28	Floyd, Fla	886	224	25	Hill, ChC-NYY	619	188	30
Burks, SF	743	122	16	Fordyce, 2Tm	601	100	17	Hocking, Min	667	109	16
Burnitz, Mil	1,170	287	25	Frye, Bos-Col	565	73	13	Holl'dsw'rth, 2Tm	859	227	26
Burrell, Phi	789	219	28	Fryman, Cle	1,081	191	18	Houston, Mil	515	118	23
Bush, Tor	622	136	22	Fullmer, Tor	991	164	17	Hundley, LA	621	139	22
Cabrera O, Mon	744	78	10	Furcal, Atl	891	120	13	Hunter T, Min	666	168	25

Player, Team	Sw	Miss	Pct	Player, Team	Sw	Miss	Pct	Player, Team	Sw	Miss	Pct
Huskey, Min-Col	604	162	27	Meares, Pit	870	174	20	Snow, SF	1,097	217	20
Jackson, SD	883	174	20	Meluskey, Hou	615	120	20	Sojo, Pit-NYY	533	40	8
Javier, Sea	646	102	16	Millar, Fla	524	79	15	Sosa, ChC	1,326	422	32
Jenkins, Mil	1,150	313	27	Miller, Ari	636	148	23	Spencer, NYY	531	91	17
Jeter, NYY	1,250	203	16	Molina, Ana	921	96	10	Spiers, Hou	571	80	14
Johnson C, 2Tm	880	262	30	Mondesi, Tor	741	205	28	Spiezio, Ana	580	105	18
Jones A, Atl	1,300	266	20	Mora, NYM-Bal	811	144	18	Stairs, Oak	843	212	25
Jones C, Atl	1,050	168	16	Morandini, 2Tm	753	95	13	Stanley, Bos-Oak	546	137	25
Jones J, Min	1,069	280	26	Morris W, Pit	955	159	17	Stevens, Mon	919	267	29
Jordan B, Atl	964	208	22	Mueller, SF	987	79	8	Stewart, Tor	1,121	191	17
Jordan K, Phi	620	86	14	Nevin, SD	1,107	280	25	Stinnett, Ari	505	128	25
Justice, Cle-NYY	1,046	217	21	Nixon, Bos	716	146	20	Stocker, TB-Ana	700	148	21
Kapler, Tex	833	131	16	O'Leary, Bos	963	187	19	Stynes, Cin	688	106	15
Karros, LA	1,112	244	22	O'Neill, NYY	1,083	183	17	Surhoff, Bal-Atl	967	100	10
Kendall, Pit	1,080	174	16	Offerman, Bos	771	96	12	Sweeney M, KC	1,194	184	15
Kennedy, Ana	1,123	181	16	Olerud, Sea	961	136	14	Tatis, StL	719	196	27
Kent, SF	1,183	251	21	OrdonezM, CWS	1,160	185	16	Tejada, Oak	1,167	204	17
Klesko, SD	971	180	19	Ortiz D, Min	839	155	18	Thomas, CWS	1,053	149	14
Knoblauch, NYY	695	53	8	Owens, SD	997	117	12	Thome, Cle	1,251	406	32
Konerko, CWS	922	145	16	Palmeiro R, Tex	1,074	164	15	Truby, Hou	524	161	31
Koskie, Min	902	211	23	Palmer, Det	1,100	307	28	Tucker, Cin	592	149	25
Kotsay, Fla	916	125	14	Paquette, StL	821	223	27	Valentin J, CWS	1,113	179	16
Lamb M, Tex	907	117	13	Payton, NYM	914	145	16	Vander Wal, Pit	701	189	27
Lankford, StL	936	336	36	Perez N, Col	1,266	147	12	Varitek, Bos	873	164	19
Lansing, Col-Bos	891	117	13	Perry H, 2Tm	827	180	22	Vaughn G, TB	970	277	29
Larkin, Cin	677	64	9	Piazza, NYM	928	193	21	Vaughn M, Ana	1,318	406	31
Lawton, Min	1,022	126	12	Polanco, StL	563	54	10	Velarde, Oak	796	135	17
Ledee, 3Tm	879	188	21	Polonia, 2Tm	628	76	12	Ventura, NYM	845	178	21
Lee C, CWS	1,117	191	17	Posada, NYY	913	241	26	Veras Q, Atl	579	63	11
Lee D, Fla	927	236	25	Quinn, KC	978	205	21	Vidro, Mon	1,152	172	15
Lee T, Ari-Phi	769	134	17	Ramirez M, Cle	958	210	22	Vina, StL	816	81	10
Lieberthal, Phi	753	120	16	Randa, KC	1,105	147	13	Vizcaino, 2Tm	524	67	13
Lockhart, Atl	503	66	13	Reese, Cin	925	171	18	Vizquel, Cle	1,007	95	9
Lofton, Cle	1,008	96	10	Relaford, Phi-SD	735	114	16	Walker L, Col	603	95	16
Long, Oak	1,014	147	14	Renteria, StL	1,076	180	17	Ward D, Hou	589	145	25
Lopez J, Atl	959	234	24	Ripken Jr., Bal	572	104	18	White R, 2Tm	703	160	23
Loretta, Mil	664	46	7	Rivera, SD	903	303	34	Widger, 2Tm	567	139	25
Lowell, Fla	1,015	132	13	RodriguezA, Sea	1,148	254	22	Williams B, NYY	959	156	16
Lugo, Hou	798	153	19	RodriguezH, 2Tm	821	238	29	Williams G, TB	1,318	277	21
Martin, SD-Sea	934	212	23	Rodriguez I, Tex	791	172	22	Williams M, Ari	695	141	20
Martinez D, 4Tm	854	99	12	Rolen, Phi	1,042	210	20	Wilson D, Sea	540	107	20
Martinez E, Sea	966	163	17	Salmon, Ana	1,235	302	24	Wilson P, Fla	1,278	411	32
Martinez F, TB	551	103	19	Sanchez, KC	867	89	10	Womack, Ari	1,234	178	14
Martinez T, NYY	1,005	147	15	Sanders R, Atl	655	170	26	Young D, Cin	1,107	237	21
Matheny, StL	836	207	25	Segui, Tex-Cle	1,140	222	19	Young E, ChC	984	75	8
Mayne, Col	631	93	15	Sexson, Cle-Mil	1,173	385	33	Young K, Pit	1,056	211	20
McGriff, TB	1,132	267	24	Sheffield, LA	961	159	17	Zeile, NYM	901	138	15
McLemore, Sea	830	104	13	Singleton, CWS	1,054	203	19	**MLB Average**			**20**

Can a Team Strike Out a Lot And Still Win? (p. 112)

Teams Leading League in Strikeouts—1946-2000
(leaders based on total strikeouts)

Year	Team	Lg	SO	Pct	Place	R/G	Rank	Lg R/G
1946	Browns	AL	713	.429	7	3.98	4	4.06
1946	Reds	NL	604	.435	6	3.35	8	3.96
1947	Browns	AL	664	.383	8	3.66	6	4.14
1947	Pirates	NL	687	.403	7t	4.77	4	4.57
1948	Indians	AL	575	.626	1	5.38	3	4.73
1948	Dodgers	NL	684	.545	3	4.80	2	4.43
1949	Browns	AL	700	.344	7	4.30	6	4.67
1949	Phillies	NL	670	.526	3	4.30	6	4.54
1950	Browns	AL	744	.377	7	4.44	6	5.04
1950	Cubs	NL	767	.418	7	4.18	8	4.66
1951	Browns	AL	693	.338	8	3.97	8	4.63
1951	Dodgers	NL	649	.618	2	5.41	1	4.46
1952	Indians	AL	749	.604	2	4.92	1	4.18
1952	Pirates	NL	724	.273	8	3.32	8	4.17
1953	Indians	AL	683	.597	2	4.97	2	4.46
1953	Cubs	NL	746	.422	7	4.08	7	4.75
1954	Nationals	AL	719	.429	6	4.08	5	4.19
1954	Pirates	NL	737	.344	8	3.62	8	4.56
1955	Orioles	AL	742	.370	7	3.46	8	4.44
1955	Cubs	NL	806	.471	6	4.06	7	4.53
1956	Nationals	AL	877	.383	7	4.21	6	4.66
1956	Cubs	NL	776	.390	8	3.80	6	4.25
1957	Indians	AL	786	.497	6	4.46	4	4.23
1957	Cubs	NL	989	.403	7t	4.03	6	4.38
1958	Yankees	AL	822	.597	1	4.90	1	4.17
1958	Phillies	NL	871	.448	8	4.31	6	4.40
1959	Senators	AL	881	.409	8	4.02	7	4.36
1959	Cubs	NL	911	.481	5t	4.34	5	4.40
1960	Senators	AL	883	.474	5	4.36	4	4.39
1960	Phillies	NL	1,054	.383	8	3.55	8	4.24
1961	Angels	AL	1,068	.435	8	4.59	4	4.53
1961	Cubs	NL	1,027	.416	7	4.42	7	4.52
1962	Indians	AL	939	.494	6	4.21	8	4.44
1962	Cubs	NL	1,044	.364	9	3.90	8	4.48
1963	Indians	AL	1,102	.488	5t	3.92	7	4.08
1963	Mets	NL	1,078	.315	10	3.09	9	3.81
1964	Senators	AL	1,124	.383	9	3.57	9	4.06
1964	Cubs	NL	1,041	.469	8	4.01	7	4.01
1965	Senators	AL	1,125	.432	8	3.65	8	3.94
1965	Mets	NL	1,129	.309	10	3.02	10	4.03
1966	Senators	AL	1,069	.447	8	3.50	10	3.89
1966	Pirates	NL	1,011	.568	3	4.69	2	4.09
1967	Yankees	AL	1,043	.444	9	3.20	10	3.70
1967	Phillies	NL	1,033	.506	5	3.78	7	3.84
1968	Angels	AL	1,080	.414	8t	3.07	9	3.41
1968	Mets	NL	1,203	.451	9	2.90	9	3.43
1969	Pilots	AL	1,015	.395	6	3.92	7	4.09
1969	Padres	NL	1,143	.321	6	2.89	12	4.05
1970	Senators	AL	989	.432	6	3.86	10	4.17
1970	Padres	NL	1,164	.389	6	4.20	11	4.52
1971	Athletics	AL	1,018	.627	1	4.29	3	3.87
1971	Giants	NL	1,042	.556	1	4.36	3	3.91
1972	White Sox	AL	991	.565	2	3.68	4	3.47

Year	Team	Lg	SO	Pct	Place	R/G	Rank	Lg R/G
1972	Mets	NL	990	.532	3	3.38	9	3.91
1973	Brewers	AL	977	.457	5	4.37	6	4.28
1973	Phillies	NL	979	.438	6	3.96	9	4.15
1974	Brewers	AL	909	.469	5	3.99	10	4.10
1974	Reds	NL	940	.605	2	4.76	2	4.15
1975	Brewers	AL	922	.420	5	4.17	9	4.30
1975	Phillies	NL	960	.531	2	4.54	2	4.13
1976	Brewers	AL	909	.410	6	3.54	11	4.01
1976	Reds	NL	902	.630	1	5.29	1	3.98
1977	Orioles	AL	945	.602	2t	4.47	7	4.53
1977	Padres	NL	1,057	.426	5	4.27	6t	4.40
1978	Orioles	AL	864	.559	4	4.09	9	4.20
1978	Reds	NL	899	.571	2	4.41	2	3.99
1979	Orioles	AL	847	.642	1	4.76	6	4.67
1979	Giants	NL	925	.438	4	4.15	9	4.22
1980	Angels	AL	889	.406	6	4.36	9	4.51
1980	Cubs	NL	912	.395	6	3.79	9	4.03
1981	Athletics	AL	647	.587	1	4.20	6	4.07
1981	Cubs	NL	611	.369	6	3.49	10	3.91
1982	Athletics	AL	948	.420	5	4.27	9	4.48
1982	Mets	NL	1,005	.401	6	3.76	10	4.09
1983	White Sox	AL	888	.611	1	4.94	1	4.48
1983	Mets	NL	1,031	.420	6	3.55	12	4.10
1984	Tigers	AL	941	.642	1	5.12	1	4.42
1984	Phillies	NL	1,084	.500	4	4.44	2	4.06
1985	Mariners	AL	942	.457	6	4.44	10	4.56
1985	Phillies	NL	1,095	.463	5	4.12	7	4.07
1986	Mariners	AL	1,148	.414	7	4.43	10	4.61
1986	Phillies	NL	1,154	.534	2	4.59	2	4.18
1987	Rangers	AL	1,081	.463	6t	5.08	5	4.90
1987	Phillies	NL	1,109	.494	4t	4.33	9	4.52
1988	Rangers	AL	1,022	.435	6	3.96	12	4.36
1988	Expos	NL	1,053	.500	3	3.85	7	3.88
1989	Angels	AL	1,011	.562	3	4.13	12	4.29
1989	Giants	NL	1,071	.568	1	4.31	2	3.94
1990	Rangers	AL	1,054	.512	3	4.17	10	4.30
1990	Expos	NL	1,024	.525	3	4.09	9	4.20
1991	Tigers	AL	1,185	.519	2t	5.04	2	4.49
1991	Padres	NL	1,069	.519	3	3.93	9	4.10
1992	Tigers	AL	1,055	.463	6	4.88	1	4.32
1992	Giants	NL	1,067	.444	5	3.54	11	3.88
1993	Tigers	AL	1,122	.525	3t	5.55	1	4.71
1993	Marlins	NL	1,054	.395	6	3.59	14	4.49
1994	Tigers	AL	897	.461	5	5.67	3	5.23
1994	Mets	NL	807	.487	3	4.48	9	4.62
1995	Tigers	AL	987	.417	4	4.54	12	5.06
1995	Giants	NL	1,060	.465	4	4.53	8	4.63
1996	Tigers	AL	1,268	.327	5	4.83	11	5.39
1996	Dodgers	NL	1,190	.556	2	4.34	12	4.68
1997	Athletics	AL	1,181	.401	4	4.72	11	4.93
1997	Cardinals	NL	1,191	.451	4	4.25	11	4.60
1998	Blue Jays	AL	1,132	.543	3	5.01	8	5.01
1998	Diamondbacks	NL	1,239	.401	5	4.10	14	4.60
1999	Athletics	AL	1,129	.537	2	5.51	4	5.17
1999	Cardinals	NL	1,202	.466	4	5.02	10	5.00
2000	Athletics	AL	1,159	.565	1	5.88	2	5.29
2000	Cardinals	NL	1,253	.586	1	5.48	4	5.00

Are Hitters Taking More Pitches These Days? (p. 114)

Pitches Per Plate Appearance—2000

Team	Pit	PA	P/PA	Record	W-L Pct
Mariners	25,527	6,444	3.96	91-71	.562
Athletics	25,171	6,432	3.91	91-70	.565
Indians	25,250	6,512	3.88	90-72	.556
Phillies	24,249	6,273	3.87	65-97	.401
Dodgers	24,298	6,312	3.85	86-76	.531
Brewers	24,073	6,355	3.79	73-89	.451
Yankees	23,846	6,311	3.78	87-74	.540
Mets	23,882	6,328	3.77	94-68	.580
Marlins	23,407	6,203	3.77	79-82	.491
Cardinals	24,005	6,369	3.77	95-67	.586
Giants	24,126	6,418	3.76	97-65	.599
White Sox	24,085	6,410	3.76	95-67	.586
Tigers	23,783	6,343	3.75	79-83	.488
Cubs	23,881	6,397	3.73	65-97	.401
Astros	24,038	6,444	3.73	72-90	.444
Padres	23,439	6,291	3.73	76-86	.469
Red Sox	23,680	6,371	3.72	85-77	.525
Angels	23,642	6,373	3.71	82-80	.506
Rangers	23,581	6,364	3.71	71-91	.438
Orioles	23,083	6,238	3.70	74-88	.457
Twins	23,249	6,283	3.70	69-93	.426
Blue Jays	23,403	6,326	3.70	83-79	.512
Pirates	23,511	6,369	3.69	69-93	.426
Diamondbacks	22,911	6,241	3.67	85-77	.525
Rockies	23,581	6,453	3.65	82-80	.506
Devil Rays	22,597	6,206	3.64	69-92	.429
Braves	22,773	6,275	3.63	95-67	.586
Reds	23,048	6,373	3.62	85-77	.525
Royals	23,083	6,394	3.61	77-85	.475
Expos	22,209	6,153	3.61	67-95	.414
MLB Totals	**711,411**	**190,261**	**3.74**		

Who Plays It Smart on the Bases? (p. 119)

"Unforced" Outs on Bases—2000, Listed Alphabetically
(minimum 3 Unforced Outs)

Player, Team	Outs	Player, Team	Outs	Player, Team	Outs
Jeff Abbott, CWS	4	Sean Casey, Cin	3	Andres Galarraga, Atl	7
Bobby Abreu, Phi	8	Vinny Castilla, TB	3	Ron Gant, Phi-Ana	4
Benny Agbayani, NYM	4	Luis Castillo, Fla	4	Nomar Garciaparra, Bos	9
Edgardo Alfonzo, NYM	5	Roger Cedeno, Hou	5	Jason Giambi, Oak	13
Luis Alicea, Tex	5	Eric Chavez, Oak	4	Benji Gil, Ana	8
Roberto Alomar, Cle	10	Jeff Cirillo, Col	10	Brian Giles, Pit	6
Sandy Alomar Jr., Cle	7	Will Clark, Bal-StL	3	Doug Glanville, Phi	7
Moises Alou, Hou	7	Royce Clayton, Tex	8	Troy Glaus, Ana	7
Brady Anderson, Bal	6	Jeff Conine, Bal	3	Alex Gonzalez, Fla	5
Brad Ausmus, Det	6	Ron Coomer, Min	5	Juan Gonzalez, Det	3
Jeff Bagwell, Hou	9	Alex Cora, LA	5	Luis Gonzalez, Ari	6
Paul Bako, Hou-Fla-Atl	3	Wil Cordero, Pit-Cle	3	Wiki Gonzalez, SD	3
Tony Batista, Tor	9	Steve Cox, TB	4	Tom Goodwin, Col-LA	5
Danny Bautista, Fla-Ari	6	Jose Cruz, Tor	3	Mark Grace, ChC	6
David Bell, Sea	3	Chad Curtis, Tex	4	Shawn Green, LA	7
Jay Bell, Ari	11	Johnny Damon, KC	8	Willie Greene, ChC	3
Albert Belle, Bal	7	Mike Darr, SD	3	Ken Griffey Jr., Cin	7
Ron Belliard, Mil	3	Brian Daubach, Bos	5	Marquis Grissom, Mil	6
Carlos Beltran, KC	5	Carlos Delgado, Tor	12	Mark Grudzielanek, LA	4
Adrian Beltre, LA	4	Delino DeShields, Bal	12	Vladimir Guerrero, Mon	10
Marvin Benard, SF	9	Einar Diaz, Cle	3	Jose Guillen, TB	4
Peter Bergeron, Mon	4	Mike DiFelice, TB	3	Ricky Gutierrez, ChC	9
Lance Berkman, Hou	4	J.D. Drew, StL	5	Cristian Guzman, Min	6
Dante Bichette, Cin-Bos	5	Shawon Dunston, StL	4	Jeffrey Hammonds, Col	5
Craig Biggio, Hou	7	Ray Durham, CWS	8	Lenny Harris, Ari-NYM	3
Henry Blanco, Mil	6	Jermaine Dye, KC	3	Todd Helton, Col	4
Tim Bogar, Hou	4	Damion Easley, Det	7	Rickey Henderson, 2Tm	4
Barry Bonds, SF	6	Jim Edmonds, StL	7	Jose Hernandez, Mil	3
Bobby Bonilla, Atl	3	Juan Encarnacion, Det	4	Ramon Hernandez, Oak	3
Aaron Boone, Cin	3	Darin Erstad, Ana	8	Richard Hidalgo, Hou	6
Scott Brosius, NYY	3	Carl Everett, Bos	9	Bobby Higginson, Det	5
Adrian Brown, Pit	4	Carlos Febles, KC	4	Glenallen Hill, ChC-NYY	6
Ellis Burks, SF	5	John Flaherty, TB	4	Todd Hollandsworth, 2Tm	5
Pat Burrell, Phi	6	Cliff Floyd, Fla	5	Todd Hundley, LA	4
Orlando Cabrera, Mon	4	Brook Fordyce, CWS-Bal	3	Torii Hunter, Min	6
Miguel Cairo, TB	3	Andy Fox, Ari-Fla	3	Damian Jackson, SD	7
Mike Cameron, Sea	7	Travis Fryman, Cle	8	Geoff Jenkins, Mil	3
Jay Canizaro, Min	7	Brad Fullmer, Tor	3	Charles Johnson, 2Tm	3
Raul Casanova, Mil	3	Rafael Furcal, Atl	7	Andruw Jones, Atl	9

Player, Team	Outs	Player, Team	Outs	Player, Team	Outs
Chipper Jones, Atl	4	Raul Mondesi, Tor	4	Luis Sojo, Pit-NYY	4
Jacque Jones, Min	6	Melvin Mora, NYM-Bal	10	Sammy Sosa, ChC	7
Brian Jordan, Atl	6	Mickey Morandini, Phi-Tor	4	Shane Spencer, NYY	3
David Justice, Cle-NYY	6	Warren Morris, Pit	4	Bill Spiers, Hou	3
Gabe Kapler, Tex	3	Bill Mueller, SF	7	Scott Spiezio, Ana	4
Eric Karros, LA	7	Phil Nevin, SD	6	Ed Sprague, SD-Bos	5
Jason Kendall, Pit	6	Troy O'Leary, Bos	6	Shannon Stewart, Tor	6
Adam Kennedy, Ana	12	Paul O'Neill, NYY	4	Kevin Stocker, TB-Ana	4
Jeff Kent, SF	10	Jose Offerman, Bos	6	Chris Stynes, Cin	5
Ryan Klesko, SD	7	John Olerud, Sea	4	B.J. Surhoff, Bal-Atl	5
Chuck Knoblauch, NYY	7	Magglio Ordonez, CWS	5	Mike Sweeney, KC	10
Paul Konerko, CWS	3	David Ortiz, Min	3	Fernando Tatis, StL	3
Corey Koskie, Min	7	Eric Owens, SD	5	Miguel Tejada, Oak	7
Mark Kotsay, Fla	8	Orlando Palmeiro, Ana	4	Frank Thomas, CWS	4
Chad Kreuter, LA	3	Rafael Palmeiro, Tex	6	Jim Thome, Cle	6
Mike Lansing, Col-Bos	4	Dean Palmer, Det	3	Bubba Trammell, 2Tm	3
Matt Lawton, Min	10	Craig Paquette, StL	4	Jose Valentin, CWS	8
Ricky Ledee, 3Tm	3	Jay Payton, NYM	6	John Vander Wal, Pit	6
Carlos Lee, CWS	3	Neifi Perez, Col	10	Jason Varitek, Bos	3
Derrek Lee, Fla	10	Juan Pierre, Col	3	Greg Vaughn, TB	4
Darren Lewis, Bos	3	Placido Polanco, StL	4	Mo Vaughn, Ana	3
Keith Lockhart, Atl	3	Jorge Posada, NYY	10	Randy Velarde, Oak	11
Kenny Lofton, Cle	7	Mark Quinn, KC	5	Robin Ventura, NYM	3
Terrence Long, Oak	4	Alex Ramirez, Cle-Pit	5	Quilvio Veras, Atl	5
Javy Lopez, Atl	5	Manny Ramirez, Cle	6	Jose Vidro, Mon	10
Mark Loretta, Mil	4	Joe Randa, KC	5	Fernando Vina, StL	10
Mike Lowell, Fla	4	Pokey Reese, Cin	7	Jose Vizcaino, LA-NYY	3
Julio Lugo, Hou	4	Desi Relaford, Phi-SD	5	Omar Vizquel, Cle	8
Dave Martinez, 4Tm	4	Edgar Renteria, StL	5	Larry Walker, Col	4
Edgar Martinez, Sea	6	Armando Rios, SF	4	Rondell White, Mon-ChC	5
Tino Martinez, NYY	5	Alex Rodriguez, Sea	3	Chris Widger, Mon-Sea	5
Mike Matheny, StL	3	Henry Rodriguez, 2Tm	3	Gerald Williams, TB	5
Brent Mayne, Col	8	Ivan Rodriguez, Tex	4	Dan Wilson, Sea	4
Dave McCarty, KC	3	Scott Rolen, Phi	4	Preston Wilson, Fla	5
Fred McGriff, TB	5	Tim Salmon, Ana	9	Tony Womack, Ari	8
Mark McLemore, Sea	6	Rey Sanchez, KC	4	Dmitri Young, Cin	9
Pat Meares, Pit	4	Reggie Sanders, Atl	5	Eric Young, ChC	14
Mitch Meluskey, Hou	3	David Segui, Tex-Cle	3	Kevin Young, Pit	6
Kevin Millar, Fla	3	Richie Sexson, Cle-Mil	9	Gregg Zaun, KC	5
Damian Miller, Ari	3	Gary Sheffield, LA	5	Todd Zeile, NYM	8
Ben Molina, Ana	4	J.T. Snow, SF	6		

Baseball Scoreboard

Has Any Pitcher Started Hotter Than Hudson? (p. 127)

Most Wins in First 39 Career Decisions—1920-2000
(minimum 25 wins)

Pitcher	W-L	Pct	Pitcher	W-L	Pct	Pitcher	W-L	Pct
Howie Krist	33-6	.846	Eldon Auker	26-13	.667	Steve Carlton	25-14	.641
Juan Guzman	31-8	.795	Gene Bearden	26-13	.667	Ownie Carroll	25-14	.641
Tim Hudson	31-8	.795	Jason Bere	26-13	.667	Phil Collins	25-14	.641
Roger Clemens	30-9	.769	Hank Borowy	26-13	.667	Rip Collins	25-14	.641
Jim Coates	30-9	.769	Jim Bouton	26-13	.667	Danny Darwin	25-14	.641
Ron Guidry	30-9	.769	Wally Bunker	26-13	.667	Jim Deshaies	25-14	.641
Tex Hughson	30-9	.769	Jim Bunning	26-13	.667	Al Downing	25-14	.641
Emil Yde	30-9	.769	John Candelaria	26-13	.667	Cal Eldred	25-14	.641
Johnny Allen	29-10	.744	Joe Cowley	26-13	.667	Carl Erskine	25-14	.641
Joe Black	29-10	.744	George Earnshaw	26-13	.667	Marvin Freeman	25-14	.641
Boo Ferriss	29-10	.744	Wes Ferrell	26-13	.667	Lefty Gomez	25-14	.641
Whitey Ford	29-10	.744	Mark Fidrych	26-13	.667	Sam Gray	25-14	.641
Larry Jansen	29-10	.744	Hersh Freeman	26-13	.667	Harvey Haddix	25-14	.641
Sal Maglie	29-10	.744	Freddy Garcia	26-13	.667	Teddy Higuera	25-14	.641
Vic Raschi	29-10	.744	Jim Hardin	26-13	.667	Larry Jaster	25-14	.641
Schoolboy Rowe	29-10	.744	Mike Henneman	26-13	.667	Chris Knapp	25-14	.641
Johnny Beazley	28-11	.718	Joe Hoerner	26-13	.667	Jim Konstanty	25-14	.641
David Cone	28-11	.718	Al Holland	26-13	.667	Ray Kremer	25-14	.641
Bruce Dal Canton	28-11	.718	Ricky Horton	26-13	.667	Johnny Kucks	25-14	.641
Ron Davis	28-11	.718	Clem Labine	26-13	.667	Barry Latman	25-14	.641
Murry Dickson	28-11	.718	Bill Lee	26-13	.667	Brooks Lawrence	25-14	.641
Atley Donald	28-11	.718	Aurelio Lopez	26-13	.667	Dennis Leonard	25-14	.641
Bob Grim	28-11	.718	Pedro Martinez	26-13	.667	Don Liddle	25-14	.641
Orlando Hernandez	28-11	.718	Ramon Martinez	26-13	.667	Billy Loes	25-14	.641
Orel Hershiser	28-11	.718	Tippy Martinez	26-13	.667	Juan Marichal	25-14	.641
LaMarr Hoyt	28-11	.718	Denny McLain	26-13	.667	Al McBean	25-14	.641
Roy Mahaffey	28-11	.718	Dick Newsome	26-13	.667	Ramiro Mendoza	25-14	.641
George Munger	28-11	.718	David Palmer	26-13	.667	Kevin Millwood	25-14	.641
George Pipgras	28-11	.718	Ron Perranoski	26-13	.667	Roger Moret	25-14	.641
Mel Stottlemyre	28-11	.718	Andy Pettitte	26-13	.667	Don Newcombe	25-14	.641
Ted Wilks	28-11	.718	Joe Price	26-13	.667	Darren Oliver	25-14	.641
Vida Blue	27-12	.692	Dick Radatz	26-13	.667	Mel Parnell	25-14	.641
Tiny Bonham	27-12	.692	Art Reinhart	26-13	.667	Jeff Parrett	25-14	.641
Harry Brecheen	27-12	.692	Rick Rhoden	26-13	.667	Johnny Podres	25-14	.641
Tim Burke	27-12	.692	Mariano Rivera	26-13	.667	Howie Pollet	25-14	.641
Spud Chandler	27-12	.692	Marius Russo	26-13	.667	Jim Ray	25-14	.641
Storm Davis	27-12	.692	Bob Shaw	26-13	.667	Elmer Riddle	25-14	.641
Scott Elarton	27-12	.692	Junior Thompson	26-13	.667	Jeff Robinson	25-14	.641
Sammy Ellis	27-12	.692	F. Valenzuela	26-13	.667	Ed Roebuck	25-14	.641
Scott Erickson	27-12	.692	Tim Wakefield	26-13	.667	Kirk Rueter	25-14	.641
Dave Fleming	27-12	.692	Montie Weaver	26-13	.667	Mike Ryba	25-14	.641
John Franco	27-12	.692	Bob Wells	26-13	.667	Jack Sanford	25-14	.641
Fred Gladding	27-12	.692	Hoyt Wilhelm	26-13	.667	Rip Sewell	25-14	.641
Dwight Gooden	27-12	.692	Mark Wohlers	26-13	.667	Larry Sherry	25-14	.641
Pat Hentgen	27-12	.692	Wilson Alvarez	25-14	.641	Bill Shores	25-14	.641
Al Hrabosky	27-12	.692	Jack Baldschun	25-14	.641	Wayne Simpson	25-14	.641
Terry Leach	27-12	.692	Frank Baumann	25-14	.641	Warren Spahn	25-14	.641
Cliff Melton	27-12	.692	Joe Beggs	25-14	.641	Chuck Stobbs	25-14	.641
Wilcy Moore	27-12	.692	Vern Bickford	25-14	.641	Steve Sundra	25-14	.641
Tom Morgan	27-12	.692	Wade Blasingame	25-14	.641	Kent Tekulve	25-14	.641
Mike Mussina	27-12	.692	Mike Boddicker	25-14	.641	Tommy Thomas	25-14	.641
Ray Narleski	27-12	.692	Pedro Borbon	25-14	.641	Jim Turner	25-14	.641
Gary Peters	27-12	.692	Jeff Brantley	25-14	.641	Bob Veale	25-14	.641
Bob Stanley	27-12	.692	Warren Brusstar	25-14	.641	Ernie White	25-14	.641
Wes Stock	27-12	.692	Ken Burkhart	25-14	.641	Earl Whitehill	25-14	.641
Lon Warneke	27-12	.692	Paul Byrd	25-14	.641	Stan Williams	25-14	.641
Bob Wickman	27-12	.692	Tommy Byrne	25-14	.641			

Who Are the Game's Best "Stoppers"? (p. 129)

Most Wins Following a Team Loss, Career—1920-2000

Pitcher	W	L	Pct	Other W	L	Pct
Phil Niekro	166	142	.539	136	120	.531
Warren Spahn	164	109	.601	194	118	.622
Tom Seaver	158	103	.605	151	99	.604
Nolan Ryan	156	155	.502	158	135	.539
Bert Blyleven	153	125	.550	131	122	.518
Gaylord Perry	153	123	.554	151	127	.543
Steve Carlton	151	117	.563	173	122	.586
Fergie Jenkins	143	103	.581	135	115	.540
Tommy John	141	106	.571	142	121	.540
Roger Clemens	139	60	.698	121	82	.596
Don Sutton	132	121	.522	188	132	.588
Ted Lyons	132	122	.520	113	88	.562
Robin Roberts	131	130	.502	144	109	.569
Frank Tanana	126	119	.514	109	115	.487
Early Wynn	124	120	.508	163	112	.593
Jim Kaat	116	106	.523	142	111	.561
Jim Palmer	116	69	.627	144	77	.652
Jerry Koosman	112	97	.536	104	106	.495
Rick Reuschel	111	101	.524	97	87	.527
Jim Bunning	111	94	.541	104	86	.547
Lefty Grove	110	60	.647	158	60	.725
Charlie Hough	109	81	.574	64	92	.410
Bob Feller	109	80	.577	149	74	.668
Red Ruffing	108	94	.535	156	117	.571
Juan Marichal	107	67	.615	130	73	.640
Bob Gibson	106	91	.538	139	79	.638
Luis Tiant	105	87	.547	113	74	.604
Burleigh Grimes	105	83	.559	114	76	.600
Claude Osteen	104	90	.536	90	103	.466
Dazzy Vance	104	68	.605	80	60	.571
Jack Morris	103	87	.542	147	93	.613
Carl Hubbell	103	62	.624	130	84	.607
Dennis Martinez	102	84	.548	126	98	.563
Mickey Lolich	102	93	.523	105	94	.528
Joe Niekro	101	94	.518	98	92	.516
Larry Jackson	100	92	.521	77	77	.500
Bucky Walters	100	81	.552	95	70	.576
Greg Maddux	99	63	.611	141	71	.665
Paul Derringer	99	101	.495	107	87	.552
Earl Whitehill	99	93	.516	106	87	.549
Randy Johnson	98	48	.671	80	47	.630
Catfish Hunter	98	72	.576	124	93	.571
Hal Newhouser	98	73	.573	90	67	.573
Sad Sam Jones	98	83	.541	84	88	.488
Jerry Reuss	96	90	.516	114	95	.545
Mel Harder	96	84	.533	105	86	.550
Bobo Newsom	95	121	.440	101	86	.540
Vida Blue	93	79	.541	112	80	.583
Wes Ferrell	93	64	.592	88	54	.620
Milt Pappas	92	66	.582	101	81	.555
Don Drysdale	92	63	.594	110	97	.531
Freddie Fitzsimmons	92	62	.597	106	75	.586
Mark Langston	91	84	.520	87	74	.540
Tom Glavine	91	59	.607	117	66	.639
Dutch Leonard	91	94	.492	72	64	.529
Red Lucas	90	71	.559	54	53	.505

Most Wins Following a Team Loss, Season—1920-2000

Pitcher, Team	Year	W	L	Pct	Other W	Other L	Other Pct
Red Faber, CWS	1921	19	11	.633	5	3	.625
Steve Carlton, Phi	1972	18	9	.667	8	1	.889
Dazzy Vance, Bro	1924	17	4	.810	10	2	.833
Howard Ehmke, Bos	1923	16	9	.640	4	8	.333
Bob Feller, Cle	1941	16	8	.667	9	4	.692
Hal Newhouser, Det	1945	16	1	.941	9	8	.529
Bob Feller, Cle	1946	16	9	.640	10	6	.625
Bobby Shantz, Phi	1952	16	4	.800	8	3	.727
Jim Maloney, Cin	1963	16	4	.800	7	3	.700
Larry Jackson, ChC	1964	16	4	.800	8	6	.571
Sandy Koufax, LA	1966	16	4	.800	11	5	.688
George Uhle, Cle	1923	15	6	.714	9	10	.474
Dazzy Vance, Bro	1925	15	7	.682	7	2	.778
Hal Carlson, Phi	1926	15	8	.652	2	4	.333
Wes Ferrell, Bos	1935	15	4	.789	10	7	.588
Thornton Lee, CWS	1941	15	10	.600	7	1	.875
Jerry Koosman, NYM	1968	15	7	.682	4	5	.444
Fergie Jenkins, ChC	1971	15	4	.789	9	9	.500
Mickey Lolich, Det	1971	15	5	.750	10	9	.526
Andy Messersmith, Cal	1971	15	7	.682	4	6	.400
Ross Grimsley, Mon	1978	15	7	.682	5	4	.556
Roger Clemens, Bos	1992	15	5	.750	3	6	.333
Eddie Rommel, Phi	1922	14	5	.737	5	7	.417
General Crowder, StL	1928	14	3	.824	7	2	.778
Larry Benton, NYG	1928	14	2	.875	11	6	.647
Lefty Gomez, NYY	1934	14	2	.875	11	1	.917
Tommy Bridges, Det	1936	14	6	.700	9	5	.643
Bobo Newsom, StL	1938	14	10	.583	6	6	.500
Johnny Vander Meer, Cin	1948	14	9	.609	3	5	.375
Johnny Sain, Bos	1950	14	5	.737	6	8	.429
Ned Garver, StL	1951	14	5	.737	4	6	.400
Bud Daley, KCA	1960	14	11	.560	1	4	.200
Mel Stottlemyre, NYY	1965	14	7	.667	6	2	.750
Don Drysdale, LA	1965	14	4	.778	9	8	.529
Fergie Jenkins, ChC	1968	14	7	.667	6	8	.429
Jim Palmer, Bal	1972	14	2	.875	7	7	.500
Claude Osteen, LA	1972	14	2	.875	6	9	.400
Fergie Jenkins, Tex	1974	14	5	.737	11	7	.611
Catfish Hunter, Oak	1974	14	4	.778	11	8	.579
Ed Figueroa, Cal	1975	14	8	.636	1	4	.200
Catfish Hunter, NYY	1975	14	8	.636	9	6	.600
Phil Niekro, Atl	1976	14	6	.700	3	5	.375
Mark Fidrych, Det	1976	14	6	.700	5	3	.625
Phil Niekro, Atl	1978	14	9	.609	5	9	.357
Steve Carlton, Phi	1980	14	4	.778	10	5	.667
Roger Clemens, Bos	1986	14	1	.933	10	3	.769
Danny Jackson, Cin	1988	14	2	.875	9	6	.600
Kent Bottenfield, StL	1999	14	5	.737	4	2	.667
David Wells, Tor	2000	14	5	.737	6	3	.667
Burleigh Grimes, Bro	1921	13	8	.619	9	4	.692
Dixie Davis, StL	1921	13	7	.650	3	9	.250
Dutch Ruether, Bro	1922	13	7	.650	8	5	.615
Jimmy Ring, Phi	1923	13	8	.619	5	6	.455
Burleigh Grimes, Bro	1923	13	11	.542	8	6	.571
Sloppy Thurston, CWS	1924	13	9	.591	7	4	.636
George Uhle, Cle	1926	13	4	.765	13	6	.684
Tommy Thomas, CWS	1928	13	10	.565	4	5	.444
Dazzy Vance, Bro	1928	13	4	.765	8	5	.615
Red Lucas, Cin	1929	13	7	.650	6	5	.545
Wes Ferrell, Cle	1930	13	8	.619	10	3	.769

Which Pitchers Love Home Cookin'? (p. 136)

Home-Road ERA Differentials—1998-2000, Listed Alphabetically
(minimum 450 IP)

Pitcher	Home	Road	Diff	Pitcher	Home	Road	Diff
Brian Anderson	3.69	5.00	+1.31	Pedro Martinez	2.36	2.14	-0.22
Rolando Arrojo	5.62	3.73	-1.89	Brian Meadows	4.48	6.19	+1.71
Andy Ashby	3.66	4.35	+0.69	Kevin Millwood	3.48	4.04	+0.56
Pedro Astacio	7.05	4.11	-2.94	Eric Milton	5.10	4.83	-0.27
James Baldwin	5.83	4.27	-1.56	Dave Mlicki	4.51	5.19	+0.68
Andy Benes	4.71	4.33	-0.38	Brian Moehler	4.13	4.88	+0.75
Willie Blair	4.68	6.38	+1.70	Jamie Moyer	4.06	4.25	+0.19
Brian Bohanon	5.73	3.61	-2.12	Mike Mussina	3.22	4.02	+0.80
Kent Bottenfield	4.66	4.51	-0.16	Charles Nagy	5.50	5.44	-0.07
Kevin Brown	1.94	3.38	+1.44	Denny Neagle	4.40	3.67	-0.73
Dave Burba	4.39	4.12	-0.27	Hideo Nomo	4.24	5.20	+0.95
John Burkett	6.16	4.69	-1.46	Omar Olivares	4.16	5.19	+1.03
Chris Carpenter	5.13	4.95	-0.18	Darren Oliver	5.45	5.55	+0.09
Roger Clemens	3.35	3.94	+0.59	Russ Ortiz	3.80	5.33	+1.53
Bartolo Colon	4.13	3.55	-0.59	Chan Ho Park	3.32	4.82	+1.50
David Cone	3.29	5.80	+2.51	Jim Parque	4.37	5.25	+0.88
Francisco Cordova	3.95	4.19	+0.25	Carlos Perez	4.16	5.68	+1.53
Omar Daal	4.33	4.04	-0.30	Andy Pettitte	4.17	4.66	+0.49
Darren Dreifort	4.79	3.76	-1.03	Sidney Ponson	4.47	5.37	+0.90
Scott Erickson	4.62	5.25	+0.62	Brad Radke	4.04	4.29	+0.25
Shawn Estes	3.27	6.26	+3.00	Pat Rapp	5.86	4.45	-1.41
Jeff Fassero	4.96	5.36	+0.40	Rick Reed	3.17	4.83	+1.67
Chuck Finley	3.37	4.61	+1.24	Shane Reynolds	3.95	4.09	+0.14
Mark Gardner	4.71	4.96	+0.25	Kenny Rogers	3.42	4.53	+1.12
Tom Glavine	3.30	3.37	+0.07	Kirk Rueter	3.86	5.28	+1.42
Mike Hampton	2.45	3.93	+1.48	Curt Schilling	3.43	3.59	+0.16
Pete Harnisch	4.17	3.36	-0.81	Jason Schmidt	3.98	4.64	+0.66
LaTroy Hawkins	5.95	4.86	-1.10	Aaron Sele	4.14	4.97	+0.83
Jimmy Haynes	5.78	5.25	-0.53	Mike Sirotka	4.05	4.57	+0.51
Rick Helling	4.94	4.28	-0.66	Jeff Suppan	4.59	5.19	+0.60
Pat Hentgen	5.32	4.50	-0.81	Kevin Tapani	4.39	5.45	+1.06
Dustin Hermanson	4.31	3.78	-0.53	Brett Tomko	3.67	5.60	+1.93
Livan Hernandez	4.01	4.73	+0.73	Steve Trachsel	4.73	5.16	+0.43
Orlando Hernandez	3.94	4.05	+0.11	Ismael Valdes	3.04	5.80	+2.76
Randy Johnson	2.82	2.76	-0.05	Javier Vazquez	4.65	5.26	+0.61
Scott Karl	5.95	4.40	-1.55	Tim Wakefield	4.89	5.09	+0.20
Darryl Kile	5.57	4.75	-0.82	David Wells	4.08	4.24	+0.17
Al Leiter	3.10	3.56	+0.46	Woody Williams	3.79	4.68	+0.89
Jon Lieber	3.96	4.48	+0.52	Steve Woodard	5.18	4.42	-0.76
Jose Lima	4.05	5.00	+0.94	Jamey Wright	5.61	4.35	-1.26
Esteban Loaiza	4.56	5.00	+0.44	Masato Yoshii	4.50	4.92	+0.42
Greg Maddux	2.58	3.30	+0.72				

Who Are Baseball's Best-Hitting Pitchers? (p. 139)

Career Hitting Statistics—Active Pitchers, Listed Alphabetically
(minimum 50 career PA)

Pitcher	Avg	AB	H	HR	RBI	Pitcher	Avg	AB	H	HR	RBI
Acevedo	.081	62	5	0	0	Dotel	.071	56	4	0	1
Aguilera	.201	139	28	3	11	Dreifort	.195	190	37	5	20
Anderson B	.145	173	25	1	6	Elarton	.156	96	15	0	1
Anderson J	.169	59	10	0	2	Eldred	.111	63	7	0	4
Ankiel	.231	78	18	2	9	Estes	.171	263	45	2	19
Ashby	.138	457	63	0	21	Farnsworth	.082	49	4	0	2
Astacio	.134	509	68	0	23	Fassero	.076	224	17	0	5
Aybar	.152	66	10	1	5	Fernandez A	.175	126	22	3	14
Batista	.089	79	7	1	3	Fernandez O	.073	96	7	0	2
Belcher	.124	388	48	2	25	Gardner	.128	485	62	1	21
Benes A	.163	123	20	0	8	Glavine	.196	899	176	1	64
Benes A	.139	675	94	7	44	Gooden	.196	741	145	8	67
Benson	.123	130	16	0	8	Hamilton	.117	300	35	4	20
Bere	.200	75	15	0	3	Hampton	.231	372	86	0	31
Bergman	.113	133	15	3	11	Harnisch	.125	502	63	2	29
Blair	.075	146	11	0	5	Haynes	.110	73	8	0	4
Bohanon	.215	200	43	3	27	Hentgen	.115	78	9	0	0
Bottenfield	.164	177	29	0	10	Heredia G	.209	86	18	0	3
Brantley	.118	68	8	0	5	Hermanson	.100	219	22	2	6
Brocail	.164	67	11	0	1	Hernandez L	.227	264	60	3	25
Brock	.190	58	11	1	7	Hershiser	.201	810	163	0	50
Brown	.120	374	45	0	23	Hill	.150	333	50	1	21
Burba	.145	173	25	3	12	Hitchcock	.093	183	17	0	4
Burkett	.093	471	44	0	17	Holt	.087	173	15	0	6
Byrd	.146	103	15	0	6	Isringhausen	.196	97	19	2	11
Castillo	.111	334	37	0	13	Jarvis	.135	96	13	0	2
Charlton	.092	87	8	0	1	Jimenez	.111	63	7	0	4
Chen	.042	48	2	0	2	Johnson R	.128	235	30	0	16
Clark	.058	242	14	1	9	Jones B	.131	352	46	1	14
Clement	.070	114	8	0	3	Jones B	.177	79	14	0	8
Cone	.155	407	63	0	22	Karl	.142	134	19	2	7
Cook	.266	109	29	2	9	Kile	.135	564	76	1	36
Cordova	.121	231	28	0	8	Leiter	.093	290	27	0	11
Cormier	.185	184	34	0	12	Lieber	.152	342	52	0	18
Cornelius	.129	62	8	0	1	Lima	.124	217	27	0	8
D'Amico J	.083	48	4	1	2	Loaiza	.180	161	29	0	11
Daal	.193	176	34	1	12	Maddux G	.179	1070	191	4	57
Dempster	.079	139	11	0	4	Maddux M	.065	92	6	0	4
Dessens	.113	53	6	0	3	Martinez P	.098	255	25	0	11

Pitcher	Avg	AB	H	HR	RBI	Pitcher	Avg	AB	H	HR	RBI
Martinez R	.154	591	91	1	33	Sanchez	.175	120	21	0	5
Meadows	.139	144	20	0	6	Schilling	.157	541	85	0	25
Mercker	.115	244	28	1	18	Schmidt	.082	233	19	0	8
Millwood	.116	199	23	1	9	Schourek	.164	269	44	2	20
Mlicki	.117	154	18	0	5	Silva	.114	88	10	0	5
Morgan	.109	497	54	0	15	Springer D	.106	66	7	0	2
Morris M	.171	105	18	0	9	Stephenson	.073	124	9	0	5
Moyer	.144	160	23	0	4	Stottlemyre	.210	238	50	1	11
Mulholland	.114	606	69	2	23	Swindell	.188	245	46	0	13
Nathan	.167	60	10	2	4	Tapani	.133	211	28	2	20
Navarro	.145	152	22	0	10	Tavarez	.100	50	5	0	0
Neagle	.153	419	64	3	34	Telemaco	.104	77	8	0	3
Nomo	.149	322	48	1	19	Thompson	.154	104	16	1	3
Nunez	.133	45	6	1	5	Thurman	.034	89	3	0	0
Olivares	.242	215	52	4	23	Tomko	.149	148	22	0	8
Oliver	.226	106	24	0	9	Trachsel	.172	355	61	2	23
Orosco	.169	59	10	0	4	Urbina	.096	52	5	0	1
Ortiz R	.210	157	33	2	15	Valdes I	.121	322	39	1	11
Painter	.156	64	10	0	5	Vazquez	.226	159	36	0	11
Palacios	.045	88	4	0	0	Villone	.114	88	10	0	4
Park	.176	272	48	2	19	Wakefield	.114	79	9	1	3
Parris	.160	156	25	0	15	Wall	.176	68	12	0	1
Pavano	.123	106	13	0	5	Watson A	.257	175	45	0	19
Perez C	.152	250	38	4	15	Weathers	.108	130	14	2	4
Person	.123	122	15	0	3	Wetteland	.167	42	7	1	8
Peters	.233	90	21	0	7	Williams B	.176	85	15	0	9
Petkovsek	.163	86	14	0	3	Williams M	.159	107	17	0	7
Pulsipher	.123	81	10	0	4	Williams W	.223	139	31	1	15
Quantrill	.098	61	6	0	0	Wilson P	.080	50	4	1	4
Rapp	.120	242	29	1	13	Witt	.115	52	6	1	5
Reed R	.178	253	45	2	20	Wolf	.207	87	18	0	4
Rekar	.151	53	8	0	1	Wood	.181	94	17	3	12
Remlinger	.077	104	8	0	8	Woodard	.120	125	15	0	6
Reynolds	.160	419	67	4	33	Worrell	.113	71	8	0	4
Reynoso	.150	327	49	3	11	Wright J	.120	209	25	1	9
Ritchie	.183	115	21	0	3	Yoshii	.137	153	21	1	13
Rueter	.151	358	54	0	26	**MLB Average**	**.145**				
Rusch	.054	56	3	0	1						

Who's Toughest to Pull? (p. 141)

Pitcher Pull Percentages—2000, Listed Alphabetically (minimum 400 BFP)

Pitcher, Team	Th	Pull	Hit	Pct	Pitcher, Team	Th	Pull	Hit	Pct
Abbott, Sea	R	213	563	37.8	Erickson, Bal	R	140	346	40.5
Anderson B, Ari	L	244	703	34.7	Escobar, Tor	R	234	551	42.5
Anderson J, Pit	L	173	496	34.9	Estes, SF	L	189	569	33.2
Ankiel, StL	L	140	426	32.9	Fassero, Bos	L	171	412	41.5
Appier, Oak	R	234	616	38.0	Finley, Cle	L	229	629	36.4
Armas Jr., Mon	R	111	281	39.5	Gagne, LA	R	117	307	38.1
Arrojo, Col-Bos	R	193	541	35.7	Garcia F, Sea	R	170	379	44.9
Ashby, Phi-Atl	R	282	667	42.3	Gardner, SF	R	159	480	33.1
Astacio, Col	R	224	573	39.1	Glavine, Atl	L	218	748	29.1
Baldwin, CWS	R	208	565	36.8	Glynn, Tex	R	123	322	38.2
Bell, Cin	R	180	412	43.7	Gooden, Hou-TB-NYY	R	147	353	41.6
Benes A, StL	R	197	497	39.6	Grimsley, NYY	R	152	323	47.1
Benson, Pit	R	235	636	36.9	Halama, Sea	L	221	576	38.4
Bere, Mil-Cle	R	197	506	38.9	Hampton, NYM	L	261	649	40.2
Blair, Det	R	200	547	36.6	Harnisch, Cin	R	162	439	36.9
Bohanon, Col	L	230	572	40.2	Hasegawa, Ana	R	110	308	35.7
Bottenfield, Ana-Phi	R	192	558	34.4	Haynes, Mil	R	240	668	35.9
Brock, Phi	R	105	284	37.0	Helling, Tex	R	277	681	40.7
Brown, LA	R	243	629	38.6	Hentgen, StL	R	228	604	37.7
Burba, Cle	R	205	552	37.1	Heredia G, Oak	R	319	674	47.3
Burkett, Atl	R	168	427	39.3	Herges, LA	R	114	326	35.0
Carpenter, Tor	R	205	575	35.7	Hermanson, Mon	R	241	684	35.2
Castillo, Tor	R	164	392	41.8	Hernandez L, SF	R	272	770	35.3
Chen, Atl-Phi	L	133	379	35.1	Hernandez O, NYY	R	227	599	37.9
Clemens, NYY	R	185	583	31.7	Holt, Hou	R	274	679	40.4
Clement, SD	R	252	603	41.8	Hudson, Oak	R	265	572	46.3
Colon, Cle	R	160	481	33.3	Jarvis, Col	R	154	396	38.9
Cone, NYY	R	185	507	36.5	Johnson J, Bal	R	143	348	41.1
Cordova, Pit	R	134	306	43.8	Johnson M, Mon	R	140	319	43.9
Cornelius, Fla	R	192	424	45.3	Johnson R, Ari	L	183	543	33.7
D'Amico J, Mil	R	216	494	43.7	Jones B, NYM	R	213	515	41.4
Daal, Ari-Phi	L	219	572	38.3	Karl, Col-Ana	R	120	326	36.8
Davis D, Tex	L	113	313	36.1	Kile, StL	R	263	680	38.7
Dempster, Fla	R	243	642	37.9	Leiter, NYM	L	260	557	46.7
Dessens, Cin	R	176	491	35.8	Levine, Ana	R	108	327	33.0
Dotel, Hou	R	112	331	33.8	Lidle, TB	R	133	324	41.0
Downs, ChC-Mon	L	126	329	38.3	Lieber, ChC	R	313	772	40.5
Dreifort, LA	R	186	564	33.0	Lima, Hou	R	306	676	45.3
Eaton, SD	R	148	419	35.3	Lira, Mon	R	150	361	41.6
Elarton, Hou	R	232	599	38.7	Loaiza, Tex-Tor	R	254	651	39.0
Eldred, CWS	R	115	325	35.4	Lopez A, TB	R	224	615	36.4

Pitcher, Team	Th	Pull	Hit	Pct	Pitcher, Team	Th	Pull	Hit	Pct
Maddux G, Atl	R	290	748	38.8	Rogers, Tex	L	359	765	46.9
Mahomes, NYM	R	103	285	36.1	Rose, Bos-Col	R	132	395	33.4
Martinez P, Bos	R	187	470	39.8	Rueter, SF	L	215	627	34.3
Martinez R, Bos	R	183	414	44.2	Rupe, TB	R	95	319	29.8
Mays, Min	R	218	543	40.1	Rusch, NYM	L	202	566	35.7
Meadows, SD-KC	R	298	697	42.8	Sanchez, Fla	L	237	576	41.1
Mercedes, Bal	R	173	478	36.2	Schilling, Phi-Ari	R	210	621	33.8
Miller W, Hou	R	120	308	39.0	Schoeneweis, Ana	L	210	579	36.3
Millwood, Atl	R	188	647	29.1	Schourek, Bos	L	145	350	41.4
Milton, Min	L	226	606	37.3	Sele, Sea	R	245	671	36.5
Mlicki, Det	R	201	430	46.7	Silva, Pit	R	170	461	36.9
Moehler, Det	R	242	617	39.2	Sirotka, CWS	L	260	621	41.9
Morgan, Ari	R	141	341	41.3	Smith C, Fla	R	134	330	40.6
Moyer, Sea	L	223	502	44.4	Snyder, Mil	R	137	422	32.5
Mulder, Oak	L	234	536	43.7	Sparks S, Det	R	153	355	43.1
Mulholland, Atl	L	223	562	39.7	Stein, KC	R	113	310	36.5
Mussina, Bal	R	284	706	40.2	Stephenson, StL	R	239	641	37.3
Nathan, SF	R	117	283	41.3	Stottlemyre, Ari	R	91	286	31.8
Neagle, Cin-NYY	L	246	652	37.7	Sullivan, Cin	R	113	277	40.8
Nitkowski, Det	L	120	355	33.8	Suppan, KC	R	276	711	38.8
Nomo, Det	R	229	539	42.5	Suzuki, KC	R	228	595	38.3
Olivares, Oak	R	136	374	36.4	Tapani, ChC	R	227	604	37.6
Oliver, Tex	L	149	387	38.5	Tavarez, Col	R	132	400	33.0
Ortiz R, Ana	R	139	330	42.1	Thurman, Mon	R	118	299	39.5
Ortiz R, SF	R	180	562	32.0	Tollberg, SD	R	150	370	40.5
Park, LA	R	233	589	39.6	Tomko, Sea	R	115	288	39.9
Parque, CWS	L	181	622	29.1	Trachsel, TB-Tor	R	274	674	40.7
Parris, Cin	R	223	645	34.6	Valdes I, ChC-LA	R	113	341	33.1
Pavano, Mon	R	87	291	29.9	Vazquez, Mon	R	253	658	38.4
Penny, Fla	R	134	370	36.2	Villone, Cin	L	177	456	38.8
Perez C, LA	L	208	508	40.9	Wakefield, Bos	R	249	518	48.1
Perisho, Tex	L	151	354	42.7	Weaver J, Det	R	241	626	38.5
Person, Phi	R	208	460	45.2	Wells D, Tor	L	266	745	35.7
Pettitte, NYY	L	242	677	35.7	Wells K, CWS	R	139	327	42.5
Ponson, Bal	R	241	704	34.2	White R, TB-NYM	R	112	300	37.3
Quevedo, ChC	R	107	282	37.9	Williams W, SD	R	194	518	37.5
Radke, Min	R	308	763	40.4	Williamson, Cin	R	87	271	32.1
Rapp, Bal	R	204	594	34.3	Witasick, KC-SD	R	178	480	37.1
Redman, Min	L	160	474	33.8	Wolf, Phi	L	209	606	34.5
Reed R, NYM	R	220	590	37.3	Wood, ChC	R	120	357	33.6
Reichert, KC	R	190	489	38.9	Woodard, Mil-Cle	R	210	491	42.8
Rekar, TB	R	228	592	38.5	Wright J, Mil	R	210	507	41.4
Reynolds, Hou	R	180	432	41.7	Yan, TB	R	178	444	40.1
Reynoso, Ari	R	213	554	38.4	Yoshii, Col	R	226	561	40.3
Ritchie, Pit	R	236	610	38.7	**MLB Average**				**38.0**

Which Pitchers Scored the Highest? (p. 143)

Highest Game Scores—2000

Pitcher, Team	Date	Opp	W/L	IP	H	R	ER	BB	SO	Score
Martinez P, Bos	5/12	@Bal	W	9.0	2	0	0	0	15	98
Mussina, Bal	8/1	Min	W	9.0	1	0	0	2	15	98
Martinez P, Bos	8/29	@TB	W	9.0	1	0	0	0	13	98
Colon, Cle	9/18	@NYY	W	9.0	1	0	0	1	13	97
Park, LA	9/29	@SD	W	9.0	2	0	0	1	13	95
Hudson, Oak	8/28	CWS	W	9.0	1	0	0	1	8	92
Villone, Cin	9/29	@StL	W	9.0	2	1	0	5	16	92
Brown, LA	9/23	SD	W	9.0	2	1	1	1	13	91
Johnson R, Ari	4/9	Pit	W	9.0	5	0	0	0	13	90
Martinez P, Bos	7/23	CWS	W	9.0	6	0	0	0	15	90
Hentgen, StL	9/14	ChC	W	9.0	3	0	0	0	9	90
Trachsel, TB	5/6	@Bos	W	9.0	3	0	0	3	11	89
Dempster, Fla	5/7	NYM	W	9.0	1	0	0	4	8	89
Martinez P, Bos	6/8	Cle	W	8.0	1	0	0	1	10	89
Brown, LA	6/15	Ari	W	9.0	4	0	0	0	10	89
Leiter, NYM	8/13	SF	W	8.0	2	0	0	1	12	89
Baldwin, CWS	5/9	@Bos	W	9.0	3	0	0	1	8	88
Glavine, Atl	4/25	LA	W	9.0	3	0	0	1	7	87
Martinez P, Bos	5/6	TB	L	9.0	6	1	1	1	17	87
Benson, Pit	5/19	StL	W	9.0	3	1	1	1	11	87
Martinez P, Bos	5/28	@NYY	W	9.0	4	0	0	1	9	87
Hernandez L, SF	8/18	Atl	W	9.0	4	0	0	2	10	87
Johnson R, Ari	8/30	@Mon	W	9.0	5	0	0	0	10	87
Loaiza, Tor	9/8	Det	W	9.0	5	0	0	1	11	87
Hudson, Oak	9/9	TB	W	9.0	2	0	0	0	4	87
Park, LA	9/24	SD	W	8.0	2	0	0	4	13	87
Holt, Hou	4/28	@Mil	W	9.0	1	0	0	2	3	86
Dreifort, LA	5/12	@StL	W	9.0	2	0	0	3	6	86
Eldred, CWS	4/24	Bal	W	9.0	2	2	2	1	11	85
Astacio, Col	5/8	@Hou	W	9.0	3	1	1	2	10	85
Lieber, ChC	5/29	Atl	L	8.0	2	1	1	1	12	85
Brown, LA	7/19	Col	W	8.0	1	1	0	1	8	85
Maddux G, Atl	9/7	Ari	W	9.0	4	0	0	0	6	85
Zito, Oak	9/10	TB	W	9.0	5	0	0	0	8	85
Maddux G, Atl	9/23	@Mon	W	7.0	2	0	0	1	13	85
Harper, TB	9/24	@Tor	W	9.0	2	0	0	1	3	85
Dessens, Cin	9/28	@Mil	W	9.0	2	1	1	0	6	85
Johnson R, Ari	4/14	@SF	W	9.0	5	1	1	0	11	84
Finley, Cle	4/16	Tex	W	9.0	5	1	0	4	13	84
Johnson R, Ari	4/20	Col	W	9.0	4	0	0	3	8	84
Hampton, NYM	6/25	Pit	W	9.0	5	0	0	2	9	84
Ritchie, Pit	6/27	ChC	W	9.0	3	0	0	3	6	84
Cooper, Ana	6/30	Oak	W	9.0	3	0	0	1	4	84
Lieber, ChC	7/3	Pit	W	9.0	2	0	0	2	3	84
Ashby, Atl	7/23	NYM	W	9.0	4	0	0	2	7	84
Leiter, NYM	9/10	Phi	W	9.0	5	0	0	2	9	84
Schilling, Ari	9/22	@SF	W	9.0	4	1	1	1	10	84

What If a Staff Has Quality, But Not Quantity? (p. 145)

Quality Start Percentages—2000, Listed Alphabetically
(minimum 15 GS)

Pitcher, Team	GS	QS	Pct	Pitcher, Team	GS	QS	Pct	Pitcher, Team	GS	QS	Pct
Abbott, Sea	27	13	48.1	Hampton, NYM	33	18	54.5	Quevedo, ChC	15	7	46.7
Anderson B, Ari	32	20	62.5	Harnisch, Cin	22	12	54.5	Radke, Min	34	17	50.0
Anderson J, Pit	26	10	38.5	Haynes, Mil	33	13	39.4	Rapp, Bal	30	15	50.0
Ankiel, StL	30	16	53.3	Helling, Tex	35	22	62.9	Redman, Min	24	14	58.3
Appier, Oak	31	17	54.8	Hentgen, StL	33	15	45.5	Reed R, NYM	30	17	56.7
Armas Jr., Mon	17	7	41.2	Heredia G, Oak	32	20	62.5	Reichert, KC	18	9	50.0
Arrojo, Col-Bos	32	12	37.5	Hermanson, Mon	30	15	50.0	Rekar, TB	27	13	48.1
Ashby, Phi-Atl	31	14	45.2	Hernandez L, SF	33	21	63.6	Reynolds, Hou	22	11	50.0
Astacio, Col	32	14	43.8	Hernandez O, NYY	29	16	55.2	Reynoso, Ari	30	17	56.7
Baldwin, CWS	28	13	46.4	Hill, Ana-CWS	17	5	29.4	Rigdon, Cle-Mil	16	8	50.0
Bell, Cin	26	11	42.3	Holt, Hou	32	12	37.5	Ritchie, Pit	31	18	58.1
Benes A, StL	27	18	66.7	Hudson, Oak	32	17	53.1	Rogers, Tex	34	17	50.0
Benson, Pit	32	19	59.4	Jarvis, Col	19	7	36.8	Rose, Bos-Col	24	8	33.3
Bere, Mil-Cle	31	14	45.2	Johnson R, Ari	35	25	71.4	Rueter, SF	31	19	61.3
Blair, Det	17	6	35.3	Jones B, NYM	27	13	48.1	Rupe, TB	18	4	22.2
Bohanon, Col	26	11	42.3	Kile, StL	34	20	58.8	Rusch, NYM	30	18	60.0
Bottenfield, 2Tm	29	12	41.4	Leiter, NYM	31	19	61.3	Sanchez, Fla	32	14	43.8
Brown, LA	33	26	78.8	Lieber, ChC	35	19	54.3	Schilling, Phi-Ari	29	16	55.2
Burba, Cle	32	16	50.0	Lima, Hou	33	11	33.3	Schoeneweis, Ana	27	11	40.7
Burkett, Atl	22	9	40.9	Loaiza, Tex-Tor	31	16	51.6	Schourek, Bos	21	7	33.3
Byrd, Phi	15	8	53.3	Lopez A, TB	24	12	50.0	Sele, Sea	34	16	47.1
Carpenter, Tor	27	11	40.7	Maddux G, Atl	35	25	71.4	Silva, Pit	19	9	47.4
Castillo, Tor	24	12	50.0	Martinez P, Bos	29	25	86.2	Sirotka, CWS	32	21	65.6
Chen, Atl-Phi	15	6	40.0	Martinez R, Bos	27	7	25.9	Smith C, Fla	19	11	57.9
Clemens, NYY	32	21	65.6	Mays, Min	28	10	35.7	Snyder, Mil	23	9	39.1
Clement, SD	34	16	47.1	Meadows, SD-KC	32	13	40.6	Sparks S, Det	15	8	53.3
Colon, Cle	30	19	63.3	Meche, Sea	15	6	40.0	Stein, KC	17	8	47.1
Cone, NYY	29	10	34.5	Mercedes, Bal	20	11	55.0	Stephenson, StL	31	13	41.9
Cooper, Ana	15	4	26.7	Miller W, Hou	16	7	43.8	Stottlemyre, Ari	18	7	38.9
Cordova, Pit	17	6	35.3	Millwood, Atl	35	18	51.4	Suppan, KC	33	15	45.5
Cornelius, Fla	21	9	42.9	Milton, Min	33	19	57.6	Suzuki, KC	29	13	44.8
D'Amico J, Mil	23	18	78.3	Mlicki, Det	21	8	38.1	Tapani, ChC	30	16	53.3
Daal, Ari-Phi	28	14	50.0	Moehler, Det	29	16	55.2	Thurman, Mon	17	6	35.3
Dempster, Fla	33	20	60.6	Moyer, Sea	26	13	50.0	Tollberg, SD	19	10	52.6
Dessens, Cin	16	9	56.3	Mulder, Oak	27	15	55.6	Trachsel, TB-Tor	34	14	41.2
Dotel, Hou	16	6	37.5	Mulholland, Atl	20	8	40.0	Valdes I, ChC-LA	20	6	30.0
Downs, ChC-Mon	19	6	31.6	Mussina, Bal	34	21	61.8	Vazquez, Mon	33	24	72.7
Dreifort, LA	32	15	46.9	Nathan, SF	15	7	46.7	Villone, Cin	23	10	43.5
Durbin, KC	16	5	31.3	Neagle, Cin-NYY	33	18	54.5	Wakefield, Bos	17	5	29.4
Eaton, SD	22	12	54.5	Nomo, Det	31	17	54.8	Weaver J, Det	30	16	53.3
Elarton, Hou	30	17	56.7	Olivares, Oak	16	2	12.5	Wells D, Tor	35	19	54.3
Eldred, CWS	20	8	40.0	Oliver, Tex	21	5	23.8	Wells K, CWS	20	5	25.0
Erickson, Bal	16	5	31.3	Ortiz R, Ana	18	8	44.4	Williams W, SD	23	15	65.2
Escobar, Tor	24	10	41.7	Ortiz R, SF	32	15	46.9	Witasick, KC-SD	25	6	24.0
Estes, SF	30	13	43.3	Park, LA	34	23	67.6	Wolf, Phi	32	19	59.4
Fassero, Bos	23	7	30.4	Parque, CWS	32	15	46.9	Wood, ChC	23	13	56.5
Finley, Cle	34	19	55.9	Parris, Cin	33	16	48.5	Woodard, Mil-Cle	22	6	27.3
Gagne, LA	19	9	47.4	Pavano, Mon	15	11	73.3	Wright J, Mil	25	14	56.0
Garcia F, Sea	20	11	55.0	Penny, Fla	22	8	36.4	Yan, TB	20	7	35.0
Gardner, SF	20	13	65.0	Perez C, LA	22	9	40.9	Yoshii, Col	29	11	37.9
Glavine, Atl	35	26	74.3	Person, Phi	28	15	53.6	**MLB Average**			46.3
Glynn, Tex	16	6	37.5	Pettitte, NYY	32	17	53.1				
Halama, Sea	30	7	23.3	Ponson, Bal	32	13	40.6				

Who Gets the Red Barrett Trophy? (p. 147)

Fewest Pitches in a Nine-Inning Complete Game—2000

Pitcher, Team	Date	Score	Opp	W/L	IP	H	R	ER	BB	SO	Pit	Time
Halama, Sea	5/17	4-0	Min	W	9.0	4	0	0	0	2	87	2:13
Carpenter, Tor	4/21	8-3	NYY	W	9.0	5	3	3	0	3	88	2:20
Wells D, Tor	4/8	4-0	@Tex	W	9.0	9	0	0	1	5	89	2:52
Maddux G, Atl	9/13	4-0	Fla	W	9.0	4	0	0	0	4	89	2:36
Maddux G, Atl	9/7	4-0	Ari	W	9.0	4	0	0	0	6	90	2:20
Kile, StL	9/2	2-1	NYM	W	9.0	5	1	1	0	2	94	2:39
Hudson, Oak	9/9	10-0	TB	W	9.0	2	0	0	0	4	94	2:05
Estes, SF	8/6	7-1	Pit	W	9.0	10	1	0	1	4	95	2:23
Maddux G, Atl	6/24	1-2	Mil	L	9.0	6	2	2	1	5	96	2:28
Hernandez O, NYY	9/16	6-3	Cle	W	9.0	4	3	3	0	6	98	3:02
Glavine, Atl	9/25	6-0	@Mon	W	9.0	8	0	0	0	3	98	2:37
Ritchie, Pit	6/27	6-0	ChC	W	9.0	3	0	0	3	6	99	2:05
Mercedes, Bal	8/30	5-1	Det	W	9.0	2	1	1	1	5	99	2:57
Mendoza, NYY	5/25	7-0	@CWS	W	9.0	4	0	0	1	4	100	2:21
Sele, Sea	4/12	4-0	@Det	W	9.0	3	0	0	1	1	101	2:24
Johnson R, Ari	4/20	3-0	Col	W	9.0	4	0	0	3	8	101	2:26
Baldwin, CWS	5/9	6-0	@Bos	W	9.0	3	0	0	1	8	101	2:22
Ponson, Bal	9/22	3-1	@Bos	W	9.0	4	1	1	1	3	101	2:17
Dessens, Cin	9/28	8-1	@Mil	W	9.0	2	1	1	0	6	101	2:35
Escobar, Tor	4/22	8-2	NYY	W	9.0	9	2	2	0	4	102	2:24
Radke, Min	5/19	3-2	@Oak	W	9.0	3	2	2	3	5	102	2:35
Baldwin, CWS	5/20	6-2	@Tor	W	9.0	7	2	2	0	3	102	2:22
Schilling, Ari	8/18	11-2	ChC	W	9.0	6	2	2	0	10	102	2:35
Kile, StL	8/27	7-2	@Atl	W	9.0	8	2	2	0	5	102	2:37
McKnight, Hou	9/27	10-1	@Pit	W	9.0	4	1	1	1	7	102	2:34
Holt, Hou	4/28	7-0	@Mil	W	9.0	1	0	0	2	3	103	2:49
Lopez A, TB	6/14	3-2	Ana	W	9.0	7	2	2	1	7	103	2:09
Ortiz R, Ana	9/24	9-2	@Tex	W	9.0	5	2	2	2	5	103	2:51
Reynoso, Ari	9/28	12-3	@Col	W	9.0	7	3	3	1	4	103	2:37
Maddux G, Atl	7/18	8-2	@TB	W	9.0	7	2	2	1	6	104	2:16
MLB Average											116	

Most Pitches in a Game—2000

Pitcher, Team	Date	Score	Opp	W/L	IP	H	R	ER	BB	SO	Pit	Time
Villone, Cin	9/29	8-1	@StL	W	9.0	2	1	0	5	16	148	2:59
Appier, Oak	7/3	3-8	@Tex	L	7.0	5	4	3	5	4	146	3:41
Johnson R, Ari	7/30	3-4	@Fla	ND	7.0	7	2	2	1	11	146	3:08
Hernandez L, SF	5/30	7-3	Phi	W	8.1	8	3	3	1	7	143	2:39
Davis D, Tex	8/20	6-2	@Bos	W	9.0	9	2	1	4	5	142	2:51
Stephenson, StL	7/25	7-3	Ari	W	8.0	5	3	3	4	2	141	2:59
Bohanon, Col	9/13	11-0	@SD	W	9.0	9	0	0	3	3	140	2:56
Mussina, Bal	4/29	3-1	Tex	W	9.0	9	1	1	1	6	138	2:46
Holt, Hou	5/23	10-2	Phi	W	9.0	8	2	2	4	7	138	2:41
Hitchcock, SD	4/30	4-7	Atl	L	7.1	6	5	4	5	10	137	3:07
Rapp, Bal	6/24	1-2	@Sea	L	7.0	4	2	2	3	8	137	2:37
Helling, Tex	7/3	8-3	Oak	W	6.0	6	1	1	4	3	137	3:41
Cone, NYY	8/5	5-6	Sea	ND	6.0	7	3	3	5	6	137	3:13
Helling, Tex	5/2	8-1	@TB	W	7.1	1	1	0	6	6	136	3:14
Ashby, Atl	7/23	1-0	NYM	W	9.0	4	0	0	2	7	136	2:59
Leiter, NYM	9/10	3-0	Phi	W	9.0	5	0	0	2	9	136	2:40
Johnson R, Ari	9/25	6-4	@Col	W	7.2	10	4	4	4	8	136	3:12
Lopez A, TB	10/1	3-2	Bos	ND	8.0	8	2	2	4	1	136	3:25

Whose Heater Is Hottest? (p. 149)

Strikeouts Per Nine Innings—2000, Listed Alphabetically
(minimum 162 IP for starters, 50 IP for relievers)

Pitcher, Team	SO	IP	SO/9	Pitcher, Team	SO	IP	SO/9
Abbott, Sea	100	179.0	5.0	Fetters, LA	40	50.0	7.2
Acevedo, Mil	51	82.2	5.6	Finley, Cle	189	218.0	7.8
Adams, LA	56	84.1	6.0	Foulke, CWS	91	88.0	9.3
Alfonseca, Fla	47	70.0	6.0	Franco, NYM	56	55.2	9.1
Almanzar, SD	56	69.2	7.2	Frascatore, Tor	30	73.0	3.7
Anderson B, Ari	104	213.1	4.4	Fultz, SF	62	69.1	8.0
Anderson M, Det	71	74.1	8.6	Fussell, KC	46	70.0	5.9
Ankiel, StL	194	175.0	10.0	Fyhrie, Ana	43	52.2	7.3
Appier, Oak	129	195.1	5.9	Garces, Bos	69	74.2	8.3
Arrojo, Col-Bos	124	172.2	6.5	Garibay, ChC	46	74.2	5.5
Ashby, Phi-Atl	106	199.1	4.8	Glavine, Atl	152	241.0	5.7
Astacio, Col	193	196.1	8.8	Gomes, Phi	49	73.2	6.0
Aybar, Col-Cin-Fla	45	79.1	5.1	Graves, Cin	53	91.1	5.2
Baldwin, CWS	116	178.0	5.9	Grimsley, NYY	53	96.1	5.0
Batista, Mon-KC	37	65.1	5.1	Groom, Bal	44	59.1	6.7
Benes A, StL	137	166.0	7.4	Guardado, Min	52	61.2	7.6
Benitez, NYM	106	76.0	12.6	Guthrie, ChC-TB-Tor	63	71.1	7.9
Benson, Pit	184	217.2	7.6	Halama, Sea	87	166.2	4.7
Bere, Mil-Cle	142	169.1	7.5	Hampton, NYM	151	217.2	6.2
Blair, Det	74	156.2	4.3	Hasegawa, Ana	59	95.2	5.6
Bohanon, Col	98	177.0	5.0	Hawkins, Min	59	87.2	6.1
Bones, Fla	59	77.1	6.9	Haynes, Mil	88	199.1	4.0
Bottalico, KC	56	72.2	6.9	Helling, Tex	146	217.0	6.1
Bottenfield, Ana-Phi	106	171.2	5.6	Henry, Hou-SF	62	78.1	7.1
Brantley, Phi	57	55.1	9.3	Hentgen, StL	118	194.1	5.5
Brocail, Det	41	50.2	7.3	Heredia F, ChC	52	58.2	8.0
Brock, Phi	69	93.1	6.7	Heredia G, Oak	101	198.2	4.6
Brown, LA	216	230.0	8.5	Herges, LA	75	110.2	6.1
Buehrle, CWS	37	51.1	6.5	Hermanson, Mon	94	198.0	4.3
Burba, Cle	180	191.1	8.5	Hernandez L, SF	165	240.0	6.2
Cabrera, Hou	41	59.1	6.2	Hernandez O, NYY	141	195.2	6.5
Carpenter, Tor	113	175.1	5.8	Hernandez R, TB	61	73.1	7.5
Carrasco, Min-Bos	64	78.2	7.3	Hoffman, SD	85	72.1	10.6
Chen, Atl-Phi	112	134.0	7.5	Holt, Hou	136	207.0	5.9
Clemens, NYY	188	204.1	8.3	Howry, CWS	60	71.0	7.6
Clement, SD	170	205.0	7.5	Hudson, Oak	169	202.1	7.5
Colon, Cle	212	188.0	10.1	Isringhausen, Oak	57	69.0	7.4
Cook, NYM	53	59.0	8.1	James, StL	41	51.1	7.2
Cordero, Tex	49	77.1	5.7	Jimenez, Col	44	70.2	5.6
Cormier, Bos	43	68.1	5.7	Johnson M, Mon	70	101.1	6.2
Crabtree, Tex	54	80.1	6.0	Johnson R, Ari	347	248.2	12.6
Creek, TB	73	60.2	10.8	Johnstone, SF	37	50.0	6.7
D'Amico J, Mil	101	162.1	5.6	Jones D, Oak	54	73.1	6.6
Daal, Ari-Phi	96	167.0	5.2	Jones T, Det	67	64.0	9.4
Darensbourg, Fla	59	62.0	8.6	Kamieniecki, Cle-Atl	46	58.0	7.1
Davis D, Tex	66	98.2	6.0	Karsay, Cle	66	76.2	7.7
de los Santos, Mil	70	73.2	8.6	Kile, StL	192	232.1	7.4
DeJean, Col	34	53.1	5.7	Kim, Ari	111	70.2	14.1
Dempster, Fla	209	226.1	8.3	Kline, Mon	64	82.1	7.0
Dessens, Cin	85	147.1	5.2	Koch, Tor	60	78.2	6.9
Dotel, Hou	142	125.0	10.2	Leiter, NYM	200	208.0	8.7
Dreifort, LA	164	192.2	7.7	Leskanic, Mil	75	77.1	8.7
Elarton, Hou	131	192.2	6.1	Levine, Ana	42	95.1	4.0
Embree, SF	49	60.0	7.4	Lidle, TB	62	96.2	5.8
Erdos, NYY-SD	34	54.2	5.6	Lieber, ChC	192	251.0	6.9
Escobar, Tor	142	180.0	7.1	Ligtenberg, Atl	51	52.1	8.8
Estes, SF	136	190.1	6.4	Lima, Hou	124	196.1	5.7
Farnsworth, ChC	74	77.0	8.6	Lira, Mon	51	101.2	4.5

Pitcher, Team	SO	IP	SO/9	Pitcher, Team	SO	IP	SO/9
Loaiza, Tex-Tor	137	199.1	6.2	Santana J, Min	64	86.0	6.7
Looper, Fla	29	67.1	3.9	Santana J, Mon	58	66.2	7.8
Lopez A, TB	96	185.1	4.7	Santiago, KC	44	69.0	5.7
Lowe D, Bos	79	91.1	7.8	Sasaki, Sea	78	62.2	11.2
Lowe S, CWS	53	70.2	6.8	Sauerbeck, Pit	83	75.2	9.9
Maddux G, Atl	190	249.1	6.9	Schilling, Phi-Ari	168	210.1	7.2
Mahomes, NYM	76	94.0	7.3	Schoeneweis, Ana	78	170.0	4.1
Manzanillo, Pit	39	58.2	6.0	Sele, Sea	137	211.2	5.8
Martinez P, Bos	284	217.0	11.8	Shaw, LA	39	57.1	6.1
Mathews, Oak	42	59.2	6.3	Shuey, Cle	69	63.2	9.8
McElroy, Bal	50	63.1	7.1	Silva, Pit	98	136.0	6.5
Meadows, SD-KC	79	196.1	3.6	Simas, CWS	49	67.2	6.5
Mecir, TB-Oak	70	85.0	7.4	Sirotka, CWS	128	197.0	5.8
Mesa, Sea	84	80.2	9.4	Slocumb, StL-SD	46	68.2	6.0
Miller T, Min	62	67.0	8.3	Slusarski, Hou	54	77.0	6.3
Millwood, Atl	168	212.2	7.1	Speier, Cle	69	68.1	9.1
Milton, Min	160	200.0	7.2	Spradlin, KC-ChC	67	90.0	6.7
Moehler, Det	103	178.0	5.2	Springer R, Ari	59	62.0	8.6
Morgan, Ari	56	101.2	5.0	Stanton, NYY	75	68.0	9.9
Morris M, StL	34	53.0	5.8	Stephenson, StL	123	200.1	5.5
Mulholland, Atl	78	156.2	4.5	Sturtze, CWS-TB	44	68.1	5.8
Mussina, Bal	210	237.2	8.0	Sullivan, Cin	96	106.1	8.1
Neagle, Cin-NYY	146	209.0	6.3	Suppan, KC	128	217.0	5.3
Nelson, NYY	71	69.2	9.2	Suzuki, KC	135	188.2	6.4
Nen, SF	92	66.0	12.5	Swindell, Ari	64	76.0	7.6
Nitkowski, Det	81	109.2	6.6	Tam, Oak	46	85.2	4.8
Nomo, Det	181	190.0	8.6	Tapani, ChC	150	195.2	6.9
Ortiz R, SF	167	195.2	7.7	Tavarez, Col	62	120.0	4.7
Osuna, LA	70	67.1	9.4	Telford, Mon	68	78.1	7.8
Padilla, Ari-Phi	51	65.1	7.0	Timlin, Bal-StL	52	64.2	7.2
Painter, Tor	53	66.2	7.2	Tomko, Sea	59	92.1	5.8
Paniagua, Sea	71	80.1	8.0	Trachsel, TB-Tor	110	200.2	4.9
Park, LA	217	226.0	8.6	Trombley, Bal	72	72.0	9.0
Parque, CWS	111	187.0	5.3	Valdes M, Hou	35	56.2	5.6
Parris, Cin	117	192.2	5.5	Van Poppel, ChC	77	86.1	8.0
Patterson, Det	29	56.2	4.6	Vazquez, Mon	196	217.2	8.1
Percival, Ana	49	50.0	8.8	Venafro, Tex	32	56.1	5.1
Perisho, Tex	74	105.0	6.3	Veres, StL	67	75.2	8.0
Person, Phi	164	173.1	8.5	Wakefield, Bos	102	159.1	5.8
Petkovsek, Ana	31	81.0	3.4	Walker K, SD	56	66.2	7.6
Pettitte, NYY	125	204.2	5.5	Wall, SD	29	53.2	4.9
Pichardo, Bos	37	65.0	5.1	Wasdin, Bos-Col	71	80.1	8.0
Ponson, Bal	152	222.0	6.2	Weathers, Mil	50	76.1	5.9
Pote, Ana	44	50.1	7.9	Weaver J, Det	136	200.0	6.1
Quantrill, Tor	47	83.2	5.1	Wells B, Min	76	86.1	7.9
Radke, Min	141	226.2	5.6	Wells D, Tor	166	229.2	6.5
Ramsay, Sea	32	50.1	5.7	Wendell, NYM	73	82.2	7.9
Rapp, Bal	106	174.0	5.5	Wetteland, Tex	53	60.0	8.0
Reed R, NYM	121	184.0	5.9	White G, Cin-Col	84	84.0	9.0
Reed S, Cle	39	56.0	6.3	White R, TB-NYM	67	99.2	6.1
Reichert, KC	94	153.1	5.5	Wickman, Mil-Cle	55	72.2	6.8
Rekar, TB	95	173.1	4.9	Wilkins, Pit	37	60.1	5.5
Remlinger, Atl	72	72.2	8.9	Williams M, Pit	71	72.0	8.9
Reynoso, Ari	89	170.2	4.7	Williams W, SD	111	168.0	5.9
Rhodes, Sea	77	69.1	10.0	Williamson, Cin	136	112.0	10.9
Ritchie, Pit	124	187.0	6.0	Wolf, Phi	160	206.1	7.0
Rivera M, NYY	58	75.2	6.9	Worrell, Bal-ChC	57	69.1	7.4
Rocker, Atl	77	53.0	13.1	Wright J, Mil	96	164.2	5.2
Rodriguez F, SF	95	81.2	10.5	Wunsch, CWS	51	61.1	7.5
Rogers, Tex	127	227.1	5.0	Yan, TB	111	137.2	7.3
Rueter, SF	71	184.0	3.5	Yoshii, Col	88	167.1	4.7
Rusch, NYM	157	190.2	7.4	Zimmerman, Tex	74	69.2	9.6
Sanchez, Fla	123	182.0	6.1	**MLB Average**			**6.5**

Has Anyone Ever Dominated Hitters Like Martinez Did in 2000? (p. 151)

Strikeout-Hit Ratios—2000, Listed Alphabetically
(minimum 162 IP)

Pitcher, Team	SO	H	SO/H	Pitcher, Team	SO	H	SO/H
Abbott, Sea	100	164	0.61	Lopez A, TB	96	199	0.48
Anderson B, Ari	104	226	0.46	Maddux G, Atl	190	225	0.84
Ankiel, StL	194	137	1.42	Martinez P, Bos	284	128	2.22
Appier, Oak	129	200	0.65	Meadows, SD-KC	79	234	0.34
Arrojo, Col-Bos	124	187	0.66	Millwood, Atl	168	213	0.79
Ashby, Phi-Atl	106	216	0.49	Milton, Min	160	205	0.78
Astacio, Col	193	217	0.89	Moehler, Det	103	222	0.46
Baldwin, CWS	116	185	0.63	Mussina, Bal	210	236	0.89
Benes A, StL	137	174	0.79	Neagle, Cin-NYY	146	210	0.70
Benson, Pit	184	206	0.89	Nomo, Det	181	191	0.95
Bere, Mil-Cle	142	180	0.79	Ortiz R, SF	167	192	0.87
Bohanon, Col	98	181	0.54	Park, LA	217	173	1.25
Bottenfield, Ana-Phi	106	185	0.57	Parque, CWS	111	208	0.53
Brown, LA	216	181	1.19	Parris, Cin	117	227	0.52
Burba, Cle	180	199	0.90	Person, Phi	164	144	1.14
Carpenter, Tor	113	204	0.55	Pettitte, NYY	125	219	0.57
Clemens, NYY	188	184	1.02	Ponson, Bal	152	223	0.68
Clement, SD	170	194	0.88	Radke, Min	141	261	0.54
Colon, Cle	212	163	1.30	Rapp, Bal	106	203	0.52
D'Amico J, Mil	101	143	0.71	Reed R, NYM	121	192	0.63
Daal, Ari-Phi	96	208	0.46	Rekar, TB	95	200	0.48
Dempster, Fla	209	210	1.00	Reynoso, Ari	89	179	0.50
Dreifort, LA	164	175	0.94	Ritchie, Pit	124	208	0.60
Elarton, Hou	131	198	0.66	Rogers, Tex	127	257	0.49
Escobar, Tor	142	186	0.76	Rueter, SF	71	205	0.35
Estes, SF	136	194	0.70	Rusch, NYM	157	196	0.80
Finley, Cle	189	211	0.90	Sanchez, Fla	123	197	0.62
Glavine, Atl	152	222	0.68	Schilling, Phi-Ari	168	204	0.82
Halama, Sea	87	206	0.42	Schoeneweis, Ana	78	183	0.43
Hampton, NYM	151	194	0.78	Sele, Sea	137	221	0.62
Haynes, Mil	88	228	0.39	Sirotka, CWS	128	203	0.63
Helling, Tex	146	212	0.69	Stephenson, StL	123	209	0.59
Hentgen, StL	118	202	0.58	Suppan, KC	128	240	0.53
Heredia G, Oak	101	214	0.47	Suzuki, KC	135	195	0.69
Hermanson, Mon	94	226	0.42	Tapani, ChC	150	208	0.72
Hernandez L, SF	165	254	0.65	Trachsel, TB-Tor	110	232	0.47
Hernandez O, NYY	141	186	0.76	Vazquez, Mon	196	247	0.79
Holt, Hou	136	247	0.55	Weaver J, Det	136	205	0.66
Hudson, Oak	169	169	1.00	Wells D, Tor	166	266	0.62
Johnson R, Ari	347	202	1.72	Williams W, SD	111	152	0.73
Kile, StL	192	215	0.89	Wolf, Phi	160	210	0.76
Leiter, NYM	200	176	1.14	Wright J, Mil	96	157	0.61
Lieber, ChC	192	248	0.77	Yoshii, Col	88	201	0.44
Lima, Hou	124	251	0.49	**MLB Average**			**0.69**
Loaiza, Tex-Tor	137	228	0.60				

Highest Strikeout-Hit Ratios, Season—1876-2000
(pitcher worked as many TOTAL innings during season as the number of games played by team with which he worked the most innings)

Pitcher	Year	SO	H	SO/H	Pitcher	Year	SO	H	SO/H
Pedro Martinez	2000	284	128	2.22	Sandy Koufax	1963	306	214	1.43
Kerry Wood	1998	233	117	1.99	J.R. Richard	1979	313	220	1.42
Nolan Ryan	1991	203	102	1.99	Nolan Ryan	1978	260	183	1.42
Nolan Ryan	1972	329	166	1.98	Rick Ankiel	2000	194	137	1.42
Randy Johnson	1997	291	147	1.98	Nolan Ryan	1981	140	99	1.41
Pedro Martinez	1999	313	160	1.96	Floyd Youmans	1986	202	145	1.39
Pedro Martinez	1997	305	158	1.93	Sid Fernandez	1990	181	130	1.39
Hideo Nomo	1995	236	124	1.90	John Smoltz	1996	276	199	1.39
Nolan Ryan	1989	301	162	1.86	Nolan Ryan	1984	197	143	1.38
Randy Johnson	1995	294	159	1.85	Tom Seaver	1971	289	210	1.38
Sam McDowell	1965	325	178	1.83	Sonny Siebert	1965	191	139	1.37
Sandy Koufax	1965	382	216	1.77	Nolan Ryan	1983	183	134	1.37
Randy Johnson	1999	364	207	1.76	Mario Soto	1982	274	202	1.36
Nolan Ryan	1987	270	154	1.75	Roger Clemens	1994	168	124	1.35
Luis Tiant	1968	264	152	1.74	Bob Gibson	1968	268	198	1.35
Sam McDowell	1966	225	130	1.73	Dwight Gooden	1985	268	198	1.35
Nolan Ryan	1977	341	198	1.72	Roger Clemens	1988	291	217	1.34
Randy Johnson	2000	347	202	1.72	Pedro Martinez	1998	251	188	1.34
Dwight Gooden	1984	276	161	1.71	Jose Rijo	1988	160	120	1.33
Nolan Ryan	1976	327	193	1.69	Roger Clemens	1986	238	179	1.33
Nolan Ryan	1990	232	137	1.69	Ron Guidry	1978	248	187	1.33
Mike Scott	1986	306	182	1.68	Nolan Ryan	1979	223	169	1.32
Sid Fernandez	1985	180	108	1.67	David Cone	1990	233	177	1.32
Randy Johnson	1993	308	185	1.66	Sandy Koufax	1966	317	241	1.32
Nolan Ryan	1974	367	221	1.66	Al Leiter	1996	200	153	1.31
Nolan Ryan	1986	194	119	1.63	Hideo Nomo	1996	234	180	1.30
Herb Score	1956	263	162	1.62	Bartolo Colon	2000	212	163	1.30
Randy Johnson	1998	329	203	1.62	David Cone	1992	261	201	1.30
Sandy Koufax	1962	216	134	1.61	Jim Maloney	1965	244	189	1.29
Nolan Ryan	1973	383	238	1.61	Dennis Eckersley	1976	200	155	1.29
Roger Clemens	1998	271	169	1.60	Sam McDowell	1970	304	236	1.29
J.R. Richard	1978	303	192	1.58	Fernando Valenzuela	1981	180	140	1.29
Randy Johnson	1992	241	154	1.56	Tom Griffin	1969	200	156	1.28
Sam McDowell	1968	283	181	1.56	Hal Newhouser	1946	275	215	1.28
Herb Score	1955	245	158	1.55	Frank Tanana	1975	269	211	1.27
Randy Johnson	1994	204	132	1.55	Curt Schilling	1998	300	236	1.27
Curt Schilling	1997	319	208	1.53	Sandy Koufax	1961	269	212	1.27
Randy Johnson	1991	228	151	1.51	Mickey Lolich	1969	271	214	1.27
Al Downing	1963	171	114	1.50	Dutch Leonard	1914	176	139	1.27
Sid Fernandez	1988	189	127	1.49	Bob Turley	1957	152	120	1.27
Sandy Koufax	1960	197	133	1.48	Sid Fernandez	1989	198	157	1.26
Jim Maloney	1963	265	183	1.45	Dave Boswell	1967	204	162	1.26
Sandy Koufax	1964	223	154	1.45	Sam McDowell	1969	279	222	1.26
Mario Soto	1980	182	126	1.44	Bob Feller	1946	348	277	1.26
Dave Boswell	1966	173	120	1.44	Chan Ho Park	2000	217	173	1.25
Vida Blue	1971	301	209	1.44	Tom Gordon	1989	153	122	1.25
David Cone	1997	222	155	1.43	Nolan Ryan	1982	245	196	1.25
Roger Clemens	1997	292	204	1.43	Bob Turley	1955	210	168	1.25

Who Gets the Easy Saves—And Who Toughs It Out? (p. 156)

Save Conversion Rates—2000, Listed Alphabetically
(minimum 5 total Sv Opp)

Pitcher, Team	Easy Sv/Opp	Regular Sv/Opp	Tough Sv/Opp	Pitcher, Team	Easy Sv/Opp	Regular Sv/Opp	Tough Sv/Opp
Adams, LA	0/0	2/3	0/4	Mecir, TB-Oak	1/4	4/7	0/2
Aguilera, ChC	17/18	10/13	2/6	Morgan, Ari	1/1	4/5	0/0
Alfonseca, Fla	31/32	14/17	0/0	Morris M, StL	0/1	3/5	1/1
Belinda, Col-Atl	0/1	1/4	0/2	Nen, SF	31/33	10/12	0/1
Benitez, NYM	20/20	18/21	3/5	Padilla, Ari-Phi	0/1	0/1	2/5
Bottalico, KC	10/12	4/8	2/3	Paniagua, Sea	0/0	3/3	2/5
Brantley, Phi	11/13	10/12	2/3	Percival, Ana	15/20	17/22	0/0
Brocail, Det	0/0	0/4	0/1	Reichert, KC	1/1	1/4	0/1
Carrasco, Min-Bos	0/0	1/2	0/4	Remlinger, Atl	4/4	4/6	4/6
Cook, NYM	0/0	2/4	0/4	Rhodes, Sea	0/1	0/3	0/3
Crabtree, Tex	0/1	2/3	0/5	Rivera M, NYY	16/17	17/18	3/6
Dotel, Hou	6/9	5/7	5/7	Rocker, Atl	15/18	8/8	1/1
Embree, SF	0/1	1/2	1/2	Rodriguez F, SF	1/1	1/3	1/4
Farnsworth, ChC	0/0	1/2	0/4	Santiago, KC	0/0	2/5	0/3
Fetters, LA	4/4	1/3	0/0	Sasaki, Sea	25/25	9/10	3/5
Foulke, CWS	9/9	19/21	6/9	Shaw, LA	17/17	9/16	1/1
Frascatore, Tor	0/0	0/2	0/3	Shuey, Cle	0/0	0/3	0/2
Garces, Bos	0/0	1/1	0/4	Simas, CWS	0/2	0/1	0/2
Gomes, Phi	4/4	2/6	1/1	Spradlin, KC-ChC	3/3	1/5	3/3
Graves, Cin	11/11	15/18	4/6	Strickland, Mon	3/3	4/7	2/3
Groom, Bal	1/2	2/4	1/5	Sullivan, Cin	0/0	2/4	1/2
Guardado, Min	3/3	4/6	2/2	Tam, Oak	0/0	2/2	1/4
Hasegawa, Ana	1/2	7/12	1/4	Telford, Mon	0/0	0/1	3/4
Hawkins, Min	4/4	9/9	1/1	Timlin, Bal-StL	4/5	7/8	1/5
Heredia F, ChC	0/0	1/1	1/4	Trombley, Bal	3/4	1/3	0/4
Hermanson, Mon	1/2	2/3	1/2	Urbina, Mon	2/2	4/6	2/2
Hernandez R, TB	19/21	12/17	1/2	Valdes M, Hou	2/2	0/3	0/1
Hoffman, SD	25/28	16/19	2/3	Van Poppel, ChC	0/0	1/4	1/1
Howry, CWS	1/1	4/6	2/5	Veres, StL	8/9	13/16	8/11
Isringhausen, Oak	21/22	10/15	2/3	Wagner, Hou	4/5	1/6	1/4
James, StL	0/1	1/1	1/3	Wall, SD	1/3	0/1	0/1
Jimenez, Col	8/8	14/18	2/4	Weathers, Mil	0/2	1/4	0/1
Jones T, Det	27/30	11/12	4/4	Wells B, Min	2/3	6/10	2/7
Karsay, Cle	9/10	10/14	1/5	Wendell, NYM	0/0	1/2	0/3
Kim, Ari	7/8	6/9	1/3	Wetteland, Tex	16/18	18/24	0/1
Kline, Mon	6/7	7/8	1/3	White G, Cin-Col	1/1	4/8	0/0
Koch, Tor	14/15	18/22	1/1	White R, TB-NYM	2/2	1/4	0/1
Kohlmeier, Bal	4/4	9/10	0/0	Wickman, Mil-Cle	20/23	9/11	1/3
Leskanic, Mil	6/6	3/4	3/3	Williams M, Pit	16/17	8/10	0/2
Ligtenberg, Atl	8/9	2/3	2/2	Williamson, Cin	0/0	5/6	1/2
Loiselle, Pit	0/0	0/4	0/2	Worrell, Bal-ChC	1/1	2/4	0/1
Looper, Fla	0/0	2/4	0/1	Wunsch, CWS	0/0	0/2	1/3
Lowe D, Bos	20/20	20/25	2/2	**MLB Totals**	**549/635**	**510/796**	**119/371**
Mantei, Ari	6/7	11/13	0/0				

If You Hold the Fort, Will You Soon Be Closing the Gate? (p. 159)

Holds—2000, Listed Alphabetically
(minimum 2 Hld)

Pitcher, Team	Hld	Pitcher, Team	Hld	Pitcher, Team	Hld	Pitcher, Team	Hld
Abbott, Sea	4	Franklin, Hou	8	McElroy, Bal	2	Sauerbeck, Pit	13
Acevedo, Mil	7	Frascatore, Tor	13	McMichael, Atl	2	Seanez, Atl	6
Adams, LA	15	Fultz, SF	7	Mecir, TB-Oak	21	Shuey, Cle	28
Aldred, Phi	2	Fyhrie, Ana	2	Mesa, Sea	11	Simas, CWS	13
Almanza, Fla	13	Garces, Bos	17	Miceli, Fla	11	Slocumb, StL-SD	12
Almanzar, SD	8	Garcia M, Pit	2	Miller T, Min	10	Slusarski, Hou	7
Anderson M, Det	9	Gomes, Phi	4	Mills, LA-Bal	8	Speier, Cle	6
Beck, Bos	7	Gooden, 3Tm	2	Mohler, StL-Cle	4	Spradlin, KC-ChC	4
Belinda, Col-Atl	5	Grimsley, NYY	4	Morgan, Ari	5	Springer R, Ari	3
Benes A, StL	2	Groom, Bal	27	Morris M, StL	7	Stanton, NYY	15
Blair, Det	2	Guardado, Min	8	Mota G, Mon	5	Stechschulte, StL	3
Bohanon, Col	2	Guthrie, 3Tm	10	Mulholland, Atl	2	Strickland, Mon	6
Bones, Fla	6	Hasegawa, Ana	19	Mullen, KC	2	Strong, Fla	2
Borbon, Tor	12	Hawkins, Min	7	Myers M, Col	15	Sullivan, Cin	22
Boyd, Phi	2	Henry, Hou-SF	12	Navarro, Mil-Cle	2	Swindell, Ari	9
Bradford, CWS	2	Heredia F, ChC	12	Nelson, NYY	15	Tam, Oak	19
Brocail, Det	19	Herges, LA	4	Nitkowski, Det	15	Tavarez, Col	6
Brock, Phi	16	Holtz, Ana	10	Orosco, StL	3	Taylor, TB	2
Bruske, Mil	2	House, Col	2	Osuna, LA	4	Telford, Mon	11
Buehrle, CWS	3	Howry, CWS	14	Padilla, Ari-Phi	15	Timlin, Bal-StL	6
Byrdak, KC	3	Jacquez, Phi	2	Painter, Tor	5	Tomko, Sea	3
Cabrera, Hou	5	James, StL	12	Paniagua, Sea	14	Trombley, Bal	18
Cairncross, Cle	3	Jimenez, Col	2	Patterson, Det	12	Valdes M, Hou	8
Carrasco, Min-Bos	8	Johnson J, Bal	2	Perez Y, Hou	3	Van Poppel, ChC	7
Choate, NYY	2	Johnstone, SF	6	Petkovsek, Ana	16	Venafro, Tex	17
Chouinard, Col	3	Jones D, Oak	7	Pichardo, Bos	4	Vosberg, Phi	11
Christiansen, 2Tm	22	Kamieniecki, 2Tm	10	Plesac, Ari	9	Wakefield, Bos	3
Cook, NYM	10	Karsay, Cle	11	Poole, Det-Mon	2	Walker K, SD	19
Cordero, Tex	4	Kim, Ari	5	Pote, Ana	2	Wall, SD	12
Cormier, Bos	9	King, Mil	5	Powell J, Hou	5	Wallace, Pit	3
Crabtree, Tex	11	Kline, Mon	12	Quantrill, Tor	13	Ward, Phi-Ana	4
Creek, TB	2	Leskanic, Mil	11	Rain, ChC	8	Weathers, Mil	14
Cruz, Det	2	Levine, Ana	5	Ramsay, Sea	5	Weaver E, Ana	2
Darensbourg, Fla	3	Lidle, TB	2	Reed S, Cle	9	Weber, SF-Ana	2
Davey, SD	2	Ligtenberg, Atl	12	Reichert, KC	4	Wells B, Min	11
Davis D, Tex	2	Lira, Mon	2	Remlinger, Atl	23	Wendell, NYM	16
de los Santos, Mil	9	Loiselle, Pit	7	Reyes A, Bal-LA	3	White G, Cin-Col	19
DeJean, Col	7	Looper, Fla	18	Reyes C, Phi-SD	2	White R, TB-NYM	4
DePaula, Cle	2	Lowe S, CWS	6	Reyes D, Cin	10	Whiteside, SD	6
Dipoto, Col	3	Luebbers, Cin	4	Rhodes, Sea	24	Wilkins, Pit	9
Embree, SF	9	Maddux M, Hou	2	Riedling, Cin	2	Williams B, 2Tm	2
Escobar, Tor	3	Magnante, Oak	14	Rincon, Cle	10	Williams M, Mil	2
Farnsworth, ChC	6	Mahay, Oak-Fla	2	Rivera L, Atl-Bal	2	Williamson, Cin	6
Fassero, Bos	5	Mahomes, NYM	3	Rocker, Atl	4	Worrell, Bal-ChC	12
Fetters, LA	11	Manzanillo, Pit	5	Rodriguez F, SF	30	Wunsch, CWS	25
Forster, Mon	4	Mathews, Oak	9	Rodriguez F, Sea	2	Yan, TB	3
Foulke, CWS	3	Matthews, StL	2	Ryan B, Bal	7	Zimmerman, Tex	21
Franco, NYM	20	Maurer, SD	2	Santiago, KC	5		

Who Knows How to Handle His Inheritance? (p. 161)

Inherited Runners Scoring Percentages—2000, Listed Alphabetically (minimum 23 IR)

Pitcher, Team	IR	SC	Pct	Pitcher, Team	IR	SC	Pct	Pitcher, Team	IR	SC	Pct
Acevedo, Mil	27	9	33.3	Holtz, Ana	59	10	16.9	Reed S, Cle	36	6	16.7
Adams, LA	27	6	22.2	Howry, CWS	38	15	39.5	Remlinger, Atl	38	12	31.6
Almanza, Fla	65	22	33.8	James, StL	32	10	31.3	Reyes D, Cin	53	16	30.2
Almanzar, SD	45	22	48.9	Jimenez, Col	26	10	38.5	Rhodes, Sea	55	15	27.3
Anderson M, Det	47	17	36.2	Johnson M, Mon	25	10	40.0	Rincon, Cle	25	1	4.0
Belinda, Col-Atl	38	15	39.5	Johnstone, SF	27	10	37.0	Rivera M, NYY	24	10	41.7
Benitez, NYM	26	13	50.0	Jones D, Oak	47	19	40.4	Rodriguez F, SF	50	20	40.0
Blair, Det	29	12	41.4	Jones T, Det	28	7	25.0	Ryan B, Bal	37	16	43.2
Bones, Fla	43	16	37.2	Kamieniecki, 2Tm	26	2	7.7	Santiago, KC	33	21	63.6
Borbon, Tor	41	20	48.8	Karsay, Cle	33	15	45.5	Sasaki, Sea	25	5	20.0
Brewington, Cle	30	11	36.7	Kim, Ari	27	4	14.8	Sauerbeck, Pit	49	15	30.6
Brock, Phi	26	4	15.4	Kline, Mon	40	17	42.5	Shuey, Cle	40	16	40.0
Buehrle, CWS	23	12	52.2	Leskanic, Mil	31	3	9.7	Simas, CWS	43	16	37.2
Carrasco, Min-Bos	51	24	47.1	Levine, Ana	31	5	16.1	Slocumb, StL-SD	43	14	32.6
Christiansen, 2Tm	37	8	21.6	Ligtenberg, Atl	39	9	23.1	Slusarski, Hou	46	22	47.8
Cook, NYM	49	12	24.5	Lira, Mon	48	18	37.5	Speier, Cle	38	12	31.6
Cordero, Tex	72	24	33.3	Looper, Fla	56	20	35.7	Spradlin, KC-ChC	32	8	25.0
Cormier, Bos	29	10	34.5	Lowe S, CWS	43	12	27.9	Springer R, Ari	39	16	41.0
Crabtree, Tex	56	22	39.3	Magnante, Oak	48	12	25.0	Stanton, NYY	41	9	22.0
Creek, TB	33	12	36.4	Mahomes, NYM	35	20	57.1	Strickland, Mon	28	11	39.3
Cruz, Det	27	14	51.9	Manzanillo, Pit	33	10	30.3	Sullivan, Cin	50	13	26.0
Darensbourg, Fla	44	7	15.9	Martin, Cle	24	5	20.8	Swindell, Ari	26	4	15.4
de los Santos, Mil	55	13	23.6	Mathews, Oak	35	9	25.7	Tam, Oak	62	16	25.8
Dotel, Hou	25	9	36.0	McElroy, Bal	29	9	31.0	Tavarez, Col	25	7	28.0
Embree, SF	41	16	39.0	Mecir, TB-Oak	46	11	23.9	Telford, Mon	34	8	23.5
Erdos, NYY-SD	25	10	40.0	Mesa, Sea	36	20	55.6	Trombley, Bal	45	15	33.3
Farnsworth, ChC	29	13	44.8	Miller T, Min	47	19	40.4	Valdes M, Hou	35	18	51.4
Forster, Mon	26	10	38.5	Morgan, Ari	38	16	42.1	Venafro, Tex	75	20	26.7
Foulke, CWS	23	4	17.4	Mulholland, Atl	30	10	33.3	Veres, StL	45	15	33.3
Franco, NYM	23	5	21.7	Myers M, Col	64	9	14.1	Walker K, SD	48	14	29.2
Frascatore, Tor	39	14	35.9	Nelson, NYY	47	11	23.4	Wall, SD	23	4	17.4
Fultz, SF	42	17	40.5	Nitkowski, Det	67	23	34.3	Wallace, Pit	23	8	34.8
Fyhrie, Ana	29	10	34.5	Padilla, Ari-Phi	33	10	30.3	Wasdin, Bos-Col	29	16	55.2
Garces, Bos	43	15	34.9	Painter, Tor	34	13	38.2	Weathers, Mil	44	11	25.0
Gomes, Phi	38	13	34.2	Paniagua, Sea	62	22	35.5	Wells B, Min	71	20	28.2
Graves, Cin	47	17	36.2	Patterson, Det	44	15	34.1	Wendell, NYM	40	6	15.0
Grimsley, NYY	47	19	40.4	Perez Y, Hou	25	4	16.0	White G, Cin-Col	49	20	40.8
Groom, Bal	59	13	22.0	Petkovsek, Ana	43	15	34.9	White R, TB-NYM	44	8	18.2
Guardado, Min	49	14	28.6	Pichardo, Bos	31	10	32.3	Wilkins, Pit	34	11	32.4
Guthrie, 3Tm	61	23	37.7	Plesac, Ari	55	14	25.5	Williams B, 2Tm	28	16	57.1
Hasegawa, Ana	36	16	44.4	Poole, Det-Mon	25	15	60.0	Worrell, Bal-ChC	25	8	32.0
Hawkins, Min	33	6	18.2	Pote, Ana	23	10	43.5	Wunsch, CWS	70	17	24.3
Henry, Hou-SF	40	12	30.0	Quantrill, Tor	59	24	40.7	Zimmerman, Tex	66	17	25.8
Heredia F, ChC	62	17	27.4	Rain, ChC	25	9	36.0	**MLB Average**			**34.2**
Herges, LA	34	17	50.0	Ramsay, Sea	34	5	14.7				

Which Relievers Prevent the Most Runs? (p. 163)

Runs Prevented—2000, Listed Alphabetically
(minimum 50 IP and more relief appearances than starts)

Pitcher, Team	RP	Pitcher, Team	RP	Pitcher, Team	RP
Acevedo, Mil	9.6	Hernandez R, TB	7.9	Rhodes, Sea	16.9
Adams, LA	10.1	Hoffman, SD	13.4	Rivera M, NYY	15.1
Alfonseca, Fla	4.8	Howry, CWS	18.1	Rocker, Atl	5.6
Almanzar, SD	-1.4	Isringhausen, Oak	8.8	Rodriguez F, SF	14.0
Anderson M, Det	1.7	James, StL	11.0	Santana J, Mon	-0.6
Aybar, Col-Cin-Fla	11.0	Jimenez, Col	13.4	Santana J, Min	-2.7
Benitez, NYM	16.0	Johnson M, Mon	-2.0	Santiago, KC	-3.9
Blair, Det	8.2	Johnstone, SF	-9.5	Sasaki, Sea	14.0
Bones, Fla	7.0	Jones D, Oak	6.8	Sauerbeck, Pit	10.4
Bottalico, KC	7.8	Jones T, Det	10.8	Shaw, LA	7.4
Brantley, Phi	-9.4	Kamieniecki, Cle-Atl	-0.6	Shuey, Cle	9.6
Brocail, Det	6.9	Karsay, Cle	4.8	Silva, Pit	6.9
Brock, Phi	7.1	Kim, Ari	7.4	Simas, CWS	6.4
Buehrle, CWS	4.4	Kline, Mon	1.9	Slocumb, StL-SD	2.5
Cabrera, Hou	-8.0	Koch, Tor	17.4	Slusarski, Hou	4.8
Carrasco, Min-Bos	-6.6	Leskanic, Mil	24.3	Speier, Cle	5.9
Chen, Atl-Phi	9.6	Levine, Ana	19.3	Spradlin, KC-ChC	-3.1
Cook, NYM	-0.5	Lidle, TB	1.6	Springer R, Ari	-5.0
Cordero, Tex	-5.1	Ligtenberg, Atl	15.7	Stanton, NYY	9.8
Cormier, Bos	5.4	Lira, Mon	3.9	Sturtze, CWS-TB	-7.6
Crabtree, Tex	2.2	Looper, Fla	-1.6	Sullivan, Cin	25.6
Creek, TB	4.1	Lowe D, Bos	24.5	Swindell, Ari	14.9
Darensbourg, Fla	10.5	Lowe S, CWS	-2.0	Tam, Oak	27.2
Davis D, Tex	-1.9	Mahomes, NYM	-13.2	Tavarez, Col	0.4
de los Santos, Mil	6.3	Manzanillo, Pit	13.8	Telford, Mon	15.5
DeJean, Col	2.6	Mathews, Oak	-4.9	Timlin, Bal-StL	-0.6
Dessens, Cin	3.0	McElroy, Bal	-5.4	Tomko, Sea	3.0
Dotel, Hou	0.9	Mecir, TB-Oak	25.8	Trombley, Bal	6.0
Embree, SF	2.8	Mesa, Sea	-9.7	Valdes M, Hou	-11.1
Erdos, NYY-SD	-7.5	Miller T, Min	-0.5	Van Poppel, ChC	5.5
Farnsworth, ChC	-4.2	Morgan, Ari	5.2	Venafro, Tex	5.2
Fetters, LA	13.7	Morris M, StL	10.9	Veres, StL	16.5
Foulke, CWS	22.8	Mulholland, Atl	4.8	Wakefield, Bos	1.8
Franco, NYM	12.2	Nelson, NYY	21.1	Walker K, SD	6.9
Frascatore, Tor	-9.7	Nen, SF	28.2	Wall, SD	15.7
Fultz, SF	4.7	Nitkowski, Det	8.4	Wasdin, Bos-Col	-6.7
Fussell, KC	-3.6	Osuna, LA	8.4	Weathers, Mil	18.0
Fyhrie, Ana	13.1	Padilla, Ari-Phi	7.3	Wells B, Min	18.6
Garces, Bos	16.9	Painter, Tor	1.9	Wendell, NYM	23.2
Garibay, ChC	-3.8	Paniagua, Sea	10.4	Wetteland, Tex	0.2
Gomes, Phi	3.9	Patterson, Det	12.6	White G, Cin-Col	19.0
Graves, Cin	22.4	Percival, Ana	-1.0	White R, TB-NYM	20.4
Grimsley, NYY	-5.1	Perisho, Tex	-12.7	Wickman, Mil-Cle	12.7
Groom, Bal	5.1	Petkovsek, Ana	7.0	Wilkins, Pit	1.4
Guardado, Min	7.9	Pichardo, Bos	13.8	Williams M, Pit	8.3
Guthrie, ChC-TB-Tor	2.6	Pote, Ana	5.3	Williamson, Cin	8.1
Hasegawa, Ana	10.4	Quantrill, Tor	3.0	Worrell, Bal-ChC	11.5
Hawkins, Min	15.6	Ramsay, Sea	2.6	Wunsch, CWS	10.5
Henry, Hou-SF	10.8	Reed S, Cle	11.8	Yan, TB	4.0
Heredia F, ChC	0.9	Reichert, KC	2.4	Zimmerman, Tex	5.2
Herges, LA	23.0	Remlinger, Atl	10.7		

Which Catchers Catch Thieves? (p. 168)

The chart below lists the runners each catcher caught stealing (**CCS**), the stolen bases (**SB**) while he was behind the plate, the caught stealing percentage (**CS%**), the runners he picked off (**CPk**), the stolen bases allowed per 9 innings (**SB/9**), and the runners caught stealing (**PCS**) and picked off (**PPk**) by his pitchers.

Catcher Caught Stealing Percentages—2000, Listed Alphabetically (minimum 500 innings caught)

Catcher, Team	CCS	SB	CS%	CPk	SB/9	PCS	PPk
Alomar Jr., Cle	21	75	21.9	0	0.83	2	1
Ausmus, Det	32	42	43.2	1	0.31	6	3
Bako, Hou-Fla-Atl	14	41	25.5	1	0.63	7	1
Blanco, Mil	38	28	57.6	2	0.34	1	2
Casanova, Mil	9	39	18.8	1	0.67	2	0
Castillo A, Tor	16	25	39.0	3	0.45	1	0
Diaz, Cle	17	34	33.3	0	0.49	2	1
Estalella, SF	22	52	29.7	1	0.59	4	2
Eusebio, Hou	8	37	17.8	0	0.62	2	4
Flaherty, TB	27	79	25.5	1	0.78	2	1
Fletcher, Tor	20	73	21.5	0	0.72	1	5
Fordyce, CWS-Bal	11	55	16.7	0	0.68	5	2
Girardi, ChC	25	63	28.4	1	0.65	13	3
Gonzalez W, SD	23	45	33.8	2	0.60	2	1
Hernandez C, SD-StL	24	57	29.6	0	0.89	1	3
Hernandez R, Oak	19	68	21.8	1	0.58	8	3
Hundley, LA	19	76	20.0	0	0.98	5	3
Johnson C, Bal-CWS	20	54	27.0	0	0.46	4	2
Johnson M, CWS	19	38	33.3	0	0.57	9	4
Kendall, Pit	34	87	28.1	1	0.61	4	7
Kreuter, LA	14	21	40.0	0	0.32	5	3
Lieberthal, Phi	24	44	35.3	0	0.44	5	2
Lopez J, Atl	18	69	20.7	2	0.57	5	3
Matheny, StL	46	44	51.1	3	0.38	3	1
Mayne, Col	17	54	23.9	0	0.60	2	3
Meluskey, Hou	18	64	22.0	1	0.74	2	1
Miller, Ari	22	50	30.6	1	0.56	11	5
Mirabelli, SF	21	45	31.8	1	0.64	1	0
Molina, Ana	34	70	32.7	1	0.58	6	4
Piazza, NYM	16	110	12.7	0	0.96	16	7
Posada, NYY	30	70	30.0	1	0.53	4	5
Redmond, Fla	21	44	32.3	0	0.68	2	2
Reed, ChC	12	30	28.6	1	0.48	4	0
Rodriguez I, Tex	14	20	41.2	1	0.24	5	6
Santiago, Cin	12	19	38.7	0	0.28	2	1
Stinnett, Ari	19	52	26.8	0	0.77	4	5
Taubensee, Cin	12	50	19.4	0	0.76	2	5
Varitek, Bos	24	104	18.8	0	0.87	10	3
Widger, Mon-Sea	19	53	26.4	1	0.70	1	1
Wilson D, Sea	13	31	29.5	0	0.41	7	1
Zaun, KC	13	57	18.6	0	0.88	0	1
MLB Totals	**1,084**	**2,924**	**27.0**	**34**	**0.61**	**239**	**138**

Who's Best in the Infield Zone? (p. 170)

Infield Zone Ratings—2000, Listed Alphabetically
(minimum 1,000 innings played at position)

FIRST BASE

Player, Team	Innings	2000 In Zone	Outs	Zone Rating	1998-2000 In Zone	Outs	Zone Rating
Bagwell, Hou	1,362.0	290	242	.834	807	683	.846
Casey, Cin	1,079.0	226	196	.867	585	500	.855
Clark W, Bal-StL	1,011.0	216	188	.870	546	463	.848
Coomer, Min	1,064.2	201	164	.816	380	324	.853
Delgado C, Tor	1,429.1	271	228	.841	770	658	.855
Galarraga, Atl	1,078.0	165	131	.794	393	313	.796
Giambi J, Oak	1,064.1	220	194	.882	692	588	.850
Grace, ChC	1,216.1	227	201	.885	776	677	.872
Helton, Col	1,349.0	325	280	.862	910	769	.845
Karros, LA	1,331.2	299	250	.836	789	666	.844
Klesko, SD	1,126.0	233	196	.841	329	276	.839
Konerko, CWS	1,068.1	204	166	.814	385	320	.831
Lee D, Fla	1,133.0	202	174	.861	511	440	.861
Martinez T, NYY	1,290.2	235	209	.889	771	675	.875
McGriff, TB	1,255.1	215	167	.777	638	515	.807
Olerud, Sea	1,358.2	274	239	.872	832	731	.879
Snow, SF	1,273.1	208	171	.822	652	538	.825
Stevens, Mon	1,036.1	238	207	.870	508	441	.868
Vaughn M, Ana	1,265.1	217	168	.774	555	445	.802
Young K, Pit	1,071.1	205	167	.815	758	649	.856
Zeile, NYM	1,270.0	235	218	.928	235	218	.928
MLB Average				**.845**			**.845**

SECOND BASE

Player, Team	Innings	2000 In Zone	Outs	Zone Rating	1998-2000 In Zone	Outs	Zone Rating
Alfonzo, NYM	1,240.2	387	326	.842	829	704	.849
Alicea, Tex	1,048.2	355	295	.831	570	482	.846
Alomar, Cle	1,309.1	491	401	.817	1,488	1,244	.836
Bell J, Ari	1,243.2	384	305	.794	811	657	.810
Belliard, Mil	1,318.2	460	384	.835	814	674	.828
Boone B, SD	1,097.1	369	300	.813	1,339	1,079	.806
Castillo L, Fla	1,176.1	385	327	.849	871	734	.843
Durham, CWS	1,303.1	455	373	.820	1,398	1,123	.803
Easley, Det	1,069.2	467	372	.797	1,446	1,149	.795
Grudzielanek, LA	1,284.2	451	383	.849	451	383	.849
Kennedy, Ana	1,324.1	473	398	.841	547	458	.837
Kent, SF	1,258.0	447	356	.796	1,234	1,015	.823
Lansing, Col-Bos	1,098.2	374	308	.824	947	781	.825
McLemore, Sea	1,091.1	358	301	.841	1,198	996	.831
Morandini, Phi-Tor	1,002.2	308	261	.847	1,098	921	.839
Morris W, Pit	1,166.2	483	388	.803	946	773	.817
Reese, Cin	1,129.0	405	354	.874	825	733	.888
Velarde, Oak	1,032.0	438	361	.824	1,118	937	.838
Vidro, Mon	1,300.2	487	397	.815	966	775	.802
Vina, StL	1,009.0	338	298	.882	948	792	.835
Young E, ChC	1,284.2	444	377	.849	1,154	975	.845
MLB Average				**.823**			**.823**

THIRD BASE

Player, Team	Innings	2000 In Zone	Outs	Zone Rating	1998-2000 In Zone	Outs	Zone Rating
Batista, Tor	1,367.0	434	338	.779	472	367	.778
Beltre, LA	1,200.1	368	296	.804	912	721	.791
Brosius, NYY	1,150.1	331	255	.770	1,053	825	.783
Chavez E, Oak	1,206.1	377	276	.732	616	463	.752
Cirillo, Col	1,321.0	425	318	.748	1,307	1,003	.767
Fryman, Cle	1,346.1	389	284	.730	921	680	.738
Glaus, Ana	1,373.0	469	359	.765	990	742	.749
Jones C, Atl	1,311.1	416	319	.767	1,154	871	.755
Koskie, Min	1,164.1	339	265	.782	554	434	.783
Lamb M, Tex	1,137.0	358	253	.707	358	253	.707
Lowell, Fla	1,191.1	354	267	.754	571	428	.750
Mueller, SF	1,155.1	332	263	.792	974	763	.783
Nevin, SD	1,212.2	334	259	.775	511	398	.779
Randa, KC	1,361.1	405	307	.758	1,173	864	.737
Rolen, Phi	1,080.0	324	265	.818	1,049	852	.812
Ventura, NYM	1,110.2	373	290	.777	1,224	977	.798
MLB Average				**.751**			**.748**

SHORTSTOP

Player, Team	Innings	2000 In Zone	Outs	Zone Rating	1998-2000 In Zone	Outs	Zone Rating
Aurilia, SF	1,193.0	442	368	.833	1,254	1,047	.835
Bordick, Bal-NYM	1,324.1	458	392	.856	1,475	1,277	.866
Clayton, Tex	1,237.0	445	382	.858	1,407	1,201	.854
Cruz D, Det	1,355.1	525	436	.830	1,528	1,288	.843
Garciaparra, Bos	1,185.0	455	392	.862	1,356	1,137	.838
Gonzalez A, Tor	1,225.1	460	380	.826	1,061	890	.839
Gutierrez, ChC	1,018.1	328	280	.854	1,036	871	.841
Guzman, Min	1,307.0	485	391	.806	920	731	.795
Jeter, NYY	1,278.2	403	327	.811	1,266	1,055	.833
Meares, Pit	1,075.0	448	366	.817	1,013	830	.819
Perez N, Col	1,402.2	572	484	.846	1,635	1,387	.848
Relaford, Phi-SD	1,080.1	375	296	.789	983	803	.817
Renteria, StL	1,258.0	436	367	.842	1,310	1,090	.832
Rodriguez A, Sea	1,285.0	450	402	.893	1,360	1,179	.867
Sanchez, KC	1,198.0	476	418	.878	1,161	1,031	.888
Tejada, Oak	1,400.1	548	475	.867	1,455	1,214	.834
Valentin J, CWS	1,212.1	485	411	.847	1,193	989	.829
Vizquel, Cle	1,328.2	456	382	.838	1,386	1,193	.861
Womack, Ari	1,244.0	430	358	.833	478	398	.833
MLB Average				**.841**			**.840**

Who Can Turn the Pivot? (p. 174)

Pivot Percentages, Active Players—1996-2000, Listed Alphabetically (minimum 15 Opp)

Player	DP	Opp	Pct	Player	DP	Opp	Pct
Abbott K	37	79	.468	Knoblauch	217	389	.558
Alexander	22	39	.564	Lansing	217	375	.579
Alfonzo	135	205	.659	Ledesma	15	29	.517
Alicea	160	276	.580	Lewis M	100	195	.513
Alomar	239	423	.565	Lockhart	90	135	.667
Anderson M	46	83	.554	Lopez L	24	44	.545
Batista	32	49	.653	Loretta	43	65	.662
Baughman	13	27	.481	Lugo	17	26	.654
Bell D	128	215	.595	Macias	8	16	.500
Bell J	100	180	.556	Martinez R	25	29	.862
Bellhorn	9	15	.600	McEwing	31	55	.564
Belliard	113	180	.628	McLemore	248	411	.603
Benjamin	40	63	.635	Menechino	17	29	.586
Berg	19	27	.704	Merloni	9	18	.500
Biggio	262	479	.547	Morandini	217	376	.577
Boone B	230	389	.591	Mordecai	16	25	.640
Branson	29	50	.580	Morris W	95	177	.537
Bush	86	145	.593	Offerman	160	296	.541
Cairo	161	257	.626	Perez N	29	41	.707
Canizaro	33	51	.647	Perez T	36	50	.720
Castillo L	149	233	.639	Polanco	32	60	.533
Castro J	26	39	.667	Randa	10	22	.455
Catalanotto	24	48	.500	Reboulet	42	68	.618
Cordero	13	25	.520	Reese	101	152	.664
Counsell	68	103	.660	Sadler	11	19	.579
Delgado W	10	23	.435	Sanchez	31	46	.674
DeShields	170	316	.538	Santangelo	4	17	.235
Durham	305	484	.630	Sexton	7	17	.412
Durrington	14	22	.636	Sheets	6	20	.300
Easley	238	344	.692	Shumpert	28	47	.596
Febles	89	137	.650	Smith B	18	28	.643
Fox	30	56	.536	Sojo	49	80	.613
Frye	98	173	.566	Spiers	12	21	.571
Furcal	13	16	.813	Spiezio	103	171	.602
Graffanino	54	90	.600	Stynes	16	31	.516
Grebeck	63	109	.578	Valentin J	40	65	.615
Grudzielanek	54	80	.675	Velandia	11	18	.611
Guerrero W	46	97	.474	Velarde	172	269	.639
Hairston Jr.	48	79	.608	Veras Q	183	320	.572
Harris	14	28	.500	Vidro	105	170	.618
Hocking	30	47	.638	Vina	236	324	.728
Huson	23	37	.622	Vizcaino	77	113	.681
Jackson	14	30	.467	Walker T	93	168	.554
Johnson R	10	24	.417	Wilson E	8	19	.421
Jordan K	33	59	.559	Womack	113	222	.509
Kennedy	60	106	.566	Young E	204	363	.562
Kent	205	341	.601	**MLB Average**			**.591**

Which Outfielders Know How to Hold 'Em? (p. 176)

Outfield Advance Percentages—2000, Listed Alphabetically
(minimum 30 baserunner opportunities to advance)

Right Field				Center Field				Left Field			
Player, Team	Opp	XB	Pct	Player, Team	Opp	XB	Pct	Player, Team	Opp	XB	Pct
Abreu, Phi	109	45	41.3	Abbott J, CWS	35	24	68.6	Agbayani, NYM	84	28	33.3
Alou, Hou	50	25	50.0	Anderson B, Bal	86	48	55.8	Alou, Hou	65	27	41.5
Bautista, Fla-Ari	62	32	51.6	Anderson G, Ana	175	84	48.0	Bergeron, Mon	30	5	16.7
Becker, Oak-Det	32	20	62.5	Becker, Oak-Det	44	19	43.2	Berkman, Hou	36	6	16.7
Bell D, NYM	95	47	49.5	Beltran, KC	95	51	53.7	Bonds, SF	107	24	22.4
Belle, Bal	128	56	43.8	Benard, SF	138	66	47.8	Bonilla, Atl	50	20	40.0
Berkman, Hou	84	37	44.0	Bergeron, Mon	147	84	57.1	Burrell, Phi	46	14	30.4
Bichette, Cin-Bos	92	42	45.7	Bradley, Mon	54	27	50.0	Cordero, Pit-Cle	138	49	35.5
Buhner, Sea	93	43	46.2	Brown A, Pit	85	39	45.9	Curtis, Tex	58	17	29.3
Burks, SF	95	59	62.1	Buford, ChC	155	89	57.4	Damon, KC	60	21	35.0
Burnitz, Mil	157	83	52.9	Cabrera J, Cle	30	19	63.3	DeShields, Bal	30	8	26.7
Darr, SD	34	11	32.4	Cameron, Sea	175	97	55.4	Erstad, Ana	88	23	26.1
Davis E, StL	50	23	46.0	Cedeno, Hou	39	16	41.0	Floyd, Fla	107	30	28.0
Drew, StL	54	20	37.0	Cruz J, Tor	223	115	51.6	Gant, Phi-Ana	93	26	28.0
Dye, KC	138	62	44.9	Damon, KC	89	45	50.6	Giles, Pit	49	15	30.6
Giambi J, Oak	57	32	56.1	Edmonds, StL	124	64	51.6	Gonzalez L, Ari	126	37	29.4
Giles, Pit	48	22	45.8	Encarnacion, Det	158	87	55.1	Greer, Tex	130	46	35.4
Gonzalez J, Det	53	23	43.4	Erstad, Ana	34	17	50.0	Grieve, Oak	147	54	36.7
Green S, LA	140	71	50.7	Everett, Bos	140	72	51.4	Guerrero W, Mon	40	13	32.5
Guerrero V, Mon	149	60	40.3	Finley, Ari	151	77	51.0	Hammonds, Col	33	14	42.4
Guillen J, TB	69	26	37.7	Giles, Pit	113	60	53.1	Henderson, 2Tm	103	33	32.0
Hammonds, Col	67	38	56.7	Glanville, Phi	153	88	57.5	Higginson, Det	162	50	30.9
Javier, Sea	39	18	46.2	Goodwin, Col-LA	156	81	51.9	Hill, ChC-NYY	46	22	47.8
Jordan B, Atl	97	48	49.5	Green S, Tex	37	20	54.1	Javier, Sea	35	11	31.4
Justice, Cle-NYY	36	18	50.0	Griffey Jr., Cin	143	80	55.9	Jenkins, Mil	116	40	34.5
Kapler, Tex	31	15	48.4	Grissom, Mil	199	113	56.8	Jones J, Min	86	23	26.7
Kotsay, Fla	114	56	49.1	Hidalgo, Hou	110	55	50.0	Jones T, Mon	40	8	20.0
Lawton, Min	72	34	47.2	Holl'dsw'rth, 2Tm	58	31	53.4	Justice, Cle-NYY	61	19	31.1
Ledee, 3Tm	56	23	41.1	Hunter B, 2Tm	38	16	42.1	Lankford, StL	101	28	27.7
Magee, Det	35	19	54.3	Hunter T, Min	134	76	56.7	Lawton, Min	63	19	30.2
Martinez D, 4Tm	104	59	56.7	Jones A, Atl	162	77	47.5	Ledee, 3Tm	84	24	28.6
McDonald J, Tex	33	10	30.3	Jones J, Min	60	29	48.3	Lee C, CWS	157	55	35.0
Mondesi, Tor	93	28	30.1	Kapler, Tex	118	64	54.2	Martin, SD-Sea	100	38	38.0
Nixon, Bos	78	36	46.2	Lewis D, Bos	31	14	45.2	O'Leary, Bos	118	33	28.0
O'Neill, NYY	109	47	43.1	Lofton, Cle	163	88	54.0	Owens, SD	35	10	28.6
OrdonezM, CWS	127	61	48.0	Long, Oak	180	96	53.3	Quinn, KC	86	22	25.6
Owens, SD	65	25	38.5	Mateo, Tex	76	41	53.9	Rodrig'z H, 2Tm	79	30	38.0
Ramirez A, 2Tm	50	30	60.0	Matos, Bal	43	22	51.2	Sanders R, Atl	65	18	27.7
Ramirez M, Cle	72	33	45.8	Murray, SF	63	37	58.7	Sexson, Cle-Mil	57	21	36.8
Rios, SF	50	28	56.0	Payton, NYM	139	66	47.5	Sheffield, LA	95	30	31.6
Salmon, Ana	128	62	48.4	Pierre, Col	68	40	58.8	Spencer, NYY	35	6	17.1
Sosa, ChC	138	81	58.7	Rivera, SD	148	79	53.4	Stewart, Tor	169	53	31.4
Stairs, Oak	97	59	60.8	Singleton, CWS	168	87	51.8	Surhoff, Bal-Atl	124	31	25.0
Vander Wal, Pit	63	29	46.0	White D, LA	47	27	57.4	Vaughn G, TB	69	15	21.7
Walker L, Col	54	22	40.7	Williams B, NYY	157	87	55.4	Ward D, Hou	36	10	27.8
MLB Average			47.3	Williams G, TB	186	108	58.1	White R, 2Tm	93	36	38.7
				Wilson P, Fla	190	106	55.8	Young D, Cin	64	25	39.1
				MLB Average			53.6	MLB Average			31.2

Who's Best in the Outfield Zone? (p. 179)

Outfield Zone Ratings—2000, Listed Alphabetically
(minimum 1,000 innings played at position)

LEFT FIELD

Player, Team	Innings	2000 In Zone	Outs	Zone Rating	1998-2000 In Zone	Outs	Zone Rating
Bonds, SF	1,151.2	278	250	.899	847	730	.862
Cordero, Pit-Cle	1,062.0	207	181	.874	273	237	.868
Gonzalez L, Ari	1,430.2	316	285	.902	886	793	.895
Grieve, Oak	1,160.1	270	230	.852	538	452	.840
Higginson, Det	1,256.1	333	300	.901	361	327	.906
Jenkins, Mil	1,126.1	265	251	.947	662	617	.932
Lee C, CWS	1,272.2	322	264	.820	561	467	.832
O'Leary, Bos	1,182.2	265	232	.875	986	834	.846
Sheffield, LA	1,133.0	231	204	.883	507	441	.870
Stewart, Tor	1,169.0	315	283	.898	822	734	.893
Surhoff, Bal-Atl	1,152.1	305	268	.879	916	804	.878
MLB Average				**.875**			**.874**

CENTER FIELD

Player, Team	Innings	2000 In Zone	Outs	Zone Rating	1998-2000 In Zone	Outs	Zone Rating
Anderson G, Ana	1,203.0	388	341	.879	780	682	.874
Buford, ChC	1,128.0	338	302	.893	689	617	.896
Cameron, Sea	1,263.2	428	382	.893	1,184	1,070	.904
Cruz J, Tor	1,423.1	442	391	.885	999	884	.885
Edmonds, StL	1,210.2	385	343	.891	959	852	.888
Encarnacion, Det	1,212.2	403	363	.901	477	422	.885
Everett, Bos	1,063.2	311	274	.881	904	803	.888
Finley, Ari	1,283.2	377	330	.875	1,214	1,078	.888
Glanville, Phi	1,275.1	425	369	.868	1,276	1,118	.876
Goodwin, Col-LA	1,092.0	359	317	.883	1,080	947	.877
Griffey Jr., Cin	1,227.1	391	362	.926	1,308	1,157	.885
Grissom, Mil	1,258.2	381	337	.885	1,192	1,034	.867
Hidalgo, Hou	1,008.2	361	324	.898	548	495	.903
Jones A, Atl	1,430.1	471	416	.883	1,467	1,323	.902
Lofton, Cle	1,152.0	365	339	.929	1,035	937	.905
Long, Oak	1,166.1	350	321	.917	350	321	.917
Payton, NYM	1,097.0	353	304	.861	354	305	.862
Rivera, SD	1,036.2	315	291	.924	687	628	.914
Singleton, CWS	1,157.2	394	347	.881	792	702	.886
Williams B, NYY	1,170.0	397	348	.877	1,179	1,033	.876
Williams G, TB	1,216.2	393	338	.860	421	362	.860
Wilson P, Fla	1,362.2	434	375	.864	759	655	.863
MLB Average				**.888**			**.884**

RIGHT FIELD

Player, Team	Innings	2000 In Zone	Outs	Zone Rating	1998-2000 In Zone	Outs	Zone Rating
Abreu, Phi	1,330.2	366	333	.910	969	868	.896
Bell D, NYM	1,168.0	268	238	.888	807	716	.887
Burnitz, Mil	1,386.0	335	307	.916	969	880	.908
Dye, KC	1,260.1	293	269	.918	862	787	.913
Green S, LA	1,425.0	308	276	.896	970	852	.878
Guerrero V, Mon	1,268.2	319	294	.922	1,066	953	.894
Jordan B, Atl	1,108.0	304	282	.928	877	804	.917
Kotsay, Fla	1,052.1	270	246	.911	784	707	.902
O'Neill, NYY	1,153.1	319	285	.893	964	873	.906
Ordonez M, CWS	1,322.2	313	273	.872	985	883	.896
Salmon, Ana	1,069.2	296	267	.902	584	516	.884
Sosa, ChC	1,373.1	334	303	.907	1,076	948	.881
MLB Average				**.894**			**.882**

Which Fielders Have the Best Defensive Batting Averages? (p. 182)

The MLB average in each category at each position is .280.

Defensive Batting Averages—2000, Listed Alphabetically
(minimum 500 innings played at position)

First Base	ZR	FP	PR	OA	Rtng
Bagwell, Hou	.268	.283	—	—	.272
Burrell, Phi	.271	.224	—	—	.259
Casey, Cin	.296	.295	—	—	.296
Clark W, StL	.299	.260	—	—	.289
Colbrunn, Ari	.245	.235	—	—	.242
Coomer, Min	.253	.302	—	—	.265
Daubach, Bos	.302	.305	—	—	.303
Delgado C, Tor	.274	.262	—	—	.271
Galarraga, Atl	.234	.229	—	—	.232
Giambi J, Oak	.309	.299	—	—	.306
Grace, ChC	.312	.315	—	—	.313
Helton, Col	.292	.301	—	—	.294
Karros, LA	.270	.300	—	—	.277
Klesko, SD	.274	.268	—	—	.273
Konerko, CWS	.251	.259	—	—	.253
Lee D, Fla	.291	.282	—	—	.289
Lee T, Phi	.310	.308	—	—	.309
Martinez T, NYY	.315	.292	—	—	.310
McGriff, TB	.219	.276	—	—	.233
McGwire, StL	.348	.331	—	—	.343
Olerud, Sea	.301	.313	—	—	.304
Palmeiro R, Tex	.261	.303	—	—	.272
Segui, Cle	.266	.349	—	—	.287
Sexson, Mil	.310	.270	—	—	.300
Snow, SF	.258	.302	—	—	.269
Stevens, Mon	.299	.253	—	—	.287
Sweeney M, KC	.269	.263	—	—	.267
Thome, Cle	.277	.294	—	—	.281
Vaughn M, Ana	.217	.243	—	—	.223
Young K, Pit	.251	.204	—	—	.239
Zeile, NYM	.348	.271	—	—	.329
Second Base	**ZR**	**FP**	**PR**	**OA**	**Rtng**
Alfonzo, NYM	.301	.300	.273	—	.294
Alicea, Tex	.291	.262	.269	—	.281
Alomar, Cle	.278	.273	.247	—	.270
Bell J, Ari	.258	.310	.286	—	.273
Belliard, Mil	.294	.255	.285	—	.286
Biggio, Hou	.286	.309	.283	—	.289
Boone B, SD	.275	.258	.259	—	.268
Bush, Tor	.321	.301	.319	—	.318
Cairo, TB	.250	.285	.294	—	.267
Canizaro, Min	.201	.282	.296	—	.237
Castillo L, Fla	.307	.290	.321	—	.308
DeShields, Bal	.257	.249	.206	—	.243
Durham, CWS	.281	.272	.296	—	.283
Easley, Det	.260	.323	.333	—	.288
Febles, KC	.284	.266	.341	—	.296
Frye, Col	.330	.324	.249	—	.309
Grudzielanek, LA	.307	.257	.302	—	.298
Kennedy, Ana	.300	.253	.261	—	.283
Kent, SF	.260	.302	.286	—	.273
Knoblauch, NYY	.236	.167	.235	—	.225

	ZR	FP	PR	OA	Rtng
Lansing, Bos	.284	.313	.248	—	.279
Lockhart, Atl	.257	.270	.258	—	.259
McLemore, Sea	.299	.308	.279	—	.295
Morandini, Tor	.305	.316	.269	—	.298
Morris W, Pit	.266	.270	.230	—	.258
Offerman, Bos	.230	.277	.270	—	.247
Reese, Cin	.329	.274	.320	—	.318
Velarde, Oak	.285	.282	.313	—	.291
Veras Q, Atl	.294	.293	.271	—	.288
Vidro, Mon	.277	.303	.306	—	.288
Vina, StL	.335	.314	.334	—	.332
Walker T, Col	.208	.215	.252	—	.220
Young E, ChC	.307	.272	.257	—	.289
Third Base	**ZR**	**FP**	**PR**	**OA**	**Rtng**
Batista, Tor	.297	.298	—	—	.298
Bell D, Sea	.285	.267	—	—	.278
Beltre, LA	.319	.268	—	—	.299
Boone A, Cin	.289	.301	—	—	.294
Brosius, NYY	.290	.307	—	—	.297
Castilla, TB	.329	.305	—	—	.319
Chavez E, Oak	.257	.279	—	—	.266
Cirillo, Col	.271	.299	—	—	.282
Fryman, Cle	.255	.323	—	—	.282
Glaus, Ana	.286	.250	—	—	.271
Greene W, ChC	.303	.305	—	—	.304
Guillen C, Sea	.265	.214	—	—	.244
Hernandez J, Mil	.274	.277	—	—	.275
Jones C, Atl	.287	.268	—	—	.279
Koskie, Min	.300	.303	—	—	.301
Lamb M, Tex	.235	.218	—	—	.228
Lowell, Fla	.276	.307	—	—	.288
Mueller, SF	.309	.317	—	—	.312
Nevin, SD	.294	.243	—	—	.274
Palmer, Det	.200	.220	—	—	.208
Paquette, StL	.281	.264	—	—	.274
Perry H, CWS	.293	.306	—	—	.298
Ramirez A, Pit	.205	.224	—	—	.212
Randa, KC	.279	.289	—	—	.283
Ripken Jr., Bal	.292	.317	—	—	.302
Rolen, Phi	.331	.312	—	—	.323
Stynes, Cin	.309	.304	—	—	.307
Tatis, StL	.218	.283	—	—	.244
Truby, Hou	.256	.239	—	—	.249
Ventura, NYM	.296	.285	—	—	.292
Williams M, Ari	.310	.300	—	—	.306
Shortstop	**ZR**	**FP**	**PR**	**OA**	**Rtng**
Aurilia, SF	.269	.275	—	—	.270
Bogar, Hou	.301	.282	—	—	.297
Bordick, NYM	.298	.294	—	—	.297
Cabrera O, Mon	.279	.306	—	—	.284
Clayton, Tex	.301	.297	—	—	.300
Cora, LA	.353	.285	—	—	.340
Cruz D, Det	.267	.309	—	—	.275

Baseball Scoreboard

Name	ZR	FP	PR	OA	Rtng
Furcal, Atl	.282	.234	—	—	.273
Garciaparra, Bos	.305	.284	—	—	.301
Gil, Ana	.275	.251	—	—	.270
Gonzalez A, Fla	.230	.252	—	—	.234
Gonzalez A, Tor	.261	.293	—	—	.268
Gutierrez, ChC	.295	.318	—	—	.300
Guzman, Min	.237	.274	—	—	.244
Jackson, SD	.284	.246	—	—	.276
Jeter, NYY	.243	.259	—	—	.246
Larkin, Cin	.285	.289	—	—	.286
Loretta, Mil	.287	.340	—	—	.297
Martinez F, TB	.333	.295	—	—	.325
Meares, Pit	.250	.275	—	—	.255
Mora, Bal	.245	.245	—	—	.245
Perez N, Col	.286	.301	—	—	.289
Relaford, SD	.216	.217	—	—	.216
Renteria, StL	.281	.252	—	—	.275
Rodriguez A, Sea	.344	.318	—	—	.339
Sanchez, KC	.325	.338	—	—	.328
Stocker, Ana	.245	.264	—	—	.249
Tejada, Oak	.311	.286	—	—	.306
Valentin J, CWS	.287	.235	—	—	.277
Vizquel, Cle	.276	.341	—	—	.289
Weiss, Atl	.249	.233	—	—	.246
Womack, Ari	.269	.281	—	—	.272
Left Field	**ZR**	**FP**	**PR**	**OA**	**Rtng**
Agbayani, NYM	.269	.276	—	.265	.269
Bonds, SF	.302	.300	—	.340	.309
Cordero, Cle	.280	.303	—	.250	.277
Damon, KC	.297	.278	—	.261	.287
Erstad, Ana	.349	.302	—	.318	.336
Floyd, Fla	.190	.201	—	.306	.215
Gant, Ana	.296	.249	—	.298	.289
Gonzalez L, Ari	.304	.303	—	.299	.303
Greer, Tex	.251	.290	—	.251	.257
Grieve, Oak	.260	.298	—	.237	.261
Henderson, Sea	.277	.271	—	.276	.276
Higginson, Det	.303	.275	—	.278	.294
Jenkins, Mil	.344	.264	—	.265	.316
Jones J, Min	.297	.301	—	.311	.300
Justice, NYY	.291	.288	—	.280	.288
Lankford, StL	.323	.259	—	.295	.308
Lawton, Min	.229	.306	—	.280	.251
Ledee, Tex	.266	.274	—	.288	.271
Lee C, CWS	.232	.302	—	.256	.247
Martin, Sea	.280	.204	—	.229	.258
O'Leary, Bos	.281	.299	—	.293	.286
Quinn, KC	.281	.313	—	.319	.294
Rodriguez H, Fla	.252	.293	—	.237	.256
Sanders R, Atl	.263	.236	—	.305	.267
Sheffield, LA	.288	.209	—	.281	.275
Stewart, Tor	.301	.312	—	.269	.296
Surhoff, Atl	.284	.302	—	.323	.294
Vaughn G, TB	.287	.312	—	.342	.302
White R, ChC	.283	.317	—	.232	.278
Young D, Cin	.250	.271	—	.226	.249
Center Field	**ZR**	**FP**	**PR**	**OA**	**Rtng**
Anderson B, Bal	.271	.320	—	.257	.274
Anderson G, Ana	.266	.303	—	.317	.287
Beltran, KC	.314	.226	—	.287	.292
Benard, SF	.213	.323	—	.318	.261
Bergeron, Mon	.297	.261	—	.247	.276
Brown A, Pit	.221	.245	—	.360	.266
Buford, ChC	.288	.284	—	.235	.271
Cameron, Sea	.286	.275	—	.262	.277
Cruz J, Tor	.274	.307	—	.277	.280
Damon, KC	.327	.294	—	.312	.318
Edmonds, StL	.284	.291	—	.274	.282
Encarnacion, Det	.298	.280	—	.268	.286
Everett, Bos	.269	.251	—	.304	.277
Finley, Ari	.261	.302	—	.298	.278
Giles, Pit	.293	.243	—	.273	.280
Glanville, Phi	.250	.295	—	.238	.253
Goodwin, LA	.272	.300	—	.279	.278
Griffey Jr., Cin	.336	.283	—	.253	.303
Grissom, Mil	.274	.302	—	.240	.268
Hidalgo, Hou	.294	.276	—	.306	.294
Hollandsworth, Col	.304	.282	—	.285	.295
Hunter T, Min	.301	.293	—	.249	.284
Jones A, Atl	.272	.319	—	.333	.297
Kapler, Tex	.259	.191	—	.277	.254
Lofton, Cle	.340	.290	—	.276	.313
Long, Oak	.323	.212	—	.281	.294
Payton, NYM	.239	.258	—	.344	.274
Rivera, SD	.333	.271	—	.284	.309
Singleton, CWS	.269	.303	—	.292	.281
Williams B, NYY	.262	.338	—	.268	.275
Williams G, TB	.238	.267	—	.223	.238
Wilson P, Fla	.244	.285	—	.253	.253
Right Field	**ZR**	**FP**	**PR**	**OA**	**Rtng**
Abreu, Phi	.297	.299	—	.308	.301
Alou, Hou	.222	.305	—	.265	.249
Bautista, Ari	.245	.292	—	.264	.259
Bell D, NYM	.277	.297	—	.269	.277
Belle, Bal	.203	.293	—	.290	.247
Berkman, Hou	.263	.181	—	.295	.262
Bichette, Bos	.259	.241	—	.291	.268
Buhner, Sea	.231	.332	—	.285	.265
Burks, SF	.306	.280	—	.215	.270
Burnitz, Mil	.303	.272	—	.252	.280
Drew, StL	.337	.255	—	.320	.319
Dye, KC	.304	.263	—	.294	.295
Gonzalez J, Det	.301	.308	—	.290	.298
Green S, LA	.284	.273	—	.273	.279
Guerrero V, Mon	.307	.242	—	.308	.298
Guillen J, TB	.296	.267	—	.325	.302
Hammonds, Col	.289	.312	—	.235	.273
Jordan B, Atl	.313	.303	—	.272	.297
Kotsay, Fla	.298	.301	—	.269	.288
Lawton, Min	.230	.280	—	.287	.257
Martinez D, Tor	.320	.308	—	.237	.289
Mondesi, Tor	.293	.238	—	.369	.311
Nixon, Bos	.316	.304	—	.286	.304
O'Neill, NYY	.282	.312	—	.303	.294
Ordonez M, CWS	.263	.283	—	.280	.272
Owens, SD	.298	.332	—	.313	.309
Ramirez M, Cle	.241	.291	—	.284	.263
Salmon, Ana	.290	.273	—	.270	.280
Sosa, ChC	.294	.244	—	.227	.263
Stairs, Oak	.287	.272	—	.225	.263
Vander Wal, Pit	.239	.236	—	.288	.256

Is It Easier to Win in a Pitchers' Park? (p. 192)

Park Indexes (Runs Scored) For First-Place Teams—1961-2000

Year	Team	Lg	Park	Year	Team	Lg	Park	Year	Team	Lg	Park
1961	NYY	AL	86	1978	NYY	AL	94	1991	Atl	NL	129
1961	Cin	NL	106	1978	LA	NL	95	1991	Pit	NL	92
1962	NYY	AL	84	1978	Phi	NL	109	1992	Oak	AL	95
1962	SF	NL	100	1979	Bal	AL	89	1992	Tor	AL	98
1963	NYY	AL	96	1979	Cal	AL	84	1992	Atl	NL	102
1963	LA	NL	85	1979	Cin	NL	93	1992	Pit	NL	99
1964	NYY	AL	102	1979	Pit	NL	110	1993	CWS	AL	99
1964	StL	NL	127	1980	KC	AL	95	1993	Tor	AL	109
1965	Min	AL	100	1980	NYY	AL	96	1993	Atl	NL	98
1965	LA	NL	76	1980	Hou	NL	92	1993	Phi	NL	101
1966	Bal	AL	100	1980	Phi	NL	115	1994	CWS	AL	90
1966	LA	NL	86	1981	Mil	AL	91	1994	NYY	AL	83
1967	Bos	AL	133	1981	Oak	AL	89	1994	Tex	AL	89
1967	StL	NL	99	1981	Cin	NL	102	1994	Cin	NL	98
1968	Det	AL	110	1981	StL	NL	104	1994	LA	NL	78
1968	StL	NL	85	1982	Cal	AL	98	1994	Mon	NL	108
1969	Bal	AL	102	1982	Mil	AL	86	1995	Bos	AL	101
1969	Min	AL	102	1982	Atl	NL	116	1995	Cle	AL	87
1969	Atl	NL	106	1982	StL	NL	105	1995	Sea	AL	103
1969	NYM	NL	96	1983	Bal	AL	98	1995	Atl	NL	109
1970	Bal	AL	89	1983	CWS	AL	104	1995	Cin	NL	95
1970	Min	AL	93	1983	LA	NL	98	1995	LA	NL	81
1970	Cin	NL	106	1983	Phi	NL	100	1996	Cle	AL	105
1970	Pit	NL	91	1984	Det	AL	89	1996	NYY	AL	101
1971	Bal	AL	103	1984	KC	AL	97	1996	Tex	AL	114
1971	Oak	AL	98	1984	ChC	NL	121	1996	Atl	NL	107
1971	Pit	NL	96	1984	SD	NL	95	1996	SD	NL	91
1971	SF	NL	99	1985	KC	AL	101	1996	StL	NL	96
1972	Det	AL	127	1985	Tor	AL	97	1997	Bal	AL	98
1972	Oak	AL	89	1985	LA	NL	82	1997	Cle	AL	97
1972	Cin	NL	83	1985	StL	NL	87	1997	Sea	AL	102
1972	Pit	NL	102	1986	Bos	AL	97	1997	Atl	NL	98
1973	Bal	AL	111	1986	Cal	AL	90	1997	Hou	NL	87
1973	Oak	AL	70	1986	Hou	NL	101	1997	SF	NL	94
1973	Cin	NL	83	1986	NYM	NL	86	1998	Cle	AL	117
1973	NYM	NL	98	1987	Det	AL	92	1998	NYY	AL	94
1974	Bal	AL	82	1987	Min	AL	91	1998	Tex	AL	115
1974	Oak	AL	97	1987	SF	NL	89	1998	Atl	NL	100
1974	LA	NL	80	1987	StL	NL	95	1998	Hou	NL	97
1974	Pit	NL	94	1988	Bos	AL	119	1998	SD	NL	73
1975	Bos	AL	119	1988	Oak	AL	86	1999	Cle	AL	106
1975	Oak	AL	82	1988	LA	NL	110	1999	NYY	AL	82
1975	Cin	NL	105	1988	NYM	NL	75	1999	Tex	AL	108
1975	Pit	NL	95	1989	Oak	AL	103	1999	Ari	NL	94
1976	KC	AL	98	1989	Tor	AL	86	1999	Atl	NL	88
1976	NYY	AL	96	1989	ChC	NL	117	1999	Hou	NL	89
1976	Cin	NL	105	1989	SF	NL	92	2000	CWS	AL	111
1976	Phi	NL	112	1990	Bos	AL	109	2000	NYY	AL	107
1977	KC	AL	98	1990	Oak	AL	77	2000	Oak	AL	91
1977	NYY	AL	94	1990	Cin	NL	100	2000	Atl	NL	100
1977	LA	NL	95	1990	Pit	NL	93	2000	SF	NL	83
1977	Phi	NL	99	1991	Min	AL	109	2000	StL	NL	100
1978	KC	AL	103	1991	Tor	AL	117	Avg (1961-2000)			97

Which Teams Were 2000's Biggest Overachievers And Underachievers? (p. 197)

Pythagorean Winning Percentages—2000

Team	W-L	Pct	Pyth W	Pyth Pct	+/-
Blue Jays	83-79	.512	76.7	.473	6.3
Mets	94-68	.580	88.2	.545	5.8
Marlins	79-82	.491	73.6	.457	5.4
Orioles	74-88	.457	69.8	.431	4.2
Braves	95-67	.586	91.2	.563	3.8
Cardinals	95-67	.586	92.3	.570	2.7
Expos	67-95	.414	65.0	.401	2.0
White Sox	95-67	.586	93.3	.576	1.7
Padres	76-86	.469	74.5	.460	1.5
Angels	82-80	.506	80.5	.497	1.5
Rangers	71-91	.438	69.9	.431	1.1
Yankees	87-74	.540	85.9	.534	1.1
Twins	69-93	.426	68.0	.419	1.0
Brewers	73-89	.451	72.1	.445	0.9
Royals	77-85	.475	76.4	.472	0.6
Diamondbacks	85-77	.525	85.0	.525	0.0
Devil Rays	69-92	.429	69.4	.431	-0.4
Red Sox	85-77	.525	85.9	.531	-0.9
Giants	97-65	.599	98.1	.605	-1.1
Tigers	79-83	.488	80.6	.498	-1.6
Athletics	91-70	.565	92.7	.576	-1.7
Reds	85-77	.525	87.1	.538	-2.1
Mariners	91-71	.562	93.1	.575	-2.1
Dodgers	86-76	.531	88.3	.545	-2.3
Cubs	65-97	.401	67.5	.417	-2.5
Pirates	69-93	.426	71.9	.444	-2.9
Indians	90-72	.556	93.2	.575	-3.2
Phillies	65-97	.401	68.2	.421	-3.2
Rockies	82-80	.506	87.2	.538	-5.2
Astros	72-90	.444	80.5	.497	-8.5

Glossary

Batting Average (Avg)
Hits divided by At-Bats.

Career Assessments
Once known as the Favorite Toy, this method is used to estimate a player's chance of achieving a specific goal. In the following example, we'll say 3,000 hits. Four things are considered:

1. Need Hits, the number of hits needed to reach the goal. (Of course, this also could be Need Home Runs, Need Doubles, etc.)

2. Years Remaining. The number of years remaining to meet the goal is estimated by (42 minus Age) divided by two. This formula assigns a 20-year-old player 11.0 remaining seasons, a 25-year-old player 8.5 remaining seasons, a 30-year-old player 6.0 remaining seasons, and a 35-year-old player 3.5 remaining seasons. Catchers remaining seasons are multiplied by a factor of 0.7. Any active player is assumed to have at least half a season remaining, regardless of his age. Additionally, if a player is coming off a year with at least 100 hits *and* an offensive winning percentage of at least .500, he's assumed to have at least 1.5 remaining seasons. And if a player is coming off a year with at least 100 hits *or* an offensive winning percentage of at least .500, he's assumed to have at least 1.0 remaining seasons.

3. Established Hit Level. For 1999, the established hit level would be found by adding 1996 Hits, (1997 Hits multiplied by two) and (1998 Hits multiplied by three), then dividing by six. A player can't have an established performance level that is less than 75 percent of his most recent performance. In other words, a player who had 200 hits in 1998 can't have an established hit level less than 160.

4. Projected Remaining Hits. This is found by multiplying Years Remaining by the Established Hit Level.

Once you get the projected remaining hits, the chance of getting to the goal is figured by dividing Projected Remaining Hits by Need Hits, then subtracting .5. Thus if Need Hits and Projected Remaining Hits are the same, the chance of reaching the goal is 50 percent. A player's chance of continuing to progress toward a goal can't be more than .97 raised to the power of years required to reach the goal based on the player's established production level. This prevents a player from figuring to have a 148 percent chance of reaching a goal.

Component ERA (ERC)
A statistic that estimates what a pitcher's ERA should have been, based on his pitching performance. The steps in calculating an ERC are:

  1. Subtract Home Runs from Hits.
  2. Multiply step 1 by 1.255.
  3. Multiply Home Runs Allowed by 4.
  4. Add steps 2 and 3 together.
  5. Multiply step 4 by .89.
  6. Add Walks and Hit Batsmen.
  7. Multiply step 6 by .475.
  8. Add steps 5 and 7 together.

This yields the pitcher's total base estimate (PTB), which is:

$$(((H - HR) \times 1.255) + (HR \times 4)) \times .89) + ((BB + HB) \times .475)$$

If intentional walk data is available, adjust the formula as follows:

$$(((H - HR) \times 1.255) + (HR \times 4)) \times .89) + ((BB + HB - IBB) \times .56)$$

9. Add Hits and Walks and Hit Batsmen.
10. Multiply step 9 by PTB.
11. Divide step 10 by Batters Facing Pitcher. If BFP data is unavailable, approximate it by multiplying Innings Pitched by 2.9, then adding step 9.
12. Multiply step 11 by 9.
13. Divide step 12 by Innings Pitched.
14. Subtract .56 from step 13.

This is the pitcher's ERC, which is:

$$(((((H + BB + HB) \times PTB) / BFP) \times 9) / IP) - .56$$

If the result after step 13 is less than 2.24, adjust the formula as follows:

$$(((((H + BB + HB) \times PTB) / BFP) \times 9) / IP) \times .75$$

Defensive Batting Average (DBA)

A composite statistic incorporating the standard deviations of various defensive statistics to arrive at a number akin to batting average. The statistics used for each position are as follows:

Pos	Statistics
1B	Zone Rating (75%), Fielding Percentage (25%)
2B	Zone Rating (60%), Pivot Percentage (25%), Fielding Percentage (15%)
3B	Zone Rating (60%), Fielding Percentage (40%)
SS	Zone Rating (80%), Fielding Percentage (20%)
LF	Zone Rating (65%), Outfield Advance Percentage (20%), Fielding Percentage (15%)
CF	Zone Rating (55%), Outfield Advance Percentage (30%), Fielding Percentage (15%)
RF	Zone Rating (50%), Outfield Advance Percentage (35%), Fielding Percentage (15%)

Earned Run Average (ERA)

Earned Runs multiplied by nine, divided by Innings Pitched.

Fielding Percentage

(Putouts plus Assists) divided by (Putouts plus Assists plus Errors).

Game Score

A tool that quantifies how well a starting pitcher performed in a single game. To calculate, start with 50. Add one point for each out recorded, two points for each inning completed after the fourth and one point for each strikeout. Subtract one point for each walk, two points for each hit, four points for each earned run and two points for each unearned run. A score of 50 is about average. Anything above 90 is outstanding. Kerry Wood's 105 game score for his 20-strikeout one-hitter against the Astros in 1998 is the record for a nine-inning game.

Go-Ahead RBI (GARBI)

Any RBI which gives a player's team the lead.

Go-Ahead RBI Opportunities

The total of a player's Go-Ahead RBI and the number of times he made an out with the go-ahead run in scoring position (excluding sacrifice hits and sacrifice flies).

Holds

A Hold is credited any time a relief pitcher enters a game in a Save Situation (see definition, except for point 3c.), records at least one out and leaves the game never having relinquished the lead. Note: a pitcher can't finish the game and receive credit for a hold, nor can he earn a hold and a save in the same game.

Inherited Runner (IR)

Any runner on base when a reliever enters a game is considered inherited by that pitcher.

Offensive Winning Percentage (OWP)

A player's offensive winning percentage equals the percentage of games a team would win with nine of that player in its lineup, given average pitching and defense. The formula is the square of Runs Created per 27 Outs, divided by the sum of the square of Runs Created per 27 Outs and the square of the league average of runs per game.

On-Base Percentage (OBP)

(Hits plus Walks plus Hit by Pitch) divided by (At-Bats plus Walks plus Hit by Pitch plus Sacrifice Flies).

On-Base Plus Slugging Percentage (OPS)

On-Base Percentage plus Slugging Percentage.

Outfield Advance Percentage

A statistic used to evaluate an outfielder's throwing arm. It's computed by dividing extra bases taken by baserunners by the number of opportunities. For example, if a single is hit to center field with men on first and second, and one man scores while the other stops at second, that's one extra base taken on two opportunities, a 50.0 advance percentage.

Park Index

A method of measuring the extent to which a given ballpark influences a given statistic. Using home runs as an example, here's how the index is calculated (using intraleague games only):

1. Add Home Runs and Opponent Home Runs in home games.
2. Add At-Bats and Opponent At-Bats in home games. (If At-Bats are unavailable, use home games.)
3. Divide step 1 by step 2.
4. Add Home Runs and Opponent Home Runs in road games.
5. Add At-Bats and Opponent At-Bats in road games. (If At-Bats are unavailable, use road games.)
6. Divide step 4 by step 5.
7. Divide step 3 by step 6.
8. Multiply step 7 by 100.

An index of 100 means the park is completely neutral. A park index of 118 for home runs indicates that games played in the park feature 18 percent more home runs than the average park.

Pivot Percentage

The number of Double Plays turned by a second baseman as the pivot man, divided by the number of Double Play Opportunities. A Double Play Opportunity is any situation with a runner on first and less than two out, where a groundball is hit to an infielder and the second baseman takes the throw.

Plate Appearances (PA)

At-Bats plus Walks plus Hit By Pitch plus Sacrifice Hits plus Sacrifice Flies plus Times Reached on Defensive Interference.

Predicted ERA

Opponent On-Base Percentage multiplied by Opponent Slugging Percentage multiplied by 31.

Pythagorean Theory

A formula for determining the expected winning percentage for a team. The formula is the square of Runs, divided by the sum of the square of Runs and the square of Opponent Runs.

Quality Start (QS)

Any start in which a pitcher works six or more innings while allowing three or fewer earned runs.

Range Factor

If Defensive Innings are available, use (Putouts plus Assists) multiplied by 9, divided by Defensive Innings. If not, use (Putouts plus Assists) divided by Games.

RBI Opportunities

The number of RBI a hitter would have accumulated if he had hit a home run every time up, given the total number of men that were on base when he batted. No RBI Opportunities are charged if the batter reaches base via a walk, hit by pitch or defensive interference, unless a runner scores as a result of the play.

Relativity Index

A method of comparing the effectiveness of a player versus his league. For hitters, the most common relativity index is Runs Created per 27 Outs multiplied by 100, then divided by league runs per game. For pitchers, it's Component ERA multiplied by 100, then divided by league ERA. A relativity index of 100 indicates a league-average player. An index greater than 100 indicates an above-average player.

Runs Created (RC)

Bill James has devised 24 different Runs Created formulas, depending on the statistics available in a given year. The current method is as follows:

1. Add Hits plus Walks plus Hit by Pitch.
2. Subtract Caught Stealings and Grounded Into Double Plays from step 1. This is the A Factor.
3. Add Unintentional Walks plus Hit by Pitch.
4. Multiply step 3 by .24.
5. Multiply Stolen Bases by .62.
6. Add Sacrifice Hits plus Sacrifice Flies.
7. Multiply step 6 by .5.
8. Add Total Bases plus step 4 plus step 5 plus step 7.
9. Multiply Strikeouts by .03.

10. Subtract step 9 from step 8. This is the B Factor.
11. Add At-Bats plus Walks plus Hit by Pitch plus Sacrifice Hits plus Sacrifice Flies. This is the C Factor.

To summarize:

$$A = H + BB + HBP - CS - GDP$$
$$B = ((BB - IBB + HBP) \times .24) + (SB \times .62) + ((SH + SF) \times .5) + TB - (SO \times .03)$$
$$C = AB + BB + HBP + SH + SF$$

Each player's Runs Created is determined as if he were operating in a context of eight other players of average skill. The final steps are:

12. Multiply C by 2.4.
13. Add A plus step 12.
14. Multiply C by 3.
15. Add B plus step 14.
16. Multiply step 13 by step 15.
17. Multiply C by 9.
18. Divide step 16 by step 17.
19. Multiply C by .9.
20. Subtract step 19 from step 18.

Expressed as an equation, that's:

$$(((((C \times 2.4) + A) \times ((C \times 3) + B)) / (C \times 9)) - (C \times .9)$$

Where home runs with men on base and batting average with runners in scoring position are available, we make further adjustments. First, figure out the player's home-run percentage by dividing his home runs by his at-bats. Then multiply that number by his at-bats with men on base to find his expected home runs in that situation. Subtract the expected total from the real total, and add the result to his Runs Created. For example, a player with 20 homers in 600 overall at-bats who hit 10 homers in 150 at-bats with men on base would get an extra five Runs Created because he would have been expected to hit five. If he hit three homers in 150 at-bats with men on base, he would lose two Runs Created.

The runners-in-scoring-position adjustment works in similar fashion. Multiply a player's batting average by his at-bats with runners in scoring position to determine his expected hits in that situation. Subtract the expected number from the real number, and again add the result to his Runs Created. A .300 hitter who batted .350 in 200 at-bats with runners in scoring position would get 10 extra Runs Created (70 hits minus 60 expected hits). If he batted .280 in that situation, he would lose four Runs Created (56 hits minus 60 expected hits).

The second-to-last step is to round a player's Runs Created to the nearest integer. Finally, once all of a team's individual players' Runs Created have been calculated, compare their total to the team's Runs Scored and reconcile the difference proportionally. For instance, if a team's players created 700 runs and the club scored 728 runs, increase each player's Runs Created by 4 percent (728 / 700 = 1.04) and round each off to the nearest integer once again.

Runs Created Per 27 Outs (RC/27)

This statistic estimates how many runs per game a team made up of nine of the same player would score. The name is actually a misnomer, however, because Bill James has based his revised formula on the number of league outs per team game rather than 27. The calculation is Runs Created multiplied by League Outs per Team Game, divided by

Outs Made (the sum of a player's At-Bats plus Sacrifice Hits plus Sacrifice Flies plus Caught Stealings plus Grounded Into Double Plays, less his Hits), or:

((RC x ((3 x Lg Outs) / (2 x LgG))) / (AB - H + SH + SF + CS + GDP)

Runs Prevented

A linear-weights system that measures how many runs a reliever prevents, by estimating the difference between the opposition's scoring potential when he enters and exits the game and subtracting any runs allowed while he was on the mound. The scoring potential depends on the number of outs, the number of men on base and the bases they occupy, and any subsequent errors. The Run Expectation for each situation is:

Runners	0 Outs	1 Outs	2 Outs
None	.56	.30	.12
1st	.95	.57	.25
2nd	1.19	.72	.34
3rd	1.45	.99	.39
1st & 2nd	1.57	.98	.47
1st & 3rd	1.87	1.21	.54
2nd & 3rd	2.04	1.43	.60
Loaded	2.38	1.64	.79

(based on MLB, 1996-2000)

Runs Prevented are calculated as follows:

1. Determine the Run Expectation when reliever enters the game. This is the Initial Run Expectation Value (IREV).
2. Subtract one run from step 1 for every run that scores while the pitcher is on the mound, regardless of whether the run is charged to him.
3. If an error is made while the reliever is in the game, find the Run Expectation for the situation that results.
4. Reconstruct that play as if the error hadn't occurred, as the official scorer would do when determining runs. Find the Run Expectation for that hypothetical situation.
5. Subtract step 4 from step 3. This is the Error Run Expectation Value (EREV).
6. Add step 2 and step 5.
7. Determine the Run Expectation when the reliever either finishes the inning (in which case it would be zero) or leaves the mound. This is the Final Run Expectation Value (FREV).
8. Subtract step 7 from step 6.
9. Repeat this process for each inning the reliever pitches.

To summarize, Runs Prevented = IREV - R + EREV - FREV. For example, assume a reliever enters the game in the eighth inning with a runner on second and one out. His IREV is .71. If his shortstop boots the next play, putting runners on the corners with one out instead of a runner on second and two out, the EREV is 1.19 - .34 = .85. If the reliever gets out of the inning and allows one run, his Runs Prevented = .71 - 1 + .85 - 0, which means he prevented .56 runs. If he pitches a scoreless ninth as well, he would get another .54 Runs Prevented and finish with 1.1 for the game.

Saves (Sv)

A relief pitcher is credited with a save if he:

1. Finishes a game won by his team, and
2. Isn't the winning pitcher, and

3. Qualifies under one of three conditions: a) he enters the game with a lead of no more than three runs and pitches at least one inning; b) he enters the game with the potential tying run on base, at bat or on deck; or c) he pitches effectively, in the opinion of the official scorer, for at least three innings.

Saves: Easy, Regular and Tough

These distinctions are made to gauge the difficulty of a save. An Easy Save occurs when the first batter faced doesn't represent the tying run and the reliever pitches one inning or less. A Tough Save occurs if the reliever enters with the tying run anywhere on base. A Regular Save is one that doesn't fall into the Easy or Tough category.

Save Opportunities/Situations

A relief pitcher is in a Save Opportunity (or Save Situation) if he enters the game with the club leading, isn't the pitcher of record and qualifies under one of three conditions: a) he has a lead of no more than three runs and the potential to pitch at least one inning; b) the potential tying run is on base, at bat or on deck; or c) he pitches effectively, in the opinion of the official scorer, for at least three innings and is credited with a save.

Save Percentage

Saves divided by Save Opportunities.

Secondary Average (Sec)

A way to look at a player's extra bases gained, independent of his Batting Average. The formula is (Total Bases minus Hits plus Walks plus Stolen Bases minus Caught Stealing) divided by At-Bats.

Similarity Score

A method of measuring the degree of similarity of two statistical lines for a player or a team. Two identical stat lines would generate a score of 1,000.

Slugging Percentage (Slg)

Total Bases divided by At-Bats.

Total Bases (TB)

Hits plus Doubles plus (Triples multiplied by two) plus (Home Runs multiplied by three).

Winning Percentage (Pct)

Wins divided by (Wins plus Losses).

Zone Rating

A Zone Rating is an estimate of a player's efficiency in fielding balls hit into his typical defensive zone, as measured by STATS reporters. Picture the playing field as a piece of pie. Fair territory is sliced up into 22 equal and rather narrow parts, extending from home plate to the outfield fence. The first slice, running along the left-field line, is Zone C. Like any piece of pie, it grows wider as you approach the "crust" (in this case, the outfield fence). Zone C is about six or seven feet wide at the third-base bag, and about 20 feet wide at a distance of 300 feet from the plate. The next 21 Zones extend from Zone C to the edge of the right-field line, which is Zone X. The dividing line between Zones M and N runs over second base, splitting the field in half. (Zones A, B, Y and Z are in foul territory.)

The first baseman is responsible for covering Zones V through X, the three rightmost zones on the field. This includes all grounders hit within approximately 20 feet of the right-field line, as well as all bunts that travel more than 40 feet.

The second baseman is responsible for Zones O through T. Remember, the left boundary of Zone N is midfield. The right boundary of Zone N, where it meets Zone O, is the left edge of the second baseman's territory. It lies about eight feet to the right of second base. The second baseman's area runs through Zone T, and the first baseman's area begins at Zone V. Zone U, in between, belongs to neither fielder.

The respective areas of responsibility for the third baseman and shortstop are mirror images of the first and second baseman's zones. The third baseman is responsible for Zones C through F, and the shortstop is assigned Zones H through L. Zone G lies in between and belongs to neither fielder. The two middle zones, M and N, lay between the second baseman and shortstop and also are unassigned.

An infielder's Zone Rating is equal to the number of balls he converts into outs divided by the number of balls hit into the player's zone. Only groundballs are considered when Zone Rating is calculated. Line drives, popups and flyballs are ignored. An infielder is credited with an out made for every ball fielded that is turned into an out. When a player fields a ball outside his zone and turns it into an out, it is counted as a ball in his zone for the purposes of calculating his Zone Rating. Infielders no longer get credit for two outs when they start a double play.

Each outfielder is given two separate zones, one for flyballs and popups another one for line drives. Because liners remain in the air for a shorter amount of time, outfielders are assigned a smaller zone for them. For a batted ball to be assigned to an outfielder, it must travel a certain distance. Corner outfielders are responsible for all line drives in their area that travel between 280 and 340 feet. They also are responsible for all flyballs and popups that travel over 200 feet. The center fielder is responsible for all liners between 300 and 370 feet, and all flies and pops over 200 feet.

The left fielder's area covers Zones F through H on line drives and Zones C through I on flyballs and popups.

The right fielder's zones are the mirror image of the left fielders: Zones S through U on liners and Zones R through X on flies and pops.

The center fielder is responsible for Zones L through O on liners and Zones K through P on flies and pops.

An outfielder's Zone Rating equals the balls hit into his zone which don't result in hits, divided by the number of balls hit into his zone. As with infielders, an outfielder who catches a ball outside of his zone is credited with both an out and a ball in his zone for purposes of calculation his Zone Rating.

Any defender's ability to get to balls outside his zone can boost his Zone Rating. Therefore, Zone Rating shouldn't be interpreted simply as the percentage of balls hit into a player's zone that the fielder was able to turn into outs.

Index

A

Hank Aaron
    chances of HR record being broken 88

Age
    26-year old rookies 6
    home runs hit between age 31-35 40
    lowest batting average through age 26 75
    most runs created through age 24 36
    oldest 20-game winners 124
    rookie season as a teenager 42
    young sluggers 11

Rick Ankiel
    poor BB/9 IP ratios 72

B

Ballparks
    Comerica Park 16
    pitchers' and hitters' parks 192
    role in increased offense 188

Baserunning
    unforced outs 119

Tony Batista
    lightest 40-HR hitters 38

Batting average
    highest, as a teenager 42
    lowest through age 26 75
    with 1,000 games caught 65

Carlos Beltran
    sophomore slump 19

Bunts
    base-hit percentage 105
    sacrifice percentage 105

C

Career assessments
    chances at 756 home runs 88
    chances at 2,298 RBI 88

Luis Castillo
    highest AB/RBI rate 52

Catchers
    as leadoff hitter 70
    caught-stealing percentage 168, 204
    hitting with 1,000 games caught 65

Eric Chavez
    best young SS/3B combo 28

Chicago White Sox
    postseason sweep 195
    young sluggers 11

Cincinnati Reds
    teams without a 13-game winner 47

Jeff Cirillo
    home vs. road hitting 80

Cleveland Indians
    OBP for first three hitters in lineup 14

Clutch hitters
    most home runs 83
    veterans 86

Coors Field
    effects on Rockies hitters 80

D

Defense
    catcher caught-stealing percentage 168, 204
    defensive batting average 182
    infield zone ratings 170
    outfield advance percentage 176
    outfield assists 176
    outfield zone ratings 179
    pivot ratings 174
    STATS Gold Gloves 204

Detroit Tigers
    lowest home-run indexes 16

E

ERA
    at Coors Field 49
    home-road differential 136

Darin Erstad
    biggest single-season hit improvements 4

F

Steve Finley
home runs hit between age 31-35 40

First Inning
winning percentage by run differential 68
worst run differentials 68

Rafael Furcal
rookie season as a teenager 42

G

Game scores 143

Go-ahead RBI 96, 204

Juan Gonzalez
OBP for first three hitters in lineup 14

Marquis Grissom
compared to Jeffrey Hammonds 61
worst on-base plus slugging 61

Vladimir Guerrero
power and plate discipline 63

H

Jeffrey Hammonds
compared to Marquis Grissom 61

Mike Hampton
pitching in Coors Field 49

Hearts of the order 101

Enzo Hernandez
highest AB/RBI rate 52

Hit by Pitch
highest hit batsman-walk ratio, pitchers 9

Hits
biggest single-season hit improvements 4

Hitters
20 HR, .320 batting average seasons 31
26-year old rookies 6
biggest single-season hit improvements 4
catchers hitting leadoff 70
chances at 756 home runs 88
chances at 2,298 RBI 88
go-ahead RBI 96, 204
hearts of the order 101
highest AB/RBI rate 52
hitting with 1,000 games caught 65
home runs hit between age 31-35 40
largest decrease in runs created 19
longest home runs 108
most strikeouts as a .300 hitter 44
OBP for first three hitters in lineup 14
offensive winning percentage 91
pitchers as hitters 139
pitches per plate appearance 114
pitches per plate appearance, postseason .. 117
power and plate discipline 63
RBI per opportunity 98, 204
runs created 91
secondary average 93
swings and misses 110
veterans in the clutch 86

Holds 159, 204

Home runs
20 HR, .320 batting average seasons 31
chances at 756 88
clutch 83
hit between age 31-35 40
lightest 40-HR hitters 38
longest 108
lowest home-run indexes 16
power and plate discipline 63

Hottest heaters 149, 204

Tim Hudson
most wins in first 39 decisions 127

Human air conditioners 110

I

Infielders
zone ratings 170

Inherited runners scoring percentage 161

J

Bill James
300-win candidates 122
role of ballparks in increased offense 188

K

Tom Kelly
worst manager winning percentages 21

Jason Kendall
leadoff hitter as a catcher 70

Jeff Kent
best seasons as second baseman 77

L

Leadoff hitters
   catchers 70
   on-base percentage 103

Jose Lima
   20-game winners with 2.00 ERA rises 55

M

Managers
   experience vs. inexperience 59
   worst winning percentages 21

Edgar Martinez
   20 HR, .320 batting average seasons 31

Pedro Martinez
   highest hit batsman-walk ratio 9

Mark McGwire
   chances of hitting 756 homers 88

N

Denny Neagle
   pitching in Coors Field 49

New York Yankees
   projected rotation for 2001 24

O

Oakland Athletics
   best young SS/3B 28

Offensive winning percentage 91

On-base percentage
   highest, as a teenager 42
   highest combined, primary SS/3B 28
   leadoff men 103
   first three hitters in lineup, team 14
   with 1,000 games caught 65

On-base plus slugging percentage
   best as second baseman 77
   worst in 2000 61
   worst up the middle, 2000 34

Outfielders
   advance percentage 176
   assists 176
   zone ratings 179

Overachieving teams 197

P

Philadelphia Phillies
   worst first innings 68

Mike Piazza
   hitting with 1,000 games caught 65

Pitch counts
   2000 .... 147, 204
   estimated 204

Pitchers
   20-game winners with 2.00 ERA rises 55
   300-game winners 199
   300-win candidates 122
   as hitters 139
   biggest home-road ERA differential 136
   by height 133
   ERA at Coors Field 49
   highest hit batsman-walk ratio 9
   highest winning percentage following
      team loss 129
   most wins following team loss 129
   most wins in first 39 decisions 127
   oldest 20-game winners 124
   platoon splits 153
   poor BB/9 IP ratios 72
   pull percentage 141
   strikeout-hit ratio 151
   strikeouts per nine innings 149, 204
   teams without a 13-game winner 47
   Yankee's projected 2001 rotation 24

Pivot ratings 174

Platoon splits
   pitchers in 2000 153

Postseason
   pitches per plate appearance 117
   series sweeps 195

Pull percentage 141

Pythagorean theorem 197

Q

Quality starts 145

R

RBI
   chances at 2,298 88
   go-ahead RBI 96, 204

highest AB/RBI rate 52
per opportunity 98, 204

Red Barrett Trophy 147, 204

Relievers
   easy, regular and tough saves 156
   holds 159, 204
   inherited runners scoring percentage 161
   runs prevented values 163

Chris Richard
   26-year old rookies 6

Ruben Rivera
   lowest batting average 75

Alex Rodriguez
   most runs created through age 24 36

Rookies
   26-year old rookies 6
   best season, as a teenager 42
   largest decrease in runs created 19

Runs created
   most, 2000 91
   most, as a teenager 42
   most through age 24 36

Runs prevented values 163

S

Saves
   easy, regular and tough 156

Second basemen
   best seasons 77
   pivot ratings 174

Secondary average
   hitters 93

Slidin' Billy Trophy 103, 204

Slugging percentage
   with 1,000 games caught 65

Sammy Sosa
   most strikeouts as a .300 hitter 44

Sophomore slump
   largest decrease in runs created 19

Starting pitchers
   game scores 143
   highest hit batsman-walk ratio 9
   pitch counts 147, 204

quality starts 145
Yankee's projected 2001 rotation 24

STATS awards 204

STATS FlatBat 105, 204

STATS Gold Gloves 204

Stolen bases
   catcher caught-stealing percentage 168, 204
   most, as a teenager 42

Strikeouts (hitters)
   most strikeouts as a .300 hitter 44
   teams leading league in strikeouts 112

Strikeouts (pitchers)
   per nine innings 149, 204
   strikeout-hit ratio 151

Swings and misses 110

T

Tampa Bay Devil Rays
   offense up the middle 34

Miguel Tejada
   best young SS/3B combo 28

Jim Tracy
   experience vs. inexperience as manager 59

U

Underachieving teams 197

Unforced outs
   players 119
   teams 119

W

Walks
   poor BB/9 IP ratios 72

David Wells
   oldest 20-game winners 124

Winning percentage
   by first-inning run differential 68
   by park type 192
   by teams leading league in strikeouts 112
   highest winning percentage following
      team loss 129
   worst as a manager 21

Wins
- 20-game winners with 2.00 ERA rises 55
- 300-game winners 199
- most wins following team loss 129
- most wins in first 39 decisions 127
- oldest 20-game winners 124
- teams without a 13-game winner 47

Z

Zone ratings
- infield 170
- outfield 179

About STATS, Inc.

STATS, Inc., a News Corporation company, is affiliated with Fox Sports. STATS collects and disseminates most, if not all, of the information found within these pages, in addition to the statistics you might find on your favorite web site. STATS, Inc. is the nation's leading sports information and statistical analysis company, providing detailed sports services for a wide array of commercial clients.

As one of the elite companies in sports, STATS provides the most detailed, up-to-the-minute sports information to professional teams, print and broadcast media, software developers and interactive service providers around the country. STATS' network of trained sports reporters records the details of more than 3,800 sporting events across the four major sports annually. Some of our major clients include Fox Sports, the Associated Press, America Online, *The Sporting News*, ESPN.com, Yahoo!, Electronic Arts, MSNBC, SONY and Topps.

STATS Publishing, a division of STATS, Inc., produces 11 annual books, including the *Major League Handbook*, *The Scouting Notebook*, the *Pro Football Handbook*, the *Pro Basketball Handbook* and the *Hockey Handbook*. In 1998, we introduced two baseball encyclopedias, the *All-Time Major League Handbook* (recently updated) and the *All-Time Baseball Sourcebook*. Together they combine for more than 5,000 pages of baseball history. We added the *Pro Football Sourcebook* in 2000. Also available is *From Abba Dabba to Zorro: The World of Baseball Nicknames*, a wacky look at monikers and their origins. All of our publications deliver STATS' expertise to fans, scouts, general managers and media around the country.

In addition, STATS Fantasy Sports is at the forefront of the booming fantasy sports industry. We develop fantasy baseball, football, basketball, hockey, golf and auto racing games for a host of sites. We also feature the first historical baseball simulation game created specifically for the Internet—FOX Diamond Legends. No matter what time of year, STATS Fantasy Sports has a fantasy game to keep even the most passionate sports fan satisfied.

Information technology has grown by leaps and bounds in the last decade. STATS will continue to be at the forefront as a supplier of the most up-to-date, in-depth sports information available. For those of you on the information superhighway, you always can catch STATS in our area on America Online or at our Internet site.

For more information on our products, or on joining our reporter network, contact us via:

America Online — Keyword: STATS

Internet — www.stats.com

Toll Free in the USA at 1-800-63-STATS (1-800-637-8287)

Outside the USA at 1-847-470-8798

Or write to:

STATS, Inc.
8130 Lehigh Ave.
Morton Grove, IL 60053

The Web Comes Alive!

Introducing Diamond Legends Internet Baseball Simulation game. It's the state-of-the-art baseball simulation that will blow you away! Diamond Legends is the first Web-based game to actually transport you back in time.

Featuring all the greats of the game and even some of the more recent baseball heroes like Don Mattingly and Kent Hrbek. Diamond Legends is the latest must-play gem in the STATS arsenal of fantasy sports.

www.diamondlegends.com

STATS Power Hitters

STATS Major League Handbook 2001
✖ Career stats for every 2000 major leaguer
✖ Bill James' & STATS' exclusive player projections for 2001
✖ Fielding stats, managerial tendencies, leader boards and more
Item #HB01, $19.95, Available Now
Comb-bound #HC01, $24.95, Available Now

STATS Minor League Handbook 2001
✖ Career data for all Double-A and Triple-A players
✖ Bill James' exclusive Major League Equivalencies
✖ Team USA composite and boxscores from the Olympics in Sydney
Item #MH01, $19.95, Available Now
Comb-bound #MC01, $24.95, SOLD OUT!

STATS Player Profiles 2001
✖ Exclusive 2000 breakdowns for pitchers and hitters, over 30 in all: lefty/righty, home/road, day/night, grass/turf, clutch situations, ahead/behind in the count, month-by-month batting in various spots, pitching with various days rest
✖ Complete breakdowns by player for the last five seasons
Item #PP01, $19.95, Available Now
Comb-bound #PC01, $24.95, SOLD OUT!

STATS Minor League Scouting Notebook 2001
✖ Evaluations of every organization's top prospects
✖ Essays, stat lines and grades for more than 1,200 prospects
✖ Recap of the 2000 amateur draft
Item #MN01, $19.95, Available Now

STATS Player Projections Update 2001
✖ Projections featuring players in new ballparks
✖ Forecasts to account for spring and winter trades
✖ More accurate playing-time projections
Item #PJUP, $9.95, Available Now

STATS All-Time Major League Handbook
Updated through the 1999 season, this is the ONLY baseball register featuring complete year-by-year career stats for EVERY major league batter, pitcher and fielder in baseball history.
Item #ATHB, $79.95, Available Now

1-800-63-STATS   847-470-8798   www.stats.com

Clearing the Bases!

The Scouting Notebook 2001
* Detailed reports and tendencies for all major league regulars
* More than 400 of the minor leagues' top prospects
* In-depth manager and ballpark analysis

Item #SN01, $19.95, Available Now
Comb-bound, #SC01, $24.95, Available Now

STATS Batter Versus Pitcher Match-Ups! 2001
* Career stats for pitchers vs. batters with 5+ match-ups
* Leader boards with best and worst match-ups
* Batter and pitcher performances for each major league ballpark

Item #BP01, $24.95, Available Now

Backlist Baseball

From Abba Dabba to Zorro: The World of Baseball Nicknames
* STATS reveals the unusual and funny stories behind player nicknames
* The All-Food Team, All-Body Parts Team and many more
* Baseball celebrities including Bob Costas, Ernie Harwell and Jim Palmer pick out their favorite baseball nicknames

Item #ABBA, $9.95, Available Now

STATS Ballpark Sourcebook: Diamond Diagrams
* Analytical essays and historical summaries for more than 100 major and minor league parks
* Extensive playing characteristics, anecdotes and accounts of memorable players and events at each playing field
* Photos, charts and diagrams detail every featured ballpark

Item #BSDD, $24.95, Available Now   (1st printing sold out!)

STATS Baseball's Terrific 20
* Perfect for baseball fans ages 7-12. Features Mark McGwire, Ken Griffey Jr., Sammy Sosa and more
* Awesome color action photos of kids' favorite players

Item #KID1, $9.95, Available Now

★★★★★ **Previous editions of all our annuals available for $9.95** ★★★★★

1-800-63-STATS   847-470-8798   www.stats.com

Full Coverage of the NFL, NHL and NBA!

STATS Pro Football Handbook 2001
✖ A complete season-by-season register for every active player in the NFL
✖ Numerous statistical breakdowns for hundreds of NFL players
✖ Leader boards in both innovative and traditional categories
✖ Exclusive evaluations of offensive linemen
Item #FH01, $19.95, Available in April

STATS Pro Football Sourcebook 2001
✖ Perfect fantasy tool!
✖ Multi-year player situational statistics
✖ Extensive team stats
✖ Three-year weighted averages show how players likely will perform in 2001
Item #PF01, $19.95, Available in June
2000 edition currently available, $9.95

STATS Pro Basketball Handbook 2001-02
✖ Career stats for every player who logged minutes in 2000-01
✖ Team game logs with points, rebounds, assists and more
✖ Season and five-year player profiles and leader boards
Item #BH02, $19.95, Available in September 2001
2000-01 edition currently available for $9.95

STATS Hockey Handbook 2001-02
✖ Career stats for every player who made an appearance in 2000-01
✖ In-depth player profiles identifying strengths and weaknesses
✖ Leader boards for forwards, defensemen and goaltenders
✖ Team game logs
Item #HH02, $19.95, Available in August 2001
2000-01 edition currently available for $9.95

1-800-63-STATS   847-470-8798   www.stats.com

Books (Free first-class shipping for books over $10)

QTY	Product name	Item Code	Price	Total
	STATS Major League Handbook 2001	HB01	$19.95	
	STATS Major League Handbook 2001 (Comb-Bound)	HC01	$24.95	
	STATS Minor League Handbook 2001	MH01	$19.95	
	STATS Minor League Handbook 2001 (Comb-Bound)	MC01	SOLD OUT!	
	STATS Player Profiles 2001	PP01	$19.95	
	STATS Player Profiles 2001 (Comb-Bound)	PC01	SOLD OUT!	
	The Scouting Notebook 2001	SN01	$19.95	
	The Scouting Notebook 2001 (Comb-Bound)	SC01	$24.95	
	STATS Minor League Scouting Notebook 2001	MN01	$19.95	
	STATS Batter Vs. Pitcher Match-Ups! 2001	BP01	$24.95	
	STATS Baseball Scoreboard 2001	SB01	$19.95	
	STATS Player Projections Update 2001	PJUP	$ 9.95	
	STATS All-Time Major League Handbook 2nd edition	ATHB	$79.95	
	STATS Ballpark Sourcebook: Diamond Diagrams	BSDD	$24.95	
	STATS Pro Football Handbook 2001	FH01	$19.95	
	STATS Pro Football Handbook 2001 (Comb-Bound)	FC01	$24.95	
	STATS Pro Football Sourcebook 2001	PF01	$19.95	
	STATS Hockey Handbook 2001-02	HH02	$19.95	
	STATS Pro Basketball Handbook 2001-02	BH02	$19.95	
			TOTAL	

Books Under $10 (Please include $2 S&H for each book)

QTY	Product name	Item Code	Price	Total
	From Abba Dabba to Zorro: The World of Baseball Nicknames	ABBA	$ 9.95	
	STATS Baseball's Terrific 20	KID1	$ 9.95	
	STATS Player Projections Update 2001	PJUP	$ 9.95	
			TOTAL	

Previous Editions (Please circle appropriate years and include $2 S&H for each book)

QTY	Product name	Years	Price	Total
	STATS Major League Handbook	'91 '92 '93 '94 '95 '96 '97 '98 '99 '00	$ 9.95	
	The Scouting Notebook/Report	'94 '95 '96 '97 '98 '99 '00	$ 9.95	
	STATS Player Profiles	'93 '94 '95 '96 '97 '98 '99 '00	$ 9.95	
	STATS Minor League Handbook	'92 '93 '94 '95 '96 '97 '98 '99 '00	$ 9.95	
	STATS Batter Vs. Pitcher Match-Ups!	'94 '95 '96 '97 '98 '99 '00	$ 9.95	
	STATS Diamond Chronicles	'97 '98 '99 '00	$ 9.95	
	STATS Baseball Scoreboard	'92 '93 '95 '96 '97 '98 '99 '00	$ 9.95	
	Pro Football Revealed: The 100 Yard War	'94 '95 '96 '97 '98	$ 9.95	
	STATS Pro Football Handbook	'95 '96 '97 '98 '99 '00	$ 9.95	
	STATS Pro Football Scoreboard	'99 '00	$ 9.95	
	STATS Pro Football Sourcebook	'99 '00	$ 9.95	
	STATS Hockey Handbook	'96-'97 '97-'98 '98-'99 '99-'00 '00-'01	$ 9.95	
	STATS Pro Basketball Handbook	'93-'94 '94-'95 '95-'96 '96-'97 '98-'99 '99-'00 '00-'01	$ 9.95	
	All-Time Major League Handbook (Slightly dinged)	First Edition	$45.00	
	All-Time Major League Sourcebook (Slightly dinged)	First Edition	$45.00	
			TOTAL	

TOTAL

Mail:
STATS, Inc.
8130 Lehigh Avenue
Morton Grove, IL 60053

Phone:
1-800-63-STATS
(847) 677-3322

Fax:
(847) 470-9140

Bill To:
Company_____
Name_____
Address_____
City_____State_____Zip_____
Phone (   )_____Ext.____Fax (   )_____
E-mail Address_____

Ship To: *(Fill in this section if shipping address differs from billing address)*
Company_____
Name_____
Address_____
City_____State_____Zip_____
Phone (   )_____Ext.____Fax (   )_____
E-mail Address_____

Method of payment:
All prices stated
in U.S. Dollars

❑ Charge to my *(circle one)*
   Visa
   MasterCard
   American Express
   Discover

❑ Check or Money Order
   (U.S. funds only)

Please include credit card number
and expiration date with charge orders!

[ ][ ][ ][ ][ ][ ][ ][ ][ ][ ][ ][ ][ ][ ][ ][ ]

Exp. Date [/   ]
           Month Year

X_____
Signature *(as shown on credit card)*

Totals for STATS Products:	
Books	☐
Books Under $10 *	☐
Prior Book Editions *	☐
order 2 or more books/subtract: $1.00/book *(Does not include prior editions)*	☐
Illinois residents add 8.5% sales tax	☐
Sub Total	☐

Shipping Costs		
Canada	Add $4.00/book	☐
* All books under $10	Add $2.00/book	☐
	Grand Total	☐
	(No other discounts apply)	

(Orders subject to availability)

Free First Class Shipping For Books Over $10